THE LEGACY OF KENNETH BURKE

Kenneth Burke

The Legacy of Kenneth Burke

EDITED BY HERBERT W. SIMONS &

TREVOR MELIA

THE UNIVERSITY OF WISCONSIN PRESS

The University of Wisconsin Press
114 North Murray Street
Madison, Wisconsin 53715

The University of Wisconsin Press, Ltd.
1 Gower Street
London WC1E 6HA, England

5 4 3 2 1

Printed in the United States of America

Library of Congress Cataloging-in-Publication Data
The Legacy of Kenneth Burke.
   (Rhetoric of the human sciences)
   Includes bibliographies and index.
   1. Burke, Kenneth, 1897–   –Influence.
2. Criticism—History—20th century. 3. Literature
and society. 4. Literature—Philosophy. I. Burke,
Kenneth, 1897–   . II. Simons, Herbert W., 1935–
III. Melia, Trevor. IV. Series.
PN75.B8L44   1988   818'.5209   88-40197
ISBN 0-299-11830-4
ISBN 0-299-11834-7 (pbk.)

CONTENTS

A gallery of photographs begins on p. 152

PREFACE

Born May 5, 1897, Kenneth Burke is nearing the end of a long and incredibly productive career. Over the course of that career he has functioned as poet, aphorist, short story writer, translator, composer, music critic, social theorist, literary critic, and more. Best known for his theory of dramatism, he is also credited with having anticipated many of the currents in contemporary critical theory, including the "rhetorical turn" in the human sciences.

This book was born of a conference on Burke, Temple University's fifth annual Discourse Analysis conference, held March 6–8, 1984. Hosted by Temple's Rhetoric and Communication program (now a separate department) and co-sponsored by the Speech Communication Association, the conference brought together Burkophiles from a dozen or more disciplines for a combination love fest and careful dissection of the Burke corpus. Between toasts to 65 + years of scholarly work and meetings to organize a Kenneth Burke Society, the conferees paid Burke the ultimate tribute by taking critical aim at his works, clarifying his more elusive concepts, comparing and contrasting him with other theorists, and assessing the uses and limitations of his central ideas. This they did by way of discussions of some ninety papers presented at plenary and small group seminar sessions. Burke's official role at the conference was as "Critic-at-Large," in which capacity he held forth, not just at the regularly scheduled sessions, but well into the night. Not bad for someone who is often labeled a "thirties" writer, one who, in Burke's own words, is "this side of an o'er ripe melon."

Like other books in the Temple conference series, *The Legacy of Kenneth Burke* has become very much its own thing. Early on we decided to gear the book to the University of Wisconsin Press series on the Rhetoric of the Human Sciences. Thus, some excellent papers on tangential themes had to be left out. Especially needed, we believed, were essays that might provide rereadings of Burkean theory in light of reconceptualizations of inquiry currently taking place within both the humanities and social sciences. Hence the particular significance attached in this volume to Burke's writings on rhetoric, dialectic, and logology, to possible applications of Burkean theory in the social sciences, and to comparisons between Burke and such contemporary theorists as Barthes, Derrida, Gadamer, and Jameson. Our intention was to build upon but also move beyond Hayden White and Margaret Brose's *Representing Kenneth Burke* (1982), showing, as one prepublication reviewer put it, that "Burke's real significance as a culture critic may just be emerging, but in disciplines other than the literary ones."

At the Burke conference we asked participants to assess, not just Burke's contributions to their own varied disciplines, but also the potential of Burkean theory as a unifying force across disciplines. In that spirit we have added to the conference collection an essay by Melia that extends Burkean theory beyond the social sciences into the higher reaches of mathematics and the physical sciences. Also added are a concluding poem by Burke in defense of pluralism as well as an appendix and an extensive bibliography. The Appendix consists of the text of an oft-mentioned but seldom seen speech that Burke delivered at the communist-led Writers' Congress of 1935, a sharp exchange on the controversial speech, reprinted from the conference proceedings, and an analysis of the speech from Frank Lentricchia's *Criticism and Social Change*. Lentricchia offers the speech as Exhibit A in defense of his case for Burke as exemplary culture critic, a model for those who, in Burke's terms, would use criticism as equipment for living.

The Legacy of Kenneth Burke is intended for a wide range of readers. For those still cutting their teeth on Burke we especially recommend the essays by Gusfield, Melia, Blankenship, and Rueckert. For those familiar with current issues in contemporary literary and discourse theory, but not as familiar with Burke, the essays by Oravec, Damrosch, Leff, Lentricchia, and Nelson should prove especially helpful.

All books are group efforts, collections of original essays more so than others. Our contributors not only prepared articles; they also served as critics for each other. David Damrosch and William Rueckert deserve special mention in this regard. Other reviewers included C. Douglas Atkins, Barbara Biesecker, John Angus Campbell, Charles Dyke, Richard Gregg, Lawrence Grossberg, Kevin Moore, Susan Stewart, and Susan Wells. We were fortunate too in having secured excellent advice from the consultants to the University of Wisconsin Press. Our special thanks to Richard Thames, both for his extensive bibliographic work and for his help, with Dori Segal, in organizing the Burke conference. Segal coordinated a large Temple team, too numerous to mention by name. We also thank SCA as well as our respective universities. Temple University's Lectures and Forums Committee was especially forthcoming, Dorothy Mewha & Co. were generous as usual, and Temple provided Simons with a much needed summer fellowship. The University of Pittsburgh was generous with both the time and clerical services involved in adjudicating ninety contributed conference papers. Acknowledgment is made also to International Publishers for permission to publish excerpts from *American Writers' Congress* and to the University of Chicago Press for permission to excerpt from *Criticism and Social Change.*

THE LEGACY OF KENNETH BURKE

INTRODUCTION

KENNETH BURKE AND THE

RHETORIC OF THE

HUMAN SCIENCES

HERBERT W. SIMONS

Marianne Moore reminded us that he was, to begin with, a poet.[1] Of Burke's translation of Thomas Mann's *Death in Venice*, W. H. Auden said simply, "This is it."[2] Denis Donoghue referred to the novel *Towards a Better Life* as "one of my desert-island books, a beautiful thing."[3] William Rueckert chose to begin his essay "Some of the Many Kenneth Burkes" with the aphorisms—reflecting a mind, he said, "that cannot help but think ironically, seeing around corners to crooked vision, seeing through to the ends of things where they reverse and become something else (god as goal and goad), perceiving that, whether we like it or not, our ideas perfect themselves, and we are 'rotten with perfection.' "[4]

"All living things are critics," Burke has said. But of course some critics are more discerning than others. Auden said of Burke that he was "unquestionably the most brilliant and suggestive critic now writing in America." Stanley Edgar Hyman said he was the greatest critic since Coleridge. Harold Bloom could find no American critic who matched his genius, save perhaps Emerson.[5]

Burke is not just a literary critic, certainly not in any ordinary sense of the term, but it is not easy to say what he is. On the occasion of Burke's receipt of the National Medal for Literature from the American Academy of Arts and Sciences in 1981, Richard Kostelanetz wrote that while he had no difficulty classifying *Counter-Statement* (1931), *The Philosophy of Literary Form* (1941), and *Language as Symbolic Action* (1966) as literary criticism, the six other nonfictional works in the Burke corpus, *Permanence and Change* (1935), Attitudes toward History (1937), *A Grammar of Motives* (1945), *A Rhetoric of Motives* (1950), *The Rhetoric of Religion: Studies in Logology* (1961), and *Dramatism and Development* (1972) were "something else...sociology a bit, the theory of language a bit less, the contemplation of life a bit more." These last books, he said, "are so diffuse, so unsystematic that they are not 'philosophy' in any formal sense but something thoroughly idiosyncratic: Burkology."[6]

Part of the problem in defining "Burkology" is that Burke, a college dropout who never held a tenured academic position, has resisted being "disciplined."[7] Here, as at a conference entitled "The Legacy of Kenneth Burke" from which this book originated, we have attempted to secure readings of the Burke corpus by scholars in a variety of fields, this so that readers might better appreciate what Burke has been about. Thus, for example, Joseph Gusfield casts Burke as a sociologist in the symbolic interactionist tradition but notes linkages as well to ethnomethodology. Somewhat more mischievously, Donald McCloskey casts Burke as an economist of the Austrian school.

But while Burke's distinct blend of theory and social commentary has ranged over a dizzying array of subject matters—among them anthropology, linguistics, religion, oratory, fiction, history, economics, philosophy, and politics—it would be a mistake to think of any of his writings as purely disciplinary contributions, for he invariably brings to each object of his scrutiny an overarching interdisciplinary framework, and he consistently takes from his engagements with the texts of a given field ideas that might help fertilize another. Said Wayne Booth, "What Burke has done better than anyone else is to find a way to connect literature with life without reducing either."[8]

Burke's initial focus was upon the aesthetics of imaginative works, but by the thirties and forties he had greatly extended his reach with rhetorical, dramatistic, and dialectical conceptions of language as symbolic action that circumscribed all life and all literature within their domains. Building on the classical trivium—rhetoric, by which to glimpse nonobvious meanings, methods, and motives; grammar, by which to discern structures and transformations; and dialectic, by which to reach ever higher without loss of conceptual baggage—Burke's own dialectic has taken him to the higher reaches of "logology," the study of words about words, wherein vocabularies are seen as having "entelechial" potentialities for development and transformation, and wherein correspondences, say, between theological and secular conceptions of creation, sacrifice, conversion, salvation are studied "in their sheer formality" as observations about language per se.

With the recent republication by the University of California Press of Burke's two fictional and nine nonfictional major works, Burke's stock is clearly on the rise. He seems, moreover, to have always had an uncanny capacity to anticipate new movements in contemporary critical and social theory. Said Ben Yagoda, the various critical doctrines that have sprung up since the decline of the New Criticism "sometimes seem to have one thing in common: Kenneth Burke thought them up nearly fifty years ago."[9] As "critical pathfinder" (to borrow Hayden White's term), Burke has been credited with being the chief architect of the New Rhetoric, the inventor of dramatism, a forerunner of French structuralism, a prefashionable deconstructionist, and—of special significance to this book and to the series of which it is a part— a founding father of the current movement to reconceive the human sciences in rhetorical terms. Before previewing the essays in this book it might be helpful, then, to consider in a general way Burke's role in relationship to the new movement.

Kenneth Burke and the Rhetoric of the Human Sciences

Elsewhere, I have characterized the phrase "the rhetoric of the human sciences" as ironic in the comedic sense, presuming as in all such irony a literal-minded fool over whose head the irony works.[10] The fool in this case is the "objectivist" (whether a scientist, historian, journalist, or what have you), a philosophical stick-in-the-mud who clings to such antiquated notions as the fact-value split, the mind as a "glassy essence," and language as a potential mirror of reality; and who holds correspondingly to traditional distinctions such as between literal language and figurative language, or certified true knowledge and mere belief, used to distinguish science from literature and "true" science from "pseudoscience." The term "human sciences" is in itself a provocation, suggesting in one breath both that the business of science is never entirely free of human foibles, prejudices, passions, and the like, and also, more particularly, that the time-honored Anglo-American distinction between the humanities and the social sciences no longer makes a great deal of sense.

But to speak generically of the *rhetoric* of the human sciences is the unkindest cut of all, inviting images of scholars as flatterers and deceivers, con artists and propagandists, and raising all manner of embarrassing questions about relationships between science and ideology, scholarship and political practice. Never mind, then, that

Herbert W. Simons

the term "rhetoric" is often used neutrally and even eulogistically as the study of how one ought to persuade; its very link to persuasion is a step down from images of "proof," "demonstration," "verification," and "falsification" that have been the watchwords of objectivism. And while our objectivist might be heartened to learn that the project to reconceive the human sciences has a reconstructive aspect—that it is not all criticism and deconstruction—still, it must seem a bit strange to objectivists that their "rhetorician" colleagues are forever "decentering" scholarly texts, casting behaviors as texts, data as symbolic constructions, theories as narratives, and applying to even the best-intentioned, least objectionable discourses a "hermeneutics of suspicion." Thus, although the term "rhetoric" currently has no fixed or precise meaning as applied to the human sciences, and might be said, even, to constitute an essentially contested term[11] in debates among competing schools of thought (including various strands of structuralism and poststructuralism, neopragmatism, Kuhnian postpositivism, and social constructionism), our objectivist might legitimately conclude that while the news from the rhetoric front is somewhat mixed, it is generally bad.

What now of Burke's contributions to what these days is being referred to as the "rhetorical turn" in the human sciences? Clifford Geertz credits Burke's writings on dramatism, rhetoric, and dialectic with having had a major influence on the "refiguration" of social thought, a shift, as he puts it, "in analytical rhetoric, the tropes and imageries of explanation."[12] Accompanying this shift "in the way we think about the way we think" has come renewed interest in sophistic habits of mind, reflected in unabashedly contrived category schemes, in field-dependent, even situation-dependent logics of justification, and in a corresponding sense of humility as regards the possibilities for "capturing" human nature or "compelling" belief through "coercive" arguments. That all philosophers are persuaders of a sort and that they are most rhetorical while purporting to be not rhetorical at all are starting points for Burke's "perspectivism," a metacritical perspective that Burke promotes as a pluralistic alternative to objectivism and relativism. Perspectivism is an attestation of the value of dialectic, as Burke explains in his highly provocative essay in *A Grammar of Motives*, "The Four Master Tropes." The essay may be read in a variety of ways (and is in this volume), but there is no question of its considerable influence on the "rhetorical turn," both directly, and via such important works as Wayne Booth's *The Rhetoric of Irony*, Sapir and Crocker's *Social Use of Metaphor*, and Hayden White's *Tropics of Discourse*. Here Burke piles irony atop irony as he casts irony itself—in the form of dialectical reversal—as the trope of tropes, thus relegating the perspectives provided by metaphor, the reductions accomplished by metonymy, and the microcosmic representations exhibited by synecdoche to the status of but "partial truths" or "subcertainties."

To many rhetoricians and especially to those of us reared in the American pedagogical tradition of rhetoric as an art of public address, Burke's "The Four Master Tropes" has been an eye-opener. That the Greek and Roman rhetoricians should have prepared extensive catalogues of figures and tropes had always seemed to us a bit bizarre, and the more than casual interest in these catalogues displayed by some literary critics and teachers of composition had often been taken as evidence of the low state into which rhetoric had fallen in English departments, reflecting a preoccupation with style over substance, form over content. Burke, along with the European structuralists and poststructuralists, has made us aware of the content in form, and, in particular, of the power of tropes as forms of thought and not mere stylistic devices. These and other parallels with the Europeans, discussed in various essays in this book, no doubt prompted John Nelson to classify Burke as part of a countertradition to objectivism that has been taking shape since Vico, and that includes such figures as Nietzsche, Freud, Wittgenstein, Heidegger, Foucault, and Derrida.[13] The "new sophistic," as he calls it, has been a diffuse, unselfconscious movement, consisting in the main of theorists who have rarely referred to their ideas in the jargon of that ancient craft, but who nevertheless bear close resemblance to the Greek sophists, especially by contrast with modernist conceptions of the scholarly enterprise.

Mention of Nelson's characterization of Burke brings to mind Dilip Gaonkar's portrayal of Burke's "Traditional Principles" essay in *A Rhetoric of Motives* as a rescue operation, an attempt at extending rhetoric's reach and reclaiming its history without at the same time depriving it of its "mereness," its lack of epistemic or substantive grounding, its status as a Derridean supplement.[14] Other contemporary writers, says Gaonkar, have found rhetoric's formal emptiness intolerable, but in seeking to provide it with a grounding they have denied it its unique potential as a critical perspective on other disciplines. Gaonkar singles Burke out as one who has not sought to remake rhetoric into something more respectable. To the contrary, his rescue operation involves a "return of the repressed," a confrontation with rhetoric's dark, unheralded, sophistic side, as reflected in the writings of the early sophists, as well as those of such as Marx and Machiavelli, Ovid and Carlyle, whom Burke was at pains to include as part of rhetoric's intellectual history. Maintains Gaonkar, Burke has helped ensure a future for the "rhetorical turn" in the human sciences by giving it a past.

Without considering Gaonkar's intriguing case in detail, I think it can be said that Burke's reconceptualization of rhetoric's nature and scope, as well as his reconstitution of its history, is far more compatible with current thinking about the human sciences than is the traditional view. The reconceptualization takes rhetoric well beyond the artificial confines imposed upon it by neo-Aristotelians who have sought to tame it, Platonists who haughtily dismissed it, and post-Enlightenment scholars who generally managed to ignore it or emasculate it. Said Burke,

> In part, we would but *rediscover* rhetorical elements that had become obscured when rhetoric as a term fell into disuse, and other specialized disciplines such as esthetics, anthropology, psychoanalysis, and sociology came to the fore (so that esthetics sought to outlaw rhetoric, while the other sciences we have mentioned took over, each in its own terms, the rich rhetorical elements that esthetics would ban).[15]

Burke's consideration of rhetoric's nature and scope in the "Traditional Principles" essay begins traditionally enough with a review of Greco-Roman conceptions of rhetoric. There is, he notes, the dominant view of rhetoric as an art of persuasion for the civic arena; dependent on ethics and politics for its judgments—the counterpart, as Aristotle put it, of dialectic. But even as Burke presents this traditional view, one begins to discern problems with its demarcation criteria that will resurface with renewed importance in the nontraditional texts that he examines later in the essay. There is rhetoric as persuasion, but there is also rhetoric as invention, the principles of which may guide inquiry and judgment—and not just on matters of civic concern. There is the sense of rhetoric as persuasion to action, but there is also persuasion to attitude, implying a freedom of choice for the audience that might admit of poetic devices as part of rhetoric's arsenal of techniques. Similarly, there is the sense of rhetoric as designed to bend another (*flectere*) but also to move, form, and mold another's opinions (*movere*). There is rhetoric as matter and manner, substance and form (in Cicero's terms, wisdom married to eloquence), and there is rhetoric as technique only. There is rhetoric as rational reason-giving, and there is rhetoric as appeal to emotion or sentiment, in place of reason. There is rhetoric as "the competitive use of the cooperative," but there is also advantage-seeking through rhetoric for the sake of the other *and* oneself.

In surveying rhetoric's traditional range of meanings, Burke seems to delight in its ambiguities, its dialectical potential for merger with or division from such other key concepts in Western thought as reality and appearance, reason and unreason, compulsion and choice, style and substance. Rhetoric is thus positioned as a central philosophical concept, raising for us many of the same questions as the sophists considered two thousand years ago. "Perhaps we should make clear," says Burke:

> We do not offer this list as a set of ingredients all or most of which must be present at once, as the test for the presence of the rhetorical motive. Rather, we are considering a wide range of meanings already associated with rhetoric, in ancient texts; and we are saying that one or another of these meanings may be uppermost in some particular usage. But though these meanings are often not consistent with one another, or are even flatly at odds, we do believe that they can all be derived from "persuasion" as the "Edenic" term from which they have all "Babylonically" split, while "persuasion" in turn involves communication by the signs of consubstantiality, the appeal of *identification*. (*RM*, pp. 61–62)

Typical of Burke's approach of rhetoric is his treatment of Marx and Bentham in the "Traditional Principles" essay. Of *A Rhetoric of Motives* Burke had written that it would "help us take delight in the Human Barnyard, with its addiction to the Scramble, an area that would cause us great unhappiness were we not able to transcend it by appreciation, classifying and tracing back to their origins in Edenic simplicity those linguistic modes of suasion that often seem little better than malice and the lie."[16] As rhetorical critic, Burke's own "hermeneutic of suspicion" (he called it "linguistic skepticism," or, after Nietzsche, "the Art of mistrust") was by no means reserved for the more obvious Scramblers in the Human Barnyard; it was brought to bear in equal measure on the discourse of the Academy, and especially those, such as Marx and Bentham, who purported to have privileged ways of knowing or communicating.

Typically, however, Burke has been a reclother rather than an unclother; his analyses demystify but do not debunk. While the objects of his analyses are often reclothed in comic dress, he is less interested in pronouncing a favorable or unfavorable judgment on a given work than in learning from it. Thus, as with Marx and Bentham, Burke repeatedly gleans ideas for rhetorical theory from unlikely contributors, managing to cast them not only as rhetoricians (theorists of persua-

sion) but as rhetors (persuaders) in their own right. Of both Marx and
Bentham, Burke writes that while rhetorical theory has traditionally
presented itself as a science of speaking well on issues of civic concern, their "polemic emphasis might rather have led them to define
rhetoric (or those aspects of it upon which they centered their attention) as: the knack of speaking ill in civic matters" (_RM_, p. 101). Marx's
major contribution to rhetorical theory, he argues, was to expose the
workings of ideology (by which Marx meant capitalist ideology), and
this he did quite well, little realizing, apparently, that the general principles of mythification and mystification that he articulated might apply equally well to Marxism itself.

But, of course, Marx's debunking project required that he present
his own analysis as "science"—hence, _above_ ideology—an objective
ground against which capitalist ideology as figure could be seen for
what it was. Bentham, like Marx, emerges as a rhetor in disguise and
as a rhetorician despite himself—able to see other writings as rhetorical, but not his own, yet hardly to be dismissed for so ubiquitous a
failing. Says Burke, Bentham's major contribution was to show how
interests, attitudes, sentiments, and the like are revealed in the most
innocent-seeming terms and expressions. Bentham called these "falla-
cies," "prejudices," "allegorical idols," and he sought in their place to
formulate a scientifically neutral vocabulary of interests. But while
Bentham was unable to do so, and indeed could not possibly have
done so, he thereby wound up providing far better evidence of the
rhetorical imperative than he would have had that been his intention.

Central to Burke's own theory of rhetoric is the concept of identification, understood broadly to include both appeals to common ground
and selective namings of a thing's ostensible properties. The concept
of identification informs not just Burke's writings on rhetoric, per se,
but also his analyses of fictional works as well as his dialectics. Beginning as he does with the dialectical pair of being and appearance that
was of such pivotal concern to the sophists, Burke's writings on dialectical merger (a kind of identification between ideas) and division
should be of special interest to rhetoricians of scholarly discourse. As
a social critic, writing out of his experience of two world wars and a
depression, Burke has been particularly attuned to forms of _"misidentification"_ (i.e., "the knack of speaking ill"), including seemingly innocent or unintended forms of deception that lie outside rhetoric's
traditional purview of concern. Hence his incorporation of Marx and
Bentham into the "Traditional Principles" essays as well as a host of
other figures not ordinarily accorded the status of rhetoricians. These
include Carlyle on the tactical uses of clothing, Ovid on sexual games-

manship, Empson on pastoral poetry as a social strategy, Diderot on courtly pantomimes, Rochefoucauld on hypocrisies, Gourmont on the dissociation of ideas, Pascal on "directing the intention," Machiavelli on administrative rhetoric. Burke writes:

> Particularly when we come upon such aspects of persuasion as are found in "mystification," courtship, and the "magic" of class relationships, the reader will see why the classical notion of clear persuasive intent is not an accurate fit, for describing the ways in which the members of a group promote social cohesion by acting rhetorically upon themselves and one another. (*RM*, p. xiv)

About This Book

The foregoing should provide some sense of what the Burkean legacy holds for humanists and social scientists, and especially for those interested in the rhetoric of the human sciences.[17] The essays gathered together in this volume should further illuminate Burke's contributions to the rhetoric of the human sciences while suggesting other implications and applications of Burkean theory as well as extensions and refinements of his basic ideas. Various essays introduce key concepts and help clarify difficult or ambiguous notions. Others provide not just a reading of Burke but a rereading in light of recent developments in critical theory.

The importance of this last function is related to the other two. Although Burke's reputation as a critical pathfinder is secure, and although his credentials as a virtuoso reader and critic have been vouchsafed by the likes of Auden, Hyman, Bloom, and Booth, the fact is that he is also among the most elusive of contemporary writers; and the passage of time since the initial publication of his major works has not made the mining of his rich deposits any easier. Readers have difficulty putting his ideas together coherently and assigning him a place among contending critical theories, let alone figuring out how to do what he does so well.

No doubt part of the reason Burke has not reached a wider audience is academic encrustation. Said Frank Lentricchia,

> Until recent years the canons of truth and sanity that govern the writing of critical theory in the United States have implicitly decreed that much of what Kenneth Burke does is a deviation from good sense. Which I translate: disturbing, different,

Herbert W. Simons

> perhaps dangerous. Burke is the great either/or of
> contemporary theory for he cannot be accepted in small,
> bearable doses. He must be taken all at once or not at all. But
> to take him all at once would require a radical reconception of
> the basis of what is usually called humanistic study.

True enough; yet we are convinced that this is not the whole story. From another perspective, more likely the dominant one, Burke is "undisciplined" to the point of appearing eccentric or even perverse. An inveterate "convolutionist," as his friend Malcolm Cowley described him, Burke is as apt to treat a pun seriously as a piety mockingly. Burke is forever inventing new terminologies or giving new twists to old ideas.[19] Worse yet, to many readers, he seems to delight in "gratuitous asides," "benign casuistries," "felicitous distortions," "perspectives by incongruity": his pen refuses to be penned in. Add to these qualities a tendency for his ideas to double back upon themselves tautologically in what Burke himself has called "the heads-I-win-tails-you-lose" method of argument.

Moreover, while Burkean theory may appear at times to be tautological, there are other times when it appears blatantly inconsistent, often intentionally so. It is not simply that Burke's ideas have changed over the years, or that the various terminologies tend to get intermixed; it is rather the case that "this mind that cannot stop exploding," as Howard Nemerov described him, is liable to erupt when we least expect it, oftentimes blowing to smithereens ideas that he has been at pains to construct on the page before.

These considerations lead us back to the question of Burke's contribution to the central issues of contemporary critical theory. Among Burke's detractors—and there are many—his alleged misuses of language and logic are proof positive of the ultimate vacuousness of his philosophy. Said Robert M. Adams, "He is the most explanatory of writers, and his explanations never quite add up; he is ridden by a thesis which so far has never failed to question, subvert and frustrate its own accomplishment."[20]

By another way of thinking, however, this self-questioning, "stable instability," as Michael Leff puts it in this volume, is the true mark of Burke's genius. Although many question the result, few doubt that Burke's comedic style—his puns and twists and extensions and asides—are an essential part of his method.

At the University of Iowa Humanities Symposium on the Rhetoric of the Human Sciences, Paul Hernadi singled out Burke as one who has managed to be ironically self-reflexive without at the same time being self-deconstructive.[21] I read Hernadi as saying that the various poststructuralist efforts at deconstructing foundationalism, objectivism, realism, and the like, as well as the equally hopeful semiotic and hermeneutic enterprises that came into prominence in the wake of the discrediting of objectivism, have trapped the deconstructionists themselves in the vortex of their own ironic reversals. Part of the attraction of the "rhetorical turn" in the human sciences and, in particular, of Kenneth Burke's brand of "new sophistic" is that it offers a humanistic alternative to an unreflexive objectivism and a self-debilitating nihilism, one that builds dialectically on an ironic recognition of our inherent limitations. Of the contributors to this volume who comment on Burke's relation to other critical theories, I believe only Cary Nelson would demur from Hernadi's claim, although Damrosch, Leff, Lentricchia, Oravec, and Williams offer quite different reasons for their concurrence with it.

How can Burke's musings about rhetoric and dialectic be put to use by research-minded social scientists? Sociologist Joseph Gusfield provides an introduction to Burke that should be of particular value to social scientists. In the process of familiarizing some readers with basic concepts and distinctions, Gusfield also manages to suggest the uses that have been made of Burke by such writers as Erving Goffman, Peter Manning, and Murray Edelman. Gusfield himself has made good use of Burke in such works as *Symbolic Crusade* and *The Culture of Social Problems*, but this has not deterred him from voicing what is probably a major source of resistance to Burke by social scientists: i.e., Burke's failure to account in "scenic" terms for the symbols we employ and the attitudes they express. Says Gusfield, "I look for some way of linking up particular ways of placement, particular God-terms, with historical periods, with classes, nationality groups, or social structures."

One possible rejoinder to Gusfield is that Burke, while not entirely indifferent to conditions giving rise to particular forms of discourse, is simply less interested in causes per se than in the accounts people provide of causation. Even during his most strongly Marxist period he recognized that material conditions of existence do not achieve their full social significance until they are inscribed in accounts. In this respect Burke bears strong affinity with ethnomethodologists and with attribution theorists in psychology. In *A Grammar of Motives*, Burke takes special delight in laying bare the rhetoric of accounts; i.e., the ways they exploit the "resources of ambiguity" in language.

More fundamentally, perhaps, *A Grammar of Motives* may be read as an extended argument for a view of linguistic causation much closer to Aristotle's than to mechanistic reductions of the role of human agency

Herbert W. Simons

in the name of science. So maintains sociologist/anthropologist Vito Signorile in his comparison between Aristotle's tetrad and Burke's pentad. The pentad, he argues, is a much-needed reconceptualization of Aristotle's tetrad, put in contemporary terms. Signorile takes special pains to defend what is probably most controversial in Burke, the notion of a logological entelechy in language paralleling Aristotle's more animistic conception of a telos or purpose in nature. The social sciences, he observes, had all but reduced Aristotle's four causes to one—efficient cause—thus finding it necessary to smuggle in other causes, often by way of teleological metaphors.

Donald McCloskey places Burke in the company of other critical theorists who treat scientific discourse in much the same terms as they might *Anna Karenina* or *Madame Bovary.* McCloskey finds Burke uncommonly "economistic" and also exceptionally shrewd for a layman on matters economic. McCloskey's own writings on the rhetoric of scholarly discourse have been profoundly disturbing to many social scientists, and especially to his colleagues in economics. They will not be cheered any the more by his intimation in this volume that the law of demand obeys Burke's "law" of good form: "yielding to the form prepares assent to the matter identified with it." Says McCloskey, "If there is a Law of Supply—there are many reasons to think so—it is hard to resist the symmetrical attractions of a Law of Demand."

Together these essays help confirm Burke's observation that "The error of the social sciences has usually resided in the attempt to appropriate the scenic calculus for a charting of the Act." But, maintains my coeditor, Trevor Melia, Burke is not antiscience or antimathematics by any means; indeed, his dramatism, his method of cluster analysis, his thought experiments exhibit a "scientific-mathematic streak." As a rhetorician of science (not just of the rhetoric of the social sciences), Melia is particularly interested in Burke's distinctions between motion and action, animality and symbolicity. These he applies to illustrative problems in mathematics and in the biological and physical sciences.

Several contributors to this volume comment on sources of Burke's own ideas. Among the major influences on Burke have been Aristotle, Plato, Spinoza, Marx, Freud, Nietzsche, Emerson, William James, Coleridge—as well as the many literary-left bohemians with whom he "co-haggled" (his term) during the twenties and thirties. In this volume Jane Blankenship compares Burke with Coleridge while Michael Leff declares Burke to be a Ciceronian. Leff's claim is especially interesting in that the received opinion among rhetoricians has always been that Burke's primary classical legator was Aristotle. It turns out, however, that Leff is less interested in direct influences than in certain features that Burke and Cicero share in common.[22] Indeed, from Leff's own perspective by incongruity, Cicero is also a Burkean. Most fundamentally, says Leff,

> Both drive the philosophy of language as action to a point that demands self-reflexive discourse about the theory of the discourse. This position, in turn, yields two related consequences. The first, and most obvious, is that since their texts aim to embody more than they state, they would teach less by abstract dicta than by example. . . . The second consequence is that the work of both authors culminates in irony. (P. 119)

Central to Burke's thinking, but occasioning widely varying interpretations of its meaning and implications, is Burke's theory of language. Helping readers better understand that theory is the aim of Blankenship's essay on "magic and mystery." Blankenship offers a cataloguing of the many insights about language that Burke gleaned from Coleridge, including his concept of entitlements. Together, she argues, Burke and Coleridge remind us that "if we have the profound propensity via our linguistic entitlements to constitute estrangements, we also have the sometime knack for creating alchemic moments which allow us to transcend divisiveness" (p. 144).

A pivotal issue as regards Burke's theory of language, ultimately engendering controversy on a variety of fronts, concerns the extent to which the human being, as the "symbol-using/symbol-misusing" animal, is also the "symbol-used" animal. Signorile places Burke in the post-Kantean symbolist tradition of Cassirer, Mead, and Langer, while Melia and Blankenship trace Burke's symbolist roots to Nietzsche, Coleridge, and Bergson. The issue is complicated, raising questions about the relationship between ontology and epistemology. For simplicity's sake, then, we might distinguish between weak and strong versions of the symbolist position, the former attesting in various ways to the influence of language on perception, thought, judgment, action, and the like, the latter to its necessity and sufficiency. Both symbolists would insist that, far from being a mirror of reality, language may in some respects be constitutive of reality. *Who* we are as individuals and as people, *how* we understand ourselves to be joined in time and space, *what* we consider to be problems or nonproblems, all depend on the language we select to "create," as it were, the worlds we inhabit. However, for "strong" symbolists there can be no reality, or any account of reality (or any account of that account), that is not mediated, indeed constituted, by language; and there can be no action in the world that is not language-driven.

That humans differ most essentially from other animals and from machines by dint of their capacity to symbolize and to symbolize about symbols is a cardinal principle in Burke. In fact, his distinction between symbolic action and nonsymbolic motion is said to be a literal one. Burke understands language in part as a repository of possibilities for thought or expressions. By one's choice of language one may conceal or reveal, magnify or minimize, simplify or make complex, elevate or degrade, link or divide, create a sense of breadth or of specificity.

However, Burke sometimes pushes the symbolist position to the point where language is said not only to provide resources which communicators may exploit, but also to exhibit its own *resourcefulness*—impelling us, for example, to call imaginary worlds into being by the magical act of naming; or to bureaucratize our best and most noble ideas, making them "rotten with perfection"; or, goaded by a dialectical impulse, to convert differences into oppositions and oppositions into war. Does this mean, then, that far from enabling us to act freely upon the world, our symbol-using capacity may actually be running us? There is certainly a tension between these ideas in Burke, as there is in structuralist and poststructuralist thought and in certain strands of literary Marxism and Freudianism as well.

Indeed, as I suggested earlier, there may be no tension more central in current efforts to reconstitute the human sciences. Shapiro credits Heidegger with having foregrounded the question of linguistic determinism in contemporary philosophical thought:

> According to Heidegger, Kant turned the question, "What is a thing?", into the question, "Who is man?". Kant's new formulation was liberating inasmuch as it frees us from the tyranny of the object. Rather than looking for meaning in the world of things, Kant turned the gaze inward, positioning the structure of human consciousness as the formal, *a priori* condition for our apprehension of things. But Kant's reorientation remained quarantined within the relentless grammatical metaphor of Enlightenment philosophy. Knowledge remained for Kant a relationship between subjects and objects. . . . What Kant neglected, and what science as a whole brackets, are the social practices or ways of being in the world that constitute man in any historical period. . . . What science neglects, according to Heidegger, is what he called the "ground plan," that which is embedded in the practices of the age and which links and constitutes man, determining being in

such a profound way that it gives rise to the questions of research. Heidegger displaces the ego subject, the subject of consciousness from the center of knowledge and puts in its place an historical, changing subject constituted as a set of skills and/or practices, including (and especially) linguistic practices which "house" human existence.[23]

But is there meaning in such a view? And what is the ontological status of both the subject and the object of inquiry? Is the "historical, changing subject" anything more than a linguistic representation? Or is there perhaps some validity in the notion of a "recovered" or "transcendent" self, capable of acting effectively upon the world, as inquirer, interpreter, critic, activist?

Here readings of Burke differ, just as representatives of contending schools differ among themselves. Many readers have seen affinities between Burke's theory of dramatism and French structuralism, which Lentricchia has recently labeled a "critical structuralism" in the manner of Roland Barthes. But Burke's interpretation of the Coleridgean dictum that language does our thinking for us might step beyond structuralism into the labyrinth of deconstructionism.

So argues Nelson in an essay explicitly intended as offering a "counter-Burke" to the "humanistic Burke" of Marie Nichols, Bernard Brock, Leland Griffin, Lloyd Bitzer, and, more recently, Wayne Booth and Denis Donoghue. Early on, suggests Nelson, Burke came to realize that texts convince in part "by establishing structured and hierarchized relations between their key terms" (p. 159). Later, he recognized "both the thoroughness of the motives of particular languages and the structural similarities of all terministic screens" (p. 159). Burke also understood that the self is in many respects "a semiotic subject" (p. 160), and he attempted, independently of Levi-Strauss and other French structuralists, "to work out the persuasively binary basis of complex idiolects."

But, insists Nelson, Burke's fit with structuralism was always a bit strained and became increasingly so in his later writings. In contrast with classical structuralism, Burke's acting subject is "radically historicized" (p. 170). Moreover, Burke, like Derrida, "continually marks and undermines his own agency by way of difference with his own work, so that intent is recuperable only as a sequence of self-regarding displacements and totality is deferred" (p. 163). By Nelson's reading—he admits it may be a misreading—Burke came to believe "that language is *all* there is, that no material world exists for us" (p. 169).

In casting Burke as a deconstructionist, Nelson seems quite aware of the consequences of his reading. Pushed to the Derridean extreme, language becomes an agent rather than an agency, and we become its servants. Moreover, nothing can exist outside the text, where truth is in effect a trope. Placed in jeopardy, then, by this most extreme version of the symbolist position are any and all claims by Burke, or others, as to the literal status of concepts (including his own central concept of dramatism), or the decidability of alternative readings, or the possibility that the paradoxes that confront us can be resolved by dialectical means (including Burke's much-vaunted perspectivism).[24] According to Nelson, Burke's promise of dialectic as an "orderly parliamentary development" is belied by Burke's own style of writing which is more like a series of dislocations than an orderly progression. Moreover, in what may be the ultimate provocation to those who have long identified with Burke's view of criticism as an instrument for social progress ("Towards a Better Life"), Nelson offers a "counter-Burke" who has always satirized our myths of progress and who, in his later works, "where the sense of the fatefulness of linguistic determinism is so strong," exhibits little faith that the satirist's project will accomplish anything. Says Nelson, Burke is perhaps "the modern Swift who knows his modest proposal will be taken literally" (p. 167).

Lest these evidences of skepticism (by Nelson?; by Burke?) be interpreted as grounds for utter and complete despair, Nelson hastens to suggest that being placed "in the Derridean paradox of using the language of Western metaphysics to call Western metaphysics into question...may not be a particularly disadvantageous place for a Burkean to be. For one of the striking things that have happened to Burke's texts in the past fifteen years is that the rest of criticism, or at least *some* of the rest of criticism, has grown into Burke and into an acceptance of the Burkean position that criticism can be exemplary *and* arbitrary, informative *and* undecidable" (pp. 166–67).

I have featured Nelson's essay in this section in part because it so effectively frames many of the other essays in this book. Though certainly not intended as such, the essays by Lentricchia, Oravec, Williams, and Damrosch may be viewed as partial or qualified refutations of Nelson—qualified because none of the contributors denies the importance of irony to Burke, and, indeed, all would agree with Nelson that Burke is never more Burkean than when he is undercutting his own schemata.

Lentricchia concedes that Burke has effectively called into question the privileging by liberal humanists of the autonomous actor-subject. But, says Lentricchia, "when he is finished he has not destroyed the humanistic impulse of his dramatism; he has only (and this by design) relocated the 'free subject' within a system that is now understood in more complex fashion than his bare-bones formulation of dramatism would admit."[25] Most important, the actor or agent is seen as operating within a constraining context and as being "the not-always-knowing carrier of historical and ideological forces." At the same time, however, the actor "acts within and upon the present and thereby becomes an agent of change."[26]

Lentricchia's perspective is that of the literary activist seeking to use criticism as a counter-hegemonic instrument of social change. Rather than regard politics as "something that somehow goes on somewhere else"[27]—outside the university—Lentricchia would have academics bring their learning, their cultural insights, their rhetoric to bear upon the rhetoric of the civic arena. Lentricchia's model of cultural activism is Kenneth Burke, and the Burke that he chooses to highlight, then, is a leftist, a Marxist of sorts, but one who is steeped in American pragmatism. Lentricchia sees Burke's entire career as exemplary, but he focuses, appropriately enough, on Burke's activist period and in particular on a highly controversial address by Burke, entitled "Revolutionary Symbolism in America," which Burke delivered in 1935 to the Communist-led American Writers' Congress.[28] Here Burke made direct application of his own theorizing about rhetoric in proposing what to many of his more orthodox allies was absolute heresy: first, "that we take 'the people' rather than 'the worker' as our basic symbol of exhortation and allegiance"; second, "that the imaginative writer seek to propagandize his cause by surrounding it with as full a cultural texture as he can manage, thus thinking of propaganda not as an over-simplified, literal, explicit writing of lawyer's briefs, but as a process of broadly and generally associating his political alignment with cultural awareness in the large" (p. 273). Although a close reading of the speech is rewarding in its own right, it is also a perfect vehicle for Lentricchia's argument that the critic-as-rhetor may indeed serve as a powerful engine of progressive change. In contravention of our general rule of limiting this volume to essays not published elsewhere, we have included the Burke speech and the ensuing discussion of the speech at the congress, as well as Lentricchia's analysis of it, in the Appendix to this book.

In the headnote which accompanies his essay in this volume, Lentricchia allows that it could be read as a response to Fredric Jameson's critique of Burke, although it was not initially intended as such. Jameson had argued in *Critical Inquiry* that Burke may have unwittingly collaborated in the ideology of bourgeois individualism by reiterating "American myths of the self and of its identity crises and ultimate regeneration." "The dramatistic modes," he maintained, "are all categories of consciousness, open to the light of day in classical, well-nigh Aristotelian fashion; the Burkean symbolic act is thus always serenely transparent to itself, in lucid blindness to the dark underside of language, to the ruses of history or of desire."[29]

While Lentricchia merely invites a reading of his essay as a response to Jameson's, Christine Oravec leaves little doubt that Jameson is her antagonist. Consistent with Lentricchia, she argues that Burke's subject, while perhaps linguistically constructed, is also constructing and thus quite capable of serving as a generative social force. The possibilities for transcendental freedom within the constraints of language are nowhere better exhibited, she argues, than in Burke's analyses of Milton's *Samson Agonistes* and Plato's *Phaedrus*. Here Burke builds on his theory of associations, showing how the authors' identities emerge from their respective rhetorics of identification. Just as Milton "as an authorial subject is constructed by the determining power of language," says Oravec, so "Plato is produced as an author through his traces in the Socratic dialectic." Of course the emergent subjects have ironic aspects, thus revealing Burke's own highly sophisticated sense of the relationship between identity, language, and historical determination:

> Milton, the pious Protestant, becomes the self-obsessed and passively murderous rebel, a figure not unlike his own Satan. Plato becomes the seductive and effective rhetor, of the kind which he himself castigates in the *Gorgias* and other dialogues. But by deriving the subject from its own language, Burke criticizes the received view of both Milton and Plato without reducing their positioning to random, arbitrary events in the subtext of history, or mere reflections of their material circumstances. (P. 190)

Williams' essay is a highly complex but exceptionally lucid exploration of the "margins of overlap" between Burke and Derrida and simultaneously of the relationship between nihilistic criticism and annihilation by nuclear war. To this bi-leveled dialectic, Williams offers a third component, a dialectical analysis of dialectic itself. Are Burke and Derrida opposed in their treatments of the relationship between critical warfare and military warfare? This, argues Williams, is an error that the form of dialectical reasoning too easily impels us to make. Williams laments the tendency within both academic and societal arenas to convert differences into oppositions and oppositions into wars, and he congratulates both Burke and Derrida for their efforts to reconstitute oppositions as differences. There are, says Williams, important differences between the two writers, most notably that

> Burke's system, encompassing both logology and dramatism, fights to avoid the progressive deconstruction ad infinitum which Derrida accepts with the understanding that there will always be a remainder, a trace, a living on. Burke grounds his perspective in what I call the "ontological loop" of dramatism; that is, dramatism, as Burke has decreed, is an ontological perspective: it tells us who we *are* in a substantial, constitutive sense. We *are* the symbol-using animal, suggesting that we inhabit, enact, dramatize the problematics of language, the duplicities of dialectic. (P. 216)

Still, Williams chooses not to play up this difference between Burke and Derrida; he recognizes for one thing that, while the "ontological loop" in dramatism affords it a ground on which to stand, "it is a ground of paradox, a molten and liquid ground wherein transformations are likely to occur" (p. 218). "In a sense," concludes Williams,

> Derrida's ontodeconstruction and Burke's ontological construction revolve around each other, arguing with each other in ways that...seem to place them in opposition. But since each problematizes the rigidity of structures of opposition, the margin between—the margin of overlap—reasserts itself. In the end there is no end to the conversation: the revelation of the end, the apocalypse of the end is to begin again, to engage in the endless process of interpretation, and to find what joy, what affirmation we may in it, for to cease the process of interpretation is to invite the Apocalypse without remainder, to enact the end that awaits at the end of the oppositional line. (P. 218)

David Damrosch's ostensible concern is with Burke's reading of Augustine in *The Rhetoric of Religion*. Is it a deconstruction of Augustine, as John Freccero has argued,[30] or is it something else—an allegory perhaps? Why, asks Damrosch, did Burke choose Augustine as the basis of his study in moving from dramatism to logology when, in principle at least, he could have chosen any theologian and certainly one less hostile to drama than Augustine?

Like Oravec, Damrosch is interested in the relationship between a text and its implied author, but in this case the object of interest is Burke himself. Damrosch argues that Burke's reading of the *Confessions* is deeply autobiographical. Moreover, the Burke/Augustine relation is synecdochic of the larger claim of logology that "what we say about *words*, in the empirical realm, will bear a notable likeness to what is said about *God*, in theology."[31] Parodying Burke's own parody of Augustine, Damrosch offers as a definition of logology "the perception that anything that can be said about God can also be said about Kenneth Burke" (p. 224).

Damrosch's logological reading of Burke on Augustine takes numerous twists and turns, just as does Burke's reading of Augustine on God. The sense of allegory which Burke uses is derivable, says Damrosch, from *A Rhetoric of Motives* wherein Burke writes:

> The new equivalent of "moral" or "tropological" criticism would probably be found in a concern with the poem as a ritual that does things for the writer and reader. . . . Any sense in which one order is interpreted as the sign of another would probably be the modern equivalent of the "allegorical."

In general, Damrosch sees far greater continuities between the earlier and later Burkes than is suggested by Nelson. There is, he maintains, "a natural affinity between dramatism and logology, between a dramatic reading of rhetoric and a theological reading." Furthermore, he suggests, "This affinity can also be observed in the other major dramatistic theoretician of interpretation, Hans-Georg Gadamer" (p. 224).

What emerges from Damrosch's reading is a view of Burke as far more Gadamerian than Derridean. Burke, like Gadamer, finds a natural grounding for his dramatism in religious experience. Moreover, each allows for a range of meaning in texts while asserting "that some defined truth persists in the range of meaning" (p. 225).

The essays previewed thus far should help clarify Burkean theory and locate it within the larger corpus of contemporary critical theories; they should provide a sense of the uses of Burkean theory both within individual disciplines and as a unifying force across disciplines; and they should suggest implications and applications of Burkean concepts as well as extensions and refinements of his basic ideas. Immodestly, we believe that no other anthology is as reflective of the scope of application of Burke's own concerns.

Still, neither this nor any other such book can adequately represent the Burkean legacy, and we have focused our efforts on the rhetorical/dialectical/logological Burke. Richard Thames's bibliography does a thoroughgoing job of bringing the reader up to date on other critical reflections on Burke's writings, a project initiated by Armin Paul Frank and Mechthild Frank in a book edited by William Rueckert.[32] However it is to Rueckert himself that we have here turned for a more rounded picture of Burke's legacy. His concluding essay in the main portion of this book offers a guided tour of the major works, and through them, a reading of the man himself. Rueckert's personal asides on how he has been moved by Burke recalled our own moments with Burke, including a visit Melia and I made recently to his home in Andover. Being readied for the occasion was a pot of what I dubbed "Burke Soup." The basic ingredients, he explained, were cabbage and broccoli; he'd been using these, he said, since he'd begun making the soup more than sixty years ago. Aside from these ingredients—the symbolic action and nonsymbolic motion of his concoction?—there was very little permanence and a great deal of change in the soup from one day to the next. A recurring theme in our conversation was Burke's "double vision," expressed metaphorically in the many dualisms that he wrestled with, but also experienced psychosomatically in times of great stress, and particularly as he was working out the implications of his own linguistic creations. Burke here offers powerful testimony to his having been used by language, but there is clear evidence as well of the autonomous agent. Indeed, the most incredible story he tells is about the logological equivalent of the "Good Book."

At age six or seven, he reports, he was kept back from school; the doctors feared that he had become learning-disabled from a fall off a second-story perch. While the other kids were learning their ABCs, Burke was twiddling his thumbs—until one day, out of a perverse sense of irony, his mother gave him a dictionary.

"That's right," said Burke, "she gave me the 'Good Book,' but with no instructions on how to figure out what was inside it." And so Burke poked around in it, and carried it around as he might have a doll or a panda bear. Eventually, he reports, "the damn thing began to make sense. And before long I had it pretty well figured out."

"Many people," says Burke, "have remarked on what a terrible thing it was for my mother to have given me that dictionary and not instructed me in it. But looking back, I was damned fortunate. Y'see, lots of kids who learn to read the easy way don't get much out of it, but I had to develop a theory of language!"

When reading Burke, it is easy to get caught up in a world of symbols—as happened to me one night after a visiting lecture at another university. In preparing for the lecture, I had come across an essay of Burke's that I had never read, "Mind, Body, and the Unconscious" (in *LSA*), and I had been particularly taken with his classification of the five symbolic dogs:

> First, along psychoanalytic lines, there is the "primal" dog, the first dog you knew, or loved, or were frightened by, or lost. . . .
> Next there's the "jingle" dog. It concerns the sheerly accidental nature of the *word* dog, what it rhymes with in English as distinct from what the corresponding word rhymes with in other languages. . . .
> Third, comes the "lexical" dog. This is the one defined in the dictionary, "by genus and differentia." It is the most public, normal, and rational of all dogs—and the emptiest of all, as regards the attitude of either poets or neurotics. . . .
> Fourth, there's an "entelechial" dog. This is the "perfect" dog *towards which* one might aspire. . . .
> Finally, there is the "tautological" dog. We here have in mind the fact that a dog involves a particular set of associations which, in a sense, reproduce his spirit. . . .

After returning home from lecturing about the five dogs, I prepared to take my own dog for her nightly walk. It was not until I was halfway down the block that I realized I had become so caught up in Burke's symbolic dogs that I had forgotten my nonsymbolic dog.[33]

On doing his own rereading of the major works in preparation for this assignment, Rueckert concluded that "criticism as a way of life, rather than system-building, is what accounts for the logic of Burke's career." Burke himself, at our recent meeting, spoke with pride of his always having played a "middleman" role, helping readers better appreciate and thus cash in on one perspective by translating it—transforming it—into the currency of another.

For a critic, and especially one who has fought so many political battles, Burke has emerged astonishingly mellow. In Burke's double vision there is room enough for scientists and solipsists, capitalists and communists (both at the mercy of technology anyway), atheists and religionists. Asked whether it is possible to reconcile the oppositions with which he and the rest of the world must currently contend, he asked us to imagine an academy in which, on any given issue, the many voices in the Platonic-cum-Burkean dialogue might be heard to provide the strongest arguments for their respective positions. On a number of issues about which we expected to find him insistent on this point or that, we found Burke flexible to the point of apparent indifference. We doubt, for example, whether Burke cares a whit whether subsequent generations label him a structuralist or a poststructuralist.

But Burke does have his essentials—the cabbage and broccoli of his theory. Their place in what otherwise is a critical pluralism is suggested by Burke in the title of an essay which he prepared for a conference on pluralism at the University of Nebraska in 1984: "When Pluralist Necessarily, When Decidedly Not." With Burke's permission we have concluded the main portion of this book with a previously unpublished poem from that essay.[34] It serves as an addendum of sorts to Burke's "Definition of Man."

NOTES

1. On dust jacket of Burke's *Collected Poems* (Berkeley: University of California Press, 1968).
2. Reported by Burke in "Counter-Gridlock: An Interview with Kenneth Burke," *All Area*, no. 2 (1983), p. 7.
3. Cited on dust jacket of Burke's novel, *Towards a Better Life* (Berkeley: University of California Press, 1966).
4. William Rueckert, "Some of the Many Kenneth Burkes," In Hayden White and Margaret Brose, eds., *Representing Kenneth Burke*. (Baltimore: English Institute and Johns Hopkins University Press, 1982), p. 3.
5. These and other tributes to Burke the critic are assembled by Ben Yagoda in "Kenneth Burke: The Greatest Literary Critic since Coleridge?" *Horizon*, 23 (June 1980), 66–69.
6. Richard Kostelanetz, "About Kenneth Burke: A Mind That Cannot Stop Exploding," *New York Times Book Review*, March 15, 1981, p. 11. Coinage of the term Burkology is Hyman's—to which Burke replied in a poem that this was one subject he consistently flunked. Hyman had defined it as an attempt "to do no less than to integrate all man's knowledge into a workable, critical frame."
7. A useful resource on this and other biographical matters is the *All Area* interview, pp. 4–35. Also see the special issue of *Pre/Text* 6, nos. 3–4 (1986).
8. Quoted by Yagoda, "Kenneth Burke," p. 67. See also Wayne Booth's *Critical Understanding: The Powers and Limits of Pluralism* (Chicago: University of Chicago Press, 1979).
9. Yagoda, "Kenneth Burke," p. 67.
10. See Herbert W. Simons, "Chronical and Critique of a Conference," *Quarterly Journal of Speech*, 71 (1985), 52–64.
11. For a discussion of other such "essentially contestable terms," see W. B. Gallie, *Philosophy and the Historical Understanding* (London: Chatto and Windus, 1964), pp. 91–157.
12. See Clifford Geertz, "Blurred Genres: The Refiguration of Social Thought," *American Scholar*, 49 (1980), 165–79. See also Geertz' tribute to

26

Herbert W. Simons

Burke in *Works and Lives: The Anthropologist as Author* (Palo Alto: Stanford University Press, 1988), p. vi.

13. J. S. Nelson, "Political Theory as Political Rhetoric," in Nelson, ed., *What Should Political Theory Be Now?* (Albany: SUNY Press, 1983), pp. 176–93.

14. Dilip Gaonkar, "Rhetoric and Its Double: Reflections on the Rhetorical Turn in the Human Sciences," in H. W. Simons, ed., *The Rhetorical Turn: Invention and Persuasion in the Conduct of Inquiry* (Chicago: University of Chicago Press, scheduled for 1989).

15. Kenneth Burke, *A Rhetoric of Motives* (Berkeley: University of California Press, 1969), p. xiii.

16. Kenneth Burke, *A Grammar of Motives* (Berkeley: University of California Press, 1969), p. 442.

17. I hope it is clear that in casting Burke as a rhetorician of the human sciences (and a sophistic one to boot), I in no way wish to minimize his accomplishments as literary critic, aesthetician, dialectician, etc. Rather, I have sought to use the rhetoric of the human sciences as a filter, a terministic screen through which to look out upon his many contributions. Burke himself has objected, in a recent issue of *Pre/Text*, to my field's overidentification of him with the field of rhetoric. But as *Pre/Text's* editor, Victor Vitanza, observed, Burke himself frequently treats rhetoric as an overarching frame, much as Richard McKeon did in his well-known essay on an architectonic view of rhetoric. By my admittedly perverse reading, much of contemporary literary and discourse theory, particularly poststructuralism, can be understood as contributions to the new movement. See Victor J. Vitanza, "A Mal-Lingering Thought (Tragic-Comedic) about KB's Visit," *Pre/Text*, 6 (Fall/Winter 1985), 163–67.

18. Frank Lentricchia, *Criticism and Social Change.* (Chicago: University of Chicago Press, 1983), p. 53.

19. Of Burke's "idiosyncratic and irridescent" terminologies, Robert M. Adams has written that "while they may account in part for the rage felt by professional philosophers with Burke's work, they delight the practicing Burkeist with a sense of metaphoric amplitude, of language taxed to the utmost." See *TLS*, July 8, 1983, p. 717.

20. Ibid., p. 715.

21. Paul Hernadi, "Literary Interpretation and the Rhetoric of the Human Sciences." Presented at the Iowa Symposium on the Rhetoric of the Human Sciences, March 28, 1984.

22. Donald McCloskey has furnished additional support for Leff's view of Burke as Ciceronian with this wonderful quotation from Plutarch's *Lives*: "By contrast with the bitterness and sullenness [of Demosthenes], Cicero was often carried away by his love of jesting into scurrility [*bomologon*], and when, to gain his ends in his cases, he treated matters worthy of serious attention with ironical mirth and pleasantry, he was careless of propriety." (trans. B. Perrin, [Cambridge: Loeb Classical Library, Harvard University Press, 1971], pp. 212–13).

23. See Michael Shapiro, "Literary Production as a Politicizing Practice," in H. W. Simons and A. A. Aghazarian, *Form, Genre, and the Study of Political Discourse* (Columbia: University of South Carolina Press, 1986), pp. 159–94.

24. I have also called into question the literal status of dramatism in Burke's system. See our exchange in "Dramatism as Ontology or Epistemology: A Symposium," *Communication Quarterly*, 33 (1985), 17–33.

25. Lentricchia, *Criticism and Social Change*, pp. 71–72.

26. Ibid., pp. 159–60.

27. Ibid., p. 7.

28. See Appendix for speech and discussion. Looking back on the speech from the perspective of fifty-plus years, Burke told us that he wouldn't change a single word. But it was not this way in the immediate aftermath of the speech, as Burke recounts in the *All Area* interview. "I really felt the ostracism. I was *out*....I lay down and I'd hear 'Burke! Burke!' My own name had become a curse word. I'd wake up and finally, my god, just this side of an hallucination: my tongue...shit dripping from my tongue. Horrible" (p. 16). Some sense of the negative reaction to the speech at the time is found in the discussion of the speech that took place the next day of the congress. The connections Burke makes and that Lentricchia underscores between politics and education seem to us a fitting ending to a book emphasizing Burke's contribution to the rhetoric of the human sciences.

29. The essay is reprinted in White and Brose's *Representing Kenneth Burke*. See Fredric Jameson, "The Symbolic Inference; or, Kenneth Burke and Ideological Analysis," pp. 68–91. Quote is on p. 88.

30. See John Freccero, "Logology: Burke on St. Augustine." In White and Brose, *Representing Kenneth Burke*, pp. 52–67.

31. Kenneth Burke, *The Rhetoric of Religion* (Berkeley: University of California Press, 1970), pp. 13–14.

32. See William Rueckert, ed., *Critical Responses to Kenneth Burke, 1924–1966* (Minneapolis: University of Minnesota Press, 1969), 495–512.

33. Evidently Burke has had similar experiences confusing the symbolic and nonsymbolic in respect to his own terms. On puzzling over how he'd come to a pentad rather than, say, a hexad featuring attitude as the sixth term, Burke recalled a letter in which he referred to his five children as my "five terms." Correspondingly, the terms were his five children. They had become personalities. See the *All Area* interview, p. 19.

34. Our thanks to James Ford for making the essay available to us.

1

THE BRIDGE OVER

SEPARATED LANDS

KENNETH BURKE'S

SIGNIFICANCE FOR

THE STUDY OF SOCIAL ACTION

JOSEPH R. GUSFIELD

Among his many talents, Kenneth Burke is a master of the oxymoron, that figure of speech which unites incongruous or contradictory terms. I think he would regard "social science" as an example of the oxymoron. The concept of the "social," inherently a human, dramatic form of action, is coupled with "science," a method most successfully used with inanimate objects, animals, and the animality in humans. The resulting term must seem to him both comedic and contradictory.

Burke has had a persistent, even though limited, impact on social scientists. While he has yet to be given recognition as a major sociological "theorist," for some of us he has played that role for several decades. In anthropology, sociology, and political science he has deeply influenced a number of scholars and their studies.[1] In the past decade, the emergence of several movements in both social science and literary criticism has given Burke's thought increased importance. Structuralism, linguistic analysis, critical theory, symbolic anthropology, and cognitive sociology have all focused the gaze of sociologists on modes of presentation and interpretation and on the central importance of language to human action. Burke's dramatism and dialectical method, developed in the 1930s and 1940s, seem suddenly to be in crowded company.

Why Burke? To judge by the audience of his readers he has been primarily viewed as a literary critic.[2] With some exceptions, including the very important one of Hugh Dalziel Duncan, there have been few major commentaries on Burke by social scientists.[3] A number of us have made use of Burkean concepts and methods in empirical research, as will be described in this paper. In general, social scientists have shown small interest in literary criticism, regarding critics as an intriguing breed, necessary to any self-respecting intellectual community, and fun to read, but hardly the sort to teach one's daughter or welcome as members of one's own department. Why Burke? What is there in Kenneth Burke that should make his work so significant for the social scientist?

Distinctions between science and art and between literature and sociology are deeply entrenched in modern thought. These distinctions have also served to keep content separated from form. Until quite recently the linguistic and cognitive categories that we use to express and communicate have been viewed as the provinces of art. Imagination and rhetoric have been regarded as jurisdictions of literature. Sociology described life in "realistic," not imaginative terms. By this view, human beings are chiefly utilitarian creatures guided by material interests or nonlogical people whose atavistic sentiments motivate actions. Thus, the symbols of the artist were assumed to be pertinent only to the special realms of the aesthetic, religious, and mystical sides of life.

Burke has effectively undermined these distinctions. What I find so vital in Burke's writings is the recognition of unity between art and human action which constitutes the bridge between sociology and literature. Both are necessarily involved in the use of language to describe and interpret human action. Both can be seen as strategies operating within and upon situations and audiences and, thus, as necessarily rhetorical. Of imaginative literature Burke has shown that it is a form of communication, something that takes place between writer and readers, and that it is strategic or rhetorical in the sense that it must order and encompass situations in ways that make sense to readers. Moreover, just as imaginative works may be said to have a sociological side, so life itself may be understood dramatistically, as though it were a literary text.

Burke is perhaps the preeminent pioneer in what Clifford Geertz has characterized as the "blurring of genres,"[4] a blurring in which the lines between the social sciences and the humanities are becoming less distinct and more permeable. But Burke is much more than a pioneer, who may be remembered on ceremonial occasions but need not be read. I find in the corpus of his work a detailed approach to the interpretation of human action and to the analysis of the terminologies of such interpretations in use in the social sciences. Because Burke insists on the paramount importance of language and symbolism in framing and defining the experiences of our world, he may be seen as a precursor of the contemporary emphasis in the social sciences on cultural forms in the construction of reality, including social structure itself. He brings to these perspectives the approach of the literary analyst. For Burke, drama is not simply a useful metaphor for describing human action. It is a literal description of what we do in social acts. This is why the two domains of literature and social science can be mutually fertilizing.

To be more precise I want to suggest four aspects of Burke's thought that have an impact on sociology and the social sciences:

1. An understanding of language as a form of action. The assertion here is that the modes of symbolizing experience are a central part of human behavior. Symbolic representations constitute the ways in which experience is made possible, and different forms of symbolic usage create different experiences. Action responds to meanings of situations, and those meanings are reflections of the language frames we use.
2. An understanding of human action as dramatic in form and, consequently, as amenable to analysis in the same framework as literary work. Burke's emphasis is on the performative character of much of human action and communication as well as the ritualistic and symbolic nature of much human interaction and institutional forms.
3. An understanding of human actions as rhetorical; as strategies developed to cope with situations involving a performer and an audience.
4. A program for analysis of human behavior which is pluralistic and dialectical. In its focus on the partial character of perspectives, Burke's method emphasizes the values of dialogue among diverse perspectives and the unities that exist across the boundaries of the social sciences and the humanities.

Anyone who reads much of Burke knows both the frustration and the joy of experiencing a writer who seems at first and even at third reading to lack organization, system, and all those good things we were led in Freshman Composition to believe were essential to coherent writing. Knowing where to begin in Burke is often, for the novitiate, a genuine problem. But first and even third impressions are misleading. Methinks there is much method in his madness. There is a definite system of thought in Burke's work, and while it has broadened over the years, it has remained quite consistent.[5]

Language as Action

It is as a theorist of language that Burke's major contribution to sociology must be seen. His is an exhortation to take language seriously and a demonstration of what that means. As in so much of Burke, form cannot be separated from content. On the first page of his *Philosophy of Literary Form (PLF)* he points out that if you know that a man said "Yes," you still do not know what was said unless you know what preceded the "Yes" and to what situation his word was addressed.[6] The terms we use are ways of naming and sizing up the situations to which we address ourselves.

I will begin with the subject matter of much of Burke's work: the nature of human beings. His view is expressed most saliently in his paper "Dramatism" in the *Encyclopedia of the Social Sciences (ESS)*, Burke's sole contribution to a social science publication, and in the chapter "Definition of Man" in *Language as Symbolic Action (LSA)*. In the latter essay he presents a definition which is, in many ways, a précis of his viewpoint:

> Man is the symbol using (symbol-making, symbol-misusing) animal, inventor of the negative (or moralized by the negative), separated from his natural condition by instruments of his own making, goaded by the spirit of hierarchy (or moved by the sense of order) and rotten with perfection.[7]

ANIMAL MOTION AND HUMAN ACTION

Human beings are animals, but they are symbol-using animals. Here Burke is squarely in a tradition that exists in the social sciences that includes Dilthey and Weber, George Herbert Mead and the Symbolic Interactionists, and the more recent influences of Alfred Schutz, the ethnomethodologists, and the renaissance of the Idealist view of how knowledge is achieved or constructed. Where human beings differ from animals is the extent of their capacity to communicate through language and to depict and understand the world by symbolizing or

Joseph R. Gusfield

placing meaning upon objects and events. Animals may be able to communicate and may even be able to reflect upon their movements, but they cannot communicate their reflections.

The implications of this for the study of human beings are enormous. Because human beings can and do affix meanings to events, the methods of the physical sciences cannot be drawn lock, stock, and laboratory into the social sciences. If the event or object to which human beings respond is one constructed by the actors, without knowing the meanings in use the sociologist or psychologist has only a partial image of humans. He or she sees them as passive beings reacting mechanistically to external conditions. They move but they do not act. Action implies those qualities by which humans assess one another and reflect upon their interests, purposes, and emotions. Human action is never certain or wholly predictable.

This is clear in Burke's frequent attack on behavioristic psychology for using as its "representative anecdote" an image of man inappropriate to much of human action. Its laboratory experiments place humans in atypical conditions to which they respond in atypical ways. Attempts to generalize from them are also necessarily flawed.[8] They reduce human action to animal motion:

> the behaviorist uses his experiments with the conditioned reflex as the anecdote about which to form his vocabulary for the discussion of human motives; but this anecdote, though notably *informative*, is not *representative*, since one cannot find a representative case of human motivation in animals if only because animals lack that property of linguistic rationalization which is so typical of human motives. (A Grammar of Motives [GM], p. 59)

SYMBOLIC ACTION

Human action is distinguished from animal motion by virtue of its symbolic character. For Burke, language is very much more than a means of pointing to referents. How we talk about things, how we name them, how we think about them and about ourselves, and how we tell others what we think are all shaped by language and by our own actions as symbol-using animals. In his essay "Terministic Screens" Burke quotes approvingly the definition of "Dramatism" in *Webster's Third New International Dictionary*: "a technique of analysis of language and thought as basically *modes of action rather than as means of conveying information*"(LSA, p. 54).

Duncan comments that what we say about what we do is as much fact as what we do.[9] This being so, a study of how we think about objects, events, and persons, and how we cast these in language and other symbolic forms, is an essential part of the study of human life. When we talk, write, wear clothes, eat foods, make love, make war, and perform the many acts of daily life we give expression to our perception of ourselves, of others, and of the world around us. We define the situations in which we act and state our relation to them—in clothing, hairstyle, and argot. The "punk rocker" is making a statement about his or her view of social authority and the response he or she has chosen to it just as clearly as the judge whose language and robes present images of authority and neutrality. Says Burke: "These strategies size up the situations, name their structures and outstanding ingredients and name them in a way that contains an attitude toward them" (*PLF*, p.4).

Burke's distinction between semantic and poetic meaning is a good place to see how symbolizing properties of language prevent the exclusive use of a scientific language after the fashion of physics, biology, or mathematics (*PLF*, pp. 121–44). Semantic meaning, which he equates with the scientific use of language, is analytic. It distinguishes and defines, aiming at clarity through placing things in distinct and exclusive categories. As Burke so charmingly puts it, the aim of semantic meaning is to give the name and address of every event in the universe. Poetic meaning utilizes the multiplicity of meanings that a given act can have. Semantically, the expression "New York City is in Iowa" is nonsense. But when we contemplate the extension of cultural influence across the nation, the statement makes sense. "As a metaphor, it provides valid insight. To have ruled it out by strict semantic authority would have been vandalism" (*PLF*, p. 126). It is his recognition of the ambiguities and multiplicities inherent in human action that makes Burke's critique of conventional positivism in social science so powerful.

What this implies is the autonomy of symbolic action as distinguished from instrumental, utilitarian activity. The judge's language and robes create the legal institution as much as does the preexistent office. What is expressed through the clothing, rituals, and material props of the courtroom is a conception of public authority. Whatever the forms of legal actions and sentencing, the symbolism provides an experience of being in the presence of legitimate and communal authority, and not of a particular person with his or her own personal likes and dislikes. The experience created by such symbols is a significant part of the legal institution often overlooked by sociologists.

One of the ways in which this insight has influenced social scientists is found both in my own work on law and in that of the political scientist Murray Edelman. My studies of the American Temperance Movement and of the public problem of drinking-driving start with a concern for the meanings expressed and symbolized in legislation. I do not assume that legislation is primarily or only a means to an end, to limit drinking or to achieve auto safety.[10] In the case of Temperance and Prohibition the legislative and legal acts are expressions of the relative status and cultural dominance of the Protestant, rural, middle-class American in conflict with the Catholic, urban, and largely working-class elements of the late nineteenth century. In Edelman's work, such acts as voting or the bargaining processes in labor-management relations are interpreted as modes of quiescence. They are dramatic representations of forms of participation only tangentially related to the utilitarian processes of governmental action or labor union decision-making.[11] Where Burke has influenced both of us is in perceiving actions as expressive and communicative and seeing in such expressions a characteristic form of institutional operation.

A clear use of the same idea is seen in Peter Manning's study of the social organization of British and American police, a study explicitly influenced by his reading of Burke.[12] Manning was interested in the ways in which police work is presented to the public, the strategies by which police obtain the necessary mandates for their authority. The "police myth," as he called it, is that of the policeman as crime fighter. A close analysis of the police showed that much of their activity was not that of preventing crime or of apprehending criminals; indeed, said Manning, there is not much that police can do about crimes. The gathering and publication of crime rates, the many events and rituals depicting police as crime fighters were the public symbolizations of police work. In Burke's terms they are the dramas through which police and their work are given meaning. I shall return to Burke's conception of action as drama shortly.

Terministic Screens

Among the many aphorisms which pepper Burke's salty prose is one that I am especially fond of: "Every way of seeing is also a way of not seeing."[13] Reality is screened through the terminologies which we utilize in interpreting and communicating. Our theories, our concepts, and our constructed contexts are always partial. The sociologist's view is "oversocialized"; the psychologist's is "overpsychologized"; the humanist's is "overhumanized"; the social scientist's is "overscientized."

Here Burke antedates Schutz in seeing how terministic screens prefigure and typify situations.[14] But Burke carries the point at least a step further in recognizing how types, like "bureaucracy" or "capitalism," become "ultimate endings" to thought and speech. Contemporary social science refers to such pure and unsullied constructions as models. Weber referred to them as "ideal types." For Burke these "perfected" ideas are "rotten with perfection" in that they impose simplistic and uniform meanings on the multifaceted, contradictory, and plural character of human acts.

Such screens are terministic, not deterministic. In another sense crucial to Burke they are terminal; they carry their users to an ultimate end, a *terminus ad quem*. Drawing analogies from theology, Burke uses the word "God" as exemplar of the ultimate terminal, the ground of everything.[15] Earlier he presented the same idea in discussing how language constructs a reality and reduces the complexity of human acts and motives to pure forms:

> Men seek for vocabularies that will be faithful *reflections* of reality. To this end they must develop vocabularies that are *selections* of reality. And any selection of reality must, in certain circumstances, function as a *deflection* of reality. (*GM*, p.59)

In selecting reality, human beings necessarily reduce the complex to the simple; the impure to the pure. Thus societies and cultures can be seen as using terms as theologies use "God," as the source and ground of being, making all else understandable. In a famous passage in *A Grammar of Motives* Burke describes "money" as a God-term in modern Western societies (pp. 91-117). It represents termination. Once action has been accounted for in terms of money, nothing further need be said.

But this is not the only sense of termination. The key words, the "God-terms," of a culture lead on to purity. Not only are they ideal types in the Weberian sense, but they become ideals as aspirations. Capitalism and socialism become terms of endearment, matters to be pursued both as explanations and as goals. Therein lies the rub that leads on to deflection. A society that valued purely money would no longer be able to recognize money because nothing else would have value. Reaching toward their terminus, terms end in termination. Even this essay deflects us from the "real," the total Burke. In order to be organized, logical, and coherent I must reduce the Burke of all of his writings to a perfect Burke, an abstract Burke, must out-Burke Burke. This is what Burke means when he says that human beings are "rotten with perfection."

Joseph R. Gusfield

The implications for social research of Burke's discussion of terministic screens are considerable. Burke's essay underscores the plural possibilities of interpretation and the necessarily limited nature of any one schematic framework. Along with other contemporary social scientists, he stands Marx on his head and restores the upturned Hegel. It is not human existence that determines consciousness but consciousness that determines existence, or at least they are coequal. Our linguistic screens prefigure experience. They frame and limit our existence. They constitute the categories through which we experience the social structures that often seem so determining.

The Dramatistic Perspective

Like most who wear the badge of literary critic Burke is absorbed with the problem of interpretation. Where he becomes so significant for sociology is in his brand of dramatistic interpretive analysis. "Drama" for him is not a metaphor to be used in certain areas of social life but a fixed term that helps us discover what the implications of the terms "act" and "person" really are.[16] In interpreting and depicting character the dramatist faces the same problems as does the sociologist. This is because human action is necessarily dramatic. Conflict, purpose, and choice are inherent in action as distinct from motion. These characteristics follow from the fact that humans use and respond to symbols in creating meanings for themselves and their situations.

Despite the clarity of his usage, Burke is often associated with the view of drama as metaphor for social action, sometimes referred to by sociologists as the "dramaturgical perspective." The perspective invites comparisons between what goes on in and out of the theater. Says Combs, for example, "The *dramatic possibility* exists in everyday life, in junctures where the social actor is called upon to utilize theatrical resources and is aware of the drama of the scene, including the scrutiny of one's own performance."[17]

Important as the influence of Burke has been on the development of the dramaturgical perspective in sociology, that concept needs to be distinguished from what Burke has termed his perspective, "the method of dramatism."

GOFFMAN'S DRAMATURGY

Erving Goffman's brilliant analyses of human interaction are frequently cited as the extension of Burke into social science. The concept of the "dramaturgical perspective" is introduced on the first page of the preface of his first book, *The Presentation of the Self in Everyday Life:*

> The perspective employed in this report is that of the theatrical performance; the principles derived are dramaturgical ones. I shall consider the ways in which the individual in ordinary work situations presents himself and his activity to others, the ways in which he guides and controls the impression they form of him, and the kinds of things he may or may not do while sustaining his performance before them.[18]

Both here and throughout his work Goffman's view of human action is dramaturgical—concerned with acting in the theatrical sense of the actor in a staged play. Goffman was drawn to the analysis of how credibility is created and how deception can occur. Consider his analysis of the merry-go-round in a classic discussion of role distance.[19] He tells us how children convey a sense of their character—as brave, foolhardy, or olympian—in how they ride, sit, mount, and dismount. Adults using the merry-go-round convey by their talk and their behavior that they are not "truly" riders but are there as guardians of a child, as satirists, or as operators. As he tells us in the excerpt quoted above, his dramaturgy is just that—the principles by which stage actors and actresses operate applied to human interaction.

In Goffman's usage the stage is a metaphor drawn on to understand and analyze interaction. The play is not the thing; the way it is played is the focal point. There is much continuity with Burke in the conception of meaning as a creation of the human being and of the audience-oriented nature of interaction. But there are also significant differences which flow from Goffman's emphasis on the stage actors and Burke's on the play itself.

Goffman's emphasis is on performances and performers; Burke's is on language and interpretation. In the first paragraph of his major summative article, written for the *International Encyclopedia of the Social Sciences,* he defines his dramatistic method:

> Dramatism is a method of analysis and a corresponding critique of terminology designed to show that the most direct route to the study of human relations and human motives is via a methodological inquiry into cycles or clusters of terms and their functions. ("Dramatism," p. 445)

Here the pentad remains both a focus of Burke's approach to interpretation and an illustration of his pluralistic method. It is central to his

Joseph R. Gusfield

view that humans approach the world with symbolic understandings and that these, like Aristotle's four causes, provide a patterned set of symbols for our ways of thinking. As dramatists know, any description of action must involve the playwright in placing the actor and his/her act in a scene, specifying an agency by which the act is accomplished, and indicating some purpose to the action. In *A Grammar of Motives* Burke elaborates on the pentad, using it to identify the forms of thought necessary to interpretations of action. In applying it to such diverse forms as poems, *The Communist Manifesto*, and constitutions, he continues the search for forms of thought which are common to seemingly disparate areas of intellectual activity.

The *Grammar* goes beyond the pentad to a general analysis of how our prefigured systems of thought emphasize some things at the expense of others. Academic disciplines, pushing their concepts to the ultimate, end by "oversociologizing," "overpsychologizing," and "overeconomizing" the human subject. Psychology can be seen as a language which emphasizes the agent; sociology as a language of scenes. Each overstates its case. Awareness of how varying schemes become limiting provides the method for analyzing the shortcomings of each perspective.

The method also provides an impressive tool for understanding how interpretive schemes work. It leads sociologists to a close analysis of the language which they use when they talk and when they write, as well as to analysis of how their subjects talk and write. Above all it helps them see the limitations of what I have elsewhere called the "windowpane" view of scientific language—the view that language can be, and ought to be, a clear window through which the scientist communicates findings and conclusions to an audience.[20]

Sociologists bring to the description and analyses of their research an already given stock of images which reflect ways of using the terms of the pentad. In my research I found that very different consequences ensue if you purport to be studying "drinking-drivers" or "drinking-driving." The first is a language of agent, of psychology, and leads to a deemphasis on context, on scene. It fits the search for personal characteristics of drivers and the neglect of scenic properties. The second emphasizes the event, including the purposes of the journey, the context of people interacting, the uses of the automobile and its place in the "world" of the driver. "Drinking-driving" leads the scholar and the reader more easily toward attending to aspects of time, social interactions, and environment. It takes attention away from the characteristics of the motorist. However the phenomena are labeled, the language is inevitably selective and partial. It is a screen and cannot be a windowpane.

Burke has thus laid the foundations for a self-critical, self-aware examination of the categories of thought and expression in the social sciences. He has provided a link between the critical analysis of literary and social science texts.

The Rhetoric of Social Action

Of greatest importance for the sociologist is Burke's conception of human action as rhetorical. The importation of rhetorical analysis into social research is enormously productive. Both the human actions which the sociologist studies and the texts in which sociological analyses are reported are perceivable as rhetorical pursuits. In Burke's terms, they involve strategies for dealing with situations by adapting ideas to audiences. Goffman has used the ideas, though not the direct language of rhetorical theory, in describing human interaction as performative. Like Goffman, Burke looks for unexpected meanings and insights in strange, often exotic places: In *A Rhetoric of Motives (RM)*, he says that "we seek to mark off the areas of rhetoric by showing how a rhetorical motive is often present where it is not usually recognized, or thought to belong."[21]

Here Burke shows us how rhetorical analysis can illuminate both literary texts and human relations in general. Identification is the key rhetorical process through which poets and ordinary people attempt to persuade others. In the selective use of symbols there are implicit, and sometimes explicit, appeals to others to join with or oppose the identities which are proffered. Burke shows how images of killing in Milton and in Matthew Arnold can become a paradigm for descriptions of change and transformation, and how they can thus illuminate the references to killing in Freud (*RM*, chap. 1). The identification of killing as transformation is the unifying element in the structure of thought created in these texts. The imagery of revolutionary violence may emerge in the clothing of death and destruction or in the vestments of the utopian Eden to be attained through it. In these texts, violence is identified as passage, as transformation, and is provided with justifications. Violence as transformation, says Burke, is a stage toward "higher" values, more acceptable than violence described in terms of destruction.

There are three aspects of Burke's rhetorical perspective that have borne juicy fruit for sociologists. The first is the enormously insightful approach to human interaction as rhetorical. The second is the understanding of social science research as affected by rhetorical elements. Last, Burke demonstrates the basic categories for seeing and interpreting social action which literature and literary analysis share with sociology.

The first has been superbly utilized in Goffman's analyses of human interaction as presentational and performative. To speak of "impression management" is to view interaction as audience-directed and adaptive. Goffman's work is filled with illuminating insights into the process by which human beings confer symbolic meanings on action otherwise interpreted as utilitarian or "meaningless." In studying institutions for persons labeled "mentally disturbed," Goffman shows that behavior seen by psychiatrists as less than sane is better understood as attempts by the patients to persuade themselves and others that they are persons of autonomy and self-control. The "stashing" of small objects in special places is interpreted as representing the extension and autonomy of the self—as a way of convincing themselves and others of their self-identity. In the asylum's institutional setting they have had to give up many other signs of their particularity. The psychiatrist identifies the "stashing" behavior as foolish and psychotic. The sociologist, in describing the behavior as a rhetorical action, confers a different identity on the act. It is not an act of "crazy people" but a strategy of managing self-identity in an institution which threatens self-esteem and recognition.[22]

Rhetorical analysis has rich usages beyond the microlevel of interactions. It is also a way of seeing how public acts and artifacts serve to persuade audiences that legal, political, and social institutions have a particular character. I have above described Manning's analysis of the "police myth," which leads the public to see crime as a matter more of individuals than of environments, as other terminologies might lead us to see it.

For Burke, the rhetorical, identifying practices are crucial ways in which the social order is created and sustained. The negative, the "thou shalt not," is essential to a view of society as social order. In Burke's often repeated sequence: if drama, then conflict; if conflict, then victimage. The idea of order implies the possibility of disorder. The guilt connected with the negative, with disobedience and rebellion, implies the need for redemption and expiation. To dramatize order, scapegoating is necessary. It is in ritual and ceremony that the drama of social life is carried out. I have argued that, whatever their utilitarian consequences, legislation, legal opinions, and courts are significant ways to dramatize the moral order of the society.[23] They state the character of the public order against which specific actions can be judged as publicly acceptable.

Anthropologists had used such ideas, as had Durkheim, in analyzing human societies, but they were little used until recently in studying contemporary societies. The recent appearance of studies of modern life as embodying the symbolic order of ritual and ceremony owes much to Burke.[24]

Rhetorical concepts are also a way of describing and discussing the languages of social sciences. The language of social science is usually presented as if it had no literary or rhetorical functions. Social scientists have generally treated their language as scientific: "Just the facts, ma'am, just the facts." Burke's influence has recently led to an analysis of the stuff of sociology, its theories and its research reports, as persuasionary attempts. In these studies, the linguistic style and the form of a text become important parts of the research. Rhetoric is a key to its structure and thought. Even the presentation of a text as "scientific" requires attention to style and literary devices which persuade and instruct the audience in how it is to be taken.[25] Science, including social science, often displays a "style of nonstyle," couching its language so as to convince audiences that it is "above" stylistic concern.

Burke's attention to rhetorical technique provides a way of understanding social theorists as well. Consider, in this connection, Burke's analysis of Marx and Mannheim in their treatments of ideology. Each offers positive, dialectical, and ultimate terms, but their dialectical theories offer different identifications and divisions. Both see ideas as developing within historical contexts in dialectical opposition; feudalism to capitalism to socialism; ideology to utopia; status quo to opposition. Marx places the dialectical conflicts in a developmental frame; he posits an ultimate—the socialist society—that transcends the dialectic. Mannheim, in not doing so, puts all ideologies on equal terms. As Burke suggests, Mannheim liberalizes Marx. (*RM*, pp. 183-207).

Burke's discovery of the ubiquitousness of rhetoric is echoed in Northrop Frye's remark:

> Anything which makes a functional use of words will always be involved in all the technical problems of words, including rhetorical problems. The only road from grammar to logic, then, runs through the intermediate territory of rhetoric.[26]

As a writer of words the social scientist cannot escape the problems of rhetoric which are embedded in the use of language directed toward an audience. Style, narrative, voice, and distance are all modes of presentation. Data, findings, and conclusions do not exist in a vacuum-packed container, without context or convention. Science is a form of literature in that it uses words to create a narrative. It is a form of rhetoric in that it uses words to persuade an audience. This is not to

equate science with rhetoric or literature but to call attention to particular forms of scientific rhetoric and to point to the place of the literary
aspects of science in the process of discovery and proof.[27] Hayden
White has done this magnificently in studying nineteenth-century
historical writing as rhetoric. Using Burkean language, among other
tools, White has presented a tropological analysis that reveals the underlying rhetorics of particular historians.[28]

To see science and social science as literary and rhetorical productions is to apply the third aspect of the Burkean method. I do not
mean the use of novels as illustrations but rather the modes of literary
analysis applied to the texts of science. I have made some preliminary
forays into the literary analysis of social science research in studying
the text of research reports on drinking-driving and in analyzing organizational documents.[29] What needs yet to be accomplished is the development of a literary criticism of factual material.[30] What is clear
from Burke is that literature is everywhere. It is not only in Culture
but also in culture. Setting aside the problems of aesthetics, there is an
intellectual need to scrutinize the stylistic and formal aspects of factual materials, of written products.

There is another sense in which the link between the humanities
and the social sciences builds on the insights that Burke's discussion
of rhetoric has given us. Burke builds bridges, as always, between the
analysis of literature and the analysis of human action. He moves, for
example, from Shakespeare's *Venus and Adonis* to Castiglione's *The
Courtier* to Kafka's *The Castle*, finding in each principles for bridging relations between classes. To find in the idea of courtship the paradigm
of how classes utilize rhetorical principles provides us with an appa-
ratus for observing how social groups interact (*RM*, pp. 208-44). In *The
Rhetoric of Motives* Burke moves from the principles of rhetoric to the
nature of social order, using courtship as a paradigm of the way in
which diverse groups persuade each other of common identifications.
His perspective of society is fundamentally rhetorical.

Dialectics, Comedy, and Dramatic Irony

"Dramatic" and "dialectic" are terms which Burke
characterizes as "equitable"(*GM*, p. 511). Each represents a partial
view of reality. "Where the agents are in action we have drama; where
the agents are in ideation we have dialectic" (*GM*, p. 512). Yet, as he
points out, the two are mutually influential. There are no ideas with-

out persons; no persons without ideas. His analysis of language leads into a methodology in which no single perspective or single term can render a complete account of experience or reality. The implications of terministic screens for social research lie in the plural possibilities of interpretation and the necessarily limited nature of any one schematic framework. The deliberate invitation to paradox, inconsistency, contradiction, and comedy are the mark of a method which, following Richard Brown, I refer to as dialectical irony—seeing something from the viewpoint of its opposite.[31] To analyze human action the analyst must consider the whole from the standpoint of each of the terms.

Wayne Booth refers to Burke as a "lumper" rather than a "splitter."[32] Lumpers find similarities where others find only differences. Splitters are the opposite; they find differences where others find similarities. (Parsons was a splitter; Goffman was a lumper.) For the thoroughgoing dialectician nothing is as it seems to be. Burke's discussion of substance prepares us for this. Nothing, except God, can exist without a context. To define, to "split," necessitates a negation—saying what the object is not in order to say what it is.

> With the dialectic substance the irony is explicit. For it derives its character from the systematic contemplation of the antinomies attendant upon the fact that we necessarily define a thing in terms of something else. (*GM*, p. 33)

Such a dialectical method has far more profound implications for social science than the Hegelian-Marxian version. Unlike that well-worn shibboleth of contemporary coffeehouses, Burke's has no synthesis except as its method is its absolute. It directs us toward the ambiguities and complexities which are lost when we adopt a utilitarian logic and a positivist method. The exclusive search for cause and effect, treating human action as animal motion, leads us again to the partiality and monism which dialectical perspective overcomes.

Burke presents a good illustration of what this means for the social sciences in discussing what a dialectical history would look like:

> History, in this sense, would be a dialectic of characters in which, for instance, we should never expect to see "feudalism" overthrown by "capitalism" and "capitalism" succeeded by some manner of national or international or non-national or neo-national or post-national socialism—but rather should note elements of all such positions (or "voices") existing always, but attaining greater clarity of expression or imperiousness of proportion of one period than another. (*GM*, p. 513)

THE COMEDIC STANCE

Here then is the clue to the Burkean style of puns, jokes, and down-right comedy, sometimes descending into buffoonery. Comedy is the art of criticism, as irony is the trope of dialectics. The search for the opposite is the method of the dialectician. Burke's admonition to adopt a "perspective by incongruity" is a logical (or logo-logical) conclusion to his dialectical perspective.[33]

Perspective by incongruity is more than style in Burke. It is an exhortation to see the limited nature of any one cognitive framework. The terminologies in use are terministic screens that shield us from the multiplicity of possibilities. The wise observer recognizes that opposites are not so different after all. Comedy points up the limits of intelligence and knowledge. As Burke says in *Attitudes toward History*, people are not vicious but they are often mistaken and necessarily mistaken: "*every* insight contains its own special kind of blindness."[34]

This is a source of Burke's predilection for the oxymoron, for terms like "secular conversion," or his fondness for Veblen's "trained incapacity." These terms enable us to recognize the paradoxes, ambiguities, and multiple facets of actions and events.

A DIALOGIC SOCIAL SCIENCE

What Burke's perspective by incongruity implies for the social sciences is precisely the blurring and blunting of the sharply defined edges of typologies. The logic and method of the hard sciences depend upon just that precise and rigid definition which a pluralistic method denies. It is an implicit assumption of causal analysis that there is a "right" answer. That one answer be the true answer while others are false is the ideal toward which, in their Enlightenment spirit, the social sciences have aspired.

A deeply held pluralism recognizes two barriers in the way of this ideal. The first is the limitations of language and of theory in representing the multifold character of the real world. The second is the importance of the researcher to the total project. His or her theories, biases, attitudes, and dramatistic categories are essential to the process of selectivity. But, at the same time, they prevent social science from being even an approximation of the model of knowing in use in the natural sciences.

What emerges is a dialogic picture of the social sciences in place of the monistic model that is even today the accepted standard. No one perspective, no single study can do justice or mercy to the complexity of human behavior. The sociologist is then the supreme ironist, the critic whose task is to point to the multiple understandings, the alternative possibilities inhering in situations, and to bring new meanings and metaphors to bear on taken-for-granted assumptions.[35] Our aim, as Burke suggests in his discussion of dialectic and irony, is to include all the relevant terms of development in a perspective of perspectives.[36] But even as we do so, we must recognize that no one designation, no one solution, no one answer is final, encompassing, or ultimate. The dialogue of all voices is itself the answer and not a road to one.

Armed with Burkean method, the sociologist's trope is that of irony. Sociology can achieve a form of criticism that reveals the limits, the assumptions of what is taken for granted in culture. It can do so by incongruity, by seeing the world from as many vantage points as possible. As Rueckert put it: "Burke admonishes us that, if we want to see something accurately, we should at least try to see it whole."[37]

What this implies is a reach for a kind of wisdom rather than the goal of certain knowledge. Knowledge is a scientific term and implies a finality that is belied by the conception of human action as symbolic. Wisdom stems from a humility that recognizes, through comedy, the human limitations on knowledge. Being self-critical, the sociologist realizes that his own designations, his own metaphors are also ways of constructing and creating a way of seeing and are always in need of correction. Burke put the matter well in *Attitudes toward History* when he likened our innocent error-making to characters in a play:

> The audience, from its vantage point, sees the operation of errors that the characters in the play cannot see; thus seeing from two angles at once, it is chastened by dramatic irony.
> (P. 41)

The sociologist is like the child watching the stage. Knowing more parts and having read the script the child cries out to the players and tries to warn them to avoid the ending as it has been written. Alternatively the sociologist provides the playwright with several other possible ways to bring the play to its last curtain.

An Image of Society

Burke's depiction of human action as symbolic terminates in a view of society in which naming and ritual are central to social cohesion and consistency. Here again, the unity of art and sociology is proclaimed.

In his approach to the study of society as a coordinated set of human relationships, Burke builds on his view of the dramatic character of action. Describing scenes, he tells us in *The Philosophy of Literary Form*, is the province of the physical sciences; describing dramas is the role of the social sciences. The remark appears in a chapter whose title is an introduction to the Burkean conception of society: "Ritual Drama as 'Hub.' " If drama is the central term in the study of social action, then ritual is the clearest form of drama and the essential form. Human acts take on recurrent meanings through stylization of content. Here society exists in the affirming order which ritual celebrates and supports.

SOCIAL STRUCTURE AND CONSCIOUSNESS

In his image of society, Burke has antedated the current turn toward the importance of language and culture. As suggested earlier, Marx's famous proposition that existence determines consciousness has for very long been the grand aphorism written over the symbolic doors of sociological houses. It made sociology the scenic discipline par excellence. The determinism and reductionism that Burke so rightly complains about have been, with notable exceptions, conventional wisdom among sociologists. The characteristic method of sociology has been to derive action from context; to find in classes, status groups, or institutions the ground for human behavior, and in the processes (forces) of historical change the motor of social dynamics.

In many of the intellectual currents of the past two decades, from Levi-Strauss and Alfred Schutz on, there has been a standing on its head of the Marxian aphorism; Hegel has had his sweet vengeance! Our interpretations, our social constructions become the reified institutions and groups which we then use to explain our actions. Hugh Duncan characterizes this reification in describing Burke's insistence on the role of social dramas: "Such dramatic enactment does not 'reflect' social structure but creates it."[38] We become members of a class, of an ethnic group, or of a family as we have names for them, and we identify ourselves within them. A history of groups would show how the perception of community is built up out of the terminologies, ceremonies, and rituals through which we compose our consciousness of ourselves as joining with others.

AUTHORITY AND ACCEPTANCE

Burke's view of society is congruent with both his emphasis on symbolic acts and the implicit criticisms of social determinism in his dialectics. One can picture much of his work as an attempt to rid us of the view of appearances as understandably ordered and to go beyond the disorder of appearances to perceive the forms which are constant. This form of structuralism is found in his characterization of his *A Grammar of Motives* as a book concerned with basic forms of thought "in accordance with the nature of the world as all men necessarily experience it."[39] These basic forms comprise the "social structure" which prefigures the way in which a society is experienced.

The problem of order is central to Burkean sociology. Just as language frames provide us with order in interaction, so too the terminologies we develop create frames of acceptance and rejection of authority. It is the fact of authority (hierarchy) that is the source of order and rejection in society. Humans, being talkers and writers, can conjure up "Thou shalts" and "Thou shalt nots." The acceptance and rejection of morals, of authority, and of division is ever present. We are capable of thinking the negative and are also "goaded by the spirit of hierarchy."

Relations between groups, between classes, between the powerful and the powerless, and between the priest and the parishioner are thought about and organized through our terms. Frames of acceptance are, as Burke puts it in the title of the book *Attitudes toward History* (1937), not forms of passivity but the terms of relationship. He uses two seminal thinkers as examples. Both Aquinas and Marx saw the existence of classes. For Aquinas they were punishment for the fall of man; for Marx a consequence of capitalist exploitation. Aquinas' program was one of passive acceptance; Marx's a program for revolution. Both are forms of order and hierarchy, for in each there is a higher and a lower state of being. Each forms a mode of understanding and explanation. Aquinas justifies the order of class. Marx attacks it.

If there is hierarchy and social order, there is also the rejection of order and consequent guilt. Here is the foundation of Burke's society: if drama, then conflict; if conflict, then hierarchy; if hierarchy, then guilt; if guilt, then redemption; if redemption, then victimage. Rejection means the need to expiate the resulting guilt. Ritual—dramatic enactments—provides us with visible symbols in which hierarchy is built up and in which rejection is atoned for. The scapegoat, the victim, is essential to the order of society. The sacrificial principle is essential. The Christian drama is enacted again and again. Even Manning's "police myth" is a form for accepting policing as the drama of good against evil in which police represent the potential sacrificial lambs redeeming the citizenry from the guilt of criminality.

Joseph R. Gusfield

Hierarchy is constant in Burke's perception of society because in every area of life there is an orderliness of principle, of higher and lower, nobler and baser. Diversity, conflict, and division portend the disruption of order, the clash of frames. The fact of hierarchy itself dictates the need for disorder as well.

The Limits of Burke's Sociology: A Critique

Despite the critique of positivist determinism, sociologists still look at context as the key word of social analysis. Indeed Burke's view of human action, including literature, as strategies for acting in situations is especially congenial to the sociologist. But it is an analysis of interaction in which the context is, in its scope and circumference, strangely narrow or unaccounted for. I look for some way of linking up particular ways of placement, particular God-terms, with historical periods, with classes, nationality groups, or social structures.

THE REPRESSION OF SOCIAL STRUCTURE

The problem of social structure remains, even though the conventional wisdom of a deterministic framework is rejected. Sociologists refer to it as the problem of the micro and the macro levels of analysis.[40] Burke's perspective, rich and productive as it is, is weakest in his perceptions of the context within which the symbols exist. These are taken for granted. At several points in his writing Burke hints at another sociology, a return of the repressed structure that has been outlawed at other stages. In an article entitled "Dramatism" he contends that "property in any form sets the *conditions* for conflict" (and hence culminates in some sort of victimage) (p. 451, emphasis added).

Strange word, "conditions," in a context of action rather than motion. In what ways does property impinge on cooperation and conflict? The problem of the role of existence remains either unexplored or accepted. Here I find Burke either mute or confusing. The sociologist wants more. Having lifted the Pandora's box I wish for Burke to provide some new wrapping.

Burke's emphasis on language places him in the same cage as the rest of us who have sought to challenge an excessively positivist intellectual domination with the idealist weapons of linguistic nominalism. If language contains the frameworks through which experience is conceived and strategies developed toward named situations, how do we account for the attitudes which the strategies express? Society becomes a cognitive world without interests or sentiments; without social structure or group loyalties; without the emotive forces of love or greed or search for glory.

SOCIETY AS HIERARCHY: ORDER AND DISORDER

Neither does Burke's view of society as hierarchy and order stand up well as a rudimentary social system. It should not surprise us, or Burke, that any one system or scheme of understanding is partial. Order and hierarchy are but one side of the many sides of social life. If human beings prize order, so too do they prize disorder; if they possess the spirit of hierarchy, so too do they possess the spirit of equality, spontaneity, and rebellion. The rational and the romantic remain dual sides of human life and social arrangements.

The anthropologist Victor Turner has given valuable insight into society with his contrast between *structure*—the hierarchical, role-allocative organization of life—and *communitas,* the sense of human similarity and solidaristic feeling.[41] A great deal of ritual celebrates the spirit of equality rather than the dividing order of hierarchy. It is strange that so dialectical a thinker as Burke should turn hierarchy and order into ultimates.

Human social life is too multiple in spirit and existence to be so readily summed up. It is in the ambiguities and ambivalences, the expressed and the unexpressed, the protests and disorder in the name of maintaining order—the paradoxes of society—that it exists. Even to describe an aggregate of people as a society is to construct a "pure" ideal belied by the situated events and activities of daily life, with its mistakes, inconsistencies, indeterminacies, and opposites.

Burke's Bridge: Literature and Sociology as Sisters under the Skin

I want to bring this paper to a close with some additional remarks about the ways in which sociology is a form of literature and what difference such a perspective makes for the sociologist. It is here that I especially see Burke as both well ahead of his time and as having made a profoundly significant gift to intellectual and scholarly thought.

In an essay by Burke with a title redolent of this idea, "Literature as Equipment for Living," he tells us that his method "breaks down the barriers erected about literature as a specialized pursuit."[42] In calling for sociological classifications to be applied to literary works, he views literature as embodying a set of strategies for dealing with situations, akin to strategies found in other areas of life. In symbolic action, art works out the manifold modes of human alternatives. Drama is not only the study of how plays are written and performed; it is the working out of principles of human action. A sociological approach to literature would provide that wider compass in its categories:

> They would consider works of art . . . as strategies for selecting enemies and allies, for socializing losses, for warding off the evil eye, for purification, propitiation and desanctification, consolation and vengeance, admonition and exhortation, implicit commands or instructions of one sort and another. (PLF, p. 262)

The implications for literary analysis, and consequently for the social sciences, of such a conception of literature are considerable. Literature is more, much more, than the works of Shakespeare or Dashiell Hammett. It applies as well to works of fact as to works of art because the line cannot be drawn when language is in use. Income tax returns, deodorant advertisements, and the latest issue of *The American Sociological Review* are subject as well to literary critique and to the analysis of rhetorical and grammatical style.

Thus the sociologist can utilize the symbolic action of literature to help provide classifications and conceptions with which to understand other actions. But so too can he or she perceive much of human action as literary, symbolic, and artistic. The one-sided view of human action as utilitarian and matter-of-fact ignores its multiple, polysemic, symbolic character. In treating both our own actions and those of the people we study as if they were devoid of art, we fail to understand much of human action.

While the reemergence of interest in Kenneth Burke may be a mere byproduct of the linguistic revolution in philosophy and, more recently, of the "interpretive turn" in the social sciences, it would be a mistake merely to honor Burke as a pioneer and then move on to more "contemporary" figures. No one since Burke has provided a more "contemporary" view of the links between life and literature, society and art. The scope and subtlety of Burke's "bridging operations" constitute a noble and enormously significant intellectual achievement.

NOTES

1. Burke's influence in the social sciences has been both specific and pervasive. A number of major studies influenced by Burke are discussed in the text of this paper. Two useful anthologies which show some of his impact on social scientists are James Combs and Michael Mansfield, eds., *Drama in Life: The Uses of Communication in Society*, Communication Art Books (New York: Hastings House, 1976), and Dennis Brisset and Charles Edgley, eds., *Life as Theater* (Chicago: University of Chicago Press, 1975). In addition to those mentioned in the paper the following are among major studies demonstrating Burke's influence: Richard H. Brown, *A Poetic for Sociology* (Cambridge: Cambridge University Press, 1977); Elizabeth Burns, *Theatricality* (London: Longman, 1972); Orrin Klapp, *Symbolic Leaders: Public Dramas and Public Man* (Chicago: Aldine, 1964) and *Collective Search for Identity* (New York: Holt, Rinehart, and Winston, 1969); Stanford Lyman and Marvin Scott, *The Drama of Social Reality*, (New York: Oxford University Press, 1975); J. David Sapir and J. Christopher Crocker, eds., *The Social Uses of Metaphor* (Philadelphia: University of Pennsylvania Press, 1977).

2. There are very few social scientists among the sixty-nine reviewers represented in the collection of contemporary reviews of Burke's works collected and edited in William Rueckert, ed., *Critical Responses to Kenneth Burke, 1924–1966* (Minneapolis: University of Minnesota Press, 1969).

3. See especially the two books by Hugh D. Duncan, *Communication and Social Order* (New York: Bedminster Press, 1962) and *Symbols and Social Theory* (New York: Oxford University Press, 1969). Another important commentary on Burke as a sociological theorist is that of Michael Overington, "Kenneth Burke and the Method of Dramatism," *Theory and Society*, 4 (1977);131–56, and his "Kenneth Burke as Social Theorist," *Sociological Inquiry*, 47, no.2 (1977), 133–41.

4. Clifford Geertz, "Blurred Genres: The Refiguration of Social Thought," *Local Knowledge* (New York: Basic Books, 1983), pp. 19–35.

5. This continuity in Burke's writings is explicitly recognized in William Rueckert's *Kenneth Burke and the Drama of Human Relations* (Berkeley: University of California Press, 1982).

6. Kenneth Burke, *The Philosophy of Literary Form* (1941; rev. abr. ed. New York: Vintage Books, 1957), p.3.

7. Kenneth Burke, *Language as Symbolic Action* (Berkeley: University of California Press, 1966), p. 16.

8. Kenneth Burke, *A Grammar of Motives* (New York: Prentice Hall, 1945), pp. 78–79.

9. Duncan, *Communication and Social Order*, chap. 10.

10. See my studies of the American Temperance Movement in *Symbolic Crusade* (Urbana: University of Illinois Press, 1963) and the public issue of drinking-driving in *The Culture of Public Problems* (Chicago: University of Chicago Press, 1981). The character of the research and the theoretical de-

velopment, as well as explicit reference to Burke, show the uses made of his ideas.

11. Murray J. Edelman's studies of political symbolism are found in his books *The Symbolic Uses of Politics* (Chicago: University of Illinois Press, 1964); *Politics as Symbolic Action* (New York: Academic Press, 1971); and *Political Language* (New York: Academic Press, 1977).

12. Peter Manning, *Police Work* (Cambridge: MIT Press, 1977). Manning is explicit about his debt to Burke and offers a clear discussion of the use of dramatism in his empirical and observational study.

13. Kenneth Burke, *Permanence and Change* (1935; rpt. Indianapolis: Bobbs-Merrill, 1965), p. 49.

14. Schutz's concern for how frames and typification prefigure experience and operate to select from among multiple realities pervades much of his work. See Alfred Schutz, *The Phenomenology of the Social World*, trans. George Walsh and Frederick Lehnert (1932; rpt. Evanston, Ill.: Northwestern University Press, 1967), chaps. 2 and 4.

15. Kenneth Burke, *The Rhetoric of Religion* (1961; rpt. Berkeley: University of California Press, 1970).

16. Kenneth Burke, "Dramatism," in *International Encyclopedia of the Social Sciences* (New York: Macmillan, 1968), p. 448.

17. James Combs, *Dimensions of Political Drama* (Santa Monica, Calif.: 1980), p. 8.

18. Erving Goffman, *The Presentation of the Self in Everyday Life* (Garden City, N.Y.: Doubleday Anchor Books, 1959), p. xi. The dramaturgical perspective pervades most of Goffman's work, especially his earlier, observational studies. These are referred to below.

19. Erving Goffman, *Encounters* (Indianapolis: Bobbs-Merrill, 1961), pp. 105-15.

20. Joseph Gusfield, "The Literary Rhetoric of Science: Comedy and Pathos in Drinking-Driver Research," *American Sociological Review*, 41 (1976), 16-34.

21. Burke, *A Rhetoric of Motives*, (New York: Prentice-Hall, 1950), p. xiii.

22. Erving Goffman, *Asylums* (Garden City, N.Y.: Doubleday, 1961), pp. 248-54.

23. This is a major conclusion in my two book-length studies of alcohol legislation and law enforcement, cited above.

24. See the review of studies in Joseph Gusfield and Jerzy Michalowicz, "Secular Symbolism: Studies of Ritual, Ceremony, and the Symbolic Order in Modern Life," in Ralph Turner and James Short, eds., *Annual Review of Sociology*, 10 (1984), 417-35. A notable exception to the absence of studies of ritual in modern life is the classic study of a New England city by W. Lloyd Warner, *The Living and the Dead* (New Haven: Yale University Press, 1959).

25. Joseph Gusfield, "The Literary Rhetoric of Science," *American Sociological Review*, 41 (1976), 16-34.

26. Northrop Frye, *Anatomy of Criticism* (Princeton: Princeton University Press, 1957), p. 331.

27. Bruno Latour and Stephen Woolgar have shown, based on field ob-

servations of a scientific laboratory, how the eventual reporting of results guides the activities and organization of ideas throughout the experimental processes. See their study *Laboratory Life: The Social Construction of Fact* (Beverly Hills: Sage Publications, 1979).

28. See Hayden White, *Metahistory: The Historical Imagination in Nineteenth-Century Europe* (Baltimore: Johns Hopkins University Press, 1973), chap. 1.

29. I have used Burke's pentad, as well as concepts drawn from Wayne Booth, Northrop Frye, and others to analyze the fictions, metaphors, styles, and voice in the dramatic presentation of drinking-driving research studies. See especially chaps. 3 and 4 of my *The Culture of Public Problems.* Also see Hayden White's most useful essay on the study of "fact" as a potential area of literary analysis, "The Fictions of Factual Representation," in Angus Fletcher, ed., *The Literature of Fact* (New York: Columbia University Press, 1976).

30. I mean by this not the analysis of classic social science theorists, such as Marx, Weber, etc., but the use of literary concepts to examine how fact is constructed in the "nitty-gritty" work of journals, monographs, and government reports. Recent work in the sociology of science moves in this direction. In addition to those reported in this paper, see Barry Barnes and David Edge, eds., *Science in Context* (Cambridge: MIT Press, 1982).

31. Brown has used the concept of irony as a central term in analyzing the impact of sociological thought. See Richard Brown, *A Poetic for Sociology* (Cambridge: Cambridge University Press, 1977), and "Dialectical Irony," in Edmond Wright, ed., *Irony* (London, 1980).

32. Wayne C. Booth, *Critical Understanding* (Chicago: University of Chicago Press, 1979), chap. 3, esp. pp. 68–74.

33. Although it is perhaps the best-known Burkean concept among social scientists, it is not much used in Burke's work after its initial presentation in part 2 of *Permanence and Change.* The method, of course, remains throughout his later work.

34. Kenneth Burke, *Attitudes toward History* (1937; rpt. Berkeley: University of California Press, 1984), p. 41.

35. See my discussion of irony as the major contribution of sociology to the study of public affairs in chap. 8 of my *The Culture of Public Problems.*

36. This is contained in the significant discussion of tropes and especially of irony and dialectic in *GM,* pp. 511–17.

37. William Rueckert, "Some of the Many Kenneth Burkes," in Hayden White and Margaret Brose, eds., *Representing Kenneth Burke,* (Baltimore: English Institute and Johns Hopkins University Press, 1982).

38. Duncan, *Communication and Social Order,* p. 113.

39. *GM,* p. xv. In referring to Burke as a "prestructuralist" I call attention to the importance he gives to how linguistic frames prefigure experience. There are many differences, I think, between Burke and the structuralists, especially in the deterministic assumptions that characterize the structuralists.

40. For analyses of this problem in sociology see the papers in Karen

54

Joseph R. Gusfield

Knorr-Cetina and Aaron Cicourel, eds., *Advances in Social Theory and Methodology: Toward an Integration of Micro- and Macro-Sociologies* (Boston: Routledge & Kegan Paul, 1981).

41. See especially Victor Turner's study of ritual in primitive tribes and in Western society in *The Ritual Process* (Chicago: Aldine, 1969).

42. This essay has been reprinted in a number of places. My reference here is to its publication in *PLF,* p. 261.

2

SCIENTISM AND DRAMATISM

SOME QUASI-MATHEMATICAL

MOTIFS IN THE WORK

OF KENNETH BURKE

TREVOR MELIA

> *Nullius in Verba*
> Motto of the Royal Society

> *Il n'y a pas de hors-texte*
> Jacques Derrida

> *Things are the signs of words*
> Kenneth Burke

In spite of well-known and ambitious programs aimed at producing a unified science, there is for the older generation of scholars probably a hint of the oxymoron about the phrase "human science." The oxymoronic quality, made more explicit if we render the locution "subjective objectivity," is largely dissolved if "science" is understood to mean only the more or less disciplined and systematic study of any set of phenomena. Many human scientists, suitably pressed, would no doubt retreat to some such weak definition of science. Still, like it or not, there remain traces of the older tradition wherein "science" means natural science and to utter the term is to conjure up the ghosts of Ptolemy, Copernicus, Galileo, Newton, Einstein, and Bohr and to make allusions to physics, astronomy, and mathematics. Insofar as these men are indisputable members of the scholarly pantheon, and their disciplines, Kuhn et al. notwithstanding, custodians of our most secure knowledge, human scientists are likely to be the beneficiaries of an "unearned increment."

Kenneth Burke must be numbered among those students of the human situation who have resolutely refused to attach the honorific "science" to their endeavors. Indeed, the flattest distinction in all Burke's work is that between "things that move" and "persons who act"— between the realm of science and that of drama. The failure of human scientists to observe the distinction led Burke to complain that "the error of the social sciences has usually resided in the attempt to appropriate the scenic calculus for a charting of the *Act*."[1] It is this attempt to extend scientific methodology into regions where its use is inappropriate that Burke calls scientism. And scientism, it is here maintained, both historically and logically provides the context for the Burkean text, the constitution beneath the dramatistic constitution, the statement that calls forth Burke's counterstatement. He has said, "I would set 'Dramatism' against 'Scientism'"; but he goes on to caution, "In so doing I do not necessarily imply a distrust of science as such."[2]

In this essay I hope to show that Burke's critique of scientism does not in fact proceed from a flat antipathy to science but rather anticipates misgivings increasingly expressed by human scientists themselves. I shall, moreover, try to show that while Burke's hexadic analysis derives from a very different metaphysical base, it retains key features of at least some of the statistical procedures it seeks to replace. And, finally, I want to suggest that Burke's logological analysis, in proposing to replace an arithmetic method with a "qualitative algebra," not only makes a contribution to a rhetoric of the human sciences but bears also on contemporary literary theory.

Burke's Critique of Scientism

It would be a mistake to allow Burke to be too easily assimilated to that humanistic critique of social science that is all too often compounded of equal parts of hostility towards, and ignorance of, "natural" science.[3] For while Burke insists on a distinction between the realm of motion (science) and that of action (drama), he acknowledges what humanists are prone to forget—that humanity is itself, from a transcendent point of view, part of the scene. Without motion, there can be no action. Unless something like the biblical account is true (and dramatism is powerless to decide), all that existed in the eons before man evolved lies in the realm of nonsymbolic motion—a condition that our technology is soon likely to restore.[4] In the infinites-

imally small interim "nature containing the principle of speech" produced the symbol-using animal.[5] The symbol-using *animal* is entirely
subject to the forces that control nature and, as such, is *a part of* the
scene. Such is man's genus. But, according to Burke, man is
differentiated—is *apart from* the scene—in his unprecedented symbol-
using abilities. Such is man's genius.[6] Our genius drives us to produce
"science," to name the scene from which we arose, and even to so endow that scene with the spirit of our own genius that *things* can become, for us, the signs of *words*.[7] In the human sciences, we name
ourselves and our relations with each other. Discovering that the act of
naming is itself the essence of humanity (and herein lies a powerful
rationale for the humanities), we name our naming in grammar, logic,
and rhetoric—the trivium, and all its latter-day derivatives. In poetry
we indulge in naming for its own—and hence for our own—sake. Attempting to name a "farther shore," we create theology and its coy
counterpart, metaphysics. Characteristically, we attribute to God our
own most central feature, and He becomes the Logos who creates *His*
universe by *verbal* fiat—by naming.

Those who, searching for a theory of knowledge rather than a theory of action, view language more as an instrument than as an end are
likely to object to Burke's thoroughgoing emphasis on man's symbolicity. But even they must conceive of, and couch, their objections in
symbolic terms. Burke, for his part, acknowledges that since all action
presupposes motion and all acts take place in a scene, drama is contained within science. Nevertheless, insofar as all human accounts of
the scene are necessarily rendered symbolically, and dramatism is first
and foremost a theory of symbols, science is contained within
dramatism—and a dramatistic critique of science becomes, at least in
principle, possible.[8]

In his essay on William Carlos Williams, Burke comments on a
poem that poignantly illustrates the limits of science. That poem de-
picts a child, presumably a patient of Williams, who, in attempting to
catch a bouncing ball, has plunged from a balcony to his "old back
yard" six floors below. Says Burke, "When the child, *successfully
clutching the ball*, hits 'the old back yard' by God he is home" (*LSA*, p.
288, emphasis added). Here for Burke is an example of the symbol-
using animal "rotten with perfection" pursuing God knows what
symbol-generated purpose to his own premature doom. Here, too, is
the seminal conjunction—that between nonsymbolic motion and symbolic action—that has preoccupied Burke from the beginning.

Burke would grant that an accurate description of the motion of the
falling, clutching child (initial and terminal velocities, acceleration,

and forces at impact, etc.) lies well within the abilities of contemporary science. So it should! Dynamics (thermo, hydro, aero, electro, quantum-electro, quantum-chromo, etc.), the study of bodies in motion, has been the central preoccupation of scientists from *their* beginning. Geometry, the measurement of the "old back yard," is one of man's earliest successes in the science of quantification. But, having granted science its very considerable due, Burke would ask, How account for the falling child's desperate "clutch"?

In his attempt to account for symbolic action—the "clutch" if you will—Kenneth Burke harks back to the old philosophies of *substance*. For in those philosophies, as Burke points out, *substance* was an *act*. Indeed Spinoza, to whom Burke is greatly indebted, defined substance as "the cause of itself" (*causa sui*).[9] Dramatism, deconstructionism to the contrary notwithstanding, thus allows for—nay even insists upon—a purposive human agent with a degree (however constricted) of autonomy. It also reintroduces the expanded notion of cause (material, formal, efficient, and final) due to Aristotle and usually associated with substance philosophy.

In the physical sciences (the study of "things that move"), quite appropriate attempts to remove teleological explanations led initially to accounts of cause as the *vis a tergo*—the force from behind. This radically truncated notion of cause was fatally wounded by Hume's critique and briefly resurrected by Kant, only to be struck down once again by the discovery of non-Euclidean geometries and the development of quantum mechanics. Forced to abandon cause, science resorted to a probabilistic account of microcosm (scene). The grainy picture that emerged, in accordance with the requirements of indeterminacy, lacked resolution. It was, nonetheless, like the pointillist painting, both powerful and compelling. The corresponding "turn from causality" to what Burke calls "the cult of sheer correlation" in the attempt to describe "persons who act" has created no such synthesis.[10] Indeed, it might be argued that, proceeding almost literally by a connecting of the statistical dots, scientized social studies have at best succeeded in producing the equivalent of number painting.

The hegemony of science has, according to the sage of Andover, resulted in the "hypertrophy of the psychology of information" and the "corresponding atrophy of the psychology of form."[11] In literature, the psychology of information leads to an overemphasis on the plot that, by alternately concealing and revealing information, delivers suspense and surprise.[12] The weakness of such literature is that, like yesterday's news (or TV drama for that matter), it scarcely bears repetition. One can be really surprised only once by the same piece of information. Confusing scientific with aesthetic truth, this literature reduces art to a "trivial pursuit." Great literature—writing that can profitably be read and reread—on the other hand, exemplifies the psychology of form in its emphasis on the appeal of *eloquence.*

Driven by scientism, the psychology of information arrives at the view that "history is after all just one damn thing after another." The mechanics of acquiring a higher degree in discipline after discipline produces what Burke has called "low powered collations," the "stamp collections of an overly proliferating priesthood" (*PLF,* p. 141). In the humanities, these collations have tended to be rationalized in terms of weak or poorly understood but fashionable critical taxonomies. (And let it be admitted that Burke's dramatistic pentad has on many occasions been used in just that way.) The social sciences, no doubt influenced by a powerful rhetoric of science, have more often resorted to statistical rationalizations.

Malaise among Social Scientists

Kenneth Burke's critique of the "cult of correlation" anticipates, informs, and sometimes inspires the growing disenchantment expressed by practitioners of the human sciences themselves. Donald McCloskey's analysis of overmathematization in his influential *The Rhetoric of Economics* is a notable but not isolated case in point. Wassily Leontief, sometime president of American Economics Association and winner of the 1973 Nobel Prize in economics, writes that "page after page of professional economic journals are filled with mathematical formulas leading the reader from sets of more or less plausible but entirely arbitrary assumptions to precisely stated but irrelevant theoretical conclusions."[13] Leontief, a mathematical economist, is sufficiently discouraged to have ceased writing for the professional journals. Robert Kuttner, talking of the impact of the computer on economic research observes that "recent innovations, such as 'vector autoregressions' and 'multivariate-regressive integrative moving average' models, in effect have the computer go on automatic pilot and search for correlations almost at random."[14] The results of such procedures, decidedly in the realm of motion, are no doubt sometimes suggestive, but they cannot be said to be the product of "understanding" (literally substance). As Burke has pointed out, the stock market as a whole may be said to *move* up and down (although analysts frequently anthropomorphize this movement—"the market is taking a breather," etc.). The individual investors who compose the market are agents (*causa sui*) *acting* primarily in the name of *purpose*. Moreover, data that substance philosophy, proceeding usually from an underlying organic metaphor, would claim to be *qualitative* are rendered quantitatively in order for the computer to do its work. This is quite in keeping with the atomistic philosophy which is normally associated with the machine metaphor that informs much scientized social study. Atomistic philosophy demands as its ultimate reality discrete units, identical, unchanging, indivisible, and hence subject to counting and correlation ("arithmetic"). The "market" must thus treat indifferently the "widow's mite" and that of the "rich businessman." It must also assume that the businessman's first buck (the one that still hangs framed on the wall of his establishment) is equivalent to the last dollar he made (and with which he carelessly tips the shoeshine boy).

In sociology, Jack D. Douglas, in "The Rhetoric of Science and the Origins of Statistical Social Thought," has traced the influence of Durkheim's famous work *Suicide*. This book, says Douglas, is "very generally seen as a paradigm for all sociological work."[15] More particularly, it is Durkheim's use of the hypothetical-statistical method that has served as a model for the discipline. That model, says Douglas, has been used for two purposes both by Durkheim and sociology generally, viz., as a sotto voce "political-and-philosophical polemic" and as a "powerful (rhetorical) demonstration that sociology was scientific and must be an independent discipline."[16] Andrew Weigert similarly writes about the part played by statistics in creating an "immoral rhetoric of scientific sociology" and, citing Burke, calls for a dramatistic interpretation of social data.[17] Stanislav Andreski's somewhat polemical *Social Science as Sorcery* offers examples of the mania for mathematical symbols (n ach = the need to achieve) that can be accounted for only in terms of a powerful rhetoric of mathematics.[18]

Paul E. Meehl, past president of the American Psychological Association and fellow of the American Academy of Arts and Sciences, has registered his distress at the nature of quantification in psychology. In a critique that applies equally to research in other behavioral sciences, he comments:

> Because physical theories typically predict numerical values, an improvement in experimental precision reduces the tolerance range and hence increases corroborability. In most psychological research, improved power of a statistical design leads to a prior probability approaching $1/2$ of finding a significant difference in the theoretically predicted direction. Hence the corroboration

yielded by "success" is very weak, and becomes weaker with increased precision. "Statistical significance" plays a logical role in psychology, the reverse of its role in physics.[19]

This is hardly the criticism of a disenchanted but mathematically illiterate humanist. Meehl, like Leontief, is a distinguished and prolific contributor to statistically based research in his discipline. Moreover, Meehl unlike Andreski is not speaking of poorly designed or badly executed statistical studies but of a problem intrinsic to much of the enterprise. Imre Lakatos, an equally distinguished philosopher-mathematician, reacted to Meehl's article, and similar criticism by David T. Lykken, thus:

> After reading Meehl (1967) and Lykken (1968) one wonders whether the function of statistical techniques in the social sciences is not primarily to provide a machinery for producing phoney corroborations and thereby a semblance of "scientific progress" where, in fact, there is nothing but an increase in pseudo-intellectual garbage.[20]

Stephen J. Gould is somewhat more restrained in his conclusions but leaves no doubt about the extent to which statistical methods of correlation in the assessment of I.Q. have led to a systematic "mismeasure of man."

Burke's critique of the "cult of correlation" could be taken for a ground-clearing operation insofar as his dramatistic centerpiece, the pentad (hexad), is the logical counterpart of correlation techniques in the social sciences.[21] Roughly speaking, whereas the human scientist would design an experiment or generate a data base, the Burkean would choose a "representative anecdote." Where the one would search for sets of correlations among his/her data, the other would look for the constituents of the hexad (act, scene, agent, agency, purpose, attitude). Where the one would determine a "principal component" of a matrix of correlations, the other would "feature" one of the hexadic terms. Where the one would calculate the quantitative relationship between other components and the principal component (a sort of correlation of correlations), the other would systematically examine the ratios among hexadic terms.[22] Rotation of axes, which allows the statistician essentially to rename his various components, is matched by variations in "scope" which offer the same resource in hexadic analysis.

In factor analysis—one of the most powerful and admired statistical techniques in the inventory of social scientists—the principal component "resolves" a maximum amount of data. Each subsequent component successively "mops up" the remaining data. The number of components used, and hence the amount of aberrant data left unaccounted for, is arbitrarily chosen. The Burkean analyst may choose which key term to feature and what is to be the scope of the analysis, but the number of "components" is fixed, and the hexad is in principle exhaustive. Indeed, it might be argued that in keeping with its emphasis on the dramatic, hexadic analysis is likely to highlight the seemingly aberrant datum. Ironically, correlation techniques, unlike hexadic analysis, may tend to suppress the very "anomalies" that have been the departure point for much productive theoretical development in the exemplary physical sciences.

Whatever the similarities and dissimilarities at the level of symbolic operations, the two procedures are underwritten by the profoundly different rationalizations of scientism and dramatism. Whereas the one searching for shared behavioral attributes must be content to show that we are all in one way or another _correlated_, the other seeking a common substance proclaims that we are all _consubstantial_. In renouncing substance (_causa sui_), scientism finishes by surrendering cause. Gould points out that cause cannot be derived from correlation, adding that "it is not even true that intense correlations are more likely to represent cause than weak ones."[23] The "old Adam," the hankering for understanding (substance), runs very deep, however, and as Gould observes, "The invalid assumption that correlation implies cause is probably among the two or three most serious and common errors of human reasoning."[24] Even if human scientists kept their vows of metaphysical chastity, and they don't, it is inevitable that policymakers mobilizing the data of the social sciences will mistake high correlations for remediable causes. And let it be noted that the legislator charged with finding solutions _must_ assign causes, and frequently does so, using data generated by a technique whose philosophical assumption is that no such phenomenon as a cause exists.

Moreover, lacking a legitimate concept of cause, scientism must always be somewhat surprised and mystified when the manipulation of arbitrary mathematical symbols provides, as it sometimes does, a "resonant" account of the human behavior it hopes to describe. The situation is analogous to that of the "natural" scientist who, turning on his television set, knows that Hertz's description of electromagnetic waves is thereby "confirmed." He also knows that, well before Hertz discovered them, electromagnetic waves were predicted and required by Maxwell's Equations. His metaphysics, however, prevent him from accounting for this amazing symmetry between reality and the symbolic representation thereof in terms of cause. He may not logically take refuge in any modern secular analogue of the ancient announcement that "God is a mathematician."

Denied any such rationalization, the scientist can only be left to wonder about what the eminent physicist Eugene Wigner has called "the unreasonable effectiveness of mathematics in the natural sciences."[25] Dramatism, on the other hand, having proclaimed that all human action *is* symbolic action, can reasonably anticipate that a hexadic treatment thereof will contain elements of causal analysis. For Burke at least, scientism in its analysis of human nature is crudely metaphoric (metonymic), whereas he believes that dramatism, postulating that symbolism is constitutive of human nature and action, is *not* a metaphor.

Because he refuses to abandon "cause" and embrace "mere correlation," Kenneth Burke's posture in the human sciences bears a striking resemblance to that of Albert Einstein in natural science. Einstein, refusing to believe the "God plays dice," rejected the probabilistic version of nature that underwrites the Bohr-Heisenberg account. Interestingly, Burke also explicitly suggests that Heisenberg's indeterminacy principle—a principle that leads directly to a "cult of correlation"—is a sign more of epistemological embarrassment than of ontological truth.[26] And, he says, "Dramatism would feel safest if one could prove beyond all doubt (as one doubtless never will) that everything in the realm of physics and biology is inexorably determined."[27] It is ironic that both thinkers are apt to be treated as great relativizers. It is true that Einstein and Burke have both pointed out the relativity of much that had hitherto been taken for absolute and thus earned credit as originators of the "New Physics" and "New Rhetoric," respectively. Nonetheless, both are classical thinkers who in grounding their system on an absolute (the absolute velocity of light; dramatism as literally true) avoid the vertigo of thoroughgoing relativism. It is interesting, too, that having rejected statistical accounts of reality, Einstein features "thought experiments" in much the same way that Burke features "representative anecdotes." It is perhaps not coincidental that both men are symbolsmiths. Einstein, who, working with blackboard and chalk, manipulated mathematical symbols, infrequently if ever entered a laboratory! Burke, except in his poetry, rarely deals directly with social data but rather analyzes *texts* about social data. He has quite properly asked, "What am I but a wordman?"

Burke's distrust of the "cult of correlation," however, should not be mistaken for antipathy to mathematical reasoning generally. In regretting the hypertrophy of the "psychology of information," Burke also urged the virtues of the "psychology of form." A number of commentators have noted (and frequently regretted) a formal-mathematical streak in Burke's literary criticism.[28] In addition to its obviously Aristotelian elements, dramatism owes a good deal to Leibniz and Spinoza, both of whom tended to reason *more geometrico*. And the original manuscript for *A Grammar of Motives* contained a section dealing with mathematics. Speaking of his "Dramatist terms," Burke himself comments that "here a poor mathematician seeks in his way to attain the generalizing ways of pure mathematics." (*CS*, p. 218). But these generalizing ways are not to be achieved by "mere correlation." The hexadic terms, Burke says, are a "set of blanks to be filled out" and "an algebra not an arithmetic" (*RR*, p. 26n). Whereas "arithmetic" here amounts to counting and correlating, in algebra, according to Burke, "You've got *equations* (this equals that); you've got *implications* (if this, then that); you've got *transformations* (from this, to that)."[29]

Burke's own analyses typically exemplify the quasi-algebraic method implicit in the hexad. He writes, for instance, of the pivotal point in the history of philosophy when Spinoza pairs the two terms "God" and "Nature." When paired terms are made equal ($x = y$), he points out that algebraically one can be substituted for the other. Spinoza, thus, in equating "God" and "Nature" prepared the way for a "naturalist" dropping of "God" as unnecessary (y is substituted for x) (*GMRM*, p. 413). Debunking, says Burke, is the process wherein x, a higher value, is said to equal y, a lower value. ("Property is theft!") Pointing out that Shakespeare's Falstaff would never crudely steal a purse, Burke says of the charming miscreant, "He converts 'thine' into 'ours'—and it is 'circumstances over which he has no control' that go to convert this 'ours' into a 'mine' " (*GMRM*, p. 515n). Here the formula is "Thine is ours" ($a = b$); "Ours is mine" ($b = c$); therefore, "Thine is mine" ($a = c$). And the method is that of what may be called a "qualitative algebra."

Viewed as a qualitative algebra, then, dramatism, without reducing action to motion, acknowledges the mathematical dimension in science. Paradoxically, this same qualitative algebra in Burke's work also lends some comfort to that poststructural movement in contemporary criticism which would, by making man a docile instrument of language, problematize his status as "authorial *agent*." The extent to which Burke's mathematical tendency raises issues (and eyebrows) in contemporary criticism is best illustrated by an excursus into algebra proper.

A cursory examination of a basic algebra text produces the following word problem (this is an example of what, significantly enough, used to be known as *rhetorical algebra*):

> During one afternoon a clerk at a soda fountain sold a certain number of drinks at 10 cents each and twice as many at 15 cents each. He took in $20. Find the number that he sold at each price.[30]

Allowing for inflation since the text was written, the description, though truncated, is realistic enough. One can well imagine that the clerk has forgotten to keep track and that the missing information is important for, say, bookkeeping purposes. A relatively simpleminded application of the hexad produces: an agent—the clerk; a scene—the soda fountain; an act—selling; an agency—the drinks; a purpose (and here we have to speculate a little)—profit; an attitude—e.g., avarice. Questions of "scope" might lead us to wonder whether the soda fountain is part of a department store or drugstore. Is the store located in a small town or perhaps a large city? Can we safely assume that these transactions are taking place in a capitalistic rather than a communist "scene"? Does the clerk work for a fixed wage or does he get a percentage of sales? Perhaps he also owns or leases this soda fountain; if so, the quality of his act may be radically changed. Again, the act may be performed in the context of a universal scene that is materialistically conceived of as "a fortuitous collocation of atoms," or more ominously, the universe may be one in which the making of a higher profit is directly correlated with the chances of going to hell! The hexadic analysis may, for want of further information, be mistaken in its details. It cannot be mistaken in its overall thrust. Each of these hexadic components must be present and must be related to each of the other elements in specifiable ways.

A dramatist of a more literal sort might perhaps wish to add narrative elements to this account. Our clerk is, let us suppose, to get ten percent of the sales. Two dollars, however, is insufficient to purchase the medicine which would perchance serve to keep his beloved wife this side of death's door (the algebra text is just about *that* vintage). Our hero, though basically honest, would perhaps be driven by circumstances to steal the fifty cents that lies between here and a happy outcome...only to get caught...and suffer penalties disproportionate to the nature and extent of his crime, etc., etc. In thus dramatizing the algebra problem we have come a long way in the direction of what Burke would call the "temporizing of essence" (*GMRM*, p. 430). Quite in keeping with the dramatistic impulse we have emphasized a sentient agent (*causa sui*), in conflict, *acting* purposively, in a contingent situation to produce change over time.

From Dramatism to Logology

In recent years, Burke has supplemented dramatism (his ontology) with logology (his epistemology).[31] Asked what is the ultimate nature of human *being* Burke unhesitatingly replies in dramatist terms. Faced with the question how shall we know a reality whose very essence is change (drama) when knowing must necessarily involve identifying stable features, Burke "essentializes the temporal." Thus the "qualitative algebra" more or less implicit in dramatism is made manifest in logology as the dramatistic emphasis on temporal change surrenders to a logological drive toward atemporal permanence.

A "logological" approach to the algebra problem would thus urge us to "essentialize the temporal"—to remove the dramatic elements. We do so thus: Let a symbol (n) represent the number of ten-cent drinks. Twice n therefore equals the number of fifteen-cent drinks. Ten times n is the amount paid for ten-cent drinks. Thirty times n is the amount paid for fifteen-cent drinks. Thus:

$$10n + 30n = 2000$$
$$40n = 2000$$
$$n = 50; 2n = 100$$

Voila! By making equations, implications, and (nontemporal) transformations, we now know that the clerk sold one hundred and fifty drinks, fifty of the cheaper and one hundred of the more expensive. Those facts, so elusive in the sweaty classroom of yesteryear, were there all the time—implicit in the equations that were implicit in the anecdote. Indeed, it is quite likely that the author (malevolent he!) began with the atemporal essential—the equations—and temporized them to the very edge of drama, full well knowing the childish (human?) tendency to overdramatize. "What kind of drink?" "Was that afternoon a hot one?" "I wish I had a soda right now!"

The sweaty young student contemplating the delights of a large, cold drink on a hot afternoon (and for that very reason making no headway with the algebra problem) must overcome his no doubt natural propensity for drama and undertake a logological analysis. He must abandon the linear narrative in favor of a detemporalized cycle of terms and move from the rhetorical realm of the merely plausible or probable into the realm of terminological necessity. Since an agent to be an agent must have the freedom to choose, the *agent* must be "erased." And if the agent is banished, so, too, is the *act*. Moreover, if there is no sensing agent, there can be no seductive *image:* the large, cool drink must become an even "cooler" abstraction—"2*n*."

In the *The Rhetoric of Religion*—subtitled "Studies in Logology"—the consummate logologer sets himself an algebraic problem of cosmic proportions; Burke undertakes to render the narrative (mythic) account of Creation in the "First Three Chapters of Genesis" in logological terms. In accordance with the dictates of a *qualitative* algebra, Burke moves immediately toward linguistic abstraction, attenuating agent, act, and image and removing temporal considerations. *Genesis*, he says, is logologically concerned with the principles of governance as achieved by a *covenant*. The covenant is "backed by a perfect authority" (God), and the covenant seeks to impose order (*RR*, p. 180). Proceeding by a series of "equations, implications, and transformations," Burke develops the "cycle of terms tautologically implicit in the idea of *order.'' Order* as a dialectical term requires its negative, *disorder.* And, if order and disorder, then by implication the necessity of *obedience* and/ or *disobedience*. If obedience and disobedience, then the necessity of *reward* and *punishment*, respectively. And if punishment then the necessity of *atonement*.

Whereas the narrative account (the temporalized essence) is unidirectional (if the story is to make sense it must proceed through time from beginning to end); the logological rendition (essentialized temporal) suffers from no such limitation. While the exigencies of presentation require (as with the algebra problem) that one equation precede the next, the equations are in fact eternally co-present—each implicit in the other. This is but another way of noting that narrative has a degree of *freedom*, whereas logology is in the realm of *necessity*.

Narratively, the author of the algebra problem could have chosen to exemplify his equation—his "principle—as a prince," or a pauper, or a drugstore clerk for that matter. Logologically, having decided that *n* is to equal fifty, he must designate twice *n* as equal to one hundred, and forty times *n* as equal to two thousand, etc. Similarly, the narrative account of creation can be, and has been, developed in any number of different ways. Once a cosmology adopts the notion of "governance by covenant," however, no matter how it is developed narratively it must confront "the cycle of terms tautologically implicit in the idea of order." Burke describes the relations between the narrative realm of freedom and that of logological necessity thus:

Trevor Melia

> Theologically, Adam could have chosen *not* to sin. He could
> have said yes to God's thou-shalt-not. But logologically, Adam
> *necessarily* sinned. For if he had chosen *not* to sin, the whole
> design of the Bible would have been ruined. (*RR*, p. 252)

The ruination alluded to here is not simply the spoiling of a good story but something directly analogous to a "mistake" in the solving of an algebra problem. The logic of language (logologic) is for Burke no less stringent in this respect than that of algebraic terms. But to say as much is also to imply that the "author" of the biblical account, while "free" to choose narrative detail (like the author of the algebra problem), was linguistically "driven" with regard to the underlying architecture of the text. And we are thus confronted with a variant on the bête noire of the social sciences—symbolic *action* threatens to reduce to symbolic *motion*.

Again the algebra analogy renders the issue graphic. We can well imagine the long-suffering student, having finally renounced drama in favor of a logological method, triumphantly arriving at a solution— and since it is *his* solution, signing his name to certify ownership. The low-grade writer whom we have previously imagined to have *dramatized* the algebra problem would almost certainly have appended an authorial signature to *his* dubious narrative. But Burke is fond of reminding us of Coleridge's observation "that language itself does as it were *think* for us." And that fact is nowhere more obvious than in logological/mathematical operations. The student will, therefore, soon be informed that *his* solution was already implicit in the arbitrary and *socially* generated symbol system with which he is working. Ironically, the now "decentered," and no doubt disconcerted, student, while he will not be regarded as the "author" of his success, will certainly and justly be charged with the failure should he make a mistake. For even as it is our *sins* that theologically certify that we are free *agents (causa sui)*, so an algebraic "sin" would be evidence of a culpable "creative" streak in our student. A teacher perceiving such a "break" in the solution of an algebra problem would not hesitate to infer the operation of an individuated *agent*.

If Kenneth Burke ultimately refuses to reduce symbolic action to symbolic motion, and his position on *this* reduction is much less clear, it is because of his emphasis on linguistic "breaks" (an emphasis increasingly shared by poststructural critics). Much to the chagrin of the "New Critics," Burke, ever sensitive to logological anomalies in symbolic expositions (texts), be they poetic, scientific, or philosophic, has never hesitated to attribute such breaks to the idiosyncrasies of the author. Thus Burke, having considered internal aspects of poems by Milton, Coleridge, and Keats, finds that an exhaustive treatment must take account of the poets' blindness, drug addiction, and fever, respectively. It is significant, too, that in each instance a "disturbance" in the poetic text points directly to a bodily disease in the poetic agent.[32] For Burke maintains that the principle of individuation is to be found ultimately in the privately experienced central nervous system of each symbol-using *animal*. What some of Burke's critics fail to notice is that his departure from the text is not motivated by *critical* idiosyncracy but by hermeneutic scruples that would do honor to a mathematician. "Cluster analysis" in its examination of linguistic equations is in its own way as rigorous as the techniques used by the mathematician to check the solution to an algebra problem.

The intrusion of the authorial agent into "text," if not, as the deconstructionists would have it, an illusion, is at least a logological (mathematical) "mistake." Marxist literary critics, viewing the autonomous "romantic" agent as a capitalist "mystification," find Burke's logological attenuation of "agent" correspondingly congenial. They also approve of his frequent "Marxist" excursions from text to social context. But Burke's "qualitative algebra" not only attenuates *agent*, it detemporalizes the narrative and in so doing leaves the Marxists ambivalent.

Frank Lentricchia, who welcomes the social relevance of Burke's literary theory and quite correctly credits him with anticipating many of the insights of "deconstructionism," does so by denying "Dramatism" its central place in the Burke corpus.[33] Troubled by the "synchronic voraciousness" of the hexad, Lentricchia emphasizes Burke's early Marxoid (diachronic) works and fails altogether in an otherwise seminal essay to mention the logological turn in *The Rhetoric of Religion*. This is surely a "misreading." Acknowledging the ahistorical, mathematical leitmotif in Burke's work, Fredric Jameson, on the other hand, treats him as a Marxist manqué.[34] Jameson accuses Burke not only of failing to conduct "ideological" analysis but of reluctance to use the very word. He is wrong on both counts.[35] In the introduction to an early edition of *The Rhetoric of Motives*, Burke issued an unmistakable invitation: "May other analysts join me in tracking down the ways in which the realm of sheerly worldly powers becomes endowed with the attributes of 'secular divinity' " (*GMRM*, p. 523). And it is clear that from his earliest comments on the economic upheavals of the twenties and thirties to his current trenchant critiques of technology, Burke has carried out his own program. But he has also warned of two great temptations that beset modern man. Confronted by seemingly mindless, inexorable, and destructive forces, we tend to resort on the one hand to fanaticism (single-minded Marxism?) or on the other to dissipation (rampant deconstructionism?). Burke has seen the attractions of both and surrendered to neither. He has rather suggested that salvation, if such there be, lies in the realm of "adequate ideas."

His Marxist critics sense that Burke, who began dramatistically by proclaiming the centrality of *act*, in adopting Spinoza's formula finishes logologically by stressing *attitude*.[36] And while attitude can be regarded as *incipient* action, it can also be thought of as *arrested* action. What René Wellek has said of Burke's criticism of poetry is perhaps more true of his social criticism—it tends to be "bloodless." The detemporalization of the narrative, implicit in dramatism, explicit in logology, is more likely to lead to an understanding of the human situation than to an undertaking to change it. Herbert Simons has observed that Burke's system "prevents the expression of warrantable outrage." That point, I think, must be granted; it need not be regretted.

Some years ago, Daniel Bell, recognizing no doubt that much that claims to be social science is in fact thinly veiled social rhetoric, called for an end to ideology. And, he said:

> If the end of ideology has any meaning, it is to ask for the end of rhetoric, and rhetoricians, of "revolution", of the day when the young French anarchist Vaillant tossed a bomb into the Chamber of Deputies, and the literary critic Laurent Tailhade declared in his defense: "What do a few human lives matter; it was a *beau geste*."[37]

Almost three decades later, the *beau geste* (manifestly a very bad joke) is still with us. As an announcement, "the end of ideology" was transparently premature. And, far from celebrating "the end of rhetoric," we are now confronted by proposals for a Rhetoric of the Human Sciences. But in evaluating such proposals, we must distinguish, as Bell does not, between rhetoric as a call to arms and rhetoric as a mode of analysis. The scientistic impulse that perhaps seeks to expunge the ideological component from social science more often succeeds in hiding it. A rhetorical *analysis*, perhaps of social data, certainly of texts about those data, far from adding to the ideological element, should, by throwing it into sharp relief, somewhat mitigate its effect. It is precisely the virtue of Burke's mathematical attitude that it tends toward the detachment that has traditionally distinguished the scientist from the engineer—even as it acknowledges that we are not objects in *motion* but human beings in *action*.

NOTES

1. Kenneth Burke, *The Philosophy of Literary Form* (New York: Vintage Books, 1957), p. 99.

2. Kenneth Burke, *The Rhetoric of Religion* (Boston: Beacon Press, 1961), p. 38.

3. Two other assimilations are also to be resisted. Burke's "dramatism," although congenial, should not be identified with Erving Goffman's notion. Goffman, treating drama as a metaphor, systematically exploits the insight that "All the world's a stage." Burke's dramatism rather derives from the observation that the most central symbol in the vocabulary of "bodies that learn language" is the term *act*. Dramatism with much more comprehensive results works out the cycle of terms implicit in that central term. Ernst Cassirer, of course, also defines man as *animal symbolicum*. He deals with the insight, however, in the context of a theory of knowledge. Burke, emphasizing the linguistic negative generally and the hortatory negative particularly, produces a theory of action.

4. If it turns out that Creation is the result of divine verbal command, then all that is from the human point of view nonsymbolic motion would be God's symbolic action.

5. And we symbol specialists need always to remember that Burke is as insistent about our animality as he is about our symbolicity.

6. Burke views technology as a logical and even, granted our "rottenness with perfection," an inevitable outcome of our symbol-using genius. He has been warning since at least as early as 1937 about the danger of ecological disaster, and nowadays, as our symbols coalesce into more and more powerful technology, he contemplates the possibility that we are not only *apart from* but *against* nature (counternature).

7. Burke, *Language as Symbolic Action* (Berkeley: University of California Press, 1966), part 3, chap. 4.

8. Burke states unequivocally that the *Grammar* is concerned with "terms alone." That statement is much less modest than it seems, however, when it is understood in the context of a theory of symbolic action wherein man is taken to be (to paraphrase) the "terminological" animal. A theory of terms *is* in some sense a theory of man!

9. For an extended treatment of Spinoza's influence on Burke see Richard Thames, "Mystical Ontology in Kenneth Burke," Ph.D. Diss., University of Pittsburgh, 1979.

10. Kenneth Burke, *A Grammar of Motives* (New York: Prentice-Hall, 1945), p. 183.

11. Kenneth Burke, *Counter-Statement* (Chicago: University of Chicago Press, 1957), p. 33.

12. It is notable that Burke in his scintillating, and neglected, novel, *Towards a Better Life* (Berkeley: University of California Press, 1966) follows Flaubert in attempting to write a virtually "plotless" novel.

13. Quoted in Robert Kuttner, "The Poverty of Economics," *Atlantic Monthly*, February 1985, p. 78.

14. Ibid.

15. Jack D. Douglas, "The Rhetoric of Science and the Origins of Statistical Social Thought: the Case of Durkheim's *Suicide*," in Edward A. Tiryakian, ed., *The Phenomenon of Sociology* (New York: Appleton-Century-Crofts, 1971), p. 47.

16. Ibid., p. 55.

17. Andrew J. Weigert, "The Immoral Rhetoric of Scientific Sociology," *American Sociologist*, 5 (1970), 111–19.

18. Stanislav Andreski, *Social Sciences as Sorcery* (New York: St. Martin's Press, 1972).

19. Paul E. Meehl, "Theory-Testing in Psychology and Physics: A Methodological Paradox," *Philosophy of Science* (June 1967), p. 103.

20. Imre Lakatos, "Falsification and the Methodology of Scientific Research Programmes," in Lakatos and Alan Musgrave, eds., *Criticism and the Growth of Knowledge* (Cambridge: University Press 1970), p. 176.

21. I shall hereafter use *hexad* instead of pentad. The sixth term, "attitude," has been implicit in the pentad from the beginning, and it is clear that were Burke writing the *Grammar* today, he would treat the term separately.

22. I'm here following Gould's description of "factor analysis" in I.Q. assessment. See Stephen J. Gould, *The Mismeasure of Man* (New York: W. W. Norton, 1981), chap. 6. For a more technical discussion see, for instance, Jac On Kim, "Factor Analysis," in Norman H. Nie, ed., *Statistical Package for the Social Sciences* (New York: McGraw Hill, 1975).

23. Gould, *Mismeasure of Man*, p. 242.

24. Ibid., p. 242.

25. Eugene P. Wigner, "The Unreasonable Effectiveness of Mathematics in the Natural Sciences," *Communications on Pure and Applied Mathematics*, 13, no. 1 (February 1960), 1–14.

26. Burke, *A Grammar of Motives and A Rhetoric of Motives* (New York: World, 1962), p. 260.

27. Kenneth Burke, *Dramatism and Development* (Worcester, Mass.: Clark University Press, 1972), p. 31.

28. See particularly the essays by Charles I. Glicksberg and John Crowe Ransom in William H. Rueckert, ed., *Critical Responses to Kenneth Burke, 1924–1966* (Minneapolis: University of Minnesota Press, 1969).

29. Kenneth Burke, "*Counter-Gridlock:* An Interview with Kenneth Burke," *All Area*, no.2 (Spring 1983), p. 21.

30. Raleigh Schorling and Rolland R. Smith, *Algebra: First Course* (New York: World, 1949), p. 121.

31. Kenneth Burke, Letter to the Editor, *TLS*, August 12, 1983.

32. It is worth noting that Burke autobiographically reports that the formula can be reversed, that is, a bodily disease can be traced to a symbolic disturbance. This fact, of course, is quite consistent with the notion that

"symbol using" is partly constitutive of the human animal. It may not be irrelevant, either, that Burke as a child was a Christian Scientist.

33. Frank Lentricchia, "Reading History with Kenneth Burke," in Hayden White and Margaret Brose, eds., *Representing Kenneth Burke* (Baltimore: Johns Hopkins University Press, 1982), p. 120.

34. Fredric R. Jameson, "The Symbolic Inference; or, Kenneth Burke and Ideological Analysis," *Critical Inquiry,* 4 (Spring 1978), 507-23.

35. See Burke's response to Jameson, "Methodological Repression and/or Strategies of Containment," *Critical Inquiry,* 5 (Winter 1978), 401-16.

36. It is significant that Burke says, "Attitude designates the point of *personal mediation* between the realms of non-symbolic motion and symbolic action." Kenneth Burke, *Attitudes toward History* (Berkeley: University of California Press, 1984), p. 394.

37. Daniel Bell, quoted in Chaim Waxman, ed., *The End of Ideology Debate* (New York: Simon and Schuster, 1969), p. 103.

3 RATIOS AND CAUSES

THE PENTAD AS AN

ETIOLOGICAL SCHEME IN

SOCIOLOGICAL EXPLANATION

VITO SIGNORILE

> *A new period in the history of science commences with a*
> *backward movement that returns us to an earlier stage.*
> *. . . This backward movement is not just an accident. . . it*
> *is essential if we want to overtake the status quo.*
> Paul Feyerabend

There is a conception of cause—one that might be termed "mechanical"—which has managed to persist through an amazingly wide range of treatises on philosophical and scientific explanation.[1] According to Lakoff and Johnson this mechanistic sense is one of the "metaphors we live by," and constitutes the dominant mode of thinking in modern science.[2] They note that the scientific conception is the result of a "purifying" process in which all the "peculiarly human aspects are factored out."

Thus, in science—and this would include the human sciences—causation has come down to us in a slimmed-down version of a wider notion more widely held. There is a lucid discussion of this in Stocks, who describes the gradual narrowing of the sense of "cause" from a much richer conception, going back to Aristotle's fourfold distinction of final, formal, material, and efficient causes.[3] These four can roughly be characterized as resulting from four basic questions which Aristotle felt had to be answered before we could acquire a complete explanation of the occurrence of some object, phenomenon, or state of affairs:

what shape or structure does it have? (formal cause); what is it composed of, what are its constituents? (material cause); how did it come about? (efficient cause); and what does it accomplish, what purpose does it serve? (final cause).[4]

Stocks shows that, in contrast to the older notion in which form was *the* cause, by Descartes's time formal and final causes were expunged from philosophical and scientific thought while material cause was already fading entirely away, leaving efficient cause to carry the burden of explanation.

Now, society is a distinctly human affair, and the ambition to eliminate "the peculiarly human aspects" in the explanatory efforts of the social sciences seems a curiously self-defeating conceit.[5] To use Burke's terminology, if the modern scientific approach is the result of systematic efforts to "objectify" causation as *sheer motion*, then, in the social sciences, we are in danger of losing sight of the *action*.[6]

This lesson can be gleaned from the vagaries of structural/functional analysis. Confronted with the need to explain human events and, at the same time, constrained to explain them "mechanistically," the functionalists among social scientists never managed to satisfy their critics. On the one hand, being faithful to the "facts" of human life, they were wont to produce a class of theories which Popper would have considered more "mythic" than scientific.[7] On the other hand, attempting to meet the requirements of mechanistic explanation, they were never able to incorporate a cogent theory of human motivation.[8] Summing up the experience of a generation of anthropologists, Jarvie allowed that functionalism was useful as a method, but entirely bankrupt as an explanatory theory.[9]

But the problem is a generic one. Reserving the term "cause" for the kind of productive factor that precedes an event and is lineally linked to it through some concept of "force," science was gradually led by the complexity of events to employ such auxiliary causal concepts as "necessary," "sufficient," and "conditional." This can be seen in Bunge's treatise on causation. A cause, he observes, could be quite a complex affair, ramifying into "conditions" and "primary agents," as well as "necessary" and "sufficient" causes.[10] Even Hempel, after weeding out the nonmechanistic conceptions he found in functionalist vocabulary, was obliged to augment the purely mechanistic perspective he was promoting with such concepts as "necessary" and "sufficient" conditions.[11]

Thus, what functionalists were castigated for doing more openly by bringing structures and functions into the scheme of explanation,

Vito Signorile

their critics wound up doing on the sly. It is the argument of this essay that, embedded within these ad hoc distinctions are notions of final, material, and especially formal causation.[12] It is in this expanded circumference of analysis that we find the relevance—a relevance Burke himself saw—of the pentad for causal explanation.[13] The strategy is to take the view that human phenomena are essentially the result of symbolic action, which, in turn, suggests that a radically symbolist approach to the question of social causation is called for.

The idea that the labor of causation is divided roughly along the lines Aristotle described for it is becoming ever more explicitly acknowledged. Mention has already been made of Bates's perception of this fact in developmental psychology (end of note 4). Bates is drawing from the work of Piaget. On this work, Kuhn notes that Piaget's distinction between "narrow" and "wide" conceptions of cause is tantamount to the difference between efficient and formal causes.[14] Kuhn considers this distinction quite valid, and finds it very much alive—albeit unrecognized—in modern physics. Describing the way in which later states of physical systems cannot be predicted from earlier states without postulating the continuous operation of the structural relationships that prevail among the constituents of the system, he comments: "the structure of physical explanation closely resembles that which Aristotle developed in analyzing formal causes."[15]

It would seem that modern science has only managed to bring Aristotle back in disguise. If this is so, then perhaps a more direct, less coy restoration of the Aristotelian tetrad could open up a new paradigm of explanation—in Burkean terms, a new *strategy*. What I will try to show is how a symbolist approach to social phenomena can find in Burke's dramatistic pentad a socially relevant specification of Aristotle's tetrad of causes.

Assumptions for a Symbolist Strategy

CAUSATION AS SYMBOLIC REQUIREDNESS

We can begin by considering the symbolist view that causes are, not components of the concrete empirical world, but rather *concepts*, or *ideas*, concerning the constituents of this world.[16] In this view, the criterion by which we judge the presence of causes is logical requiredness or necessity. Our explanation of an object or event is complete when "it stands to reason."

Objections to this way of formulating causation come from two sources: one is Kantian, the other Wittgensteinian. The Kantian objection hinges on the distinction Kant (following Leibniz) made between the *synthetic* and the *analytic* in human knowledge and reasoning. In one reading, the former has an empirical content independent of human thought, while the latter is purely conceptual. Some argue that cause is a *synthetic* datum, not analytic.[17]

Quine, on the other hand, argues that the distinction between the synthetic and the analytic is spurious, for no isolated statement in science can be empirically grounded. "The unit of empirical significance," he says, "is the whole of science."[18] This is the view of Rorty, who advances what he calls the "post-Kantian" thesis that terms do not derive their meaning from an independent reality to which they refer, but draw their meaning instead from the total conceptual matrix (school, discipline, etc.) in which they function.[19]

Such views support the symbolist assumption that knowledge is necessarily symbolic, and thus necessarily removed from things-in-themselves—or, as Burke puts it, the "wordless universe." We may *impute* a necessity to things-in-themselves, but this imputation is itself a symbolic act. For Burke, this is an ineluctable state of affairs. In his "definition of man," he notes that the human being is "separated from his natural condition by instruments of his own making." And these "instruments" are, of course, symbols and the products of symbols.[20] We can, indeed, conceptualize *sheer motion*, but this conceptualization is itself a symbolic *act*, and as such exists in the realm of symbolic structures (of which, of course, the pentad is an important example).

The Wittgensteinian objection stems from Ludwig Wittgenstein's conclusion, found in his *Philosophical Investigations*, that there is no compelling reason to accept the compulsions of logical necessity, such as one would find in the "truth table" or a syllogism.[21] This issue has been discussed by a number of writers who have picked up Wittgenstein's challenge.[22] But a definitive resolution remains elusive. There is, it would seem, the paradox of employing a compellingly logical argument showing why we are not compelled to accept logical conclusions. This puts the argument on a par with other celebrated "vicious circles."[23]

The belief is, as expressed by Dummett, that there must be a middle-ground explanation between Platonism and conventionalism, between the argument which states that logical necessity is an eternal verity existing in the nature of timeless ideas, and the assumption which sees logical necessity as a product of culture—in particular, an artifact of language.[24]

Vito Signorile

Again, the symbolist position is that there is no distinction here. Both the Platonic and the conventional exist in a matrix of symbols. As Susanne Langer expresses it, the "symbol-mongering" mind immediately transforms experience into concepts, which, in turn, serve to present things to our minds, not our hands.[25] That logical compulsion—that is, the compelling argument of a syllogism—may turn out to be not so compelling after all should be of no great consequence to the symbolist. For logic may very well share in the degree of compulsion which characterizes symbol systems in general: a culturally determined specification of what it is that all sane minds *must* accept. On this view, the question of logical necessity reduces to the question of symbolic requiredness. And, in turn, the necessity of causation reduces to the necessity of propositional logic. Thus, Hempel can state that "causal explanation is a special type of deductive nomological explanation,"[26] Roy Francis can argue that cause is a logical property of 2×2 tables,[27] and Karl Popper can point out that "to give a causal explanation of an event means to deduce a statement which describes it."[28]

REQUIREDNESS AND MOTIVE IN NONDISCURSIVE SYMBOLS

The compelling nature of symbols is precisely what is implied in Burke's "principle of perfection," in what he calls "logological entelechy." The idea of "entelechy" derives from Aristotle, who conceived of it as a general principle governing all natural phenomena. All things, he asserted, seek to attain their immanent perfection (*per-fect*: "make-through, thoroughly"), to bring to completion the kinds of things they happen to be. Without subscribing to its Aristotelian physical sense, Burke saw the relevance of this principle for understanding how language can move us. There may or may not be an entelechy in things, but there surely is one in words. This principle, says Burke, "is central to the nature of language as motive."[29] Hidden in our vocabularies are a tangle of motives,[30] and one important way in which they motivate is through the principle of perfection. The entelechy of words drives human action to achieve perfectly the state of affairs they symbolize. Thus driven, the human being, as Burke observes, can become "rotten with perfection," for the "best" can become the enemy of the merely "good" (*LSA*, p. 16).

Yet, as far as human motivation is concerned, this is not the whole story. For Burke also observes that "motives are subdivisions in a frame of meanings."[31] This larger frame of meanings encompasses more fully the circumference of human symbolization. What is needed to round out the symbolist analysis of human action is yet one more expansion. We need to consider structures that are made up of "wordless" symbols.

Burke often speaks of the "wordless universe" as the realm of "sheer motion." Yet to concede that this is true is to concede too much. Burke has in fact pointed out that, besides language, "there are other symbol systems, such as music, dance, painting."[32] While "sheer motion" is, indeed, located in the "wordless universe," the wordless world is not entirely devoid of symbolization. There are symbols out there in the tacit dimension, and the symbolic requiredness of language has its counterpart in the symbolic requiredness of wordless symbols.

The necessity of linguistic requiredness, of which logic is the purest example, flows from what Langer calls the "discursive" form of symbolic expression.[33] In the discursive mode the structure of the symbols is based on the alignment found in temporal sequences. This lineality of the discursive mode lends itself to the conceptualization of events unfolding in nature as analogous to sentences logically unfolding in speech, which leads Langer and others to conclude that the idea of chains of cause and consequent is an artifact of language.[34]

There is, as we have seen, another form of symbolization. It is a wholly nondiscursive form of symbolism, which Langer calls the "presentational." The limits of language, she writes, "are not the last limits of experience.... things inaccessible to language may have their own forms of conception, that is to say, their own symbolic devices."[35] In contrast to the discursive, presentational symbolism transcends time. In the presentational mode it is possible for the later to account for the earlier or for an immanent, mutual accounting to take place in a timeless, simultaneous reciprocity. Langer finds a rich source of presentational symbolism in the arts. It represents, in fact, the foundation of her theory of art.[36]

That the wordless does not necessarily mean the unknown is an important conclusion from Michael Polanyi's studies of the "tacit dimension." Polanyi's concern was to examine the implications of the fact that we can "know more than we can tell." In doing so, he, like Langer, points to an area of experience that lies outside the domain of language. If we can, indeed, "know more than we can tell," it is because another, nonlinguistic, region of symbolic experience is available to us.[37]

Vito Signorile

This nonlinguistic realm of symbolic experience is familiar to us in the form of the *irrational*. The irrational is not just the illogical but, in a more positive sense, the nondiscursive. Irrational motives, if they are truly motives, come from the operation of presentational symbols. Such motives are compelled, not by the force of the lineal required-ness found in conventional logic, but by the force of symbols whose influence cannot be reduced to this kind of logic. This, surely, is the spirit in which Weber proffered the concept of "elective affinities." The decisions of historical actors cannot always be accounted for by an analysis which depends on the discovery of rational (in the sense of logical) motives. There are often nonrational "elective affinities" at work.[38]

Weber could not achieve a systematic incorporation of elective affinities in his theory of human action. Freud, on the other hand, based the whole edifice of his theory on this irrational component of human acts. It is no accident that, in pursuing the phenomena of irrational motives, Freud was led to the "discovery" of the unconscious. While the rational tends generally to be a conscious activity, the irrational action compelled by nondiscursive symbols is primarily subterranean, subconscious.

To be sure, the range of things denoted by the "unconscious" is exceedingly large. As Burke has shown, this term is used to denote such disparate things as the True Self operating behind the scenes, the hidden physiological processes of the body, and sheer ignorance (*LSA*, chap. 4). A term whose function is to denote that of which we are unaware manages to imply a great deal.

In Freudian mythology the various nonconsciousnesses (un-, sub-, and pre-) represent a change of *frame*. To use Goffman's terminology, it was a change from the "natural" framework to the framework[39] of "guided doings." What in early Freud (and his contemporaries) were considered events in nonsymbolic "nature" became, in later Freud, events located in the sphere of symbolic "action."

Freud, however, retained a rationalist bias. In making the irrational rational, he continued to pursue his analysis in the discursive mode. The patient's irrationality is explained through the therapist's rationality. The influence of the linguistic mode in Freud's thought is considered by some psychoanalysts to be the decisive source of his insight into human psychology. The French psychoanalyst Jacques Lacan claims that an unbiased study of Freud's methods would show that he respected the influence of language on the mind. His, after all, was a "talking cure," in which the resources of language were a central factor. As they matured, it would seem that Freud's theories began to take on the semblance of a theory of language. So much so that Lacan is able to declare that the psychoanalytic method must begin with the realization that "what the psychoanalytic experience discovers in the unconscious is the whole structure of language."[40]

In any attempt to achieve an understanding of the unconscious, the unconscious functioning of language is a strategic point of departure. The fact that language compels its speakers to articulate structures largely unconscious to them provided an important window through which to view the much larger sphere of unconsciously followed patterns of *social* activity. This was one source of Emile Durkheim's insight into the nature of "social facts" as external and compelling forces in the production of human action.[41] In his classic essay on the "unconscious patterning of human behavior," the linguist Edward Sapir made a similar observation.[42] The symbolist strategy is to expand the circumference of this insight and view the "irrational" play of motives as largely unconscious compulsions emanating from the domain of presentational symbols. Nondiscursive, presentational symbols compel human acts in the same way that language compels speech-related acts.[43]

RATIOS AS CAUSE

Burke's pentad can be taken as a specification of Goffman's *social frame*. Of the two primary frameworks Goffman identified—the "natural" and the "social"—only the latter is characterized by the presence of "guided doings." Explanation in this framework is not unlike esthetic explanation, and the pentad is our entré into the detailed analysis of the myriad factors at work in the social framework. To sort out the scene, purpose, act, agent, and agency embedded in the frame of "guided doings" is to answer the question Goffman poses as the generating motif of the frameworks: "What is it that's going on here?"[44]

The causal significance of the pentad comes from the ways in which each of its elements has implications for the others. Burke expresses this as the *ratios* of propriety, suitability, or compulsion that prevail among the elements. There exists, in other words, a mutual round of requiredness among them (elsewhere I have suggested calling these pentadic elements "pentodes").[45] They are, as Burke says, "principles of determination" (*GMRM*, p. 15). An *act* can require a particular *scene* insofar as that scene is appropriate to that specific act. In this way, along with the other pentodes, scene can help explain the act. All the ratios carry within them a degree of symbolic requiredness. Indeed, although the pair-wise fit in any given case may be a loose one, the

Vito Signorile

complex ratios of all five pentodes at once (which is, in fact, how social life gets done) exact much more stringent demands of fit.

The Tetrad in the Pentad

Nevertheless, even in the pair-wise case there is a much more compelling character to the ratios than is immediately apparent. Burke notes, for example, that the scene-act ratio is important enough in literature to have its own name: *genius loci* (*GMRM*, p. 6). The ratios are the result of symbolic structures which operate *causally*, in a generally unconscious manner, within a situation as framed by those who participate in it. It must be remembered that in identifying the degree of fit it is necessary to remain within a given frame (or circumference) of action. A change in frame signals a change in the whole identity of the action under analysis. Furthermore, within any given frame we must endeavor to take account of the full range of symbols which the situation comprises, discursive *and* presentational.

Because the causation is nonlineal, the question whether one element in the ratio provokes the other to appear is not usually appropriate. With the possible exception of *act*, as will be discussed below, any one pentode does not, in principle, have priority over the others. A scene may, in fact, determine what the agent shall be, such as when the kind of person you are depends on whether you are at work or at home. But it is also true that an agent can determine the scene, as is nicely illustrated by those comedies in which a "boy" turns out to be a "girl," or a "pauper" is revealed to be a "prince," and so on, to infinite permutations. What gives way to what cannot be decided beforehand. In operating as causal compulsions the ratios work like the round-robin of causes in Aristotle's schema: they are more immanent and mutual than they are lineal; they can be driven by esthetic requirements as well as logical ones.

The proper equation to follow in translating the pentad of terms to the tetrad of causes is not clear. I can't agree with the translation Burke gives in *A Grammar of Motives*. He argues that the conversion should be made along the following lines: *Agent* is "efficient" cause, *purpose* is "final" cause--a function it shares with *agency* (although he notes that the instrumental aspect of *agency* enables Aquinas to shift it from the category of "final" to "efficient" cause)—*scene* is "material" cause, and *act* is "formal" cause (*GMRM*, pp. 227-29).

I suggest organizing the correspondences in a somewhat different pattern. There is no argument about agent as efficient cause, nor about purpose as final cause. But I think agency is better conceived as material cause and scene as formal cause. Now, act is not a superfluous ingredient in this conversion. In the Aristotelian scheme, the four causes converge to bring about a thing, an entity. In the Burkean framework, four of the pentodes result in one of them: the act. Just as a physical entity is explained by its four sources of causation, an act is explained by its four component pentodes. A refinement of the details of this schema is obviously needed, but this is not the place to pursue such an analysis. In the remainder of the essay, I will confine myself to some general statements describing how final, material, and formal causes can be placed in a symbolist, Burkean, framework.

FINAL CAUSE

Perhaps it is best to begin with the most unpopular of the Aristotelian causes. No doubt it is still professionally risky to bring the idea of purpose into discussions of scientific explanation. Very few social scientists are willing to go beyond conceding, as Bergmann does, that purpose is a demonstrable factor in conscious human motivation or mental activity, but has no role to play in our understanding of the events of "nature." Hempel, taking the example of a speed-regulating device, argues that to explain why it functioned to regulate speeds, "we would have to refer to the construction of the machine and to the laws of physics, not to the intentions and beliefs of the designer." One could, however, change the circumference of the question in such a way as to *include* the "intentions and beliefs of the designer." Nevertheless, intentionality is still considered to be a psychological, in-the-mind datum. Even R. M. MacIver, whose monograph on causation greatly expanded the concept in social science, limited teleology to the range of "psychological" causes.[46]

According to the *Oxford English Dictionary*, the teleological was the original use of the word "cause." To the Romans it connoted the interests of a litigant in a court of law. This sense of aim or goal survives today in such phrases as "to fight for a cause."[47] One can only speculate whether, by some remote punning coincidence, the resonant phonetic similarity between *theology* and *teleology*, the decline of the former lead to the demise of the latter in scientific circles.

In the common conception, not only is purpose in the mind, but it is conscious as well. To be sure, Freud's "discovery" of the unconscious opened up the possibility of considering unconscious purposes, but it still located the business inside the individual. Can anyone seriously suggest that scientists consider a nonindividual, possibly nonconscious kind of teleology? Indeed, does not purpose automatically imply a process going on in individual minds? Aristotle himself took pains to clarify the matter. According to G. E. R. Lloyd, Artistotle was

> well aware that there is no *conscious* purpose in nature. In an important passage in the Physics (199b26 ff.) he considers an objection that might be made to his conception of the final cause in nature, namely that nature does not deliberate, but maintains nevertheless that one can speak of "ends" in nature, or "that for the sake of which" natural processes take place.... [nature] exhibits order and regularity, and if order and regularity, then "ends" although not conscious ends.[48]

Burke, in *A Grammar of Motives*, considers Aristotle's use of *purpose* more "realistic" than the "mystical" use in Plato (*GMRM*, pp. 292–93). Whether there actually are conscious ends in nature is, of course, a question we need not pursue. We can proceed quite confidently on the basis of what Richard H. Brown calls "symbolic realism."[49] This position rejects the proposition that things-in-themselves are knowable.[50] All knowledge is necessarily from a point of view, necessarily metaphorical.

It would be inconsistent for a physical scientist to object to the use of metaphor in the symbolic definition of reality. The history of the physical sciences abounds with examples of conceptualizations which were borrowed from the realm of *action* and depersonalized as descriptive of events in the realm of *sheer motion*. I have already mentioned, citing Lakoff and Johnson, how one derives the scientific concept of causation by factoring out its "peculiarly human aspects." Similarly, consider the depersonalization in such concepts as: *satellite*, which meant companion; *work*, which meant—and still does—a person's effort; and *function*, which referred to status in life or official position in government. The latter is what Leibniz had in mind when he applied the word "function" metaphorically to the operation of mathematical relationships.[51]

Once we realize that many scientific terms were derived from originally social applications, we can appreciate the metaphoric advantage gained by Aristotle when he employed the notion of purpose in his philosophy of nature. Just as Leibniz, say, was not proposing that lines and curves constituted a factual bureaucratic organization when he described their mathematical "functions," Aristotle, too, was not proposing that the idea of purpose applied to nature implied a commitment to the existence of a Personal Being imposing and supervising that purpose.

The idea of teleology in nature has continued to grace scientific discourse. The anthropologist Clyde Kluckhohn distinguished between "adjustive" and "adaptive" responses in societies, depending on whether the purpose served by the response was the survival of the individual or that of the group.[52] The biologist Ernst Mayr similarly finds two kinds of purposiveness in organisms: individual biological purposiveness, which he calls "teleonomy," and world purposiveness, which he identifies as "teleology."[53] In sociology, Wsevolod Isajiw identifies "telecausality" as a way of organizing propositions about the functioning of social systems.[54] Among philosophers, Ernest Nagel has no problem contemplating "directively organized systems,"[55] while Marjorie Grene promotes Julian Huxley's concept of the "telic" in natural phenomena.[56] C. H. Waddington perhaps sums up the scientific experience with this aspect of the phenomenal world in his description of what he calls "quasi-finalistic" causation.[57] In a whimsical dialogue, something of a cross between Plato and Lewis Carroll, Douglas Hofstadter gives a lively discussion of the problem and suggests that the difference between, say, an evolutionary explanation of ant communication and a teleological one is in the level, or point of view, from which the communication is considered.[58] That is to say, from the way in which the phenomenon is framed. In Burke's terminology, this translates as a change in circumference.[59]

The precise location of purpose in the scheme of things depends on the circumference within which these things are framed. Conscious purposes, for example, can be encompassed by unconscious ones. It is not a question of what is *the* purpose, but what is the *circumference*. This is more easily seen, perhaps, when we contrast the personal motives of an employee with the collective motives of the employer-organization. Collective unconscious purposes can be postulated of symbol systems such as language and society without violating the truth of individual conscious motives. The choice is not either-or, the choice is *which*—which frame, which circumference?

Furthermore, the symbolic structures are presentational as well as discursive. So we must learn to locate purpose in the tangle of nonlinear symbolic play. An important property of this "forest of symbols,"[60] first clearly discerned by Durkheim in his conception of the "conscience collective," is its existence as a *public* entity, not reducible to the content of individual minds. In a discussion of the nature of cultural things Geertz addressed himself to the question, where is culture located? Not in artifact, he concludes, nor in any of its specific manifestations, nor even in the minds of individual human persons. Culture is located in the sphere of *inter*persons, in the sphere of *public life*. Like language, it is a system which individual minds tap, but do not contain.[61] There are symbol systems with immanent purposes which we are moved to realize in the same way that we are moved to realize the immanent entelechy of words.

Langer notes that this purpose in-the-entity-itself is what is meant by "motive" in art. "The word does not usually refer to what motivated the artist's procedure," she writes, "but to relations of forms within the piece itself." The word *motif*, she continues, "is often used to remove the ambiguity." Thus, "motive" may be in the artist, but "motif" is in the work. It is, to use a term Langer employs in her discussion of presentational symbol systems, a "virtual" purpose. "A motif," she says, "serves to create a virtual motivation."[62]

MATERIAL CAUSE

Material causes may be found conceptualized in the literature as some set of "material conditions" under which efficient causes take effect. There is an understandable reluctance to consider these "conditions" to be causes, since they play a passive role in the production of effects. Nevertheless, these "conditions" must be present for the derivation of the effect. Unless they are omnipresent it is fatal to the process of explanation to ignore their required presence. This is as much requiredness as we find in efficient causation.

Material causes may also enter under the guise of some "instrumentality" or "medium."[63] Here it is more clearly seen that what is at play is Burke's *agency*. In the round of ends, means, agent, they are manifestly the means. However, more generally, agency can be understood as *any* means whereby an effect comes about. Agency can take place in two ways: as the medium *through* which the agent works (the instrumental), or as the medium *with* which the agent accomplishes the effect (the componential).

It is easy to see how this might work in the case of conscious human action. But the role of material causes in unconscious action is much more obscure. Some insight into how such processes might operate can be gained from Polanyi's theory of consciousness, for this theory postulates an unconscious material process underlying the conscious act of awareness.[64] The underlying process, according to Polanyi, is *necessarily* unconscious.[65] In order to attend consciously *to* some entity of awareness, we must disattend *from* those material elements of which it is composed. In Polanyi's terminology, the mind shapes a *focal, comprehensive entity* by collecting the necessary *subsidiary elements* for its construction.[66]

Polanyi observes that we cannot retain an awareness of the comprehensive entity when we shift our attention to the subsidiary elements comprised by it. Each time we shift the focal act to the elements of the composition, the comprehensive entity dissolves. For example, in conversation, the more we attend to how a person is speaking, the less we are able to follow what is being said. Langer noted this character of symbols in *Philosophy in a New Key*. Symbols work best when they least draw attention to themselves. Because symbols are arbitrary vehicles of meaning, an examination of their physical nature can only be distracting. They are most efficient when they are "transparent vehicles" for the meaning they carry.[67]

Thus, even conscious action has an unconscious substrate, which is its material cause. In the wider social system, considered as a symbol system, material causes are at work contributing to the emergence and maintenance of social forms.

EFFICIENT CAUSE

A brief word on agent as cause. We are inclined to consider the individual, physically aligned in the action, as the efficient cause of social acts. But, again, it is necessary that we not lose sight of the circumference of the act. Socially speaking, the agent causes the act, not as a biological individual, but as a role player in a dramatic situation. The biological presence of the individual is not so much the agent as the agency. For any act embedded in a social organization, insofar as it is an organizational act, the agent is the organizational role (or position), not the individual physically considered. Problems emerge in analyzing and discussing such things when there is a subtle, unrecognized shift in circumference as we go along.

FORMAL CAUSE

Modern physics, says Kuhn, has now moved in the direction of reinventing Aristotle's concept of formal cause.[68] A generation ago, Stocks saw this development coming when, in concluding his survey of the history of causal explanation in science, he wrote:

> My own philosophical inquiries, pursued over a number of years in various fields, seem to me to converge more and more on the point that if a tenable theory of the natural world is to be framed, it must be on the basis of the recovery of a conception of cause closely resembling the Aristotelian form.[69]

Vito Signorile

In the same vein, the sociologist Zygmunt Bauman noted that it is "the entirely modern demand to understand-through-allocating-in-a-structure which is at stake, not the traditional search for *the* efficient cause."[70]

What the mathematical equations governing physical phenomena involve are, not linear cause-effect properties of matter, but rather the *formal* properties of things, properties having to do with how they are structured. Knowledge of the initial states of a physical system enables us to determine its state at a later time only because of the structural, or formal, laws which the system must follow if it is to retain its identity as a system. Given the initial conditions, the outcome gets shaped by the formal relationships that prevail in—indeed, define— the system.

Nagel convincingly shows how absurd it would be to recast the formula expressing the relationship between voltage, current, and resistance in teleological terms.[71] We are quickly led to a conspiracy theory of electricity, in which voltage and current, say, collude to ensure that resistance is kept in its place. Nevertheless, the formula expressing the relationship between the three factors does constitute a formative system in which their relationships have a definite shape. When we note further that the very nature of these entities is defined by the mathematical relationships described in the formula,[72] we see that even in this science of the "concrete," we are dealing with entities which can be identified only by their location in a symbolic structure (which is what a mathematical formula amounts to).[73]

The importance of form in scientific explanation is especially noticed in biology. Waddington notes that the "secret" to any organic system's performance is in its "architecture." As this "architecture" becomes more complex, he says, "the ultimate constituents are able to conceal more and more of their own [specific] character within it." Substitutions become possible because, in the functioning of the system, "the architecture itself is more important that the constituents out of which it is built."[74]

Perhaps the most ambitious attempt to resurrect the notion of form-as-cause is Rupert Sheldrake's "hypothesis of formative causation." Again, the initial insight comes from biology. But the idea is quickly seen to generalize. Sheldrake notes the shaping influence of form in processes as widely disparate as crystal growth and primate ethology. The process is "morphogenesis"; its shaping force, Sheldrake believes, is "morphic resonance." The analogy is that of the resonant sympathetic vibrations found in mechanical systems. Forms send out what could be called "resonating fields," which influence other materials to assemble themselves into similar forms.[75] What makes it possible for Sheldrake's thesis to command serious attention is the empirical underpinning on which his claims rest. We cannot evaluate his hypothesis here, but he himself suggests the line along which appropriate experiments might be pursued in putting his hypothesis to the test.

Formative causation, or formal cause, is the essence of *scene* as a causal element in symbolic processes. It is the kind of thing Mills implied when he wrote: "Both motives and actions very often originate not from within individuals, but from the situation in which individuals find themselves."[76] We can sense the shaping influence of scene, as Burke suggests, in the Darwinian doctrine of survival of the fittest. In this doctrine the shape of the environment explains the shape of those things that dwell within it (*GMRM*, p. 6). Any conception which accepts the idea of environmental determinism shares the basic notion that scene has an effect on the shape things eventually take.

An illustrative example of the way scene may function as cause can be found in Burke's discussion of "exorcism by misnomer." In examining the case of a claustrophobic soldier, Burke construes the originating incident which the psychologist hit upon, not as a dog threatening the patient when, as a child, he was trapped in a passageway, but rather as a total situation, "the situation of being confined in a passageway without an exit at a time when a danger sign (the dog) was present" (*PC*, pp. 133-42). The form which the neurosis (claustrophobia) took, Burke is saying, came, not from some component thing in the provoking incident (e.g., the dog), but from the *scene* in which the incident occurred.[77]

It is here, perhaps, that we can place the sixth element which Burke considered adding to the pentad: attitude. By this Burke seems to mean an orientation to the action one is contemplating. It is not a simple inclination to act; rather, it is an *approach*, something more like a *style*, which guides the action. Burke goes on to explain, "agency would more strictly designate the 'means' (*quibus auxiliis*) employed in an act. And 'attitude' would designate the manner (*quo modo*)" (*GMRM*, p. 443). The manner is the way in which a thing is done, not the simple doing of it. The guiding, shaping function of attitude is clearly evident in the contrast Burke makes between "style" and its opposite, "trained incapacity." If the latter is a generalized shaping of character that renders the person incapable of "fitting," the former is characterized by a high degree of propriety, of fittingness. Thus, it is conceivable that both scene and attitude share the function of formative causation. The scene appears as the "exterior" source of formative causation, while manner, or attitude, might be considered the "internal" source.[78]

Harold Garfinkel notes how attention to the scenic features of social encounters can help explain the interaction that takes place within them.[79] What counts as scene is a question of framing. One important aspect of framing is the circumference within which the event is embedded. Such circumferences are, of course, arbitrary and flexible points of view. The significance of such points of view, arbitrary though they be, is their formative influence on the shaping of action as it ensues, just as a bilingual speaker, tapping the framework of one of the two languages, is thenceforth guided by the structure of *that* language.[80]

The story can go on and on. There is much more that needs to be said about all the issues raised here. Yet enough has already been said to point out the central role of symbolic structures in all things human. The sea change heralded by Susanne Langer's *Philosophy in a New Key* has been long in coming. Collingwood advanced his "revolutionary" claim that there are goals in nature over forty years ago, at about the same time that Langer announced the central importance of symbols for philosophical inquiry. Neither made an impression on "normal" science.[81] Indeed, when not simply ignored, there was more often derision than admiration in scientific circles. On this climate of opinion, Grene writes that such denials happen to fit "very smoothly into the metaphysical paradigm (in Kuhn's sense) of the world machine." To be skeptical of teleology, for instance, "is 'scientific,' even if this means denying what is as plain as the nose in one's face."[82] An existing mind-set served to engender the conviction that such ideas were the product of "occult" thinking and in danger of sending us back (God forbid!) to the Middle Ages. Thus it is that the odyssey of our groping for that essential insight which will afford us the "paradigm" of our time has been long and tortuous, filled with brilliant perceptions and wrong turns. Emile Durkheim, a far-sighted beginner on this journey, becomes noted for his "empirical" study of suicide, rather than his symbolist study of religion—the origin, he surmised, of all our categories of thought. Max Weber's ideal-type is faulted for its inability to explain "reality," rather than praised for its prescient recognition that concepts serve to bring things to our minds not to our hands. But we are now experiencing the fullness of time. We see now more clearly where the roads are taking us. A regnant metaphor looms ever more clearly ahead: human societies are far from finely clocked machines. They are, rather, a language expressing itself in many dialects, in poetic imagery, and a vast dance of attitudes.

And these roads: Don't you notice? They have been paved and posted a good deal of their length by one Kenneth Burke!

NOTES

1. Bergmann, for instance, advances the claim that all scientific explanation is "causal," and means by this that it is "mechanistic." Gustav Bergmann, "Purpose, Function, and Scientific Explanation," in May Brodbeck, ed., *Readings in the Philosophy of the Social Sciences* (New York and Toronto: Collier-Macmillan, 1968), pp. 211–23.

2. George Lakoff and Mark Johnson, *Metaphors We Live By* (Chicago: University of Chicago Press, 1980), pp. 69–71.

3. John L. Stocks, *Reason and Intuition* (London: Oxford University Press, 1939; rpt. Freeport, N.Y.: Books for Libraries Press, 1970), p. 63 et seq.

4. Aristotle considered the form(al) to be the essence of what a thing is, its distinguishing characteristic, that which makes it what it is. This set of distinctions has not been altogether neglected in the literature of social science. David Bidney, *Theoretical Anthropology* (New York: Columbia University Press, 1953), states: "If we, following Aristotle, distinguish between the material, formal, efficient and final causes or conditions of natural phenomena, then it becomes obvious that we may not speak of culture in general as being a cause of behavior without specifying which cause we mean. Cultural products, such as artifacts, mentifacts, or sociofacts, are the material, formal, and final causes of cultural developments; they are not the efficient causes or active agents" (p. 33).

Also compare: "The criminal law is the formal cause of crime." J. Michael and M. J. Adler, *Crime, Law and Social Science* (1933;rpt. Montclair, N.J.: Patterson Smith, 1971), p. xli. More recently, Elizabeth Bates, *The Emergence of Symbols* (San Francisco: Academic Press, 1979), pp. 14–19, has argued that explanation in developmental psychology requires distinctions borrowed from Aristotole's four-cause scheme. The most ambitious use of Aristotle's conception, in particular that of *formal cause,* is found in Rupert Sheldrake, *A New Science of Life* (Boston: Houghton Mifflin, 1981). See the discussion of "Formal Cause" below.

5. Properly modified, this argument can be extended to the whole of science, which, after all, is a distinctly human affair.

6. Kenneth Burke, "Dramatism," in *The International Encyclopedia of the Social Sciences* (New York: Macmillan, 1968), pp. 445–52.

7. Karl R. Popper, *Conjectures and Refutations* (New York: Harper and Row, 1965), pp. 33–37.

8. See, for example, Herbert Blumer, *Symbolic Interactionism* (Englewood Cliffs, N.J.: Prentice-Hall, 1969).

9. I.C. Jarvie, *Functionalism* (Minneapolis: Burgess, 1973).

10. Mario Bunge, *Causality* (New York: World, 1963), sec. 2.6.

11. Carl G. Hempel, *Aspects of Scientific Explanation* (New York and Toronto: Collier-Macmillan, 1970), chap. 11.

12. It must be noted, however, that Bunge does have a place for formal and final causes. These he places in the wider arena of *determinacy*. Causation, in the sense he wishes to employ it, is just one of a variety of ways in which the existence of things is determined (*Causality*, pp. 26–29). Because he endeavors to restrict the word *cause* to denoting the external and one-directional producer of effects, Bunge rejects the idea that feedback, and other interactional or functional models, are causal. They are, he concedes, *determinate*: "most contemporary social scientists would be prepared to admit that interaction rather than causation is the prevailing category of determination in social matters" (pp. 156–57). There is at least one social scientist—Arthur Stinchcombe—who would not agree, holding out for the ideal that even social events are ultimately explainable as chains of mechanical causes. See Arthur Stinchcombe, *Constructing Social Theories* (New York: Harcourt, Brace, and World, 1968).

13. Kenneth Burke, *A Grammar of Motives and A Rhetoric of Motives* (Cleveland: World, and Toronto: Nelson, Foster, and Scott, 1962), pp. 227–28. Hereafter cited as *GMRM*. Herbert Simons has drawn my attention to the fact that Ronald Crane's approach to literary criticism employed the Aristotelian fourfold scheme of explanation: concerning any literary work the critic must elucidate its subject matter (material), its method (efficient), its guiding principles (formal), and its purpose (final). Wayne Booth (*Critical Understanding* [Chicago: University of Chicago Press, 1979], p. 99 ff.) calls this Crane's "quadrate." Curiously, there is the worry, expressed by both Crane and Booth, that adopting a scheme as venerable as Aristotle's would trap one's analysis in static categories. Thus, they write reassuringly that they mean to apply these categories in a flexible manner. For example, what is *form* for the poet can be *matter* for the critic. Aristotle was aware of the effect created by this shifting perspective. The fault, rather, lies with disciples down through history who, routinizing the genius of the master (as Max Weber might put it), bureaucratize the imaginative (as Burke does put it!). Booth quite rightly shows that this effect of shifting points of view is also true of the *ratios* in Burke's pentad (*Critical Understanding*, p. 113). The matter is discussed later in this essay (see section entitled "The Tetrad in the Pentad").

14. Thomas S. Kuhn, *The Essential Tension* (Chicago: University of Chicago Press, 1977), chap. 2.

15. Ibid, p. 28; see also Stocks, *Reason and Intuition*, p. 77.

16. They constitute, in Max Weber's view, one of the components with which *ideal types* are constructed. On a symbolist interpretation of Weber's ideal types, see my "The Pythagorean Comma: Weber's Anticipation of Sociology in a New Key," *Human Studies*, 3 (1980), 115–36. The resort to ideal types is, for Weber, so basic that he believed it to be characteristic of all scientific explanation. He saw no essential difference between physical and social causation for, in both lines of inquiry, one seeks to discover the

"sufficient ground" for an object's existence. See Max Weber, *Roscher and Knies: The Logical Problems of Historical Economics*, trans. G. Oakes (New York and Toronto: Collier-Macmillan, 1975), p. 194. And what constitutes "sufficient ground" is *conceptually* decided, not empirically.

17. Gottfried Wilhelm Leibniz, "Necessary and Contingent Truths," and Immanuel Kant, "Introduction to the *Critique of Pure Reason*," in R. C. Sleigh, Jr., ed., *Necessary Truth* (Englewood Cliffs, N.J., and Toronto: Prentice-Hall, 1972), pp. 15–23; 24–33. Both Bunge (*Causality*, p. 39) and Alvin Plantinga consider cause to be a "synthetic" datum, or, as Plantinga prefers it, "necessity *de re*," that is, necessity inhering in the things themselves, independently of our conceptions of them. On this, see Alvin Plantinga, *The Nature of Necessity* (New York and Toronto: Oxford University Press, 1974) and "De Re et De Dicto" in *Necessary Truth*, pp. 152–72. Also see Sleigh's introduction to this volume, pp. 1–11. Kant further distinguishes the *a priori* and the *a posteriori*. It is the *a priori* that is, properly speaking, independent of experience. An adequate analysis of the issue would require that we distinguish between knowledge that we obtain independently of our experience of the "outside" world, and knowledge that is based on experience, but is about things that occur in themselves, regardless of what we think about them (Burke's "wordless universe"). It can be argued that Kant himself considered cause to be a *synthetic a priori* and, thus, a datum in which experience only *informs*, or *fills out*, what is already there. See Lewis Beck, *A Commentary on Kant's Critique of Practical Reason* (Chicago: University of Chicago Press, 1963).

18. W. V. O. Quine, "Two Dogmas of Empiricism," Sleigh, *Necessary Truth*, p. 69.

19. Richard Rorty, *Philosophy and the Mirror of Nature* (Princeton: Princeton University Press, 1979), chap. 6. On similar views, in which the sciences are seen as communities of rhetorical discourse, see Michael A. Overington, "Doing the What Comes Rationally: Some Developments in Meta-Theory," *American Sociologist*, 14 (1979), 2–12, and Richard H. Brown, "Theories of Rhetoric and the Rhetorics of Theory: Toward a Political Phenomenology of Sociological Truth," *Social Research*, 50 (1983), 126–51.

20. Kenneth Burke, *Language as Symbolic Action* (Berkeley: University of California Press, 1966), chap. 1.

21. Ludwig Wittgenstein, *Philosophical Investigations*, trans. G. E. M. Anscombe (New York: Macmillan, 1968). The *Philosophical Investigations* represents a rejection of the earlier *Tractatus Logico-Philosophicus*, trans. D. F. Pears and B. F. McGiness (London: Routledge and Kegan Paul, 1961), in which Wittgenstein argued: "There is no compulsion making one thing happen because another has happened. The only necessity is *logical* necessity" (sec. 6.37). For a collection of Wittgenstein's writings on the subject during his final years, see G. E. M. Anscombe and G. H. von Wright, eds., *Ludwig Wittgenstein On Certainty* (New York: Harper and Row, 1972). Also see Harold Brown, *Perception, Theory, and Commitment* (Chicago: University of Chicago Press, 1977), pp. 21–23, for a discussion of necessity in Hume

Vito Signorile

and Wittgenstein. The classical formulation of the problem is Hume's, which became the impetus for Kant's approach—his "Copernican revolution"—in which he took the necessity in causation out of "nature" (the "nonsymbolic" in Burke's terminology) and put it in the mind (where the Burkean might locate the process of symbolization).

22. Besides Harold Brown, cited above, see Dummett's, Chihara's, and Stroud's contributions in *Wittgenstein, The Philosophical Investigations: A Collection of Critical Essays* (Garden City, N.Y.: Doubleday, 1966).

23. Concerning which, see Patrick Hughes and George Brecht, *Vicious Circles and Infinity* (New York and Markham, Ont.: Penguin, 1978).

24. Michael Dummett, "Wittgenstein's Philosophy of Mathematics," in *Wittgenstein, The Philosophical Investigations*, pp. 420–47.

25. Susanne K. Langer, *Philosophy in a New Key*, 3d ed. (Cambridge: Harvard University Press, 1957), p. 111. In modern usage, the terms "world" and "thing" ordinarily connote what is going on "out there." I have noted elsewhere ("Man the Measure: Being a Further Postscript in the Shandean Mode," *American Sociologist*, 14 [1979], 115–18) that "world" and "thing" both have subjective, person-oriented origins. Roughly, in Old Germanic "world" (*werald*) connoted the ambience of a person's life or lifetime (see Latin *saecula* for a parallel development), while "thing" meant interest or subject matter (again, one finds a parallel development for *res, rei* in the Latin tongues).

26. Hempel, *Aspects of Scientific Explanation*, pp. 300–301.

27. Roy Francis, *The Rhetoric of Science* (Minneapolis: University of Minneapolis Press, 1961).

28. Karl Popper, *The Logic of Scientific Discovery* (New York: Basic Books, 1959), p. 59.

29. *LSA*, p. 16, and the introduction to *The Rhetoric of Religion* (Berkeley: University of California Press, 1970).

30. See C. Wright Mills, "Situated Actions and the Vocabularies of Motive," *American Sociological Review*, 5 (1940), 904–13.

31. Kenneth Burke, *Permanence and Change*, 2d rev. ed. (New York: Bobbs-Merrill, 1965), p. 19.

32. Kenneth Burke, "Above the Over-Towering Babble," *Michigan Quarterly Review*, 15 (Winter 1976), 88.

33. Langer, *Philosophy in a New Key*, pp. 79–102.

34. To be sure, not all philosophers of language agree with such a strong version of linguistic determinism. Lakoff and Johnson, for example, claim that our conceptual (metaphorical) system is grounded in physical experience, and, in particular, find the concept of cause partly "direct" (or "emergent"), that is, grounded in direct empirical experience, and, in part, more remotely metaphorical. In their words, it is an "experiential gestalt" (*Metaphors We Live By*, pp. 117–19). What is interesting about this position is that it is itself governed by a master metaphor, one, I suppose, borrowed from architecture (rather than electricity): Grounding. And that serves to highlight the problem with this approach. The epistemological concept of

"ground" is itself not directly grounded. When we add to this the objection that the word *cause* can mean an agent-purpose relationship rather than one between agent and patient (recipient), some difficulties might begin to be felt concerning the matter. The difficulty with the hypothesis of linguistic determinism is, no doubt, the discomfort we feel with the notion that ideas might, at "bottom," have *no* grounding, that they might all be found "floating" in some Platonic Empyrean. Yet, we now know enough to realize that the referential function of terms can no longer be taken for granted. Citing Clifford Geertz's solution—proposed in *The Interpretation of Cultures* (New York: Basic Books, 1973), pp. 28-29—to what can be taken as the problem of grounding in cultural anthropology, Rorty affirms the position of "Post-Kantian philosophy," that it's "turtles all the way down" (*Philosophy and the Mirror of Nature*, pp. 266-69). As far down as you please!

35. Langer, *Philosophy in a New Key*, p. 265.

36. See Susanne K. Langer, *Feeling and Form* (New York: Scribner's, 1953), and *Philosophy in a New Key*.

37. Michael Polanyi, *The Tacit Dimension* (Garden City, N.Y.: Doubleday, 1966).

38. See Richard Howe, "Max Weber's Elective Affinities: Sociology within the Bounds of Pure Reason," *American Journal of Sociology*, 84 (1978), 366-85, for a discussion of the place of "elective affinities" in Weber's theory of rationality. On this point, also see my "Pythagorean Comma," pp. 117-18.

39. Erving Goffman, *Frame Analysis* (New York: Harper and Row, 1974).

40. Jacques Lacan, "The Insistence of the Letter in the Unconscious," in Jacques Ehrmann, ed., *Structuralism* (Garden City, N.Y.: Doubleday, 1970), pp. 101-37. Also see Sherry Turkle, *Psychoanalytic Politics* (New York: Basic Books, 1978).

41. Emile Durkheim, *The Elementary Forms of Religious Life*, trans. Joseph Swain (London: George Allen and Unwin, 1976).

42. Edward Sapir, "The Unconscious Patterning of Behavior in Society," *Selected Writings of Edward Sapir*, ed. D. G. Mandelbaum (Berkeley: University of California Press, 1963), pp. 544-59.

43. On the concept of speech acts, see John R. Searle, ed., *The Philosophy of Language* (New York and Toronto: Oxford University Press, 1971).

44. Goffman, *Frame Analysis*, chap. 1.

45. "*Ratio* and Religious Motivation," unpublished manuscript. My argument is that a substantive term is needed. In deciding on this one, I follow a lead suggested by C. A. Waddington in *The Nature of Life* (New York: Harper and Row, 1961), p. 64, who employed the Greek word *hodos* (which means way, path, channel) in coining the term "creode."

46. Bergmann, "Purpose, Function, and Scientific Explanation," pp. 211-23; Hempel, *Aspects of Scientific Explanation*, p. 327; R. M. MacIver, *Social Causation* (New York: Ginn, 1942), pp. 22 and 271.

47. "Cause," *Oxford English Dictionary*, 1933 ed.

48. G. E. R. Lloyd, *Aristotle: The Growth and Structure of His Thought* (Cambridge: Harvard University Press, 1968), p. 61. Also see Marjorie

Vito Signorile

Grene: "Neither in Collingwood's nature nor in Aristotle's does *telos* or goal mean primarily, much less exclusively, conscious purpose." *Knower and the Known* (New York: Basic Books, 1966) p. 228. Grene points out that, as early as 1933, Collingwood called attention to the fact that goals-in-nature constitute an irrefutable datum, not only in biology but in chemistry and physics as well. This was a claim that Grene dubbed "Collingwood's Revolution." See R. G. Collingwood, *The Idea of Nature* (Oxford: Clarendon, 1945).

49. Richard H. Brown, *A Poetic for Sociology* (Cambridge University Press, 1977), chap. 1.

50. It might be noted that the *Ding-an-sich* is itself a point of view: the viewpoint of (or from) the thing itself. Furthermore, this concept also postulates that the "thing," animate or not, *can* have a point of view. That is, we can treat it as though it were a living object capable of "viewing" both itself and its surround. This role at one time was played by God, and captured by medieval scholars in the phrase *sub specie aeternitatis*. For a later version of this *deus ex machina*, see Leibniz's statement: "he who perfectly understood each concept as God understands it, would by that very fact perceive that the predicate is present in the subject." Leibniz, "Necessary and Contingent Truths," in Sleigh, *Necessary Truth*, p. 15.

51. See my note: "From the Loins of Leviathan: A Shandean Postscript (Of Sorts)," *American Sociologist*, 12 (1977); 95–98.

52. Clyde Kluckhohn, "Myths and Rituals: A General Theory," *Harvard Theological Review*, 35 (1942); 45–79.

53. Ernst Mayr, "Footnotes on the Philosophy of Biology," *Philosophy of Science*, 36 (1969); 197–202.

54. Wsevolod Isajiw, *Causation and Functionalism in Sociology* (London: Routledge and Kegan Paul, 1968).

55. Ernest Nagel, *Logic without Metaphysics* (Glencoe, Ill.: Free Press, 1956), p. 78.

56. Grene, *Knower and the Known*, p. 229.

57. Waddington, *Nature of Life*, p. 88.

58. Douglas Hofstadter, *Gödel, Escher, Bach: An Eternal Golden Braid* (New York: Random House, 1980), pp. 320–22.

59. As I have already intimated, this is one way of replying to Hempel's *reductio* concerning a speed-regulating device. Properly framed, the question can easily accommodate a teleological answer. A discussion of the general idea of framing and its importance for sociology in particular, but science in general, can be found in R. H. Brown's essay on "point of view" in *A Poetic for Sociology*, chap. 3. Hofstadter devotes a chapter to this question, where he states, "mental representations of situations involve frames nested within each other" (*Gödel, Escher, Bach*, p. 644). He credits Marvin Minsky with introducing the concept in the field of artificial intelligence. See Minsky, "Matter, Mind, and Models," in Minsky, ed., *Semantic Information Processing* (Cambridge: MIT Press, 1968). An important critique of Minsky's claims, as well as those of others in the field of artificial intelli-

gence, can be found in Herbert Dreyfus, *What Computers Can't Do* (New York: Harper and Row, 1972). But, of course, Goffman's *Frame Analysis* remains the most comprehensive treatment of the concept from a sociological point of view.

60. Victor Turner, *The Forest of Symbols* (Ithaca: Cornell University Press, 1967).

61. Geertz, *Interpretation of Cultures*, chap. 1. I have discussed this more fully elsewhere: "Reductio ad Idiotam: Some Observations on the Social Appropriation of Knowledge," unpublished manuscript.

62. Susanne K. Langer, *Mind: An Essay in Human Feeling*, Vol. 1 (Baltimore: Johns Hopkins University Press, 1970), p. 220.

63. It is no mere coincidence that the word *medium* also connoted an artist's material, for example, clay, oils, stone. Aristotle's own illustration of the four causes employs the analogy of sculpture. For a discussion of how art becomes science, and science art, see Brown, *Poetic for Sociology*.

64. Michael Polanyi, "The Structure of Consciousness" in Marjorie Grene, ed., *The Anatomy of Knowledge* (Amherst: University of Massachussetts Press, 1969), pp. 315–28.

65. I must note, however, that Polanyi expressly rejects the idea that the subsidiary elements are unconscious data. A kind of awareness, he argues, is present, but not *focally*. He is, of course, right, for some kind of subliminal detection must be present to supply the focusing act with the material it needs. But this paradoxical quality of the unconscious, the idea of an unaware awareness, has always been the most intriguing and significant thing about it.

66. There is an important similarity between Polanyi's *comprehensive entity* and Langer's *significant form*. See her *Philosophy in a New Key*, p. 72. The latter is the fundamental process of symbolization, and is essentially nondiscursive. This suggests to Langer that an underlying substrate of all conscious discursive activity is the articulation of nondiscursive symbolism. See *Mind*, pp. 146–47. Another convergence may be seen respecting Pike's distinction between the "emic" and the "etic" in human experience. The "emic" is the cultural entification, reification, or segmentation of things in the continuous flux of nature. It is the "act" of creation out of the raw stuff of sheer motion. See Kenneth Pike, *Language in Relation to a Unified Theory of Human Behavior* Vol. 1 (Glendale, Calif.: Summer Institute of Linguistics, 1954), and "Towards a Theory of the Structure of Human Behavior" in Dell Hymes, ed., *Language in Culture and Society* (New York: Harper and Row, 1964), pp. 54–62.

67. Langer, *Philosophy in a New Key*, p. 75.

68. See Kuhn, *Essential Tension*, chap. 2.

69. Stocks, *Reason and Intuition*, p. 80.

70. Zygmunt Bauman, "Modern Times, Modern Marxism," in Peter Berger, ed., *Marxism and Society: Views from Eastern Europe* (New York: Appleton-Century-Crofts, 1969), pp. 1–17.

71. Nagel, *Logic without Metaphysics*, p. 77.

Vito Signorile

72. See my discussion of this in "Pythagorean Comma," p. 125, esp. n. 4.

73. The formula might still be given a teleological interpretation, for we should not be lulled into the ready acceptance of the entities it postulates as truly existing. Current, Resistance, Voltage: are these three *things* interacting in wordless nature, or a construct that serves our human purposes, like the *points* of a compass? Are these empirical existents regardless of theories or worldviews, or the result of an immanent teleology (indeed, entelechy!) in the very (symbolic) structure of science?

74. Waddington, *Nature of Life*, p. 21.

75. Sheldrake, *New Science of Life*.

76. Mills, "Situated Actions and the Vocabularies of Motive," p. 9.

77. Here we can nicely avail ourselves of the convenient observation that, insofar as the scene is often a nondiscursive aspect of social action, its effects are often unconscious.

78. *PC*, chap. 4. There is a reply by Burke to Wayne Booth's critique of his method of literary criticism, in which Burke notes the strategic presence of propriety in the construction of literary works. Booth mentions a complaint against Burke's "excremental" reading of a poem by Keats to the effect that Burke attributes to Keats intentions the poet could not conceivably have entertained. Burke's response is that a poet is conceivably guided by the search for "what feels right." And, when discovered, it is a feeling which is, often enough, an unconscious appreciation (see Booth, *Critical Understanding*, pp. 104–5, and Burke's reply, pp. 127–37). The whole of Burke's treatise on "piety" can be placed in the context of formal cause. Note his definition of piety as "the sense of what goes properly with what" *PC*, p. 74). Indeed, piety could be seen as the full round of ratios taken together.

79. Harold Garfinkel, *Studies in Ethnomethodology* (Englewood Cliffs, N.J.: Prentice-Hall, 1967), chap. 1. Also see Hugh Mehan and Houston Wood, *The Reality of Ethnomethodology* (New York and Toronto: Wiley, 1975), pp. 142–43.

80. This is the essence of the distinction Wayne Booth draws between genuine pluralism and relativism. The choice of systems may be relative, but, once it is made, we are constrained by imperatives embedded within the chosen system. A particularly subtle relativist is one who switches systems when the obligatory moves within the system lead to trouble. Often this is accomplished by changing the circumference. See Booth, *Critical Understanding*, pp. 25–26, 136–43. Also see Brown, *Poetic for Sociology*, chap. 3, for a discussion of the sociological importance of taking points of view into account.

81. On the concept of "normal science" see Thomas S. Kuhn, *The Structure of Scientific Revolutions*, 2d ed. (Chicago: University of Chicago Press, 1970). See esp. the "postscript."

82. Grene, *Knower and the Known*, p. 239.

4

THE DISMAL SCIENCE

AND MR. BURKE

ECONOMICS AS A

CRITICAL THEORY

DONALD N. McCLOSKEY

One implied audience for an economist speaking on the subject would be other economists.[1] The audience would not be large. The speaker might assume the role of stern humanizer, reminding his colleagues that economics is not chiefly a matter of statistics and equations (though noting by the way that these too are handsome tropes). He would point out that economics is more a matter of trust, words, power, neurosis, and the drama of human relations. He would chide its practitioners for turning such a science away from history, literature, philosophy, and the arts.

It is a puzzle in rhetoric, though, what role to take when speaking to humanists. Surely not that of barbarizer of their humanity. What then? A puzzle. The audience must be indulgent toward the poor solution offered here. No just complaint can be made that a literary, rhetorical, and even Burkean analysis of economics is not done well. As when seeing the dog walking on his hinder legs, one should be surprised to find the trick is done at all.

The main point in fact, and the only surprise, is that the economic dog *can* walk like a human, even on Burkean legs. The dog I have in mind is the breed most popular in the English-speaking world, and of which I am an example: bourgeois, quantitative, splendidly scientific. Other breeds of economist—Marxist, institutionalist, Austrian, Gandhian—also walk about like humans, but few find this surprising, least of all the dogs themselves.

Donald N. McCloskey

Bourgeois economists like other scientists, I say, use methods of persuasion common to poets and litterateurs. Not everyone will find this surprising. Some literary intellectuals, Kenneth Burke among them, are so confident of the reach of literary thinking that they react with a shrug: So what else is new? Others are less confident. Even the Frankfurt School, an apparently self-confident bunch, divide critical from scientific thinking on what they believe to be epistemological grounds, the better to leave the science alone. Most moderns divide the world of knowing into literary and scientific thoughts, so that they can leave the other alone.

The scientists, among whom economists properly count themselves, approve of the division. Until recently I believed like most economists that literary and scientific thinking strictly alternate, the one as Burke might say the negative of the other. The scientist is to collect statistics when on duty and read literature only when off. It's assumed without much reflection that he can't be an economic scientist while reading St. Augustine or a literary man while thinking about markets.

The division rules the intellectual world, supported by other divisions said to be similar: objective/subjective, fact/value, hard/soft, male/female. The objective-fact-hard-male side stands armed as science; the subjective-value-soft-female side stands and waits as nonscience. And some on the scientific side see a more than orthographic similarity between nonscience and nonsense. Bemused by such thoughts the economist is understandably anxious to view economics as a science—imperfect perhaps or immature but a science nonetheless. His self-esteem depends on it. He worries what the physicists will think. But he believes that being a science (and here's the error) excludes being a literary study. Economic science, he reckons, differs from mere saying.

The economist would think it strange to say that the Prince of Saying, the very Kenneth Burke, has much to say about economics. Yet Burke does. Compared with most literary folk Burke is notably economistic. More than occasionally he makes remarks about money, markets, economic history, and redemption payments. Though the remarks of an amateur unabsorbed in the professional talk they are often shrewd. He argues in *The Rhetoric of Religion* that empires rise "rationalized by money (which is a language, a kind of purpose-in-the-absolute, a universal wishing well)."[2] In *A Grammar of Motives* he opines that "we should never expect to see 'feudalism' overthrown by 'capitalism' and 'capitalism' succeeded...but rather should note elements of all such positions (or 'voices') existing always, but attaining greater clarity of expression or imperiousness of proportion [in] one period than another."³ And the like.

Notably his thought at its center has economic content, and in particular it parallels the "Austrian," libertarian school of economics. A grim thought. In his article on "dramatism" in the *International Encyclopedia of the Social Sciences*, speaking about "human action" distinct from the "mere motion" the tides insensate have, Burke is speaking Austrian.⁴ His terminology is that of Austrian economics, expressing their central idea. In 1949 Ludwig von Mises entitled the manifesto of his school *Human Action*. Listen to page 10:

> Human action [Act] is purposeful behavior. Or we may say:
> Action is will put into operation and transformed into an
> agency [Agency], is aiming at ends and goals [Purpose], is the
> ego's [Agent's] meaningful response to stimuli and the
> conditions of its environment [Scene], is a person's conscious
> adjustment to the state of the universe that determines his life.⁵

It would not be easy to say whether this was page 10 of von Mises or of Burke. Both discourse on human action; both emphasize the purposefulness of human affairs; both attack the behaviorist hallucination that humans are large rats; and both disparage the loose talk of class action (as against individual action aggregated) in macrosociology and Marxism: "The resultant of many disparate acts cannot itself be considered an act in the same purposive sense that characterizes each one of such acts (just as the movement of the stock market in its totality is not 'personal' in the sense of the myriad decisions made by each of the variously minded traders)"("Dramatism"). An economist would attribute such talk unhesitatingly to von Mises or Hayek or an American approximation sui generis such as Frank Knight (with whom Burke shares some features of personality and literary style).

Burke has not read much of these writers and they have not read him.⁶ The discovery of human action was simultaneous but independent, brought about perhaps by similar intellectual scenes and purposes: *ad bellum purificandum*. There is no Burkean influence on scholarship in economics because there was no influence of scholarly economics on Burke. That is not his scene; he is no economic theorist, and it is not from the flashes of amateur brilliance that his way of talking can help the field. It is his profession that can do it, logological talk; and more broadly—perhaps more narrowly—literary-critical talk.

Donald N. McCloskey

It can help by exposing the rhetoric of economic scientists to critical view. It can help to understand economics and economists in the way it can help to understand poetry and poets.

This will be disappointing. The noneconomist might hope that literary criticism could help understand the *economy*, not just the locutions of people who study it. After all, he would say, economics is notoriously narrow in its understanding of the human condition. Surely here is an opportunity to get rid of that great stick of a character Homo Economicus and replace him with somebody real, like Madame Bovary.

It may be. But as Our Lord once put it, "It's more complicated that that."[7] True enough, the understanding of individual motivation in economics could use some complicating. The economist has from time to time inquired at the psychology shop for premises of behavior more complex than simple greed. He has seldom found any to his liking. The experimental psychologists have stick figures of their own for sale, and few enough buyers.[8] It would seem reasonable for the economist to inquire instead at the English or the communication or the speech shops. He might get them to sell a few behavioral assumptions on the sly, as for a while now they have been selling philosophy interdicted by the departments of philosophy.

To repeat: it may be. The places where literature and economics overlap are not much explored.[9] One can think of possibilities, though they are not convincing to an economist and can't be made convincing without more inquiry.

Here's one instance. Both economists and literary critics talk about "preferences." Economists mean by this simply "what people want," in the sense of wanting some candy when the price is right. Albert Hirschman and a few other economists have recently observed that stopping at mere wants causes economics to overlook higher-level preferences, wants about wants.[10] Elsewhere these are known as taste, morality, or, west of the Sierras, life-style. Hirschman's notion is that if you wish to be the sort of person who enjoys Shakespeare you will sit through a performance of *The Two Gentlemen of Verona* as part of your education. You impose a set of preferences on yourself, which you then indulge in the usual way. You have preferences about preferences: metapreferences.[11]

It would not be shocking if literary critics could teach economists a thing or two about metapreferences. Literary criticism after all is largely a discourse about them, and people like I. A. Richards, Northrop Frye, Wayne Booth, and Kenneth Burke are fair canny. One might think that the older line of critics—Sydney, Johnson, Coleridge, Arnold—would have in fact the most to teach, being more concerned than the recent kind with matters of value (matters of how well, as against simply how). But a passage from the younger line can illustrate how literary notions might be used to understand the economy of taste. Richards wrote in 1925:

> On a pleasure theory of value [that is to say, a theory using only preferences, not metapreferences] there might well be doubt [that good poetry is better than bad], since those who do enjoy it [namely, bad poetry, such as that collected in *Poems of Passion*] certainly appear to enjoy it in a high degree. But on the theory here maintained, the fact that those who have passed through the stage of enjoying the *Poems of Passion* to that of enjoying the bulk of the *Golden Treasury*, for example, do not return, settles the matter.... Actual universal preference on the part of those who have tried both kinds fairly is the same (on our view) as superiority in value of the one over the other.[12]

Economists will notice right away that the Richards test is similar to that of the philosopher John Rawls, a test of political constitutions from behind a hypothetical veil of prenatal ignorance; they will notice that it is similar to the tests of social preferences proposed earlier by Harsanyi, Sen, and others, tests which are extensions of expected utility. In a world of certainty they will notice that Richards' argument is the same as the economics of "revealed preference" or on a national level the "Hicks-Kaldor test of welfare improvements." In the jargon of economics a bundle of groceries is "revealed preferred" to another if you *could* buy either bundle (could *afford* to buy either) but in fact chose one of them. In your view evidently the bundle you could afford but did not take must be inferior.

The point is that Richards' test is a revealed preference test *for (good) taste*. In other words it is a way of ranking metapreferences. You could have read the classic comic book but in fact chose to read Dostoevski because you wanted to be that sort of person. The Dostoevski-reading personage is revealed preferred by you. That someone who has passed through the stage of enjoying "The Love Boat" on television to that of enjoying the bulk of modern drama does not return will settle the matter. That someone who has passed through the stage of enjoying modern drama to that of enjoying the bulk of Shakespeare does not return will settle it again: Shakespeare is metapreferred to modern drama, metapreferred in turn to "The Love Boat."

The same applies to nonliterary preferences, which is why Richards' notion can be used by economists. To be sure: it's more complicated than that. We do drift slowly from one metapreference to another and sometimes, gyre-like, return to elementary pleasures. But the notion is a good beginning. People who learn French cooking may never return to German. The style of life in Andover, New Jersey—that is, the preferences one chooses to indulge—may be revealed preferred to those in Pittsburgh or New York. It would be so revealed if one observed people with a choice trekking from Pittsburgh to New York and thence to Andover but never back again. In like fashion a capitalist democracy may be revealed preferred to a workers' democratic republic by the direction in which the guns on the border point.[13]

What is attractive about the test is that it replies to an argument you hear a lot from economists and other people living after virtue, that "you can't say anything about tastes." Because it lies deep in the culture, a way of preventing religious wars and of keeping ethics out of life, you hear it even from sophomores. They say in effect *de gustibus non est disputandum*, as did literally the economists Gary Becker and George Stigler.[14] To this our man Hirschman answers: *de valoribus disputandum est*.[15] Hirschman's brave counterassertion requires some test, some argument to give it persuasive weight. The Richards test will do.

The Richards test, in short, is literary criticism but it is also economics. Even by an economist's narrow standard of sayability there is nothing intrinsically can't-sayable about changes in preferences guided by taste. Or at any rate it is no more can't-sayable than ordinary remarks about ordinary choice, the heart of economic theory.

Literature and its criticism, then, might help to understand the economy. It might help understand the development of taste or the motivation of entrepreneurs or the formation of expectations. Fine. But its main use, I say, is not to understand the economy but to understand the talk by economists about the economy. The talk has become sickly. Understanding it better would be a good thing, like the understanding of one's neuroses that comes from Freud or of one's alienation that comes from Marx. Looking at economics with a literary eye will make economists more self-conscious about their rhetoric. A good and healthy thing.

The scientific paper is a literary genre. I have argued the point in "The Problem of Audience in Historical Economics," which uses a suggestive essay by Charles Bazerman, "What Written Knowledge Does: Three Examples of Academic Discourse."[16] A scientific paper like a poem or an oration depends for its effect on such things as metaphors, analogies, introspections, appeals to character, and appeals to authority. Of course it depends also on experiments, mathematics, and statistics. But even these, I say, reduce again to metaphor. Even in a cheap sense the scientist's argument rests commonly on rhetoric, as when the statistician acquires persuasiveness from the common meanings of his technical words, such as "unbiasedness," "efficiency," "robustness," and "significance" (William Kruskal, a statistician of note, argues this in "Formulas, Numbers, Words").[17] And in the ancient and honorable sense of "rhetoric," after all, a piece of scientific writing is above all meant to persuade.

In the terminology invented by J. L. Austin and John Searle the assertions of an economic scientist are not mere utterances (about which only phonology can speak) or mere propositions (about which only formal logic can speak). They are speech acts or, as they say, "illocutionary acts": attempts to persuade. As Burke would put it (and did put it before Austin and Searle), they are acts by the economist-agent in a scene of scientific conversation through the agency of master tropes and their servants for the purposes of influencing public policy or achieving eminence in the scholarly world or even on occasion satisfying a curiosity about economic events.

The point can be illustrated by any important phrase from economic literature. Take for instance "The demand curve slopes down." This conventional line of economic poetry, much used in epic and containing within it a metaphor wrapped in mathematics, means that when the price of something rises the consumers will buy less of it. When the price of oil rises the quantity of heating oil or gasoline demanded falls. People turn down their thermostats and wear sweaters indoors. They take fewer vacation trips and buy smaller cars.

The price does it, which is what makes the phrase important as social law, the Law of Demand. Laymen look on prices as extortions with no redeeming social value; economists look on them as inducements to human action. Like a law that things with mass attract, the Law of Demand is not surprising by itself, though surprising enough in its practical uses. Furthermore, economists believe it when other people do not, as they believe in the goodness of free trade and the efficacy of competition. Belief in the Law of Demand holds together the speech community of economics.

The question is how economists persuade themselves of its truth. How do they know that when the price of gasoline goes up the quantity of gasoline demanded will go down?

The ways they persuade themselves turn out to be mostly common topics, argument such as one might see in "Areopagitica" or "A Modest Proposal." Yet economists believe they believe by virtue of special topics in Economic Science:

- After a good deal of handwringing and computer squeezing certain very sophisticated statistical tests of the Law applied to entire economies, tests in which every allowance has been made for bias and incompleteness, have sometimes resulted in the diagonal elements of certain matrices being negative at the 5 percent level of significance. The jargon for this special topic is "a fully identified complete system of demand equations." Even its inventors, such as Hans Theil, have no great confidence in the result. A shift of one metaphor here, a shift of one appeal to authority there, and the "proof" would be valid no longer.

- Less ambitious but more numerous demonstrations of the law have been attempted market-by-market. Agricultural economists especially have for fifty years been fitting demand curves to statistics on corn and hogs. Again the curves sometimes give the right slope and sometimes don't. In any case the thought before calculation that forces the right slope—known as "specification"—contains elements of introspection, analogy, and other common sense embarrassing to the claims of mindless objectivity. Econometricians have begun to take heed.[18] But they need help in their rhetoric before calculation.

- Some economists have tried recently to subject the Law to a few experimental tests. After a good deal of throat clearing they have found it to be true for rats and false for humans, an interesting result which no one believes. As Harry Collins has recently argued, an experiment uses debate rather than ends it.[19]

These three arguments are properly scientific, although only the third quite matches the received view of scientific method (philosophically obsolete and historically misleading though it is). The received arguments yield mixed results. Does this leave economists uncertain about the Law of Demand? Not at all. They believe it ardently. Only part of their ardor therefore can be properly scientific. The part is small: few economists would assign a weight of more than, say, 15 percent to the statistical and experimental evidence.

The other 85 percent is patently literary:

- Introspection is an important source of belief. The economic scientist asks himself, "What would I do if the price of gasoline doubled?" If properly socialized in economics he will answer, "I would consume less." In similar fashion a poet might ask herself what she might do if she saw heather or a wave; a textual critic might ask himself how he would react to a line if "quod, o patrona virgo" were emended to "quidem est, patroni et ergo."
- Thought experiments (common in physics) are persuasive too. The economic scientist asks in view of his experience of life and his knowledge of economics what other people would do if the

price of gasoline doubled. In the same way, a novelist might ask how Huck would respond to Jim's request to come up on the raft; or a critic might ask how an audience would react to the sacrifice of Coriolanus.

- Cases in point, though not controlled experiments or large samples, persuade to some degree. The biggest recent triumph for the Law of Demand was the Oil Embargo of 1973–74: the doubling of gasoline prices caused gasoline consumption to decline, although noneconomists predicted it would not. This is narrative, not statistical, fit (although statisticians are moving toward a rhetoric that a literary person would recognize as narrative).[20] The narrative tells. In the same way, Wayne Booth remarks, "The most sensitive book-length theological account we can imagine. . . . lacks something that men know together when in answer to the question, 'What is the life of man?' they answer, 'There was once in Bethlehem. . . .' "[21]

- The lore of the marketplace persuades. Businesspeople believe that the Law of Demand is true, for they cut prices when they wish to raise the quantity demanded. They have the incentive of their livelihood to know rightly. What mere professor would dispute such testimony? Disputing it would contradict a fundamental conviction among professors of economics (and among professors of ecology and evolutionary biology too) that opportunities for profit are not usually left lying around untaken. The argument is ad hominem, an argument from the character of its audience. In the same way a literary critic might try, un-Burke-like, to defend the authority of the author—who after all has an incentive to know what he means—against the claims of the playful reader making a text out of "Beauty is truth, truth beauty."

- The lore of the academy also persuades. If many wise economists have long affirmed the Law of Demand, what mere latecomer would dispute their testimony? Any science operates this way, standing on the shoulders of giants. The argument from authority is not of course decisive. But it must be given weight. Scholarship could not make progress if all questions were reopened every fifteen years. In the same way Keats followed the tradition of pastoral as preparation for epic; and the New Criticism worked away in its tradition undisturbed by Burkeish thoughts of audience and speaker.

- Commonly the symmetry of the Law will persuade: as Burke remarked in *A Rhetoric of Motives*, "yielding to the form prepares assent to the matter identified with it."[22] If there is a Law

Donald N. McCloskey

of Supply—there are many reasons to think so—it is hard to resist the symmetrical attractions of a Law of Demand. At higher
levels of mathematical science the appeal to symmetry accounts
for a higher percentage of the persuasion. In the same way the
critic will search for structure in "Ode on a Grecian Urn" and
find it in the symmetry of beautiful act and truthful scene.

- Mere definition is a powerful argument, and again the more
powerful the more mathematical the talk. A higher price of gasoline leaves less income to be spent on all things, including gasoline (at least by one definition of income or of the Law). In the
same way the critic can define the elements of discourse dramatistically, leaving less for other metaphors.

- Above all, analogy persuades. That the Law of Demand is persuasive for ice cream and movies, which no one would want to
deny, makes it more persuasive also for gasoline. Analogy gives
the Law its majesty. The Law is persuasive for ice cream and
movies, of course, but by analogy is also persuasive for gasoline, for food, for housing, for status, for power, for love. Analogy rules the scientific world as it does the literary world: bird
thou never wert.

These are eleven good reasons for believing the Law of Demand.
Three of them look "scientific," though at bottom they too are
metaphorical—mathematics being the noblest metaphor of them all.
The rest are "literary," which is to say that they use tropes of the
language-using animal that might appear in any memorable speech.
Economic argument, being language and symbolic action, is accessible to literary criticism.

It is not the failure of economics to be really and truly scientific that
accounts for its verbality. The point is the opposite one: all science, including economics, is verbal because it is human, tropal because it is
artful, rhetorical because it has after all an honest purpose to persuade.

A good example of the rhetoric of successful science in economics is
a famous paper written in 1957 by Robert M. Solow, "Technical
Change and the Aggregate Production Function." Solow was trying to
understand the rising income of Americans from 1909 to 1949. He
wished to know in particular how much was caused by more machinery, buildings, and other physical "capital" and how much by other
things—chiefly the increasing ingenuity of people. He began:

> In this day of rationally designed econometric studies and
> super input-output tables, it takes something more than the
> usual "willing suspension of disbelief" to talk seriously of the

aggregate production function. . . . The new wrinkle I want to describe is an elementary way of segregating variations in output per head due to technical change from those due to the availability of capital per head. . . . Either this kind of aggregate economics appeals or it doesn't. Personally I belong to both schools. . . . It is convenient to begin with the special case of *neutral* technical change. . . . In that case the production function takes the special form $Q = A(t) f(K,L)$ and the multiplicative factor $A(t)$ measures the cumulated effect of shifts over time.[23]

The four master tropes which Burke and others detect in literature are here at work: metaphor, metonymy, synecdoche, and irony. The argument depends at once on a metaphor. The "aggregate production function" which Solow diffidently introduces asserts that the making of our daily bread is like a mathematical function. The jumble of responsibility, habit, conflict, ambition, intrigue, and ceremony that is our working life is supposed to be similar to a chalked curve on a blackboard. Economists are habituated to such figures of speech to the point of not recognizing that they are, but noneconomists will agree that this one is bold. No wonder that like any drama of human relations it requires willing suspension of disbelief.

The L and K in the equation are metonymies. The L reduces the human attentiveness in making bread to mere hours of work. The hour is an emblem, no more the substance of the matter than the heart is of emotions or a bottle is of the wine. The K reduces the material inheritance of the workplace to a pile of shmoos. Solow is aware of the boldness of this figure too, though defending it as conventional: he "would not try to justify what follows by calling on fancy theorems on aggregation and index numbers," referring in a footnote to Joan Robinson's exploration of "the profound difficulties that stand in the way of giving any precise meaning to the quantity of capital."[24]

The identification of $A(t)$ with "technical change" is a synecdoche, and on it the paper turns. The notation says that the multiplier A depends on time, rising as the technologists get smarter. But Solow admits that "slowdowns, speedups, improvements in the education of the labor force, and all sorts of things" will also cause it to rise. Critics of the calculation such as Evsey Domar, Theodore Schultz, and Solow himself, have called it a mere "measure of our ignorance." Calling it "technical change" as Solow does apologetically (though persistently) is a bold synecdoche indeed, taking part for the whole and running with it.

Solow runs with it into a paragraph containing a little freshman calculus and a clever exploitation of the conventions of the economists'

Donald N. McCloskey

conversation. By the second page of the article he has made his main point and has persuaded most of the economists listening. He persuades them with the symmetry of the mathematics and the appeal to the authority of scientific traditions in economics, and with the perspectival tropes: metaphor, metonymy, and synecdoche.

Especially he persuades them with irony, the "perspective of perspectives" (*GM*, p. 512). Observe his ironical bow to "rationally designed econometric studies" (he knew as did part of his audience that the rationality was in doubt, though in 1957 the econometricians were humorlessly unaware). He describes his notion as a mere "wrinkle" and as "elementary," so elementary a wrinkle that no one had thought of it before and that after Solow an intellectual industry arose to exploit it.[25] He protects himself from criticism by mocking the sobersides: "Personally I belong to both schools." The synecdoche of "technical change" is protected by ironical quotation marks when in doubt, though the marks fall away as doubt fades.

Irony is the most sophisticated of the master tropes. As Hayden White put it:

> It presupposes that the reader or auditor already knows, or is capable of recognizing, the absurdity of the characterization of the thing designated in the Metaphor, Metonymy, or Synecdoche used to give form to it. . . . Irony is in one sense metatropological, for it is deployed in the self-conscious awareness of the possible misuse of figurative language. . . . Irony thus represents a stage of consciousness in which the problematical nature of language itself has become recognized. It points to the potential foolishness of all linguistic characterizations of reality as much as to the absurdity of the beliefs it parodies. It is therefore "dialectical," as Kenneth Burke has noted.[26]

The most sophisticated economists and the most sophisticated novelists favor irony. Irony presupposes an existing conversation off of which one can score; in this and in other ways it is mature. The economist George Stigler wrote as follows about the guiding metaphor of why people purchase things: "It would be of course bizarre to look upon the typical family—that complex mixture of love, convenience, and frustration—as a business enterprise. Therefore, economists have devoted much skill and ingenuity to elaborating this approach."[27] The jest protects and persuades.

The point could be pushed further. It is that the master tropes beloved of Burke illuminate pieces of economic science as much as they do Rousseau's notion of the general will or Falstaff's character.[28] Literary criticism of a Burkean (or Richardsian, Fryean, Boothian, Fishian, Hartmanian, or Hirschian) kind is able to make clear the workings of the texts of economists as much as the texts of poets.

It is possible to go at least one step further along this curious path. I have said so far that economic theory can be enriched by literary criticism and especially that literary criticism can be used to criticize the writings of economists. The further step is to note that economic theory is itself a species of criticism. In other words, like Marxism and psychoanalysis, bourgeois economics of the school of Adam Smith is literally a critical theory. It was the first: Marxism was a conscious reaction to all its doctrines, and psychoanalysis was an unconscious reaction to its doctrine of conscious rationality.

A critical theory, to use as a checklist Raymond Geuss's synthesis in *The Idea of a Critical Theory: Habermas and the Frankfurt School*, is "a reflective theory which gives agents a kind of knowledge inherently productive of enlightenment and emancipation."[29] The false consciousness of a person lacking the theory is spoken of in medical terms, as a "delusion" from which the patient "suffers."[30] The neurosis is cured and the alienation overcome by self-consciousness and the liberation it brings. Likewise, I am saying, bourgeois economics.

"Critical theories aim at emancipation and enlightenment." This purpose was foremost in Adam Smith's mind. Smith's emancipating theory was no small contributor to the literal emancipation of the slaves in the British Empire. And of course his thinking has ever since been the foundation of one kind of anarchist politics, unpopularly antistatist in a statist world. (That Smith's thinking has occasionally been adopted by state gangsters is no more or less relevant than that Marx's has). Bourgeois economics can assert as well as can Marxism and psychoanalysis that it aims at emancipation and enlightenment. One might even argue that in actually hitting the target it has performed better.

"Critical theories ... are claimed to be 'reflective' or 'self-referential': a critical theory is itself always a part of the object-domain which it describes; critical theories are always in part about themselves."[31] This is more true of economics than it is of the others, as economists have recently begun to realize. What they have realized is that there are sharp limits imposed by economics on the ability of economists to engage in that prediction and control alleged to characterize science. The limit is the American Question: If you're so smart why ain't you rich? Economists mostly are not rich. An economist who pretends to know what will happen to the economy next year, the better to advise the prince, is claiming knowledge that can make

Donald N. McCloskey

him rich. If he knew that bond prices were going to rise next year he could invest and prosper. In fact he would have done so already; and he would surely not be telling anyone else until the information was exhausted. To imagine that tip sheets give valuable advice on bonds is no more sensible than to imagine they give it on thoroughbreds. It is an economic principle: opportunities for profit, to repeat, are not left lying around untaken. Anyone who was so smart would be quietly rich. More self-referential you cannot get.

"Critical theories are cognitively acceptable only if they survive confirmation through observation and experiment." I have mentioned the degree to which the Frankfurt School falls for the dichotomous maneuvers of its positivist enemies. The economic arguments discussed above suggest that economics falls on the nonscience side of the dichotomy, along with the other critical theories.

So it goes: if Marxism is a critical theory so also is economics. The argument will irritate Marxists (and non-Marxists too, I suppose). It removes the left lean from the idea of a critical theory: American economics, I need not emphasize, is considered "right wing" (though oddly so: no one who wants to abolish import tariffs and syndicalist monopolies outright, as most economists in the United States do, can be called exactly a "conservative," and certainly not a "fascist"). But if the idea of a critical theory is to amount to anything more than a periphrastic conjugation of Marxism it should be able to absorb this bourgeois and "right-wing" economics. In the end the idea of a critical theory should be able to absorb the idea of rhetorical criticism, as propounded by Kenneth Burke. Or maybe it will be absorbed by it. When all is said and done, rhetoric looks like the master critical theory, a sweetly American one, shorn of the fallacious economic history and antique neuroses haunting European Marxism.

No wonder, then, that rhetoric has flourished in America. And no wonder that it can be used to deconstruct and maybe reconstruct that American (and formerly Scottish) invention, the bourgeois, English-speaking science of economics. The dog walks, and dances with tears in his eyes, to a tune by Kenneth Burke.

NOTES

1. Certain passages from the following have appeared in a different form in "The Literary Character of Economics," *Daedalus* (Summer 1984), 97–120, and in *The Rhetoric of Economics* (Madison: University of Wisconsin Press, 1985). I thank the National Endowment for the Humanities and its program in Humanities, Science, and Technology for support during the writing.

program in Humanities, Science, and Technology for support during the writing.

2. Kenneth Burke, *The Rhetoric of Religion* (1961; rpt. Berkeley: University of California Press, 1970), p. 275.

3. Kenneth Burke, *A Grammar of Motives* (1945; rpt. Berkeley: University of California Press, 1969), p. 513.

4. Kenneth Burke, "Dramatism" in *The International Encyclopedia of the Social Sciences* (New York: Macmillan, 1968).

5. Ludwig von Mises, *Human Action: A Treatise on Economics* (New Haven: Yale University Press, 1949), p. 10.

6. On Frank Knight see *GM*, pp. 256–57.

7. *RR*, p. 277 and numerous times thereafter.

8. Tibor Scitovsky, *The Joyless Economy* (1976) and Ronald Heiner, "The Origin of Predictable Behavior," *American Economic Review*, 73 (1983), 560–90. Compare the Lord's stricture on "a constant procession of solemn, humorless caricatures. . . [from] various oversimplified schemes that reduce human motives to a few. . . itches"; or Satan asking whether one must "shop around among the various caricatures" (*RR*, pp. 299–300).

9. A pioneer from the literary side is Kurt Heinzelmann, whose *The Economics of the Imagination* (Amherst: University of Massachusetts Press, 1980) discusses at length how economic theory in the nineteenth century used language and how it in turn influenced the language of imaginative writers. Marc Shell has catalogued the use of (strictly) monetary metaphors in literature in *The Economy of Literature* (Baltimore: Johns Hopkins University Press, 1978).

10. Albert Hirschman, "Against Parsimony: Three Easy Ways of Complicating Some Categories of Economic Discourse," *American Economic Review*, 74 (1984), 89.

11. Jon Elster, *Ulysses and the Sirens: Studies in Rationality and Irrationality* (Cambridge: University Press, 1979).

12. I. A. Richards, *Principles of Literary Criticism* (1925; rpt. New York: Harvest/Harcourt Brace Jovanovich, n.d.), pp. 205–6.

13. Milton Friedman is recognized as a skilled orator, a *vir dicendi peritus* (the knowledgeable add the *bonus*). He uses the trope in question to support his argument against conscription in peacetime: "I have observed many persons initially in favor of the draft change their opinions as they have looked into the arguments and studied the evidence; I have never observed anyone who was initially in favor of a volunteer force reverse his position on the basis of further study. This greatly enhances my confidence in the validity of the position I have taken." See Friedman, *An Economist's Protest*, 2d ed. (Glen Ridge, N.J.: Thomas Horton and Daughters, 1975), p. 188.

14. Gary Becker and George Stigler, "De Gustibus Non Est Disputandum," *American Economic Review*, 67 (1977), 76–90.

15. To which might come the reply, "Delenda est valor." See Hirschman, "Against Parsimony," p. 90.

16. Donald McCloskey, "The Problem of Audience in Historical Econom-

ics: Rhetorical Thoughts on a Text by Robert Fogel," *History and Theory*, 24 (1985), 1–22; and Charles Bazerman, "What Written Knowledge Does: Three Examples of Academic Discourse," *Philosophy of the Social Sciences*, 11 (1981), 361–86.

17. William Kruskal, "Formulas, Numbers, Words: Statistics in Prose," *American Scholar*, 47 (1978), 223–29.

18. T. F. Cooley and S. F. Leroy, "Identification and the Estimation of Money Demand," *American Economic Review*, 71 (1981), 825–44; Edward Leamer, *Specification Searches: Ad Hoc Inferences with Non-Experimental Data* (New York: Wiley, 1978) and "Let's Take the Con Out of Econometrics," *American Economics Review*, 73 (1983), 31–43.

19. Harry M. Collins, *Changing Order: Replication and Induction in Scientific Practice* (London: Sage, 1985).

20. Fredrick Mosteller and John W. Tukey, *Data Analysis and Regression: A Second Course in Statistics* (Reading, Mass.: Addison-Wesley, 1977). See also Leamer, *Specification Searches*.

21. Wayne C. Booth, *Modern Dogma and the Rhetoric of Assent* (Chicago: University of Chicago Press, 1974), p. 74.

22. Kenneth Burke, *A Rhetoric of Motives* (1950; rpt. Berkeley: University of California Press, 1969), p. 58.

23. Robert Solow, "Technical Change and the Aggregate Production Function," *Review of Economics and Statistics*, 39 (1957), 349–50.

24. Ibid., p. 350.

25. Literally speaking it *had* been thought of before, by G. T. Jones in *Increasing Returns* (Cambridge: University Press, 1933). Solow did not know about Jones, an economic historian, though he was aware of several attempts in the 1950s by historically oriented economists such as Valavanis-Vail, Schmookler, and Abramovitz to measure the same thing. The others were less influential because they did not use the metaphor of the production function as explicitly as Solow did.

26. Hayden White, *Metahistory: The Historical Imagination in Nineteenth-Century Europe* (Balitmore: John Hopkins University Press, 1973), p. 37.

27. George Stigler, *The Theory of Price*, 3d ed. (New York: Macmillan, 1966), p. 21.

28. Hearing at the conference Michael Leff's essay reprinted in this volume sharpened my understanding here.

29. Raymond Geuss, *The Idea of Critical Theory: Habermas and the Frankfurt School* (Cambridge: University Press, 1981), p. 2.

30. Ibid., p. 12.

31. Idid., p. 55.

5   BURKE'S CICERONIANISM

MICHAEL LEFF

The motive for this paper arose from an incident that occurred some years ago in my classical rhetoric seminar. I was there delivering a warm though not entirely coherent encomium on Cicero's *De oratore*. The standard histories of rhetoric, I asserted, did a disservice to that work. *De oratore* was more than an elegant recapitulation of conventional rhetorical doctrine, more than a shrewd practicum on oratorical performance, and more even than a philosophical statement about rhetoric and oratory. In my view, it was a synthetic masterpiece that merged form and content to embody a rhetorical perspective on civic life. Both in doctrine and in texture, the work represented an alternative to the abstract, systematic Aristotelian theory of rhetoric. As I proceeded through these and other equally sweeping dicta, I was greeted by silence and stares of bewilderment. So I tried another approach, a desperate attempt to find a point of comparison. *De oratore*, I said, exhibited a special sensitivity to rhetorical form such that the concept of form was instantiated in the very act of presenting it, and a contemporary parallel to this approach could be found in the works of Kenneth Burke. In fact, I added, one might go so far as to regard Burke as a Ciceronian. At this point, bewilderment gave way to looks of disbelief. There was an uncomfortable pause and then the boldest of my students blurted out: "But Burke is an Aristotelian."

The student was repeating an old orthodoxy in the lore of Speech Communication, one that I had forgotten. I do not know how it originated. Perhaps it devolved from Virginia Holland's book *Counterpoint*, an early effort to make Burke accessible to rhetoricians by stressing affinities between Aristotle's *Rhetoric* and Burke's "new rhetoric." More likely the book itself was symptomatic of a broader motive. At the time people in speech first became aware of Burke, the field was dominated by an Aristotelian paradigm, and there was an almost irresistible temptation to chart the new in terms of the old. Burke was too important to disregard, but both his idiom and his interests seemed remote from traditional scholarship in speech departments. It was comforting, therefore, to contemplate an essential link, lurking just below the sur-

Michael Leff

face, that connected Burke with the then-unchallenged master of the field.

As Aristotle's influence has waned, this connection has become less present than it once was. Nevertheless, my student's response demonstrates that the old orthodoxy abides, and furthermore, by the normal standards of classification, it is not without foundation. The categories of intellectual history ordinarily depend on studies of influence, and the marks of Aristotelian influence on Burke are rather clear. Aristotle appears frequently in the text of Burke, far more frequently than any other author associated with the traditional rhetorical canon. Some of Burke's fundamental ideas—for example, the theory of form in *Counter-Statement*—have an Aristotelian tint; some of his own categories, most notably the tetralogy of motives, are Aristotelian in origin. And there is direct borrowing of certain important Aristotelian terms such as imitation and catharsis. These relationships are complex and equivocal, and especially since Burke relies more on the *Metaphysics* and the *Poetics* than on the *Rhetoric*, they cannot justify a simple collapse of Burkean rhetoric into an Aristotelian frame. Nevertheless, the evidence is sufficient to warrant talk about Burke's Aristotelianism.

In the case of Cicero, matters are very different. There are, to be sure, references to his work, but they are widely scattered and mainly incidental. Cicero does receive sustained attention in the appendix to *Attitudes toward History* and in the second part of the *Rhetoric of Motives*. But even in these places, there is little to suggest a fundamental or decisive theoretical interest in Cicero. In short, the influence of Cicero on Burke is minimal, if not nonexistent.

Consequently, given the orthodox entitlement and the orthodox method of entitling, to say that Burke is a Ciceronian is (and here I quote from Burke) to attach to "some name a qualifying epithet which has heretofore gone with a different order of names."[1] Or, in other words, it is a perspective by incongruity. As such, it entails no claim at all about the direction of influence of the earlier of these authors on the later. Rather my argument rests on the identification of certain features (perhaps "anecdotes") the two share in common and a rationale for classifying those features within the same cluster relative to a conceptual and not a chronological perspective on the history of rhetoric. The relationship I posit, of course, is reciprocal, and so anything I say about Burke's Ciceronianism applies with equal force to Cicero's Burkeishness.[2]

Perhaps the best way to initiate this project is to enumerate some of the points of affinity between Burke and Cicero. Since the comparison involves two subtle and prolific authors, the resulting list necessarily must simplify and flatten complex matters. Moreover, the index is fairly long, and its recitation may become tedious. But the index is loaded; if it does its work, it should gather momentum and significance as it develops.

To begin, Burke and Cicero both belong to a thinly populated category (perhaps they even exhaust it) of writers who have made important contributions to rhetorical theory without having been academic teachers of the subject. Perhaps because of their nonacademic orientation, neither places much faith in the rigid separation of departments of knowledge. Both display an extraordinary breadth of learning and a tendency to rely indifferently on any and all sources of knowledge when confronted with an intellectual problem. Perhaps more important, both resist the separation of academic from public culture; learning for them is an integral part of life, and this applies with a vengeance in respect to the language arts. For Cicero, as for Burke, the study of the aesthetics of language is intensely practical, a means of gaining equipment for living. Consistent with the breadth of their learning, both authors write in an expansive manner. Their works are packed with details, and they are notorious for digressions along the main route of the argument. Their digressions, in fact, often transform the argument as they accumulate and roll through the linear frame of the discourse.

These general characteristics of outlook and style seem related to a series of shared doctrines that impinge more directly on the conception of rhetoric. In the first place, both Burke and Cicero place a high value on eloquence. Both regard the primary function of eloquence as the direction and control of human emotions, but neither divorces the emotions from the operations of reason and argument. This tendency to unify categories that normally receive separate treatment recurs in other aspects of their thought. Thus, neither attempts to sediment content from form or to abstract form from content. Instead they hold the two in solution, viewing them as interdependent and interactive. Closely related to this point is their common commitment to the unity of expression and thought. Rueckert observes that "verbalizing and thinking, words and reason, are interchangeable terms for Burke."[3] And for Cicero the union of *res* and *verba*, of *ratio* and *oratio*, stands at the base of all his speculation about rhetoric. Moreover, both Cicero and Burke oppose the separation of the intrinsic or technical dimensions of discourse from its extrinsic social or political dimensions. Both, that is, stress the aesthetic in discourse without alienating the aesthetic from the pragmatic functions of language. All of these spe-

Michael Leff

cific points of integration help form a still more general attitude: Cicero and Burke alike regard eloquence as a unity that manifests itself in an infinite variety of forms. They contend that eloquence arises from a common fund of universal resources based in nature. For Burke, these universals arise from psychophysical constants inherent in man, from the neurological and biological rhythms of human life. For Cicero, the universals arise from a broader neo-Stoic vision of the harmony and order of nature itself. But in both cases, the universals have no human meaning apart from their manifestation in particulars. Thus, the patterns of verbalized thought that provide the resources for eloquence appear in all forms of discourse, but are embodied in different ways each time they appear. They can be apprehended and used only as they are put into practice.

This emphasis on practice summarizes and orders the other points I have reviewed, and it can be expressed in one simple proposition: discourse is an act. More specifically, every instance of eloquent speech is an act that embodies the unity of words and thoughts, of form and content, and of the intrinsic resources and the extrinsic powers of language. Such unities can occur only in a concrete, situated linguistic performance. Consequently, a theory of discourse cannot rest content in a neutral and purely abstract terminology, and it is for this reason that both Burke and Cicero ground the theory of eloquence in a model, in a specific type of discursive performance. For Burke it is ritual drama and for Cicero it is oratory that serves this function. The two models are obviously different, but that fact should not disguise the more fundamental similarity between theories that refer all eloquence to the paradigm of a certain kind of discourse. Thus, it is possible to round out the affinities between the two authors in this way: if the term dramatism characterizes Burke's system, then we might characterize Cicero's system with equal accuracy under the title "oratorism."[4]

The logic of this symmetrical, integrative pattern requires one final step. The philosophy of discourse as action achieves realization by reference to a concrete model of performance. But how is one to talk about the model itself? Or, to put the matter in other terms, the model becomes a representation of discourse in action; it is one type of action singled out from among many types, and its theoretical function is to preserve the unity of discourse that eludes disembodied theoretical analysis. But there must also be a representation of the model, a representation of the representative act. If such metadiscourse is to remain consistent with the premises of the system, it must instantiate the principles it enunciates. Thus, for Cicero and for Burke metadiscourse must fold theory into practice. Theoretical inquiry becomes an exercise in practice, and theoretical discourse becomes a substantial rather than a statistical representation of action, becomes a model that embodies the models it seeks to organize. A theory of eloquence, in sum, must be what it represents.

Here, then, we come to an essential unity in Burke and Cicero: both drive the philosophy of language as action to a point that demands self-reflexive discourse about the theory of discourse. This position, in turn, yields two related consequences. The first, and most obvious, is that since their texts aim to embody more than they state, they would teach less by abstract dicta than by example. Or, to use the classical terminology, the lessons are imparted by *imitatio*, not merely by rational method. I use the Latin word here because its English cognate, "imitation," suggests mere slavish copying. But *imitatio*, in its best sense, refers to a notion similar to Polanyi's personal knowledge or Peirce's abduction. This involves a kind of concrete abstraction where what is learned in one experience is transferred laterally to a new experience. In rhetoric or criticism, *imitatio* occurs when a reader or listener, having apprehended principles embodied in one text, reembodies them in the production or interpretation of another text. Thus, Burke and Cicero teach by example in that their methods demand reenactment rather than abstract reduction.[5]

The second consequence is that the work of both authors culminates in irony. This is an elusive notion, and I believe that it is best explained in relation to my point about *imitatio*. This relationship itself, however, is not transparent, and emerges only after a careful reading of the works of the two authors. As a result, I propose to develop my argument by reference to Burke's essay "Four Master Tropes," and Cicero's dialogue *De oratore*. Since Burke's essay both explains and enacts a concept of irony, it is appropriate to begin with it.

"Four Master Tropes" exhibits a double structure.[6] There is a straightforward topical progression from metaphor to metonymy to synecdoche to irony. And there is also a more subtle and much more important pattern of dramatic action. It is certainly not fanciful to attribute dramatic characteristics to the essay, since Burke's own equations almost mandate this kind of reading. In *Attitudes toward History*, Burke argues that "terms are characters," and that "an essay is an attenuated play," complete with "hero" terms and "villain" terms.[7] Moreover, "Four Master Tropes" concludes with irony (in more than one sense), and it explicitly connects irony with dialectic, and dialectic with drama. And the final sentence of the essay stresses the importance of peripety as a key element in dialectic. The reader is thus alerted to look for dramatic alignments and oppositions and for strategic reversals within the essay itself.

As it turns out, poetic realism is the hero, and scientific realism the villain of the piece. Burke fixes our attitude toward these two characters in respect to their treatment of substance. A science of human behavior unwittingly employs one-way metonymies and thus charts the dimensions of human life in terms of models drawn from a lower order of existence (for example, animal responses). This strategy ignores the motives and interests that inform the substance of human behavior, and it reduces all human action to naturalistic correlations, to mere processes. The result is to mistake statistical for substantial representation. Poetic realism makes use of statistical representations, and it also relies on metonymic reductions. Yet it does not end in reduction, for if the poet reduces the spiritual to the physical in making a work of art, the work is designed to guide the reader back to the spiritual realm from which it originated. Poets, therefore, characteristically use the fluid trope of synecdoche, which indifferently moves from whole to part or from part to whole, from quality to quantity or from quantity to quality, and so on through the range of shifting perspectives. Poetic realism, moreover, locates its perspective in the distinctively human medium of language, and it produces models that refer to the essential motives embedded in human speech. Poetic, then, incorporates the metonymic strategies of science, but expands and supplements them in order to engage the substance of human relations (*GM*, pp. 505–11).

The consideration of irony effects a peripety in the structure of the essay. In this respect, we might recall that classical doctrine treats metaphor, metonymy, and synecdoche as figures of speech, since they work within sentences. Irony, however, is a figure of thought, since its operation extends beyond the sentence to larger units of discourse. Burke's categories reflect a similar division of levels. His first three tropes deal with perspective, while irony is of a higher order, a perspective on perspectives. Thus, just as the perspectives of poetic subsume the strategies of science, so also does irony subsume the perspectives of poetic. This maneuver instantiates Burke's concept of irony, for he asserts that irony occurs when the interaction of terms upon one another produces a development which uses all the terms (*GM*, p. 512). Within this perspective on perspectives, no one perspective is precisely right or precisely wrong. Rather, through a kind of dialectical mortification, all competing perspectives are absorbed into the body of a totalizing form. This definition, of course, enacts itself within the text as Burke completes his progression from science to poetic to irony.

Nor is this the only respect in which Burke's treatment of irony is ironic. His argument reverses conventional attitudes about the relationship between the ambiguous statements of drama and dialectic and the scientific ideal of unequivocal statement. Dramatic irony, for Burke, is substantive, because it attempts to encompass the whole. Naive scientific realism, however, is relativistic, because its tendency toward the absolutism of one position fragments the complex unity of substance and isolates us in the subjectivism of a single perspective.[8] Thus, while other apologists for art inadvertently perpetuate the bias of science by praising the relativism of art, Burke consumes his enemy. His ironic twist shows that science uses the strategies of poetics, but the goal of science is realized only through the conscious expansion of these strategies so as to encounter the ambiguities of substance.

Finally, Burkean irony ironically perfects tropical perspectivism even as it inoculates us against its perfection. The other tropes open new perspectives, and as irony gathers them together, it yields a maximum proliferation of perspectives. In rounding out this development, irony discounts any single angle of vision and serves as an antidote to the behaviorist fallacy. Blind use of any single perspective encourages the perfection of the perspective until it becomes an abstract scheme resting content within its own reductive structure. Irony balances this tendency against the weight of other partially true perspectives; it recalls us to a broader context of motives and reminds us that substance cannot be reduced to form. Substance can come into being only through the enactment of form.

The relationship between *De oratore* and "Four Master Tropes" is chiasmatic. Burke treats irony explicitly, but its enactment is implicit. Cicero openly announces the principles of reflexive enactment, but leaves the reader to discover its ironic structure. And so a study of *De oratore* should reveal how these two concepts merge when approached from the other end of the process.

The self-reflexive eloquence of *De oratore* is widely acknowledged, but often discounted as incidental, as a mechanism simply for illustrating specific rhetorical devices. Cicero, however, repeats this theme so often and with so much emphasis that I cannot doubt its relevance to the interpretation of the dialogue as a whole. In the preface to the first book, for example, Cicero declares that, since his intent is not to produce a string of technical precepts in the manner of Greek theorists, he will construct a dialogue whose dramatis personae are men renowned for the highest achievements in eloquence (1.23). In other words, he chooses a vehicle that permits enactment as well as statement. This point is reinforced throughout the work by choral comments various interlocutors make about the performance of other interlocutors. Where praise is given, it always stresses the eloquence displayed by the speaker as he talks about eloquence (2.38, 362, 3.51, 188). And, to pass over many other indications of this same point, I would single out the delightful dialogue within the dialogue that occurs at the beginning of book 2. Two minor characters, Catulus and Caesar, attempt to goad Crassus into a theoretical discussion of oratory by arguing for the propriety of conducting philosophical disputations. Crassus resists participation in this kind of exercise, and to justify his reticence, he makes an elaborate reply to the argument of his friends. When he finishes, Caesar remarks: "I think now that I have already bestowed my pains to advantage in coming here, for to myself this very protest against disputation has been a disputation of the most pleasant character."[9] The whole scene is packed with ironies. As happens so often in the dialogue, a character assumes a kind of Socratic modesty and protests against doing the very thing that he is doing. And Caesar's last word is a pointedly ironic comment about how enactment can outstrip statement. The full force of this irony emerges in the third and final book, where it comes to dominate the structure of the whole discourse.

Crassus is the major interlocutor in book 3, and he begins by establishing a pair of related oppositions. The first consists in the tension between the technical and philosophical structuring of the dialogue. The technical structure, which determines the external order of the discourse, divides oratory into a series of discrete components and separates the content of speech from its form. The philosophical structure, developed mainly through a sequence of extended digressions, argues for the unity of eloquence and the merger of form and content. The second opposition involves a tension between the philosophical conception of the unity of eloquence and the diversity of oratorical performance mandated by the rhetorical doctrine of propriety. The remainder of Crassus' efforts is designed to overcome these interlocking problems.

The first issue surfaces as Crassus dutifully (though protesting all the while) proceeds through the four technical elements of style—purity, clarity, ornamentation, and propriety. The first two receive summary treatment—they are trivial preliminaries to eloquence. Ornamentation, however, is another matter. It raises great and complex issues vital to the orator's success. In fact, it is so weighty and encompassing that it cannot be approached through static technical precept. Eloquence requires ornaments that arise from knowledge of the subjects of discourse and the character and emotions of the audience. But to engage these matters is to enter the domain of philosophy, and so,

ironically, proficiency in what is supposed to be a technical component of style proves dependent on a general mastery of philosophical
knowledge. Moreover, Crassus insists that the separation of philosophy from rhetoric, of the tongue from the brain, is purely conventional, the product of certain historical accidents. By nature, both
rhetoric and philosophy draw from a common reservoir of knowledge, and the ornaments of speech exist as counterparts to the substance of thought. Thus, Crassus concludes with the famous
aphorism: "A full supply of matter begets a full supply of words."[10]

This preliminary synthesis, however, still leaves Crassus' task unfinished, for the philosophical tendency of the dialogue now seems to
overpower its rhetorical tendency. That is, a complete identification
between knowledge and eloquence, where the latter simply follows
the former, suggests that the art of oratory requires no special attention.[11] Consequently, Crassus must add an important qualification—
namely, philosophical knowledge is a necessary but not sufficient
condition for eloquence. Philosophy can rest content within its contemplative structures, but oratory must body forth into the contingent
world of human affairs. The orator must command the resources of
learning, but must also add something to them, and that something is
the proper rhetorical treatment of a subject. Eloquence, in this idealized sense, is substance put into action. And the orator has priority
over the philosopher because the orator's range subsumes and goes
beyond philosophy (3.142). In sum, Crassus rescues eloquence from
the static divisions of technical rhetoric, passes it through the substance of philosophy, and then raises eloquence beyond philosophy
because of its capacity to fold substance into rhetorically effective
action.

These arguments demonstrate that eloquence is a unity of form and
content that displays itself in action. But how is the orator to identify
and apply the right words and thoughts in a given case? Since the requirements for action vary in each instance, no set of abstract rules
can answer this question. Consequently, we are led back to the matter
of propriety. In one sense, this term pervades the dialogue. It recurs
frequently, sometimes in tones of marked emphasis, and it is identified as the chief element in art. Propriety is also the fourth category in
the technical division of style, and in due course Crassus addresses it
specifically. Nevertheless, consistent with earlier remarks in the dialogue, he has little to say about it other than that it defies theoretical
analysis. The chief element in art, thus, is dismissed in a single paragraph (2. 210–12).

Here we arrive at the irony of ironies. Crassus has lead us through
as ascending series of dialectical mergers, and just as we come to the

top and lay hands on the master term, that very term seems to pull us back to the ground. We cannot disentangle propriety from its manifestations, and so it cannot be captured in theoretical abstractions. It can be apprehended only as embodied in a particular discourse. But that does not mean propriety is unteachable, for where one method of instruction fails, another can succeed. And so contemplation of propriety may not pull us to the ground, but rather push us back into the fabric of the text. To return to the text in this way is to understand the propriety of its theoretical silence about propriety. The text instantiates the concept. Viewed in this light, though it retains much of the structure of academic rhetoric, and though it subsumes principles of contemplative philosophy, *De oratore* is neither a rhetorical textbook nor a philosophical treatise. It is an oration about the art of oratory, and it instructs by being what it cannot explain.

De oratore, therefore, is substantive in the complex and ironic Burkean sense of the term. The work is a verbal act that transcends itself by calling attention to its status as a verbal act. Moreover, Cicero relies on some characteristically Burkean strategies to realize this goal—that is, a dialectic that absorbs rather than discards opposing perspectives, a reliance on a master term that discounts its own hegemony, and an emphasis on self-reflexive enactment within the text of a theoretical discourse.

These similarities are striking, so striking in fact that, if the chronological placement of the two authors were reversed, our scholarship would already have produced a considerable body of literature devoted to the influence of Burke on Cicero. And even as things now stand, this paper demonstrates an ironic but very real influence of the later writer on the earlier. Experience in the present, after all, has a way of infiltrating our perspectives on the past, and my reading of *De oratore* is, in some considerable measure, the result of filtering that work through the lens of Burkean terminology. Perhaps this yields a misreading, a forced interpretation. Nevertheless, as Burke himself teaches us, all interpretation involves comparison, and comparison entails a principle of synecdoche that sanctions movement from present to past as well as from past to present. This same principle, of course, allows for the proliferation of perspectives, and encourages attention to other ways of organizing the relationship between the two authors. A reader might, for example, stress the dissimilarity between a system built on the interpretation of finished literary works and a system that looks forward to the performance of an oration. Or another reader might contrast Burke's hermeneutic for uncovering latent meaning with Cicero's scheme of invention through revelation. Still, in the economy of Burkean dialectic, these alternative perspectives merge within rather than eclipse the perspective I assume in this paper.

My own perspective emphasizes the consubstantiality of thinkers who extend the notion of discourse as act into the realm of theoretical discourse. When grouped together in this way, Burke and Cicero display a common opposition to orthodoxies that seek a perspectively neutral language, that discount the substance of language by attempting to raise it above or submerge it beneath the ambiguities of language in use. Instead, they teach us to hold discourse in solution by enacting models of its enactment. Such substantial representations ironically join with even as they rise above the substance they imitate. The whole system produces a stable instability, for a consistent stress on action cannot disarm the ambiguities of appropriate action. Thus, Burke and Cicero equip us to act by displaying the universal resources that manifest and alter their configuration each time they participate in the substance of action. Both thinkers engage us in a hopefully incomplete dialogue ripe with its own imperfection.

NOTES

1. Kenneth Burke, *Permanence and Change: An Anatomy of Purpose*, 2d rev. ed. (Indianapolis: Bobbs-Merrill, 1965), p. 90.

2. On reading a draft of this essay, one of the editors remarked that "if Burke can be called anything (and he probably can't), it is indeed an Aristotelain (as opposed to Marxian, Freudian, Spinozan, etc.)." Thus, he believes that while early attempts in the field of speech to assimilate Burke to Aristotle were "unfortunate," they were "nonetheless essentially correct. What needed to be done was to acknowledge, as I believe K.B. does, the extent of his debt to Aristotle and emphasize the extent to which he goes beyond A. Leff rather relies on what I'd call a 'creative equivocation.' If we say, and someone has, that Burke is a Gorgian (a modern Gorgias), we can mean one of two things. (1) He has read and digested what Gorgias said, profited from it, incorporated it into his own work. Or (2) he shares fundamental presuppositions, habits of thought etc. with Gorgias which would have manifested themselves had Gorgias never existed. I say K.B.'s relationship to Aristotle is of the former type. (Burke says, 'I am always uncomfortable when I disagree with Aristotle.') Leff says, Burke's relationship to Cicero is of the second type. Fair enough! (I chose Gorgias above—because I believe a similar case could be made.) If I were he, I'd not choose to appear to be combatting point No. 1." Indeed, I would not, and I cannot think of clarifying matters in a better way than the editor already has. Per-

Michael Leff

haps I would make one small change—instead of the editor's "creative equivocation" I would use the Burkean title "perspective by incongruity."

3. William Rueckert, *Kenneth Burke and the Drama of Human Relations*, 2d rev. ed. (Berkeley: University of California Press, 1982), p. 150.

4. My formulation here again provoked friendly correction from the editor. He would qualify my equation by arguing that Burke's system belongs to a "different order of pretensions" from Cicero's. Dramatism, he notes, is put forward as a literal and universally encompassing approach to human relations. Thus, it would apply to "the situation of a Trappist monk—vowed to silence—and of course the rest of mankind. 'Oratorism,' I think, would not." Strong support for the editor's argument seems to arise from the fact that through much of Western intellectual history (e.g., the entire Middle Ages) *De oratore* has been regarded either as irrelevant or as relevant only to a very limited, practical kind of activity. That is, appreciation of the philosophical breadth of *De oratore* depends upon an attitude that grants, at least in potential, serious intellectual significance to the activity of the orator, and such an attitude is not common among postclassical thinkers. For the most part, it is alien even to contemporary writers who, like Burke, seek to revive rhetorical studies, since they normally approach rhetoric via literary rather than civic discourse. Nevertheless, within the terms of Cicero's civic humanism, the idealization of oratory and its elevation to the center of human activity is a perfectly understandable mechanism for charting a certain way of living and thinking. Oratory thus becomes a microcosm by which we can understand the nature of human relations, which in turn becomes a microcosm for understanding the nature of the world itself. Burke's use of the dramatic model involves a similar set of extrapolations and is encumbered by similar limitations. That is, those who discount drama as "mere fiction" or who cannot imagine its essential representation of the human condition must find Burke's system useless or unintelligible. Within the economy of the two systems, drama and oratory function in much the same way and in that important sense do belong to the same "order of pretensions." Nevertheless, the editor's point does apply when considering the range of those systems. Cicero assumes that his model applies only to those who consciously choose to pursue a certain course of life; it is not intended to account for the domain of pure contemplation, and while Cicero argues that the active life can encompass and rise above the contemplative life, he does not doubt that the two can be separated. As I understand Burke, however, dramatism works in all regions of human experience, and though its operations are often well disguised, they can be discovered as unconscious principles of action even in the most rarefied forms of contemplation or the most austere specimens of scientific reasoning.

5. The editor raises another caveat in response to the paragraph above. The concept of *imitatio* describes the way Cicero generally intends his works to be used and the way in which they have been used by educators and writers. The same cannot be said of Burke. In fact, Burke sometimes

demonstrates a marked tendency toward abstract reductionism. (This point is ably demonstrated by Rueckert in his *Kenneth Burke and the Drama of Human Relations*.) Thus, in respect to Burke, I am advocating, not describing, a way to read and use his works. This position imposes a Ciceronian perspective on Burke, a way of reading Burke through Cicero, and it clearly involves hazards. Perhaps it is itself a form of reductionism—i.e., a reduction of Burkean abstractions to concrete Ciceronian practices. Nevertheless, as I argue below concerning the essay "Four Master Tropes," Burke sometimes invites a reading of this type, and my objective is to provoke new ways of reading Burke based on the Ciceronian key of civic discourse. My argument is that rhetoricians primarily concerned with public business might find it more profitable to assimilate Burke via the Ciceronian conception of eloquence rather than through the Aristotelian categories of rhetorical theory. This approach produces a somewhat different coloration to the ambiguities both of the Burkean text and the public discourse to which it is applied. And, of course, I am referring to a kind of general imitation of principles of thought, since Burke and Cicero obviously do not have a similar status as stylistic models.

6. The essay appears as "Appendix D" in *A Grammar of Motives* (Berkeley: University of California Press, 1969), pp. 503–18. The essay is generally regarded as one of the pivotal pieces in Burke's corpus and has attracted special notoriety since the publication of Hayden White's *Metahistory: The Historical Imagination in Nineteenth-Century Europe* (Baltimore: Johns Hopkins, University Press, 1973).

7. Kenneth Burke, *Attitudes toward History*, 2d revised ed. (Boston: Beacon Press, 1961), p. 312.

8. In the section devoted to irony, Burke makes no further reference to the contrast between scientific and poetic realism. This follows logically, since irony involves the management of poetic perspectives. Nevertheless, his comments on irony clearly imply reference to the discourse of behavioristic science. Such discourse relies upon nonrepresentative anecdotes precisely because of its use of a single, isolated perspective. The result is a reductive terminology that yields relativism, in Burke's sense of the term. Consequently, when applied to human affairs, strict scientific statement cannot manage differing perspectives, cannot achieve ironic transcendence, and thus becomes the paradigm of a relativistic terminology. (See *GM*, pp. 510–14.)

9. 2.26. The translation is by E. W. Sutton and H. Rackham in the Loeb edition (Cambridge: Harvard University Press, 1942).

10. 3.125. This is Rackham's translations of the famous Latin phrase: "Rerum enim copia verborum copiam gignit."

11. On this point, see A. D. Leeman, *Orationis Ratio: The Stylistic Theories and Practice of the Roman Orators, Historians, and Philosophers* (Amsterdam: Hakkert, 1963), 1. 124–25.

6

"MAGIC" AND "MYSTERY" IN

THE WORKS OF KENNETH BURKE

JANE BLANKENSHIP

A central part of the "legacy" of Kenneth Burke is his powerful treatment of language as constitutive of social reality. He has long tried to make us ever aware that, as symbol users and symbol creators, we are the instruments of our instrument (language). Many writers have pointed to the role of language in constituting self, institutions, culture, but Kenneth Burke approaches this study from a unique vantage point. In his analysis of language as constitutive of "reality," Burke's stress is not merely on the descriptive; his stress, rather, is on the suasive nature of all nomenclatures, including those of the sciences—on the "Thou shalt" (or shalt not) rather than merely on the "It is" (or is not). Moreover, although Burke's logological approach to the study of words about words is decidedly secular, he draws heavily from the resources of the study of words about the Word; that is, from theological explanations of creation. Further, Burke is not simply a philosopher-critic, but also a creative artist who has, himself, written poetry, short stories, music, and a novel.

This essay maintains that "magic" and "mystery" can be considered synoptic terms around (under) which we can place much of Kenneth Burke's work, particularly his theory of "entitlement" and his treatment of "social mystery." A secondary focus of this essay is to note Burke's "uses" of another philosopher-critic and creative artist, Samuel Taylor Coleridge, who with Burke not only acknowledges but celebrates the function of magic and mystery in human story. Burke's interest in Coleridge is both methodological and substantive. Although Burke's debt to Marx and Freud, among others, has been widely discussed, the Coleridgean influence has received little attention. That influence is nowhere more profoundly manifest than in Burke's treatment of "magic" and "mystery."

Magic

A defining characteristic of magic is that the magician pronounces the magic *words* and from "nothing," "something" appears. The act of magic par excellence is that of God's verbal fiat: "Let there be and there was." Burke is everywhere aware of the "dim analogue" between that act and the human act, i.e., a universe created by God and a universe of discourse. Whether by God or by ordinary mortals, each is "spoken into being" by fiat or decree. Thus, in both the sacred and the secular realms, the act of "naming" is creative. For example, in "Theology and Logology," Burke reminds us: "The story of creation in Genesis is an account of successive verbal fiats."[1] As regards the creative in the secular world, in *The Philosophy of Literary Form* he speaks of an "establishment or management by decree [which] says, in effect: 'Let there be'--and there was."[2] This parallel receives its most extended treatment in *The Rhetoric of Religion*. While the emphasis in the following essay is on the secular side of fiats, it is to Burke's discourses on logology and theology that we turn to appreciate most fully the magical principle "implicit in" fiat (*RR*, "Theology and Logology," pp. 151-84). We begin by examining the magical functions of such entitlements.

ENTITLEMENT

Burke observes early in *The Philosophy of Literary Form* that "the magical decree is implicit in all language; for the mere act of naming an object or situation decrees that it is to be singled out as such-and-such rather than as something-other" (*PLF*, p. 4). The magical decree, he says, is different from the petition or prayer. Both "size up" reality, offering strategies for encompassing situations, but whereas the first commands, the second says "please."[3] To note how the command operates, "think of the difference in magic if you confront [a] situation *in the strategic name of* 'planned economy' or, employing a different strategy, *in the name of* 'regimentation.'"[4] Such "commands" direct our attention in one way rather than another.[5] As Coleridge observes, a word is "not to convey merely what a certain thing is, but the very passion and all the circumstances which were conceived as *constituting* the perception of the thing by the person who used the word."[6]

In "What Are the Signs of What? A Theory of 'Entitlement,'" Burke reverses the commonplace that words are the "signs" of things, so as to entertain the possibility that things are the "signs" of words.[7] Is it not the case, he argues, that verbal expression may sum up, or entitle, a nonverbal situation:

> since language derives its materials from the cooperative acts of men in sociopolitical orders, which are themselves held together by a vast network of verbally perfected meanings, might it not follow that man must perceive nature through the fog of symbol-ridden social structures that he has erected atop nature? Material things would thus be like outward manifestations of the forms which are imposed upon the intuiting of nature by language, and by the sociopolitical orders that are interwoven with language.(*LSA*, p. 378)

Again, Burke refers us to the analogue between the Sacred Word and the secular word. If the Word may be said to be "a mediatory principle between this world and the supernatural," then might not words be "a mediatory principle between ourselves and nature?" Just as we may think of "the Word as the bond between man and the supernatural," might not "words (and the social motives implicit in them) be the bond between man and the natural?" Or, to put it more squarely: Might not "nature be necessarily approached by us through the gift of the spirit of words?"(*LSA*, p. 378).

Having established this additional aspect of secular "entitlement" by virtue of word magic, of "naming," Burke would take us even further into ways in which the notion of secular "entitlement" resonates with the sacred "Entitlement" of the Word. Indeed, suggests Burke, might not human symbolic action, admittedly of a very special kind, change God himself? On this matter, Burke recalls a doctrine put forth by the Lutheran theologian Streigel

> who held that Christ's work on the Cross had the effect of changing God's attitude towards mankind, and that men born after the historical Christ can take advantage of this change. Here we have something like the conversion of God himself, brought about by Christ's sacrifice (a total action, a total passion). From the godlike nature came a godlike act that acted upon God himself. And as regards mankind, it amounts to a radical change in the very structure of the Universe, since it changed God's attitude towards men, and in God's attitude towards men resides the ultimate ground of human action.[8]

Implied by that grounding, as we shall see, is that we are the instruments of our linguistic devices; moreover, they have side effects not only on ourselves but on others. Says Burke, we are driven by a "terministic compulsion" to take terms "to the end of the line."

IMPLICATIONS OF ENTITLEMENT

Among the most powerful aspects of the magic of entitlement is its power to *discriminate*, and it is precisely at this point that Burke turns our attention to Coleridge as a "truly magical writer."[9]

Burke cites several reasons for this assessment. First, Coleridge is a master of "delightful discriminations" (Letter, May 26, 1982). Burke is particularly taken with his discrimination between "fancy" and "imagination" (Letter, May 26, 1982). Second, not only does Coleridge make "delightful discriminations" but he talks about their making. Third, not only does Coleridge talk about particular desynonymizings, but he treats of desynonymizing in general—that is, in principle.[10] Indeed, Burke points us to a footnote in Coleridge's *Biographia Literaria* to suggest the full impact of the second part of that awesome fiat "LET THERE BE—and there *was*." The footnote is a long one. It comes at a point in the *Biographia* when Coleridge refers to a "recent volume of synonymes." The footnote suggests: When a distinction is made between "two or more words, that had before been used promiscuously," and becomes "naturalized" and of "general currency," then "language itself, does as it were *think* for us."[11] Burke writes of this observation:

> I take it that the footnote...is Coleridge's words for what I mean by DISCRIMINATIONS, which are the logological equivalent of the "creativity" via words as proclaimed in the first chapter of Genesis, where God said "Let there be," *and there was.*
>
> When a new Discrimination becomes generally accepted, in effect from out that vast undefinable *Definiendum*, the "Universe," it has added a new detail to some "Universe of Discourse."
>
> I see my term, "Discrimination," as applicable to both sides of that basic dualism, non-symbolic motion and symbolic action. In the realm of non-symbolic motion an infinite number of "discriminations" is occurring constantly. At some spot, for instance, water is turning from its state as a liquid to a solid (ice) or a gas (steam), etc. Speech makes its own kind of discriminations when defining the relevant boiling and freezing points. And Coleridge's proposal to "desynonymize" the terms "fancy" and "imagination" is a discrimination wholly on the symbolism side.[12]

Characteristic of the human story is the capacity to discriminate between "the honest," "the mistaken," "the downright lie"—we have, after all, created them as three not one.[13] And we are stuck with our creations until we continue our human story with new discriminations. For as Burke points out:

> We are the instruments of our instrument. And we are necessarily susceptible to the particular ills that result from our powers in the ways of symbolicity. Yet, too, we are equipped in principle to join in the enjoying of all such quandaries, until the last time.[14]

Each discrimination made in human story has implications (directs *attention* to one field rather than another). And we are quick to spin out those implications into "terministic screens," for example:

> each of our scientific nomenclatures suggests its own special range of possible development, with specialists vowed to carry out these terministic possibilities to the extent of their personal ability and technical resources. Each such speciality is like the situation of an author who has an idea for a novel, and who will never rest until he has completely embodied it in a book. Insofar as any of these terminologies happen also to contain the risks of destroying the world, that's just too bad. (*LSA*, p. 19)

Of course, as Burke points out, all is not yet lost: "there is at least the fact that the schemes get in one another's way, thus being to some extent checked by rivalry with one another" (*LSA*, pp. 19–21).

Even checked by the rivalries of terms, there remains a special powerfulness about such "magic." Inherent in the logological principle of perfection, there is a "terministic compulsion": the need to spin out the implications of our terministic screens as far as they will go.[15] Thus, the symbol user continues on as symbol constructor with ever more elaborate (and frequently self-confirming) constructions.

Not infrequently, the symbol user, symbol maker "speaks" not merely in his own name but in that of the family, of a larger constituency, of a research paradigm, of "all 'right-thinking' persons everywhere," and so on.[16] And because of our terministic compulsion, we may carry out the entelechial principle in both science and poetry to the point of "bureaucratization of the imaginative."[17]

There is within our set of terministic screens a "vibrancy of interrelated IMPLICATIONS" which may conceal as well as reveal ("[Nonsymbolic] Motion," p. 821). In our various ways, we, like Odysseus, shield "from the Cyclops the knowledge of [our] name and hence the control of [our] person."[18] The "Negative" as Burke has pointed out, is a distinctly linguistic invention.[19] And the human retains in profound ways the right to say not merely a digital "Yes" or "No" but "Maybe" as well—with all of our tendencies toward "Yes and No."

Not only do our terministic constructions reveal and conceal, but they have several kinds of what Burke calls "side-effects" on the self (the creator) and on others. In his article "On 'Creativity'—A Partial Retraction," Burke suggests that sometimes unintended by-products are in a profound way a part of the poetic process, for when a creative person gives body to the "imaginative," an institutionalization occurs.[20] Or, another side effect: Consider the author whose engrossment with his own works has "brought him closer to the fictional life than the 'real one'—whose 'catharsis' is brought on by the very condition which he sought to expel."[21] Burke describes this process as a kind of autosuggestion: "My general notion is that terms are not merely suggestive in their effects upon the readers, but also autosuggestive in their affects upon the writers who get *used* by using them."[22] Consider here the awesomeness of Coleridge's suggestion in *Anima Poetae*: "The mind that may help to unravel it, 'feels' the riddle of the world."[23] These "side-effects" are evinced not only by the creator's self but by others as well.[24] Burke observes in "Theology and Logology":

> This logological principle of perfection (which I would call "entelechial," restricting the Aristotelian concept of the "entelechy" to the realm of nomenclature, "symbolicity") can also be seen to operate in areas which we do not ordinarily associate with the idea of perfection, except in such loose usages as "perfect fool" or "perfect villain." But its powers along that line are terrifying. It showed up repeatedly in theological charges of heresy, in which the heretics were nearly always saddled with the same list of hateful vices. And in our day the Nazis did the most outrageous job with "perfection" in that sense by the thoroughness of their charges against the Jew. It takes very little inducement for us to begin "perfecting" the characters of our opponents by the gratuitous imputation of unseemly motives. Thus, all told, in my logological definition of humankind, I put a high rating on my clause, "rotten with perfection." Satan was as perfect as entelechy in one sense as Christ was in another. Doubtless Machiavelli was thinking along those lines when he told his Prince that, whereas one should be wary of hiring mercenaries, the way to get the best fighters is make the war a holy war. (P. 155)

We thus begin to glimpse the dangerous "magic" of terministic implications; frequently laden with more and more personal and institutional vested interests, they are particularly dangerous when they become imbued with an aura of the sacred. For a hint of the full range of what Burke is getting at here consider the several kinds of "toxic waste dumps" we have created for ourselves. Our association of perfection with waste, and the pride with which we advertise our "reclamation projects."

In "Towards Helhaven: Three Stages of a Vision," Burke lets us glimpse what may happen when humans are reduced to instrumentalities of their own making.[25] In Helhaven, we can live completely removed from our natural condition. Burke asks us to face up squarely to "the problem of how life on earth can manage to survive the burdens of world-wide pollution that plague the ways of industrial progress" ("Towards Helhaven," p. 19). Just as Burke has argued that humans are goaded by "terministic compulsion," so he argues that technology "is an ultimate direction indigenous to Bodies That Learn Language, which thereby interactively develop a realm of artificial instruments under... symbolic guidance."[26] Surely his vision of technology "as a compulsion" suggests new dimensions to his notion that it is possible to become "rotten with perfection" (*PC*, p. 296, "Theology and Logology," p. 155).

In sum, as human story evolves, we desynonymize, we name, that is we make "discriminations." There is a magical decree implicit in all naming; the decree, the verbal fiat "Let there be," is a command to act in one way rather than another toward that which is named.

Each discrimination has implications both for the creator of the discrimination and for others. We humans, driven by a kind of "terministic compulsion," tend to carry these implications "to the end of the line," checked only by sometimes competing sets of implications and the resonance of interrelated implications.

As humans, we may "talk," we may talk about talk, and we may talk about that which is not talk. Burke suggests that verbal expressions "sum up" nonverbal situations and that, as humans, we have constituted, symbolically, a social structure through which we perceive nature; that is, our words operate as a mediatory principle between ourselves and nature. Thus, he asks us to consider not only that words be the "signs" of things but that things may be said to be the "signs" of words. Such an "entitlement" as that may be magical, indeed.

Mystery

Were humans to exist only in the realm of nature, we might have begun this essay by examining the other key term in our title, Mystery. For one can argue that as bodies we are born into this world separated from each other, and in this sense profoundly mysterious to each other, unique in our solitary existence. Still, humans also exist in the realm of symbolic action. While nature's story existed before we were born and may well exist after we are gone, human story came into being with the first creative verbal fiat. With that fiat, social mystery came into the world. This portion of the paper is largely about social mystery, about our estrangement from and reconciliation with each other as humans. But first let us indicate how Burke places social mystery within an even larger setting.

Human story, for Burke, is a story of estrangements (mystifications) and reconciliations (demystifications). He sees us as at once a part of nature and at the same time separated from it by instruments of our own making (symbols). Although we are mostly concerned, in this piece, with human story, there also exists a story that nature itself is engaged in telling; this (extrahuman) story began without us and will likely continue without us.[27] Much of nature's story thus remains a mystery to us. Our world is not "merely" a world of (nonsymbolic) motion; it never can be fully that.[28] Thus, we may re-turn (laden with our symbol system) to nature, but we cannot return to it because our efforts at deciphering nature's plot are ultimately but reflections of our own story.

We are separated not only from the natural world but from the supernatural world as well, whether secularly, as Burke is, by dwelling in a world of logology (words about the *word*), rather than in a world of theology (words about the Word), or "sacredly," as Coleridge is by his fervent pursuit of the cosmic mystery, the enigma.[29] The supernatural is, as Burke reminds us, "by definition, *outside* the realm of Nature."[30] Even though we have the capacity for symbolic action, as bodies we remain in nature along with those creatures with the capacity only for nonsymbolic motion. Since there can be no (symbolic) action without (nonsymbolic) motion, we share nonsymbolic motion with all living creatures.[31] Thus, our estrangement from the supernatural may be even more profound, more "mysterious," than our estrangement from nature.

The Coleridge connection here has both substantive and methodological dimensions. Just as both men's sense of the magical functions of language pervades their works, so each acknowledges, even celebrates, the functions of mystery in any full understanding of language and the human condition.

Burke seems particularly attracted to two dimensions of Coleridge's treatment of mystery, first, to the palpably close relationship of the natural and supernatural and the role that closeness plays in the creative process, and, second, to the underlying dialectic of Coleridge's discussion of this matter.[32] Coleridge's poems of "fascination" reveal directly his interest in the relationship between the natural and the supernatural, from the enchantments of his childhood readings of _The Arabian Nights_, through journeys into haunted caves and the enchanted realms of Tamar, Christabel and Kubla Khan, to the nightmare terrors of the enigma so much at the center of this concern for the mysterious. Indeed, it is the cosmic mystery, God, whom Coleridge pursued most fervently.[33]

It is possible, for example, to read Coleridge's "Christabel" as a story merely of "supernatural elements":

> The night is chill; the forest bare;
> Is it the wind that moaneth bleak?
> There is not wind enough in the air
> To move away the ringlet curl
> From the lovely lady's cheek.
> There is not wind enough to twirl
> The one red, leaf, the last of its clan
> That dances as often as dance it can,
>
> Hanging so light, and hanging so high
> On the topmost twig that looks up at the sky.
>
> Hush, beating heart of Christabel!
> Jesu Maria, shield her well!
> She folded her arms beneath her cloak,
> And stole to the other side of the oak.
>   What sees she there?[34]

But it does not take us long to realize what is concealed beneath "the small revelations which every now and then take place."[35] The leap is not hard to make between Christabel's story and the human story "of the spiritual estrangement that [we must all] undergo, and which swallows some of us forever."[36] In _Attitudes towards History_, Burke points out how Coleridge may have understood very _palpably_ the mysterious: "The terror that runs through his poems...gives evidence that he was close to the 'trembling veil' of the "secret," [Coleridge's] particular core of mystery and mystification" (*AH*, p. 183).

Burke's two longest forays into Coleridge's mystery poems (or poems of "fascination") are his piece on *Kubla Khan*, reprinted in *Language as Symbolic Action*, and his equally well known piece in *The Philosophy of Literary Form* on Coleridge's "great watershed" poem, *The Rime of the Ancient Mariner*. The first focuses on the creative process; the second turns our attention to the alchemic moment of transcendent communion with other creatures and with God.

Burke is attracted not only to Coleridge's mystery poems but to his concern with permanence and change and to their underlying dialectic. The "cosmogony of good and evil" provides the grounds for much of Coleridge's writings of whatever genre; throughout his life he was to speak of "the Terrors...that precede God's love" (*PLF*, p. 99). The law of bipolarity, or bicentrality, informs much of his methodology and his terminology. Moreover, as Fogle points out, bipolarity is no sometime and no rigid mechanical juggling act.[37] True opposites "must be essential each to the other"; the "reconciliation of opposites" must be always centrally at hand.[38] Fogle goes on to point out that, for Coleridge, "reality is always organic unity or wholeness, but this reality can only be discursively revealed as two, in the form of polar opposites reconciled, or of centripetal and centrifugal forces in equilibrium."[39]

At almost every turn in Burke's work we are required to face up to the matters of "polarity," "duality." Early on in his writing, in *Attitudes toward History*, he observes:

> Man is "dualistic" at least in the sense that his sleeping self is radically dissociated from his waking self. Each morning and each night, he crosses and recrosses a threshold, thereby changing his identity.
>
> To an extent, therefore, mystery and mystification seem inevitable. Every man has his "secret," an awe too deep for the boldness and shrewdness of rational verbalization. There is the "trembling veil" of sleep, which he cannot draw without risk, usually being content, sometime before midnight, to curl himself up like an embryo, and abandon himself to that vague area of experience which, in the filing systems of day, we must put in a folder marked "Miscellaneous." (*AH*, pp. 180-81)

But he is also much concerned with the dramatistic view of life as a series of "mergers and divisions," just as the Coleridgean would look at art and life as a tension between "unity and multeity."[40]

Jane Blankenship

Burke writes: "Coleridge, as dialectician, knew there must be a concept of 'one' behind a concept of 'many,' or a concept of 'many' behind a concept of 'one.' Each implies the other. However, a radical difference in stress or accent, is possible here. You may emphasize unity in *diversity*, or you may emphasize *unity* in diversity" (*GM*, p. 400). Burke approvingly quotes Coleridge further on the difficulties of "one": "But as little can we conceive the oneness, except as the midpoint producing itself on each side; that is, manifesting itself on two opposite poles. Thus from identity we derive duality, and from both together we obtain polarity, synthesis, indifference, predominance" (*GM*, p. 412). And so we come to those famous Burkean notions of the reconciliation of opposites, and perspective by incongruity.

In the *Rhetoric of Motives*, Burke also talks of Coleridge's "systematic dissociation of [ideas]" and the "kinds of methodological oxymoron" from which his predecessor works, of "illustrating total unity by fragmentary examples" (p. 70). Coleridge himself attests to the accuracy of Burke's observation when he points out that his own thought is "like a kaleidoscope" in attempting to "reduce all the miscellaneous fragments into order."[41] Coleridge says in *Anima Poetae*:

> I would make a pilgrimage to the deserts of Arabia to find the man who could make me understand how the *one can be many*. Eternal, universal mystery! It seems as if it were impossible, yet it *is*, and it is everywhere! It is indeed a contradiction in *terms*, and only in terms. It is the co-presence of feeling and life, limitless by their very essence, with form by its very essence limited, determinable, definite.[42]

THE ORIGINS OF MYSTERY

What are the origins of mystery? One might be tempted to answer, "in the human condition," and suggest looking about everywhere in Burke for the answers. But Burke himself is clear about where we should start.

Beginning with the "purely physiological aspect of the Self (its grounding in the realm of motion)" as "characterized by the centrality of the nervous system" and separated at birth from others (the principle of 'individuation')" Burke moves us to the "Self as a 'person,' member of a community (Culture) characterized by motives in the realm of Symbolic action" ("Motion, Action," p. 83). He argues: "Whatever may be the genetic traits differentiating one individual from another, and whatever the distinct histories of individuals, the nature of symbolic action shapes the Self largely in modes of roles, of sociality" (enmeshed in notions of "remembrances or expectations," of memory and anticipation) ("Motion, Action," p. 83). In a profound way, the "nonsymbolic motions of springtime are *completed* in the symbolic action of a spring song" ("Motion, Action," p. 93, emphasis added). "The body...provides a PRINCIPLE OF INDIVIDUATION that is GROUND in the CENTRALITY OF THE NERVOUS SYSTEM. But this SEPARATENESS as a PHYSIOLOGICAL ORGANISM is 'TRANSCENDED' by the peculiar COLLECTIVE SOCIAL NATURE OF HUMAN-SYMBOL-SYSTEMS" ("Logology: Over-All View"). In sum, in "Towards a Transcendent Immanence" Burke suggests:

> Being physiologically endowed with the ability to learn an arbitrary, conventional symbol-system such as familial, tribal language, the organism matures in a realm of symbolic action, its so-called "mind" or "consciousness" being developed by such essentially public, "socialized," resources, and highly sensitive to the many discordances that are associated with the complexities and contradictions of civilization. We are "composite" creatures, living a dualistic way of life such as "dumb" animals presumably do not experience.[43]

Mystery is, thus, inherent in the generic biological divisiveness of human beings. Still, through our own invention, our human symbol system, we may become consubstantial; that is, similar but not identical; only angels communicate perfectly, or so Burke teases us (*RM*, p. 21). Mystery is inescapable whenever different kinds of beings are in communication. "Strangeness" is a prerequisite for "mystery." However, the "estranged must...be thought of as in some way *capable* of communion"(*RM*, p. 115).

Mystery is also inherent in the very nature of language wherein symbol systems may be grounded in nonsymbolic motion but where motion need not be grounded in symbolic action unless one carries "to the very end" the argument that words are the signs of things and argues that nonsymbolic motion is a "thing" constructed by symbol users. Burke does not really argue that; nor even does he argue "for" that level of "perfectability" in his theory of "entitlement." Rather, he argues, that "mystery is inescapable insofar as...symbol-systems are necessarily inadequate for the *ab intra* description of the nonsymbolic" (*RR*, pp. 307-8).

Mystery is inherent in the nature of language in yet another sense, in that by our discriminations we direct attention to one place rather than another. Terministic screens, if carried out with any vigor at all, may produce a "trained incapacity" that may unconsciously or consciously provoke estrangement. Mystery is inescapable because of "the peculiar range of intelligent ignorance" (_RR_, p. 309). Moreover, "different modes of being and living as rightly or wrongly are felt to imply different modes of thought" (_RR_, p. 309).

Not only is mystery inherent in language but it is also inherent in the nature of human knowledge. In _The Rhetoric of Religion_, Satan asks TL (The Lord): "That is, the makings of 'mystery' are to be found in any lack of knowledge?" TL replies, "Yes, by sheer definition, tautologically" (_RR_, p. 308). Mystery is "inescapable" because factual knowledge is necessarily fragmentary (_RR_, pp. 307–8).

Further, mystery is inherent in the nature of the _principle_ of "perfectability." We are always going from-through-to somewhere, unless we have managed to "bureaucratize the imaginative." Then we may be said to be at a _landing_ in our up and down "ladder" in the Dialectic of the Upward and Downward Way, but it is unlikely in _any_ event that we will go straight up or straight down; rather we will take a step up and several down or a step down and several up in our attempts to reach perfectability at either end. Burke seems to "save" us from perfectability in either direction by small and large "teases," by assuming the comic attitude toward the human condition.[44]

THE KINDS OF MYSTERIES

Burke argues that mystery's origins are everywhere (_PC_, p. 283). In an appendix to _Permanence and Change_, Burke reiterates his interest in the realm of "social mystery" (with its concerns for "Bureaucracy," "Hierarchy," "Order," "Authority" and "Propriety") but also reminds us of "the mysteries of dream, of creation, of death, of life's stages, of thought (its arising, its remembering, its diseases). There are the mysteries of adventure and love" (_PC_, pp. 227, 283). Many hints at the kinds of mystery are scattered through _A Rhetoric of Motives_ and _Permanence and Change_; for example, Burke suggests that there is mystery in the "secrecy of plans during gestation," or "fears that arise from the sense of limits," or in the "infancy of the 'unconscious,' nonverbal, postverbal and subverbal," or "in the very perfection of formal thinking," or in "bureaucracy", or in "_any_ pronounced social distinctions, as between nobility and commoners, courtiers and king, leader and people, rich and poor, judge and prisoner at the bar"—that is, in "_class distinctions_" (_RM_, pp. 115, 122, 180, 232; _PC_, p. 277). In short, as Burke says in the _Grammar_, "the mystery of the hierarchic is forever within us...and...let us observe, all about us, forever goading us, though it be in fragments" (_RM_, p. 333).

One more mystery perhaps implicit in some of the others needs to be pointed to quite squarely. Hierarchical mystery is inherent in the nature of the "turn from polytheism to monotheism" (*RR*, p. 310), for then the Mystery becomes the All (or, as Coleridge would remind us here, the *Whole*). And human knowledge, although capable of a variety of ways of coping with unity and diversity, merger and division through "creative circumferencing" and the like, remains *human* knowledge. It remains "fragmentary"; otherwise it would be divine knowledge. Human story would then become divine story, and Burke, being interested in the dialectical, may well be supremely uncomfortable and out of sorts in talking merely about the divine story.

These considerations provide us with our grounding in the term "mystery/Mystery." And now we may turn briefly to social mystery, whether as reinforced by connotations of cosmic mystery or as figuring the divine (cosmic) mystery. Although these two considerations pop up throughout Burke's works (including his forays into the works of Coleridge), they are perhaps most clearly explicated, in the first instance, in Burke's treatment of E. M. Forster's *A Passage to India*, and, in the second instance, in his treatment of Kafka in *A Rhetoric of Motives* (*LSA*, pp. 223–39; *RM*, pp. 118, 233–44).

Everywhere (very early) we are reminded that mystery functions to reveal (as when we are initiated into the mysteries) and conceal (as when we are "kept in the dark"); to facilitate congregation and segregation and/or "congregation by segregation" as Burke calls it in *Dramatism and Development*. Mystery works both as a "passive reflection of class culture and as an active way of maintaining cultural cohesion" (*DD*, p. 29).

At every turn we are led to know that the human story is a story not only of "holocausts" but of "identification" and "transcendence" as well, and it is with this latter term that we end this essay. We have, of course, at least skirted the notion of "transcendence" for some time now, and Burke and Coleridge are always bumping into one another about it. Not unexpectedly, it is in *The Rhetoric of Religion* that Burke points us to *Notes on the Pilgrim's Progress*, where Coleridge discusses his "dialectic pentad," his "*Dramatistic Grammar* at considerable length."[45] Says Burke:

> In an *ultimate* dialectic, the terms so lead into one another that the completion of each order leads to the next. Thus, a body of positive terms must be brought to a head in a titular term which represents the principle or idea behind the positive terminology as a whole. This summarizing term is in a different order of vocabulary. And if such titles, having been brought into dialectical commerce with one another, are given an order among themselves, there must be a principle of principles

> involved in such a design--and the step from principles to a
> principle of principles is likewise both the fulfillment of the
> previous order and the transcending of it. (*RM*, p. 189,
> emphasis added)

Coleridge's concern for secular-sacred transformation permeated his works, whether in prose or poetic writings. Throughout his writing and his life, as Burke reminds us, Coleridge hoped for some kind of "spontaneous virtue and the total act" (*GM*, p. 370). He sought it via sacred conversion and in his plans for a better life in a utopian, or perfect, community on the banks of the Susquehanna River (*GM*, pp. 368–71). *Towards a Better Life* is, not so coincidentally, the title of Burke's novel, and his early hopes for secular communities which would variously modify "private property in the direction of possessions that were jointly owned or jointly served" are similarly utopian.[46] Although less directly than Coleridge in his talk of a personal religious transformation, Burke agrees that "theological notions of creation and re-creation bring us nearest to the concept of total acts" (*GM*, p. 19). In a piece in the *Journal of General Education*, Burke talks persuasively of the Dialectics of the Upward and Downward Way.[47] He points out that after the ascent, there will be "a descent, a Downward Way, back into the world of particulars, all of which would now be 'identified' with the genius of the unitary principle discovered en route ("Rhetoric—Old and New," p. 204). *Precisely* because of his verbal journey, "all would be thus made consubstantial by participation in a common essence, as with objects bathed in the light of the one sun, that shines down upon them as from the apex of a pyramid" ("Rhetoric—Old and New," p. 204). One gets the distinct impression that Burke might be happier, having glimpsed that principle of oneness to return, at least from time to time, to the "purgatorial" realm of dialectic.[48] Still, whether in the secular or the sacred realm, "faith," as Coleridge observed in *The Friend*, "is a total act of the soul."[49] Both Coleridge and Burke, however, are abundantly aware that

> the very *wish* for wholeness is derived from partiality—hence
> could only be attained through the unity of all men with one
> another and all mankind with the universe. We must aim at
> congregation by devices making for segregation—*peace* is
> something we must *fight* for. The more perfect the end, the
> correspondingly more imperfect the means. (*GM*, p. 370).

Both Coleridge and Burke seek after those alchemic moments in which transcendence is possible, and, for that ultimate act of transcendence during which we, like Coleridge's "loathsome water-snakes, are proclaimed blessed and beautiful" (*PLF*, p. 63). Where more fittingly than in that great "watershed poem," the *Rime of the Ancient Mariner*, and where but in that great "watershed moment"—in the middle "where it should be"—would Burke direct us to look for so "radical a bit of alchemy" to take place? (*PLF*, p. 71 ff.) After all, "alchemy," Coleridge tells us, "is the theoretic end of chemistry: there must be a common law, upon which all can become each, and each all."[50] Where better to leave our co-authors than working at that "omnivum gatherum," celebrating with Coleridge a "communion with the universe"[51] and mindful of Burke's observation that the negative is a linguistic invention created by man and now extends via other "technologies" to still more treacherous inventions with which we have polluted the universe. These, after all, are inventions of our own making and perhaps shall be of our remaking particularly if we understand their vital nature. As Coleridge observed in his *Biographia*, "the thinking spirit within me may be substantially one with the principle of life, and of vital operation."[52] And, as Burke observes in his short story "Herone Liddell": "Meanwhile, I comb the beach for the wrench-like shape such as I dreamed of. . . . If I could dream it, the sea can make it--and having made it, the sea can toss it up."[53]

Conclusion

Kenneth Burke has long tried to make us understand the magic implicit in language as symbolic action and to make us recognize that while we are using language, it is using us. His theory of entitlement helps show us how this is so. Moreover, his treatment of specific "entitlements" (single terms, single works, or cultural "decrees") shows us the implications of those entitlements, reminding us vividly of how powerful our "discriminations," our verbal "fiats," our "magic" can be both on others and on ourselves. And he does more.

Burke's treatment of linguistic entitlements points out clearly that our own "fiats" exist in the larger human story of estrangements (mystifications) and reconciliations (demystifications) involving our relationships with nature, the supernatural, and our fellow human beings. He has provided us glimpses of the dark holocausts we have created and also set before us the moments of transcendent communion of which we are capable with our verbal "magic."

Burke reminds us that "mystery" resides in the human condition from the moment we are born into this world a separate physiological organism, but as humans, as "bodies that learn language," we have devised a peculiarly collective social nature by means of our symbol

Jane Blankenship

systems. And we have done this despite the inadequacy of symbols for the *ab intra* description of the nonsymbolic, despite the fragmentariness of "factual knowledge," and despite our propensity toward "trained incapacity." Along the way, Burke has also taken the time to illuminate not only one or two "mysteries" (e.g., "bureaucracy," "authority," "order"), but many others as well (e.g., "adventure" and "love," the fears that "arise from the sense of limits," the fears of contemplating "forever").

In his treatments of "mystery," as in his treatment of "magic," Burke also treats of the resonance between the secular and the sacred in illuminating instances in which social mystery is reinforced by connotations of cosmic mystery and instances in which it figures the divine mystery.

Through his treatment of "magic" and "mystery" and their very intimate, indeed circular, connections, Burke draws from many sources, but there seems, to this author at least, a special relationship between Burke and his sometime partner in dialogue, Samuel Taylor Coleridge. They are by no means identical in their treatment of these two very powerful terms, but these two philosophers/critics/creative artists do share some central substantive and methodological ideas which Burke often and explicitly points to in his work. Together they remind us that if we have the profound propensity via our linguistic entitlements to constitute estrangements, we also have the sometime knack for creating alchemic moments which allow us to transcend divisiveness. We will, perhaps, be better able to do that if we remember Burke's observations that to think of language as merely a "tool" is both inaccurate and potentially dangerous. As he says: "You can lay a tool down but you can't lay language down. . . . [Your] own vocabulary hypnotizes you. . . . I believe, absolutely, you do get hooked to a vocabulary. If you really do live with your terms, they turn up tricks of their own. You can't get around them. . . . [*They*] *use you*."[54] Burke's treatment of "magic" and "mystery" allows us to glimpse something of how and with what results such "use" occurs. "Coming to terms" with "terms" is, thus, an enduring part of Kenneth Burke's legacy to us.

NOTES

1. Kenneth Burke, "Theology and Logology," *Kenyon Review* n.s, 1 (1979), 153. In this respect, in *The Rhetoric of Religion* (Berkeley: University of California Press, 1970), Burke points out that Coleridge held a "semisecularized view of poetic production as . . . a 'dim analogue of Creation' "(p. 8). Col-

eridge, himself, in *Anima Poetae*, ed., Ernest Hartley Coleridge (Boston: Houghton Mifflin, 1895), admonishes us: "Admit for a moment that 'conceive' is equivalent to creation in the divine nature, synonymous with 'to beget'...admit this, and all difficulty ceases, all tumult is hushed, all is clear and beautiful. (p. 33)"

2. Kenneth Burke, *The Philosophy of Literary Form*, 3d ed. (Berkeley: University of California Press, 1973), p. 3.

3. *PLF*, p. 4. There (p. 5), he also notes: "It is difficult to keep the magical decree and the religious petition totally distinct."

4. *PLF*, p. 4. See also Kenneth Burke, "(Nonsymbolic) Motion/(Symbolic) Action," *Critical Inquiry*, 4 (1978), 809–38. Burke, indeed, extends the suasive nature of language even to "the most unemotional scientific nomenclatures." *Language as Symbolic Action* (Berekley: University of California Press, 1966), p. 45.

5. Burke also notes that the rhetor not only "commands" others to direct attention to see one way rather than another, but "commands" himself as well.

6. Samuel Taylor Coleridge, *Shakespeare Criticism*, ed. Middleton Raysor (London: Dutton, 1907), 2.74.

7. Kenneth Burke "What Are the Signs of What?" in *LSA*, pp. 359–79.

8. Kenneth Burke, *A Grammar of Motives* (Berkeley: University of California Press, 1969), pp. 19–20.

9. Letter from Kenneth Burke, May 26, 1982. Burke's special interest in Coleridge began rather early in his career and continues to this date. He "began working in earnest" on Coleridge in 1938 (*PLF*, p. xi). He tells us: "I got into Coleridge...by a kind of accident. I was asked to give a course for a summer session at the University of Chicago. I chose Coleridge; but at the time I had no notion of the gradual fascination that would take on as I began wending my way through the whole of the Shedd edition" (Letter, May 26, 1982). By 1939, Burke was writing in the *New Republic* "Each time I note the signs of the elite boom for Kierkegaard and Kafka, I am disgruntled. It should be Coleridge. Most assuredly it should be Coleridge" ("Why Coleridge?" *New Republic*, 13 [September 1939]: 163). He speculates: "[I suspect] it is largely because we are all compelled to read his poem [*Rime of the Ancient Mariner*] in high school, that those lesser figures are focusing attention at his expense" ("Why Coleridge?" p. 163). Burke himself is direct about what he thinks of this: "anyone who snoots him to that extent I class as a slob (or I'll settle for 'sadly uninformed')" (Letter, May 26, 1982).

Burke's attachment to Coleridge was "special" not only at the early stages of his career but later as well. Indeed, his "use" of Coleridge is still in progress. He observes that he recently just "noticed" a footnote in *Biographia* which lately he has been "referring to clamorously" (Letter, May 26, 1982).

When asked directly about his "uses" of Coleridge, Burke writes: "Garsh! I have referred to Coleridge in all the ways I related to him [in print]....Just leaf through Earnest Hartley Coleridge's collection, *Anima*

Jane Blankenship

Poetae, or the *Table Talk,* and you'll get the quality of Coleridge's 'usefulness.' " And, of course, tucked away in the advice are those devastating parenthetical comments, e.g., "(And by all means *note* the *footnote* to the...Shawcross edition of [*Biographia*], Vol. I, p. 63....I tie this in with 'discrimination' and 'universes of discourse,' as per...'Logology: Over-All View...' " He notes: "My seven volumes of the Shedd edition are 'indexed' to the point of morbidity."

10. Letter from Kenneth Burke, May 26, 1982. In *A Rhetoric of Motives* (Berkeley: University of California Press, 1969), Burke observes: "Coleridge's 'desynonymizing' of 'fancy' and 'imagination' was in part an attempt to dissociate these two meanings, leave for 'fancy'...the purely 'mechanical' recombinations of sensory experience, and giving to 'imagination'...creative and super-sensory meanings" (p. 79).

11. S. T. Coleridge, *Biographia Literaria,* ed. J. Shawcross (1907; rpt. Oxford: University Press, 1967), 1. 63.

12. Letter from Kenneth Burke, May 10, 1982. In a letter of 26 May 1982, he uses the phrase "the infinite wordless universe."

13. Kenneth Burke, "Logology: Over-All View," a one-page mimeographed summary sometimes provided by Burke when people ask him what logology is all about. Undated. Reprinted in *Communication Quarterly,* 33 (Winter 1985), 31-32.

LOGOLOGY: OVER-ALL VIEW

LANGUAGE IS:

THE ARBITRARY CONVENTIONAL COLLECTIVE MEDIUM OF EXPRESSION AND COMMUNICATION (WITH CORRESPONDING MODES OF ATTENTION, OR STORE OF SYMBOL-GUIDED DISCRIMINATION) MOST AMPLY EQUIPPED TO DISCUSS ITSELF AND ALL OTHER SUCH MEDIUMS.

ITS THREE OFFICES ARE: TO INFORM, PLEASE, AND MOVE THOSE PERSONS WHO ARE FAMILIAR WITH ITS CONVENTIONS.

BY ITS RANGE OF NOMENCLATURES (IN THE REALM OF SYMBOLIC ACTION) IT HAS COMPREHENSIVELY ORGANIZED, IN WAYS STILL BEING DEVELOPED, THE STUDY OF ITS NONSYMBOLIC GROUND (THE REALM OF SHEER MOTION) AND OF THE SITUATIONS, PROCESSES, AND RELATIONSHIPS THAT CONSTITUTE THE COMPLEX OF SYMBOLIC AND NONSYMBOLIC FACTORS AFFECTING ALL HUMAN CONDUCT.

It is the medium best suited to speculating on the possible best definition of ourselves.

The second clause is borrowed from Cicero (on the three offices of the orator).

***

"Magic" and "Mystery" in the Works of Kenneth Burke

THIS VIEW IMPLIES ALWAYS A DUAL RELATIONSHIP:

A COMPREHENSIVE UNDEFINABLE *DEFINIENDUM,* HERE
CALLED THE INFINITE WORDLESS UNIVERSE WITH THE
COUNTLESS UNIVERSES OF DISCOURSE THAT STORY CAN
MAKE OF IT

(AND FROM THEN ON
ALL IS DOUBLE)

We assume a time when our primal ancestors became able to go from
SENSATIONS to WORDS for *SENSATION.* (When they could duplicate the experience of tasting an orange by saying "the taste of an
orange," that was *WHEN STORY CAME INTO THE WORLD.*)

Whereas Nature can do no wrong (whatever it does is "Nature") with
Story there enters the realm of the true, false, honest, mistaken, the
downright lie, the imaginative, the fanciful, the speculative, the visionary.

***

BY LEARNING LANGUAGE THE HUMAN BODY, A COMPOSITE CREA-
TURE, COMBINES THE REALMS OF NONSYMBOLIC MOTION AND
SYMBOLIC ACTION.

The body thus provides a PRINCIPLE OF INDIVIDUATION that is
GROUND in the CENTRALITY OF THE NERVOUS SYSTEM. But
this SEPARATENESS as a PHYSIOLOGICAL ORGANISM is "TRAN-
SCENDED" by the peculiar COLLECTIVE SOCIAL NATURE OF
HUMAN SYMBOL-SYSTEMS.

***

There's a strictly *logological* counterpart of "magic." It *empirically* matches
the creative word in the first chapter of Genesis where each decree said
" 'Let there be'—and there was." See first parenthesis above referring to
discriminations. For all *discriminations* in the purely symbolic realm, the Universes of Discourse, are by definition "creative" but being creatures of sheer
symbolicity. And such nomenclatures constitute a realm of *discriminations*
that human STORY brought into the world. But in time that will all be
gone, thus undoing Emerson's complaint, "A believer in Unity, a seer of
Unity, I yet behold two," while the realm of nonsymbolic motion continues
to discriminate in ways of its own.

14. *LSA*, p. viii. See also p. 46: *"many of the 'observations' are but implica-*
tions of the particular terminology in terms of which the observations are made."

In "Theology and Logology," p. 154, he refers us to Anselm's interpretation of Isaiah 7:9, "Believe, that you may understand. . . ."

15. *LSA*, pp. 46–47. In the same work, p. 19: "A given terminology contains various *implications*, and there is a corresponding 'perfectionist' tendency for [us] to attempt carrying out those implications."

16. Some of Burke's most powerful insights on this point are tied to his "ecological" writings. Long an ecologist, Burke came, for example, to realize how mighty our "resources of guilt" are and to note how master polluters of all sorts (e.g., Hitler) claim to act "in the name of" cleansing. Thus, we "purify" our water, "re-move" our toxic wastes, "save" our energy, and talk about "clean" bombs all the while demanding our "freedom to waste and pollute" and to seek after new ways of "perfecting" ourselves.

17. Kenneth Burke, *Attitudes toward History* (Boston: Beacon Press, 1961), pp. 225–28.

18. Anya Taylor, *Magic and English Romanticism* (Athens: University of Georgia Press, 1979), p. 5.

19. *LSA*, pp. 9–13. See also Kenneth Burke, "A Dramatistic View of the Origin of Language," *Quarterly Journal of Speech*, 37 (1952), 251–64, 446–60; 38 (1953), 72–92, and "Postscript on the Negative," *Quarterly Journal of Speech*, 38 (1953), 209–16.

20. Kenneth Burke, "On 'Creativity'—A Partial Retraction," *Introspection: The Author Looks at Himself*, University of Tulsa Monograph Series, No. 12 (1971), p. 78.

21. Paraphrase by Eric Metcalf upon reading "On 'Creativity'—A Partial Retraction." See also Burke, "Theology and Logology," p. 163, regarding the role of Proust's "psychogenic" asthma and (p. 182) regarding Nietzsche's "restless hankerings." Further, see *PLF*, p. 65, regarding "homeopathic magic" capable of "transforming poisons into medicines."

22. "On 'Creativity' " p. 78. Burke's fundamental notion of bodies that learn language is so profound that, in *Permanence and Change*, 3d ed. (Berkeley: University of California Press, 1984), p. 73, he talks of Darwin's vertigo as a result of the misalignments between his emotional and intellectual attitudes toward his developing theory of evolution.

23. Coleridge, *Anima Poetae*, p. 51. See also *PC*, p. 73.

24. See *PC*, p. 75, Burke's discussion of "piety" as "a response which extends through all the texture of our lives. . . ."

25. Kenneth Burke, "Towards Helhaven: Three Stages of a Vision," *Sewanee Review*, 79 (1971), 11–25, and Burke's "Why Satire, with a Plan for Writing One," *Michigan Quarterly Review*, 13 (1974), 307–37.

26. *PC*, p. 296. See also, Kenneth Burke, "Archetype and Entelechy," *Dramatism and Development* (Worcester, Mass.: Clark University Press, 1972), especially pp. 53–54. See also Burke, "Rhetoric, Poetics, and Philosophy," in Don M. Burks, ed., *Rhetoric, Philosophy and Literature: An Exploration* (West Lafayette, Ind.: Purdue University Press, 1978), p. 33: "Now owing to technology's side-effect, pollution, mankind clearly has one unquestionable purpose; namely, to seek for ways and means (with correspondingly global

attitudes) of undoing the damage being caused by man's failure to control the powers developed by his own genius. His machines are not just the *fruits* of human rationality. They are in a sense the *caricature* of his rationality."

27. Human story came into the world only with the development of *symbol* systems. For notions of "placement" see, for example, Burke's treatment of nature, counternature, and the supernatural in "Afterward: In Retrospective Prospect," *PC,* pp. 295–336.

28. Kenneth Burke, "Bodies That Learn Language," Lecture, University of Massachusetts, Amherst, Spring 1983.

29. Coleridge yields an interesting insight into this when he observes in *Anima Poetae,* p. 51: "I would make a pilgrimage to the deserts of Arabia to find the man who could make me understand how the *one can be many.* Eternal, universal mystery! It seems as if it were impossible, yet it *is,* and it is everywhere! It is indeed a contradiction in *terms,* and only in terms. It is the co-presence of feeling and life, limitless by their very essence, with form by its very essence limited, determinable, definite."

30. *PC,* p. 299. But as Burke also points out "All Counter-Nature...is *in* Nature" (*AH,* p. 416).

31. See for example, "(Nonsymbolic) Motion," pp. 813–22, and "Motion, Action, and the Human Condition," in William E. Tanner and J. Dean Bishop, eds., *Rhetoric and Change* (Mesquite, Tex.: Ide House, 1982), pp. 78–94.

32. In this essay, we have made no attempt to include Burke's myriad of short, "referential" forays into Coleridge on magic; e.g., when Burke refers us to Coleridge's *Ancient Mariner* where "(in a magically fearsome situation) lightning is described as pouring..." (*LSA,* p. 320 n. 4.)

33. *Anima Poetae,* p. 65, illustrates at once his grasp, even as a youth, of something of the relationship between the many and the one and his realization of the incapacity of humans to "possess" it: "I saw in early youth, as in a dream, the birth of the planets; and my eyes beheld as *one* what the understanding afterwards divided into (1) the origin of the masses, (2) the origin of their motions, and (3) the site or position of their circles and ellipses. All the deviations, too, were seen as one intuition of one, the selfsame necessity, and this necessity was a law of spirit, and all was spirit. And in matter all beheld the past activity of others *or* their own—and this reflection, this echo is matter-its only essence, if essence it be. And of this, too, I saw the necessity and understood it, but I understood not how infinite multitude and manifoldness could be one; only I saw and understood that it was yet more out of my power to comprehend how it would be otherwise—and in this unity I worshipped in the depth of knowledge that passes all understanding the Being of all things—and in Being their sole goodness—and I saw that God is the One, the Good—possesses it not, but *is* it."

34. *Coleridge's Ancient Mariner, Kubla Khan, and Christabel,* ed., Tuley Francis Huntington (New York: Macmillan, 1922), p. 41.

35. Ibid., p. 102.

36. Richard Harter Fogle, *The Idea of Coleridge's Criticism* (Berkeley: University of California Press, 1962), p. 150.

37. Ibid., p. 21.

38. Ibid, pp. 5, 18.

39. Ibid, p. 4.

40. Angus Fletcher offers an illuminating insight into the "method" of both Burke and Coleridge: "One cannot survive amid what Burke recently called the 'whole great clutter of our civilization' unless one...follows the Coleridgean road of *method*. Method is not mechanistic system, it is not a positivistic program, it is certainly not dogma. Yet it is not without order—its order is that of a road—a logological route followed to its end, what ever turnings occur in the middle of the way. Coleridgean method may at first look like random wandering in a maze, but finally it reveals a different order: the perfect route through the maze—Ariadne's thread, perfectly reeled in. Method traces the logic of the maze." *Representing Kenneth Burke*, ed. Hayden White and Margaret Brose (Baltimore: Johns Hopkins University Press, 1982), p. 151.

41. See Burke on the perception of "total unity by fragmentary examples" in *RM*, p. 70. Note also in *PLF*, p. 102, his own tendency to characterize from "a myriad shifting points of view."

42. Coleridge, *Anima Poetae*, p. 51.

43. Kenneth Burke, "Towards a Transcendent Immanence," *Cross Currents*, 32 (1982), p. 334.

44. In *LSA*, p. 20, Burke expresses the "conviction that mankind's only hope is a cult of comedy." See also Burke on comic correctives in *AH*, pp. 166–75.

45. *RR*. p. 31. See Shedd edition of Coleridge's *Notes on the Pilgrims Progress* (New York: Harper, 1853), 5. 256.

Prothesis
The Word-Christ.

Thesis — The Scripture.   *Antithesis* — The Church.

Methesis
The Spirit.

Synthesis
The Preacher.

46. Kenneth Burke, *Towards a Better Life (Berkeley: University of California Press, 1968), and* Burke, *Counter-Statement* (Berkeley: University of California Press, 1986), p. 215.

47. Kenneth Burke, "Rhetoric—Old and New" *Journal of General Education*, 5 (April 1951), 204. Of course, Burke talks elsewhere of the Upward and Downward Way: e.g., *RM*, p. 311, and *RR*, p. 37. In "Quest for Oly-

mpus," he talks of the "succession of Up and Downward Way: The final apparent ascent actually being (though I did not realize this fact at the time when I wrote the story) enigmatic descent" (*The Complete White Oxen* [Berkeley: University of California Press, 1968], p. xiii).

48. William H. Rueckert, *Kenneth Burke and the Drama of Human Relations* (Minneapolis: University of Minnesota Press, 1963), pp. 138–39.

49. Samuel Taylor Coleridge, *The Friend*, Essay 15. As cited in *GM*, p. 369.

50. Samuel Taylor Coleridge, *Specimens of the Table Talk* (Edinburgh: John Grant, 1905), p. 162. New Edition.

51. *PLF*, p. 72. Here, Burke is talking about Coleridge's "The Eolian Harp." Coleridge, in *Table Talk*, p. 146, "My system, if I may venture to give it so fine a name is...[an attempt] to reduce all knowledges into harmony." The phrase "omnivum gatherum" is from J. L. Lowes, *Road to Xanadu: A Study in the Ways of Imagination* (Boston: Houghton Mifflin, 1927), p. xcix. Coleridge, it should be noted, draws a distinction between *all* and *the whole*; e.g, in *Table Talk*, p. 219: "All is an endless fleeting abstraction, the whole is a reality."

52. Coleridge, *Biographia Literaria*, p. 361.

53. Kenneth Burke, "The Anaesthetic Revelation of Herone Liddell," *CWO*, p. 310. "Herone Liddell" was first published in 1959.

54. Burke in "Counter-Gridlock: An Interview with Kenneth Burke," *All Area*, no. 2 (1983), pp. 30–31, 10.

Burke, Kenneth; American writer; b. 5 May 1897, Pittsburgh, Pa.; s. of James Leslie Burke and Liliyan May Duva; m. 1st Lily Mary Batterham 1919, 2nd Elizabeth Batterham 1933; two s. three d.; ed. Ohio State and Columbia Univs....*Leisure interests:* trying to keep from becoming too unfit, worrying about the military-industrial complex, punishing the piano. Photos courtesy of Elspeth Burke Hart

152

Four generations. On Burke's maternal side. Courtesy of Elspeth Burke Hart

Four generations. Burke likened the elements of his pentad to the personalities of his five children. Had he a sixth child, the pentad would have become a hexad, with "attitude" as the additional element. Courtesy of Elspeth Burke Hart

153

"Making a Scene." Courtesy of Elspeth Burke

With singer/songwriter grandson Harry Chapin. Among Burke's many accomplishments was the composition of a song which Chapin made famous, "One Light in a Dark Valley." Burke complained at the conference that he made more money off the recording than he did on his books. Photo by Tom Chapin

Burke with lifetime friend Malcolm Cowley at Cowley's 60th anniversary party. Photo by Sheila Lamb; courtesy of the photographer

With Joe Gusfield at the Conference. Photo by Vito Signorile

"Critic-at-Large" at the Burke conference. Photo by Vito Signorile

7

WRITING AS THE ACCOMPLICE

OF LANGUAGE

KENNETH BURKE AND

POSTSTRUCTURALISM

CARY NELSON

On going back over Coleridge's Biographia Literaria, *I ran across a footnote in which, with regard to the "desynonymizing" of the terms "imagination" and "fancy," he says: insofar as any such distinctions become accepted, "language itself does as it were think for us."*
It is a chance remark which the structuralists would make much more of,...In effect Coleridge is saying that words *are doing what the theologian would say that the "mind" is doing....With Coleridge's passing remark that, if a new distinction becomes generally established, in effect the corresponding words think for us, we are at the very center of logological inquiry.*[1]

And insofar as men "cannot live by bread alone," they are moved by doctrine, which is to say, they derive purposes from language, which tells them what they "ought" to want to do, tells them how to do it, and in the telling goads them with great threats and promises, even unto the gates of heaven and hell.[2]

My particular interest in this paper is with Burke's later work, a period beginning roughly with *The Rhetoric of Religion* in 1961 and *Language as Symbolic Action* in 1966 and continuing with the linked series of essays he has written since then, essays that reflect on and amplify the major concerns of his remarkable career. I believe that

156

Burke's work of the past twenty-five years presents a somewhat different view of rhetorical action, human agency, and language in general than that he propounded through the 1950s. It is a question, however, not of a radical break with his own past, for everything Burke says now is amply and fatefully prepared for by his work since the 1930s, but rather, if you will, of the perfection of principles already at work in Burke's writing, a movement of his own "terministically goaded vision" in the direction of those "projects that 'go to the end of the line.' "[3] In effect, we can witness the principle of entelechy working itself out in terms of Burke's own project, at least in those moments when he presses his model toward a fulfillment of its most radical implications. The synthesizing term for the entelechial development of Burke's own system is logology, a concept whose major components are in fact at work as early as *A Rhetoric of Motives*.

Before mapping out this position, however, I want to place it in the context of previous Burke studies, because the Burke I read and privilege is a different Burke from the Burke at least some of those working in communication, rhetoric, and English have read and argued for over the years. Rather than state my position with feigned innocence, then, I would rather say explicitly that I want to offer a counter-Burke to the humanistic Burke of Marie Nichols, Bernard Brock, Leland Griffin, Lloyd Bitzer, and, more recently, Wayne Booth and Denis Donoghue.[4] The Burke I want to counter is the Burke whose career, it seems, largely comes to a conclusion with *A Grammar of Motives* and *A Rhetoric of Motives* of 1945 and 1950. This is a Burke who can more easily be read to support the idealized view of communicative efficacy one finds in Lloyd Bitzer, Joseph Comprone, Virginia Holland, and Daniel Fogarty.[5] If, on the other hand, one reads the later Burke then another perspective opens up in the earlier work, one fulfilled in texts like *The Rhetoric of Religion*. Of course the later Burke can be partly assimilated to the humanistic view of man as the subject potentially in full control of language and of his own communicative intentions, but not without trivializing Burke's irony and skepticism. The most notable figure who has worked this territory is Wayne Booth, who makes Burke's structural subversions of his own enterprise, his self-reflexive perspectives by incongruity, into a harmless relativism.

Put somewhat baldly, the issue is whether one sees the symbol-using animal in Burke as an independent agent or as a figure occupying the role of agency within a verbal drama that is in a sense already written for us. There is part of Burke, surely, that believes that rational and accurate taxonomies and explanations of human motives and the workings of rhetoric are possible and necessary. That part of Burke be-

Cary Nelson

lieves that one can get such things right and thus that the interpretive project has at least a chance of being both dependably communicative and socially curative. Another part of Burke believes that language pursues its conflictual and relentlessly transformational games on its own no matter what interpretive precautions we take and thus that the wish to control the game with some ethical end in mind is itself only an effect of language and thus destined for developments already inscribed in the round of changes language works on us. That part of Burke asks whether we are free to use language as we choose and whether the structures revealed by dramatism facilitate, even guarantee, communication, or whether we are used by language in the service of its own principles of entelechy and communication is often tragic and comic as a result.

I think it is fair to say that both these positions are present in Burke's work, that his writing is dialectically structured by them. On that point I would strongly agree with Frank Lentricchia, though I would disagree with Lentricchia's claim that the comic for Burke serves as an effort to transcend this dialectic and stand outside it.[6] I would also take issue with Angus Fletcher's image of Burke's work as a spiral curriculum, since it disguises the constitutive tensions of these positions in Burke, making Burke into a sloppy version of Northrop Frye.[7] Burke is either unable or unwilling to write his own central book, on the model of Frye's *Anatomy of Criticism*. There is no explicit center to Burke's project, no secure core around which his career moves. In each book his entire project is continually erected and dismantled.

If, however, Burke does counterpoint his faith and his skepticism, then it is quite in error to use him as a guide to the efficacies of communication. Indeed Burke himself might be a bit puzzled by this image of him as the figure who helps us understand how it is we generally communicate with one another so successfully. Neither the Burke who has seen the whole of twentieth-century history populate one killing ground after another nor the Burke who has watched the sometimes delayed and misconstrued reception of his own work (recorded most recently in pieces like "As I Was Saying" and "Dancing with Tears in My Eyes") is perhaps so likely to see rhetoricity as a ballet of loving communication and full intersubjectivity.[8] Rhetoric is for Burke a community of actions based on primordial *difference*, not a means to recover primordial sameness. Rhetoric for Burke has always been the exercise of power. Language has repeatedly been at once, personally, the scene of psychoanalytic embarrassment and, collectively, the embodiment of differing interests and the idealization of oppression. Since his first efforts at satire, Burke has been at work to point out the efficient mechanisms by which language helps to convince us of our superiority and the holiness of our various destructive missions. In the process he has mapped out a small territory where one may *play* with this rhetorical power. But that is not to say either that he has always had great faith in the power of play to change human history or that he himself has entire freedom in choosing his own rhetorical moves. What becomes clear in *The Rhetoric of Religion* and since, I think, is that Burke believes one can move up and down certain rhetorical structures and thereby expose their structured, predictive, mechanistic, and determining efficacy. Indeed, one can subject these structures to endless substitution and variation, even regularly on a local level differ from particular discourses by way of negation or reversal. But one cannot really operate outside these patterns. In a very basic sense, therefore, one cannot write except as an *agent* of the very verbal structures one may want to expose and criticize.

A full discussion of these issues would involve a book-length developmental study of Burke's philosophy of language. Even in a short space, however, it is possible to describe the basic poles of his position. In his early studies of rhetorical persuasion, Burke came to realize that texts could be a powerful and often fateful source of motivation toward action, indeed that texts can convince us to adopt as our own motives that which our biology alone does not seem to entail. He also realized that texts convince in part by establishing structured and hierarchized relationships between their key terms, thereby managing to convince us that the relationships between these terms are both correct and inevitable. Realizing that no argument can escape this kind of pattern, Burke proposed as one way to avoid being disastrously persuaded (as nations often are) a critical procedure of contrasting and juxtaposing different rhetorics, thereby making the dialectician into a variously bemused, horrified, and linguistically manipulated participant in the human comedy.

This early work gave Burke an unusual capacity to describe both the social and the psychological effects of rhetorical actions. But as his career progressed he became increasingly aware of both the totalizing power of individual terminologies and the fatefulness of the linguistic structures themselves, quite apart from whatever content we might inscribe them with in any historical period: "We *must* use terministic screens, since we can't say anything without the use of terms. . . . And now where are we? Must we merely resign ourselves to an endless catalogue of terministic screens. . . . In one sense, yes."[9] At moments, indeed, he begins to suggest that language *as a whole* operates as a kind of terministic screen, one that substantially creates the world we perceive as natural. Having defined man as "the symbol-using animal," he goes on to ask: "But can we bring ourselves to realize just what that formula implies, just how overwhelmingly much of what we mean by 'reality' has been built up for us through nothing but our symbol systems?" (*LSA*, p. 5) Our world, he writes, "is necessarily inspirited with the quality of the Symbol, the Word, the Logos" by which we conceive the world (*LSA*, p. 55). "If the things of nature are, for man, the visible signs of their verbal entitlements, then nature gleams secretly with a most fantastic shimmer of words and social relationships. . . . In this sense things would be the signs of words" (*LSA*, p. 379). The next step, of course, is to recognize that what we are as humans is uniquely identified with this semiotically constructed world, that man is the "symbol-made animal" (*LSA*, p. 63). At this point, Burke is very close to structuralism's view of man as a construct of social codes: "So far as sheerly empirical development is concerned, it might be more accurate to say that language and the negative 'invented' man" (*LSA*, p. 9).

This is not, however, a position Burke is willing to maintain unequivocally. In Burke's transitional period, which I identify in particular with *A Grammar of Motives* and *A Rhetoric of Motives*, the tensions between the more conservative and the more radical positions are quite overt.[10] The final essay in *A Grammar of Motives*, "Four Master Tropes," is a useful text to use to illustrate the rhetorical reversals this tension promotes. "Metaphor, metonymy, synecdoche, and irony" are each given typically provocative and unstably Burkean definitions. Moreover, Burke announces playfully at the outset: "Give a man but one of them, tell him to exploit its possibilities, and if he is thorough in doing so, he will come upon the other three."[11] As is characteristic of Burke at this stage of his career, he wants to suggest the transformative resources of the language with this formulation, to evoke as well its connectedness, and even the fated nature of the equivalences connotation will work on usage. But he is not quite willing to see humans as *spoken by* these fated tropical progressions. Nor is he quite willing to follow through the implications of the circularity implicit in the dialectical progression from trope to trope. "It is customary to think that objective reality is dissolved by such relativity of terms as we get through the shifting of perspectives," he writes, thereby becoming devil's advocate despite himself (*GMRM*, p. 504). "But," he continues, "on the contrary, it is by the approach through a variety of perspectives that we establish a character's reality." The real risk, of course, is not that reality will disappear but that we will recognize it as a projection of our terministic screens, that reality will be suspected to be linguistically constructed, or, more accurately, that we will recognize that it is available to us, as incurable symbol-using animals, only in such linguistically structured form. Almost without quite wanting to, Burke has introduced a view of the world as textually available to us.

The problem continues to haunt him. Irony is eventually offered as the master of the master tropes, the universally transformative trope closest to the pure principle of the dialectic itself. "Irony arises," he writes, "when one tries, by the interaction of terms upon one another, to produce a *development* which uses all the terms. Hence, from the standpoint of this total form (this 'perspective of perspectives') none of the participating 'sub-perspectives' can be treated as either precisely right or precisely wrong. They are all voices, or personalities, or positions, integrally affecting one another" (*GMRM*, p. 512). The certain representational nature of language is radically at risk in this model. As is typical with Burke, he is driven to follow an argument through to its end. Language here is becoming a self-referential system, not a tool we can use with confidence in our power to limit its communicative effects, and not a trustworthy mirror of reality. Again, however, he retreats. "People usually confuse the dialectic with the relativistic," he warns us, but, even then, he cannot resist partly confirming this rejected connection: "It is certainly relativistic," he continues, "to state that any term (as per metaphor-perspective) can be seen from the point of view of any other term" (*GMRM*, pp. 512–13). The retreat from this, however comforting to those conservative rhetoricians who want, say, to use dramatism to trace precisely how Ronald Reagan's speeches work on his audiences, is very weak indeed: "terms," Burke argues, "are thus encouraged to participate in an orderly parliamentary development," this no doubt to suggest that we retain control of their transformations and that the progression can keep a positivistic correspondence with extratextual reality (*GMRM*, p. 513). But nothing in Burke's career holds with this dependable and dour progression. Rapid moves to the end of a sequence, sudden perspectives by incongruity, a patchwork structure of dislocations is more in his style. Indeed, Burke often leaps to the logical end of an argument half a sentence after introducing it.

Nonetheless, in the later work, when Burke argues that any terminology is a screen that structures reality for us, he is more likely to be led to the radical, entelechially perfected version of his position. Even there, however, he invokes more cautious, commonsensical versions of this argument: "any nomenclature necessarily directs the attention into some channels rather than others," he writes, suggesting a manageable sort of rhetorical deflection and allowing us to believe we can study the distortions and persuasions of rhetoric from a point outside their decisive influence (*LSA*, p. 45). Even in the more narrow state-

ments, however, there is a radical edge. "Nomenclatures are formative, or creative," he writes elsewhere, "they affect the nature of our
observations, by turning our attention in this direction rather than
that, and by having implicit in them ways of dividing up a field of inquiry."[12] Just how formative and how creative, of course, is the issue.
In Burke's image of the field of inquiry divided up and constituted by
discourse we have an anticipation of Michel Foucault's work in *The Ar-
cheology of Knowledge*. Obviously, if our attention is turned only in certain directions, then some elements of the world will be excluded from
our perspective. Indeed, nomenclatures create the coherence of the
world we do see. Nor is Burke able to argue that individual terminologies permit access to alternative discourses or that they can resist the
totalizing of their own projects. When he writes that "there is a kind of
'unconscious' that is sheerly a reflection of whatever terminology one
happens to be using" (*LSA*, p. 71), and that this unconscious possesses the resources to complete a terminology and indeed drives it
toward such a formal consummation, then there are no limits to the
creativity of terministic screens. Indeed, Burke calls into question his
more complacent view of terministic determination rather explicitly in
the foreword to *The Rhetoric of Religion*. There he describes logology as
the study of "words used with thoroughness" and adds that "even
when men use language trivially, the motives inherent in its possible
use are acting somewhat as goads, however vague." Thus the radically
hierarchical persuasiveness of theology is not only a model of the
"terministic enterprise in general" but also a general description of
"the nature of language itself as a motive."

In any case, Burke's whole study of rhetoric goes against the grain of
the position that we can freely choose our terms and what we will do
with them; his project is designed "to take care of those who would
define man as the 'tool-using animal' " (*LSA*, p. 13). Such "overly
'naturalistic' views conceal from us the full scope of language as motive" (*RR*, p. 10). What happens to Burke's work is in part the result of
recognizing both the thoroughness of the motives of particular languages and the structural similarities of all terministic screens. His
later work may be considered the result of placing "the rhetoric of
Hitler's battle" over "the rhetoric of religion" and asking what their
homologies reveal about "the form underlying all language" (*RR*, p.
297). What he finds is that all languages, all terminologies, embody
"the 'hierarchical psychosis' (of the 'social pyramid')" (*LSA*, p. 143).
All languages function by hierarchizing sets of terms, by idealizing
some categories and debunking others. The relations between these
terms are relations of affirmation and negation, idealization and vic-

timization. Any terminology has its scapegoats. Moreover, "once you have placed your terms in a developmental series, you have an arrangement whereby each can be said to participate, within the limitations of its nature, in the ultimate perfection ('finishedness') of the series" (*GMRM*, pp. 713–14). So, at least within a terminology, "No word is an island. In all words is every word" ("Why Satire," p. 334). All nomination within a particular language, Burke argues repeatedly in his later work, though most thoroughly in *The Rhetoric of Religion*, invokes the entitlement of the god-terms of the language. "Language," in the end, "is one vast menagerie of implications" ("Theology and Logology," p. 155). We are the agents of language use in this "menagerie of implications," but that is a more limited freedom than we have often supposed. As Burke puts it in a line he borrows to make one of his most succinct revisions of his view of agency in the linguistic situation, "The driver drives the car, but the traffic drives the driver" ("Why Satire," p. 311). We use words and exercise a certain choice in speaking (thereby driving the car), but we are ourselves *driven* by our historicized participation in the linguistic situation (the traffic).

The key texts to use in working through this stance as an argumentative position include "Five Summarizing Essays" from *Language as Symbolic Action*, the work on entelechy in *Dramatism and Development*, and *The Rhetoric of Religion*. But the issues at stake are also brought into the foreground by elements of Burke's writing practice throughout his career. I have in mind the patchwork structure of many of his books—essays, appendices, prefaces, and sometimes prefaces added in later years. At the least, we need to credit the structural displacement of the authorial subject in these documents, instead of homogenizing them by paraphrase. In other words, we need to credit the rhetorical structures Burke has actually given us, rather than try to fix, say, his dispersed, fragmented books by renarrativizing their arguments. (Consider, for example, actually making the effort to analyze the *structure* of *A Rhetoric of Motives*.)

Burke continually marks and undermines his own agency by way of difference with his own work, so that intent is recuperable only as a sequence of self-regarding displacements and totality is deferred.[13] His work is decentered in a radical way that has, regrettably, been acknowledged by his critics only with frustration, rather than with thoughtful description. The techniques Burke uses to create this decentered corpus are important enough to him that he employs them not only in structuring individual books but also in countering and resituating individual essays. Thus his satiric piece "Towards Helhaven," which appeared in 1971, was followed in 1974 by an after-

Cary Nelson

word that simultaneously declared itself to be a preface, "Why Satire, with a Plan for Writing One." The satire itself, however, includes its own introduction, as well as a poetic envoi and a prose addendum. Moreover, the satire itself can be read as a plan for the full writing of the satire. Similarly, the quite serious "satyr-play" that concludes *The Rhetoric of Religion* is described as an appendix but titled as both epilogue and prologue, a paradox appropriate to temporizing the essence of Burke's own system.

Some of Burke's recent essays add another self-reflective dimension to this writing practice. In part this is facilitated by the relative completion of Burke's lifelong differential system. The key terms of his enterprise have been established for many years. Their history and usefulness have been amply demonstrated. Now he has been free, therefore, to treat his own system as a fractured and multiply available totality, summarizing it and mocking it, playing with its implications and its intimidations. A number of important features of his method have become clearer as a result. Others, including some Burkean characteristics that have long made many of our positivist colleagues uneasy in the presence of his texts, have become increasingly foregrounded and thus inescapable. The casualness of his recent references to the terms of the pentad, for example, make it clear that it never was a fixed taxonomic system but an exploratory one; certainly the pentad was never designed to provide a securely deterministic model of textual production.

Since Burke's major terms have received elaborate explanation in his earlier work, it is now possible for him to use them in a particularly condensed, rhetorical, and, I think, dramatistic way. They can now be called on regularly to make sudden rhetorical appearances— entering from the wings, in effect, to play immediate roles on stage in an essay. Concepts like entelechy, the principle of perfection, or the negative, indeed the whole project of logology, can be invoked whenever they are useful without more than a phrase of contextualization. As a result Burke's project is pulled in two directions, one holistic and encyclopedic, one comic and self-critical. The terms, in short, at once suggest a total coherent system and a mere series of substitutions, a chain of metonymic displacements in the fragmentary rhetoric of the essays. This has always been a major element of Burke's work—the sense that his categories are willfully hypostatized and even personified, so that they become the dramatis personae of his intellectual family romance. Overdetermined, they are by choice playfully reductive. They reveal by embarrassing their objects of analysis. Burke's project becomes an *affectionate* and playful hermeneutic of suspicion, to modify slightly Paul Ricoeur's well-known description of Marxism and psychoanalysis.

Now many who were less affectionately suspicious about Burke's work have sensed this mixture of conviction and charade in his style and rejected it as a result. Commentators on Burke have often sought to rescue him from his own more rigorously comic form of self-reflection. But the recent work—especially when seen in the larger intellectual context of the general project of contemporary critical theory—makes this bowdlerizing of Burke both more difficult and strategically unnecessary. Burke's vocabulary—if one reads Burke from the vantage point of other recent theory—is at once obsessional and irreverent. Moreover, it is exemplary precisely because of this unstable paradoxicality. Burke himself, of course, is not without a strain of the positivistic scientificity he would despair at in his critics, so there is also a constitutive moment in Burke in which he would believe that his logology is all we critically symbol-using animals need and all we will ever need on earth. Yet the countermoment—in which the terms of a long and extraordinarily productive life are merely representative and thus arbitrary—is also constitutive for Burke's project.

Some of the inescapability of this dynamic is built into the style of the recent work. The most appropriate form is perhaps that of "(Nonsymbolic) Motion / (Symbolic) Action," one of the *Critical Inquiry* essays, rather than, say, that of "Theology and Logology," published in the *Kenyon Review*.[14] The first section of the former uses clusters of paragraphs separated by white space. Thus the associative, interchangeable, substitutable nature of Burke's writing is emphasized. The second section is in the form of a dialogue with another writer's published essay. "Theology and Logology," on the other hand, though it is divided into a foreword and five numbered sections, opts for a conventional prose presentation, which works against the associative and reflective shifts in perspective, though the essay as a whole is destabilized by being as well a supplementary reconstitution of *The Rhetoric of Religion*. *The Rhetoric of Religion* itself is also a key text here, not only because of the wonderful incongruity of the epilogue but also because the book develops not as a sequential argument but by way of the successive reconstitution of the project in the foreword, the introduction, each of the three chapters, and the epilogue.

With all of the recent essays, moreover, it is possible to read Burke's comments about human symbolicity self-reflexively, as comments, that is, on Burke's own method. So Burke's reference to "arbitrary, conventional symbol-systems," with its implicit judgment about the comedy of human semiosis, is a judgment on the comic and paradoxical regularity of his own work as well ("Theology and Logology," p. 152). Dramatism is equally an arbitrary terminological filling out of a linguistic structure already given to him by the culture. And the positioning of logology between nonsymbolic bodily motion and theological conviction is a self-reflexive embarrassment as well. For logology is thereby reducible to a linguistic mediator between bodily process and actual religious belief. Burke would not, if all the moments of his enterprise could read each other, be able to free logology from "the same motivational quandaries" ("Theology and Logology," p. 171). There are, for Burke, no metalanguages that transcend the linguistic situation.

For characteristic self-reflexive moments, consider these: "Thus the categories, or 'inventories,' of Whitman's poetry are unfoldings of terms that IMPLY one another, their associative interrelationship being revealed in a succession of tiny plots" ("[Nonsymbolic] Motion," p. 821). The unfolding categories in Burke's own system are equally readable as a narrative substitution of terms in a conventionalized structure. Burke's system is of necessity a mechanistic replication of the linguistic process rather than a privileged form of knowledge or a vehicle for open self-expression. Indeed, his system is also a *second* nature steeped in the desire to perfect (and replace) an original nature with technicity. "The realms of nonsymbolic motion and symbolicity (with its vast range of implications) are so related that the acquiring of skill with symbol-systems is analogous to a kind of 'fall' into a technical state of 'grace' that 'perfects' nature." Clearly, dramatism and logology are both acquired rhetorical skills. Finally, for an ironic observation about the dialectician's potential for transcending mere verbal warfare by the playful juxtaposition of multiple languages, take this passage about the somatic and the symbolic as a commentary on the pitfalls built into the logological aim to heal: "There could be a mutually reinforcing relationship (a 'feedback'?) between the author's symbolic prowess and corresponding processes of his body whereby the development of his skill at his particular mode of symbolic action would be making him sick and keeping him sick" ("[Nonsymbolic] Motion," p. 819).

Read that way, of course, that passage places us in the Derridean paradox of using the language of Western metaphysics to call Western metaphysics into question. Yet that may not be a particularly disadvantageous place for a Burkean to be. For one of the striking things that have happened to Burke's texts in the past fifteen years is that the rest of criticism, or at least *some* of the rest of criticism, has grown into Burke and into an acceptance of the Burkean position that criticism can be exemplary *and* arbitrary, informative and undecidable. This places Burke's comic skepticism at the center of his enterprise, possibly an exaggeration, but one with some strategic relevance.

In some sense, then, Burke's project has always been the project of the satirist, even when he is most serious—the satirist who *inverts* the entelechy of our myths of progress—who shows that the way to the excremental is merely the obverse of the way to transcendence and thus that our lech for transcendence is always excremental. But I don't believe, especially in his late works where the sense of the fatefulness of linguistic determinism is so strong, that he has much faith in the likelihood that the satirist's project will change anything. He is perhaps the modern Swift who knows his modest proposal will be taken literally.

Burke's own modest proposal for the disposition of the earth, his 1971 satire "Towards Helhaven: Three Stages of a Vision," is a useful case in point. Helhaven is a project, paradoxically made possible by technology, by which the pretechnological natural marvels of the earth are to be reconstructed on the moon. Technology, then, is to restore what it destroyed. Burke specifically links this essay with his 1929 satire "Waste—or the Future of Prosperity" and lets us know in this way just how hopeful he is that this new rhetorical action will bring about any change. Indeed, all he can do in "Helhaven" is to exploit cheerfully the very differences and righteous hierarchies already at work in the culture:

> Among the most deeply-probing facilities in the Culture-Bubble will be the above-mentioned Super-Lookout, a kind of Chapel, bare except for some small but powerful telescopes of a special competence. And on the wall, in ecclesiastical lettering, there will be these fundamental words from the *Summa Theologica*: "And the blessed in Heaven shall look upon the sufferings of the damned, that they may love their blessedness the more." The underlying situation here is this:
>
> In order that the Lunar Bubble be kept perfectly provisioned (and we are being frank about such matters because we want you to realize how scrupulously this entire project is being planned), there will still be the necessity that gases, minerals, and even some organic growths be reclaimed now and then from Earth. Thus the New Colonialism will entail frequent missions back to our Maternal Source for such replacements. Increased experience in the use of space-craft will make it certain that the trip itself will not be dangerous. But the

Cary Nelson

possibility of encountering a nasty band of still-surviving hominids will add risk to these forays, and give them somewhat the quality of marauding expeditions (though the expression is obviously unjust; for any Lunar Paradisiacs of the future will be but replenishing their gigantic womblike Culture-Bubble, as it were, from the placenta of the Mother Earth from which their very body-temperature is derived, and which is just as much our home, however filthy we shall have made it before clearing out, as it is the home of any scurvy anthropoid leftovers that might still somehow contrive to go on hatching their doubtless degenerate and misshapen broods back there among those seven filthy seas).[15]

What does such a project—a rhetorical project for Burke—offer us as a model of the freedom of the writer, of the subject who chooses the efficacy of what he or she writes? I believe it offers us a mode of writing as fated and ineffective play, pleasurable, worth doing as an act of witness, but not likely to change oneself or the world, not likely either to guarantee an author's subjective presence in his or her writing and finally not likely to promote an ideal of communication. That confidence in the power to alter the rhetorical situation and to stand outside its differences and know their essential nature is the liberal view of the power of rhetoric, the one we like to espouse in justifying and aggrandizing our social role as teachers and promoters of discourse. That is the conventional liberal view of the saving incongruity of satire as well, and it is one Burke allows himself to adopt as one version of his Helhaven project: "ideally, satire would enable us to contemplate a situation to which we might otherwise close our minds" ("Why Satire," p. 321). But Burke also suggests the "vatic thoroughness" of the project's own demonic vision is more likely to win out, so I'm not convinced the liberal view is actually Burke's view in this wistful and joking piece.

Perhaps Burke's deliberately duplicitous title points most economically to his late view of the rhetorical situation. "Helhaven" is a haven from hell (the earth) that is also itself hell. Indeed, in the word "Helhaven" we will also hear an echo of hell/heaven, an echo amplified in many passages in Burke's "Why Satire, with a Plan for Writing One": "Even now, the kingdom of Helhaven is within you" (p. 321); "(hail Heaven!) in Helhaven, home" (p. 337). Helhaven is a rhetorical exploitation of the god principle of technology-as-transcendence that is itself of necessity steeped in technology's dialogue with the human as excremental. As *writing*, it is a haven from our hellish myths of progress that is *itself* the hell of those very myths, their demonic perfection. And it is amused, indeed gains its marginal freedom by way of amusement, at the end of the earth, both geographically and rhetorically. If technology, in Burke's view, is in part a dream of distancing ourselves from our mortality, if its rhetoric mimics the rhetoric of religious transcendence, it is, after all, *our* dream, not truly a hoped-for identification with a godlike principle outside ourselves, but a division in our nature, a division structured into the connotative, hierarchizing web of the language. "My satire on the 'technological psychosis,' " he writes, "will be an offspring of that same psychosis" ("Why Satire," p. 317). From those connotative, determining structures, there is no escape, no outside, no other that is not already within. To ask, then, whether we speak language or language speaks us is to ask, for the late Burke, for that improbable transcendence of materiality that is itself a myth only of the language we are. The autonomy of language, I would argue, belongs to language, not to those who use it.

This leads me to my final distinction—and it is the most difficult one for me to make, because it tempts me to my own misreading of Burke. That misreading would be to say that Burke, the Burke of bodily embarrassment, psychoanalytic deflation, and the plural competitive social contract, comes to believe that language is *all* there is, that no material world exists for us. What Burke suggests instead is, first, that we see always through terministic screens; second, that language is an independent source of human motivation; and third, more deeply, that anything we can see or feel is already *in* language, given to us *by* language, and even produced *as us* by language. Moreover, language produces us as motivated subjects not through some free play of difference but as part of mobile yet always structured and hierarchized differences. Our work, then, is already written for us. In writing it anew, we make it our own but always as agents of a rhetorical situation of no one's choosing.

Working within this coherent but paradoxical view of language, Burke is able to present a rather suggestive and strikingly contemporary picture of semiosis as a process of structured but locally unpredictable binary displacements. "Discursive terminologies," he argues, "will allow for a constant succession of permutations and combinations" (*RR*, p. 282). The words produced will thereby be widely variable, but they will proceed by binary substitution: "DUPLICATION, POLARITY, NEGATION" ("Theology and Logology," p. 175). "Even pure identity," he writes, "implies the negation of non-identity," so all linguistic transformations and substitutions are differences in implicit structural opposition, differences as well with the potential to be hier-archically arrayed (*RR*, p. 283). This is a potential, of course, that is guaranteed to be realized, since we are all "*goaded by the spirit of hierar-chy (or moved by the sense of order*" (*LSA*, p. 15) structured into the con-notative, perfecting "*'entelechial' principle natural to the genius of language*" (*LSA*, p. 139). The structure of discourse is given, therefore; we are thrown into it and spoken by it, but we can, within the limits of history and character, choose the terms we speak to fill out the pat-tern, a pattern whose differences allow for virtually infinite play.

This is, of course, the Burke of my title and the Burke of poststruc-turalism. William Rueckert was the first to argue persuasively that Burke is a genuine precursor to structuralism, but there was always a good deal of awkwardness in this fit.[16] In Burke's many efforts to work out the persuasively binary basis of complex ideolects there is clearly a link with Levi-Strauss and those who have followed in his influence. In Burke's tremendously important argument that language is not simply a tool we use as we will but a structured—and hierarchically arrayed—source of motivation, there is clearly a thorough precursor to structuralism's rejection of a free and independently active subject. In-deed, in his recent essays, Burke has stated quite clearly that the self in many respects is a semiotic construct, "a product of the Culture" ("[Nonsymbolic] Motion," p. 813); the human organism acquires a self "through its protracted, informative traffic with the (learned) public modes of symbolic action" ("Theology and Logology," p. 164). The process, moreover, is a continuous one; language *thinks for* us—and in doing so urges us to fear and desire and thus substantially makes us what we are.

Yet the subject, for Burke, is also radically historicized, indeed, in a way that some will find devastating: "the principle of personality does sum up, or implicitly contain, the kind of social and political order in which it participates" (*RR*, p. 310). "Ideas of 'personality,' " Burke writes, "will draw heavily on the idea of a leader" who represents his people by seeming, within a particular historical context, to title, name, and unify their differences (*RR*, p. 305). The subject is logologi-cally constructed; it is a narrative cycle of terms arrayed hierarchically in imitation of contemporary versions of empire. This invocation of the *politics* of personality, of course, runs counter to the ahistorical ele-ment in classical structuralism, though it is powerfully antihumanistic in that it demolishes the romantic idealization of the independent subject as a unique and inwardly generated identity. The problem for a structuralist interpretation of Burke is intensified, however, in that Burke has never maintained this position unequivocally. To the more dour versions of structuralist determinism, he counters with "the indirectness that is typical of human discriminations." For the vision of culture as a static, hierarchically ordered series of binarisms, Burke substitutes the "vast gangle of symbolically, culturally engendered 'reality' above or beyond our experiences" as biological animals. For the emphatically absent subject, Burke substitutes "a Self as *personalized* by participation in its particular Culture's modes of literal (univocal), equivocal, and analogical symbol-using" ("[Nonsymbolic] Motion," p. 815). Moreover, this is a self that throughout almost all of Burke's career has been linked to bodily process and infantile motivation. In many ways, then, this is the undecidable subject of poststructuralism—a problematic but not dismissable site for discourse. It is with poststructuralism, then, in its more reflective, plural, and, at least with figures like Roland Barthes and Jacques Derrida, playful posing and problematizing of categories that Burke's work finds it true homology and its most fitting basis for comparison and contrast. As with Barthes's *S/Z*, the effort in Burke to locate linguistic and cultural determinism and to differentiate it from the subject's efforts at self-expression, even the effort to specify the cultural or logological codes in operation, will be dialectical, arbitrary, and, to make matters worse, quite reversible. Burke, of course, has always understood that polar terms are reversible, that what we cherish as freely chosen action can be embarrassed by psychoanalytic, political, or logological incongruity. And he has understood that these interpretive suspicions can in turn be recovered as symbolic actions at least to be credited to the subject's accomplishments. The interpretive positioning of these terms, both in Burke and in much poststructuralist writing, can display the logic of semiosis without *ever* decisively *naming* its components. If that is Burke's contribution, to have taken the obsessional vocabulary of forty years and subjected it to the serious and comic rigor of the seventies and eighties, a mere decade or two ahead of his time, that's rather more of a contribution than the rest of us are likely to claim as our own.

NOTES

1. Kenneth Burke, "Theology and Logology," *Kenyon Review*, n.s., 1 (1979), 156–57. The footnote Burke refers to is in chapter 4 of Coleridge's *Biographia Literaria*, ed. James Engell and W. Jackson Bate (Princeton: Princeton University Press, 1983), pp. 86–87. People interested in Burke's recent work should see the annotated bibliography in the second edition of

Cary Nelson

William Rueckert's *Kenneth Burke and The Drama of Human Relations* (Berkeley: University of California Press, 1982), and Richard H. Thames's bibliography, in this volume.

2. Kenneth Burke, *The Rhetoric of Religion: Studies in Logology* (1961; rpt. Berkeley: University of California Press, 1970), p. 274.

3. Kenneth Burke, "Why Satire, with a Plan for Writing One," *Michigan Quarterly Review*, 13 (Winter 1974), 307–37.

4. See Marie Hochmuth Nichols, "Kenneth Burke and the New Rhetoric," Bernard Brock, "Political Speaking: A Burkean Approach," and Leland M. Griffin, "A Dramatistic Theory of the Rhetoric of Movements" in William H. Rueckert, ed., *Critical Response to Kenneth Burke, 1924–1966* (Minneapolis: University of Minnesota Press, 1969); Wayne C. Booth, "Kenneth Burke's Way of Knowing," *Critical Inquiry*, 1 (September 1974), 1–22; Denis Donoghue, *Ferocious Alphabets* (New York: Little, Brown, 1981) and "American Sage," *New York Review of Books*, September 26, 1985, pp. 39–42.

5. See Lloyd F. Bitzer, "Functional Communication: A Situational Perspective," in Eugene E. White, ed., *Rhetoric in Transition: Studies in the Nature and Uses of Rhetoric* (University Park: Pennsylvania State University Press, 1980); Virginia L. Holland, *Counterpoint: Kenneth Burke and Aristotle's Theories of Rhetoric* (New York: Philosophical Library, 1959); Daniel Fogarty, S.J., "Kenneth Burke's Theory," in Rueckert, *Critical Responses to Kenneth Burke*.

6. See Frank Lentricchia, "Reading History with Kenneth Burke," in Hayden White and Margaret Brose, eds., *Representing Kenneth Burke* (Baltimore: Johns Hopkins University Press, 1982).

7. See Angus Fletcher, "Volume and Body in Burke's Criticism, or Stalled in the Right Place," in White and Brose, *Representing Kenneth Burke*.

8. See Kenneth Burke's "As I Was Saying," *Michigan Quarterly Review*, 11 (Winter 1972), 9–27, and "Dancing with Tears in My Eyes," *Critical Inquiry*, 1 (September 1974), 23–31.

9. Kenneth Burke, *Language as Symbolic Action* (Berkeley: University of California Press, 1966), pp. 50, 52.

10. To think of *A Grammar of Motives* and *A Rhetoric of Motives* as in any sense centrally transitional, that is, as leading from and to *anywhere*, is already somewhat unorthodox in Burke studies, since these books, and particularly the *Grammar of Motives*, have all the imaginable trappings of monuments in and of themselves. The *Grammar of Motives* is certainly Burke at his most relentless and visionary system-building best. Of course everyone realizes that there are problems with the system. The four master tropes, say, appear as much an alternative to the terms of the pentad as any supplement to them. The pentad itself simultaneously provides for an analysis of the terminological constitution of actions and for the dissolution of actions into terms. It is a kind of hermeneutic explosion and cyclical activation of human actions. The pentad activates a connotative cycle that throws off centrifugal effects linking an individual action to the whole of

human behavior. Of course most Burkeans handle such implications by picking and choosing from Burke's work as suits their needs, thereby honoring the image of the theoretical toolkit before Foucault was around to honor the term. Yet a number of consistently Burkean features of the *Grammar*'s style in some ways work against the cohesiveness of the book's system and indeed against what one might call the positivist moment within its descriptive aims and its worldview. These features of the book would lead us to see Burke's system not as an interpretive goal but as a more general view of the ironic transformations characteristic of verbal behavior. *A Grammar of Motives* is continually pulled in two directions—toward a radically deterministic and textualizing view of human agency and perception, and toward a more limited view that recasts our terminologically driven conflicts as comical indications that we are dramatic puppets who need to get enough distance from the dialectic to become its masters. Read this way, it becomes an investigation of the problematics of freedom and determination, a dialogue about the rhetoricity of human motivation that leaves Burke's final position open to reflection and to the balance of his career. It is certainly not a book that leaves us with a secure and empirical handbook for the study of discourse, but rather a book that gives us the tools to see more than we are, perhaps, ready to handle.

11. Kenneth Burke, *A Grammar of Motives and A Rhetoric of Motives* (New York: World, 1962), p. 503.

12. Kenneth Burke, *Dramatism and Development* (Worcester, Mass.: Clark University Press, 1972), p. 33.

13. William E. Cain, in *The Crisis in Criticism: Theory, Literature, and Reform in English Studies* (Baltimore: Johns Hopkins University Press, 1984), mistakenly reads Burke in the opposite way: "his many prefaces, forewords, introductions, expansive footnotes, and interviews signify his effort to subdue his swirling system" (p. 140). Quite to the contrary, Burke in this way insures the decentered plurality of his work.

14. Kenneth Burke, "(Nonsymbolic) Motion/(Symbolic) Action," *Critical Inquiry*, 4 (Summer 1978), 809–38.

15. Kenneth Burke, "Towards Helhaven: Three Stages of a Vision," *Sewanee Review*, 79 (1971), 22.

16. William H. Rueckert, "Kenneth Burke and Structuralism," *Shenandoah*, 21 (Autumn 1969), 19–28.

8 KENNETH BURKE'S CONCEPT

OF ASSOCIATION AND THE

COMPLEXITY OF IDENTITY

CHRISTINE ORAVEC

Kenneth Burke's concept of identification is central for understanding his views on rhetoric and persuasion.[1] Burke himself announces the importance of the term in his introduction to *A Rhetoric of Motives:*

> We emerge from the analogies with the key term, "Identification."...Thereafter, with this term as an instrument, we seek to mark off the areas of rhetoric, by showing how a rhetorical motive is often present where it is not usually recognized, or thought to belong.[2]

Identification is also an important concept in some of Burke's criticism, being the major critical term used in discussing *Samson Agonistes* in the *Rhetoric* and Plato's *Phaedrus* in *A Grammar of Motives.* Interestingly, these two critical exercises touch upon rhetorical concerns directly. The former study analyzes a dramatic poem which makes a political statement; the latter discusses a poetic dialogue on the effect of discourse.

The concept of identification, through its root term, identity, has played an even more important role in the interpretation of Burke's ideas in recent years because of its centrality to issues in critical Marxism and in deconstruction. To cite two examples of studies in a Marxist vein, Fredric Jameson's articles in *Critical Inquiry* accuse Burke of collaborating in the ideology of bourgeois individualism by reiterating "American myths of the self and of its identity crises and ultimate regeneration"; while Frank Lentricchia in *Criticism and Social Change* devotes many pages to articulating Burke's "complex" ideas on the issue

174

of identity in the course of discussing the relationship between rhetoric and social action.[3] Apparently, an initial task in assessing the relationship of Burke's work to contemporary critical theory is a reexamination of his notions of identity and identification in light of efforts to "decenter" and "demystify" the "transcendental" self.[4]

In this study, I wish to argue that Burke's notions of identity and identification do conflict with the more radical Marxist position exemplified by Jameson as articulated in the first of the articles in *Critical Inquiry*. One may, however, by a careful examination of Burke's writing, derive a complex notion of identity fully capable of engaging a contemporary critique. As Jameson himself admits, Burke anticipated many of his charges through the use of effective "strategies of containment"; indeed, in Lentricchia's terms, Burke may be the subject's "cagiest champion."[5] My purpose, then, is to analyze the Burkean strategy of containment called "identification," with an aim toward rediscovering its cogency and relevance to issues of identity in contemporary critical theory.

Such a task is made easier by the fact that Burke's notion of identification never strays very far from earlier versions of the three ruling analytical schemas of the twentieth century: Freudianism, Marxism, and structural linguistics. A complete examination of identification accounting for its relationship to each of these schema would require a book-length discussion. In lieu of that discussion, I wish to focus upon one dimension of the concept of identification, that of "association." Although "association" may seem to be one of Burke's more obscure terms of analysis, it sustains his discussion of "the rhetoric of class" in part 2 of *A Rhetoric of Motives*. Moreover, it is a key strategy by which Burke tracks the interpenetration of subject, environment, and discourse, anticipating certain directions of late-twentieth-century critical thought and placing these directions in relationship to each other. And finally, association functions in Burke's critical applications as a technique which demonstrates, if not his deconstructive powers, at least a less opaque view of the subject than may be expected.

Before pursuing further Burke's concept of association, however, I wish to sketch the dimensions of the contemporary issues surrounding the concept of identity, so as to articulate fully the efficacy of Burke's strategy of response. I do so with reference to the aforementioned arguments of Jameson and Lentricchia, reading the former as a critic of certain tendencies in Burke's view and using the latter's interpretation of Burke as a ground for introducing association as the functional elaboration of identification.

Christine Oravec

The Complexity of Identity:
Burke Situated

From Barthes to Foucault, from Lacan to Derrida, the wholeness, uniqueness, intentionality, and generative power of individual human beings, generally phrased as the "problem of identity," has been thrown into question.[6] The issue ranges, in various forms, through the critical theories of contemporary Freudianism, Marxism, and deconstructionism, though not without a great deal of variation between theories and subtheories. A common thrust that links these various approaches, however, appears to be a view of the individual subject as "constructed" rather than "constructing," that is, determined by forces, whether environmental or linguistic, which are impersonal and universal, and hence, nonproductive of uniqueness or "identity." To phrase the issue in such bald terms, however, is to ignore the dialectical subtleties of contemporary theory. Thus a more intensive examination of two of Burke's interpreters, in this case both Marxist in persuasion, may discover the precise point of engagement.

At first reading, Fredric Jameson's critique of Burke seems oddly wrongheaded, as though Jameson had not read Burke at all. After his implication that Burke is enmeshed in "American myths of the self and of its identity crises," Jameson elaborates:

> Burke's system has no place for an unconscious, it makes no room for genuine mystification, let alone for the latter's analysis or for that task of decoding and hermeneutic demystification which is increasingly the mission of culture workers in a society as reified and as opaque as our own. The dramatistic modes, if I may put it that way, are all categories of consciousness, open to the light of day in classical, well-nigh Aristotelian fashion; the Burkean symbolic act is thus always serenely transparent to itself, in lucid blindness to the dark underside of language, to the ruses of history or of desire.[7]

There are two issues here. Jameson's placement of Burke in the American pantheon of individualist authors and thinkers best exemplified by the likes of Ralph Waldo Emerson and William James of course is correct—Burke's transcendentalist and pragmatist origins pervade his thought, making possible, as Lentricchia argues, his "self-reliant" Marxism of the thirties (however contradictory the idea), and the rhetorical analysis of the late forties and fifties.[8] However, how could anyone accuse Burke of ignoring the unconscious, mystification, and the techniques which expose the "dark underside of language"?

The issue rests precisely upon Burke's concept of identification, rather than solely upon his embeddedness in the intellectual tradition of American individualism. Specifically, the issue rests in the last phrase of the quoted section from Jameson: "the ruses of history or of desire." The problem, according to Jameson, is not that Burke ignores Marxist and psychoanalytic modes of analysis, but rather that these theories place their "ultimate" emphasis upon the determinate role of material and sexual forces. Burke's notion of identification, like his notion of dramatism that is similarly attacked by Jameson later in the article, is a "strategy of containment," preempting a thoroughgoing demystification of the subject as determined by its environmental context. Identification, Jameson suggests, requires that a locus of power in history be discovered in the individual as producer and creator through the instrumental modes of a language which constructs affinities between itself and other entities similarly equipped.[9]

Thus phrased, the issue between Jameson and Burke is a real one, though it runs the risk of making Burke appear unresponsive to the power of the Marxist critique. What is required is an interpretation of Burke that is sensitive to the power of the Marxist analysis and duly alert to Burke's shortcomings, while concerned with reading Burke as situated both in his own past history and in ours. This reading comes from Frank Lentricchia, whose book *Criticism and Social Change* can be seen as an apologia in the best sense. Lentricchia argues that Burke's concept of identification implies a notion of identity neither opaque nor mystical, but dialectically complex enough to withstand much of the Marxist critique.

The key to Lentricchia's characterization of Burke's concept of identity resides in the word "complex" and its derivative, "complexity."[10] This notion of complexity is not to be confused with the New Critical concern of making explicit the complex pattern of a poem, a work of art, or an author's corpus. The complexity of identity is not to be taken as a self-contained icon, reflective yet mimetic in its representational isolation. Such a view of literature, naturally, implies an author-subject equally self-contained and isolated.[11] Rather, Lentricchia's discussion of identity in Burke implies a complex interaction of historical and situational forces with the assertive force of the individual:

Yet the liberal humanist privilege granted to the autonomous actor-subject. . . is probably the primary focus of Burke's critical

Christine Oravec

consciousness. He performs about as thorough an act of what is now called "deconstruction" as is possible, but when he is finished he has not destroyed the humanistic impulse of his dramatism; he has only (and this by design) relocated the "free" subject within a system that is now understood in more complex fashion than his usual bare-bones formulation of dramatism would permit....The humanist conception of "agent" is understood in its widest context—it is seen as *having* a constraining context, which is precisely what humanism has difficulty admitting. But such understanding (that the subject is a function of a system) cannot and should not eliminate all humanist desire for the free subject—a point that many recent anti-humanists are not yet ready to concede.[12]

Lentricchia associates Burke's complex notion of identity with the complex entanglements of the surrounding historical context; he quotes Derrida to the effect that "intention and the subject...are not destroyed, they are situated in a way so complicated as to be almost overwhelmed."[13] Such complexity supports Burke's adoption of the concept of identification, which, unlike persuasion, assumes a rhetor not by any means entirely conscious or self-contained. Thus:

Burkean rhetoric would occupy the space between the old rhetoric of pure will and modernist and postmodernist aesthetic of antiwill: between a subject apparently in full possession of itself, and in full intentional control of its expression, and a subject whose relation to "its" expression is very problematic. ...The rhetorician is the not-always-knowing carrier of historical and ideological forces, while at the same time he acts within and upon the present and thereby becomes an agent of change.[14]

Supporting such claims would require a deeper examination of Lentricchia's arguments, such as his discussion of "agent" in *A Grammar of Motives*, or of Burke's contribution to the American Writers' Congress, "Revolutionary Symbolism in America" (both Burke's speech and Lentricchia's discussion of it are included in this volume). However, enough of Lentricchia's thrust should be apparent to justify a discussion of identification as a key term articulating Burke's notion of identity and answering some of Jameson's concerns. Specifically, such a discussion should justify examining the function of association as one that establishes links between the individual subject and the complex environment in which it is embedded.

Identity and the Types of Association

Under the subheading "The Priority of the Idea" in *A Rhetoric of Motives*, where most references to "association" may be found, Burke lays out most succinctly his differences with Marxist analysis, culminating in the following statement:

> Would it then be possible to make a distinction that allowed for "ideology" within limits? That is, could we consider the Marxist critique as usefully limiting the application of the ideological, but not as wholly discrediting it? For the human mind, as the organ of a symbol-using animal, is "prior" to any *particular* property structure—and in this sense the laws of symbols are prior to economic laws. Out of his symbols, man has developed all his inventions. Hence, why should not their symbolic origin remain concealed in them? Why should they be not just *things*, but *images* of "ideas"? (*RM*, p. 136)

In the pages prior to this passage, Burke uses the concept of association to move from the "thing" to the "image" of "ideas," while shedding light on the identity of the "human mind." Further, Burke partitions association into three dimensions, the mechanical, the analogical, and the ideological, each of which represents a different critical approach to the issue of relating the subjective self to historical context. The following discussion describes the relationship of identification to its associational function, and characterizes the three approaches in terms of critical strategies.

Discussion of identification as a process of association must start, in Burke's terms, with a "metaphysics" or "ontology" of the subject.[15] A subject, whether it be a physical thing, a person, or an image, has several properties which establish its recognizable identity. On the metaphysical level, identification is an act of recognizing things by naming and classifying their various properties. The act of identification can be as simple as referring to the subject by naming one of its properties: the chair is identified as "the red chair." Or, identification may be more complex, as when a person is referred to by name, by the way she or he is dressed, or by her or his social or economic affiliations: one could identify John by saying, "John is a temperance man." As a result of identification, the chair is put into a "class," the class of "all red chairs," and John is put into the class of "temperance supporters." Burke writes:

> Metaphysically, a thing is identified by its *properties*. In the realm of Rhetoric, such identification is frequently by property

Christine Oravec

> in the most materialistic sense of the term, economic property.
> ...In the surrounding of himself with properties that name his
> number or establish his identity, man is ethical. (*RM*, pp. 23–24)

However, in addition to these more material properties, a subject
may have more general properties or "associations." Associations are
superstructural references, as distinguished from the substructural
reference of material property; they include concepts, ideas, or "clusters of attitudes."[16] For example,

> "Feast" is on the level of bodily appetite. Yet not quite. For the
> element of sociality in a feast introduces an ingredient of
> motivation beyond that of hunger.[17]

Association, then, is a type of identification that names and classifies
things according to their superstructural properties. One may associate "feast" with the class of social functions; or one may associate
"temperance" with the concept of "moderation," in addition to its
more material identification of "nonalcoholic."

Assigning something an identifying name or class is a particularly
powerful function; indeed, it may be related to the rhetorical power of
a subject. Lentricchia argues that there are two reciprocal dimensions
to the concept of identification: identification "with," and identification "of." The latter is the active rhetorical function: " 'Identification
with' requires that the critical rhetor perform the dangerous act of
'identification of' ": the political work of ideological analysis pre-
sumes a power-enabling act of cognition—an identifying that necessarily entails a knowing and a mastering." Obviously, this concept of
identification requires the notion of a rational, conscious, dominating
subject, the kind most subject to criticism from the Marxist position
for its obliviousness to determining historical factors. There is no deconstructing this form of identification; one can only estimate its external effects. But there is another dimension of identification, that is,
identification "with," which "operates at the mediating level where
Burke situates rhetoric itself. It is conscious, as when we identify ourselves with our occupations; it is also elusively unconscious, and necessarily so under advanced capitalist norms of dispersion that
encourage us to think of what we do as autonomous activity."[18] To understand this second dimension of identification one must delve into
the functioning of association in constructing the subject within the
historical context.

Burke describes three kinds of association related to the "rhetoric of
class": the mechanical, the analogical, and the ideological (*RM*, p.

132). He identifies these three kinds, however, not with Marxist theory, but with Coleridge's fancy, primary imagination, and secondary imagination.[19] Insofar as Coleridge is concerned with the explanation of "self and self-consciousness," his three-part process is a mechanism for generating identity in terms of the creative agent. Coleridge's conception of imagination as an "inter-penetration of the counteracting powers" of identity as subject and identity as object undergirds Burke's notion of "the human mind" as productive of and produced by language.[20]

Mechanical associations, like Coleridge's "fancy," are accidental juxtapositions, things which are identified with a subject merely by being in the same place at the same time. And the fancy, Coleridge states, is a passive or reflective faculty: "it must receive all its materials ready-made."[21] For example, if at a certain time "moderation" is a highly acceptable social position to take, the fact that "John is a temperance man" allows John to be readily accepted in his society. Likewise, if warm colors are "in," red chairs are highly acceptable. Speaking of Veblen's *Theory of the Leisure Class*, Burke suggests,

> Sometimes the identifications he reveals seem of the first, more accidental sort. People seem bent on doing or acquiring things simply because these things happen to have become the signs of an admired status. (*RM*, p. 134)

In this case, it is the accidental coincidence of timeliness that associates status with certain "status symbols," determined by prior social codes.

Burke goes on to discuss these mechanical associations as "signs," and states that the connection between the signs and their signifieds is arbitrary, much as do Saussurean structuralists. Since the signs are separated from their signifieds, they can become a self-sustaining system capable of shifting arbitrarily across any possible field of signifieds. "One can imagine these same people [status seekers] doing exactly the opposite, if the opposite happened to be the sign of the same status" (*RM*, p. 134).

Yet the very notion of sign systems depends in turn upon the identity of subjects: a "John" who acts temperately, or status seekers who "seem to be bent on doing or acquiring." Moreover, the significance of the action, to behave "temperately" or not, rests not in its mechanical associations but in the "intent" of the source, and any criticism of the intention becomes a criticism of individuals. As Rosalind Coward and John Ellis state:

> Structuralism tended to gravitate toward a mechanistic theory
> of the action of the structure....The relations between the
> various elements were then conceived as relations of exteriority.
> The universe of structuralism was made up of fully constructed
> objects and subjects; their "presence" was affirmed by the
> naive, empirical reference to "concrete" evidence, to "social"
> life, to culture, to anthropology, etc.

The result of such a positive structuralism is either a mechanical materialism with an entirely passive subject, or a transcendent idealism
with the subject in control of all meaning yet removed from the matrix
of the linguistic structure.[22]

Both Burke and Coleridge were aware of the tendency of mechanical
association to support the extreme of naive materialism. Yet the opposite extreme, the potential for idealism, still remains in both. Burke's
response to materialism is to develop an approach toward idealism
that derives the human subject from language, and language from an
environmentally grounded human organism. Language then serves
as a material mediator between history and the individual.

The approach to idealism can be seen in Burke's second category of
the rhetoric of class, the "analogical." Instead of separating the realms
of the signifier and the signified, analogizing associations share signification across areas of concern, such as the political, the social, or
the religious. No area of concern is exempt or prior, including the
material:

> In the surrounding of himself with properties that name his
> number or establish his identity, man is ethical....Man's moral
> growth is organized through properties, properties in goods, in
> services, in position or status, in citizenship, in reputation, in
> acquaintanceship and love. (*RM*, p. 24)

Analogizing associations depend upon similarities between the analo-
gized realms that are produced by the functioning of language. The
act of applying one set of associations to another set is "transference,"
and the end result of this transference is a "transformation."

> There are *analogizing* associations, where terms are transferred
> from one order to another. Thus, a business culture may
> become much exercised over a work's "value" as an
> aestheticized equivalent of "price." (*RM*, p. 134–35)

For example, John is materially associated with temperance, but he is
also associated with the more ideological property of temperance,
moderation. John may also be associated analogically with political or

economic groups which advocate moderation in other areas of action besides alcoholic intake. John's action on the plane of individual habit is transferred, by the association of moderation, to the plane of social interaction.

Another kind of analogizing association is Burke's notion that since "patterns of experience for all men are much alike," transference of association takes place between persons as well as between areas of an individual's own concerns. The interests of one person or group can be associated with the interests of another person or group.

> Here is perhaps the simplest case of persuasion. You persuade a man only insofar as you can talk his language... *identifying* your ways with his. (*RM*, p. 55)

In other words, John may join the Temperance Union if he is persuaded that the members' interests are similar to his. Identification that is actively brought about by transfer of associations from one individual or group to another individual or group is the first step in the process of persuasion; that is, the first step in the process of constructing a subject. As Coleridge suggests, primary imagination, parallel to analogizing association, is characterized "as a repetition in the finite mind of the eternal act of creation in the infinite I AM."[23] Significantly, rhetorical concerns, with their emphasis on agent as "speaker," originate at the analogizing level of identification, which produces identity not mechanically but through the metaphorical processes of language.[24]

In introducing language as productive of identity, Burke's second type of class rhetoric implies a "discursive reality" in discourse, which is inclusive of, yet greater than, its arbitrary and mechanical nature as linguistic sign.[25] Elsewhere in the *Rhetoric*, Burke appropriately calls this capability of signs to determine as well as indicate meaning the "dialectical" function. Though a different order of terms than the "positive," dialectical terms are not a separate category from the positive; rather,

> we come to the place where the dialectical realm of ideas is seen to permeate the positive realm of concepts.... Thus the ethical-dramatic-dialectical vocabulary so infuses the empirical-positive world of things that each scientific object becomes available for poetry. (*RM*, p. 186)

Language can, and does, actively create meaning and hence identity. Yet language is a human product, grounded in humanity's capacity to speak, and finally in a material, "biological" ground.[26]

Christine Oravec

Many passages in Burke's work affirm that his concept of identity is never isolated or merely individualistic. Even as early as 1938, in his "Twelve Propositions on the Relation between Economics and Psychology," he recognizes the social construction of the identity:

> People are neither animals nor machines...but actors and acters. They establish identity by relation to groups (with the result that, when tested by *individualistic* concepts of identity, they are felt to be moved by "deceptions" or "illusions," the "irrational"—for one's identification as a member of a group is a role, yet it is the only active mode of identification possible, as you will note by observing how all individualistic concepts of identity dissolve into the nothingness of mysticism and the absolute). If you would avoid the antithesis of supernaturalism and naturalism, you must develop the coordinates of socialism—which gets us to cooperation, participation, man in society, man in drama.[27]

Burke's more mature acknowledgment of the constructed nature of identity comes, however, in his discussion of the third type of rhetoric of class, the "ideological." This type of association occurs when a single superstructural association serves as a basis for relating different concerns "generically." For example, a concept like moderation may be the motivating principle behind all of John's actions, social, political, and personal. In the critical context, these underlying principles are called motivations. Speaking of the actions of murder and suicide in *Samson Agonistes*, Burke suggests that the motivating principle behind these two actions is change or transformation:

> You need to look for a *motive that can serve as ground for both these choices*, a motive that, while not being exactly one or the other, can ambiguously contain them both....A poet's identification with imagery of murder or suicide, either one or the other, is, from the "neutral" point of view, merely a concern with *terms for transformation in general*. (*RM*, pp. 10–11)

This quotation indicates that a general motivating principle, whether it be moderation, transformation, or whatever, is manifested in, or "embodied by," groups of concerns which are otherwise only artificially associated with each other.[28] For example, one would not associate a character's actions of murder and suicide, except perhaps mechanically; yet in Milton's Samson, the two actions are identified by sharing the same motive, transformation.

In his discussion of ideological associations, as indicated previously, Burke makes a commitment to the priority of the symbolic function:

> For the human mind, as the organ of a symbol-using animal, is "prior" to any *particular* property structure—and in this sense the laws of symbols are prior to economic laws. (*RM*, p. 136)

Yet the idealism expressed in this identification of humanity as language using is swiftly qualified. Rather than a material world dominated by superstructural texts, Burke articulates a subtle dialectical relationship between the two realms:

> Given an economic situation, there are ways of thinking that arise in response to it. But these ways of living and thinking, in complex relationship with both specific and generic motives, can go deep, to the level of *principles*. For a way of living and thinking is reducible to terms of an "idea"—and that "idea" will be "creative" in the sense that anyone who grasps it will embody it or represent it in any mode of action he may choose. The idea, or underlying principle, must be approached by him through the sensory images of his cultural scene. But until he intuitively grasps the principle of such an imaginal clutter, he cannot be profoundly creative, so far as the genius of that "idea" is concerned. For to be profoundly representative of a culture, he will imitate not its mere insignia, but the principle behind the *ordering* of those insignia. (*RM*, p. 137)

Note that ideological associations, or "ideas," are inaccessible but through "sensory images," or the material associations of language, which are in turn embedded in culture. Ideology is not so removed from its material signs as to be an independent and impenetrable source. Note, too, that the subject ("anyone") "embodies" or "represents" that idea in its own material praxis, through its life as a biological organism. Recognizing the two-sided nature of the terms "embody" and "represent" is important in reading this passage, for a subject that "embodies" or "represents" may do so passively, "in itself," or actively, "toward something else."[29] To say that identities are formed by language, through both its effect and its use, reaffirms the existence of identity but views it as a product as well as a producer of material culture. One dimension of identification, either identification "with" or identification "of," does not precede the other; only the priority of language is asserted. Language is Burke's ideal refuge, the organizing yet demonstrably ambiguous ground by which he strategizes the containment of identity. As in Coleridge's secondary imagination, which "dissolves, diffuses, dissipates, in order to re-create...[struggling] to idealize and unify," Burke's ideological association struggles to unify on the ground of language, though that ground be continually contested.[30]

As Marxist critics would point out, Burke's use of language as a medium for transcending differences of class and status, like his concept of identity, allows for the possibility of mystification. His "neutral point of view" is still a transcendent one, evocative of an omniscient God who is the archetype of the subject.[31] Yet even socialism, suggests Jameson, "should signal a transcendence of the older individualism and the appearance of new collective structures."[32] Burke's location of transcendence in the construction of the subject, while it does not avoid the problem of identity or mystification, allows for the active construction by cooperative human agents of the collective, even as the agents are constrained by their historical roles.

Language, then, is the strategy of transcendence by which the unification of subject/object, self/other, and in Jameson's terms, individual/collective can occur. What may look like a break or a separation between two underlying principles of association becomes a transformation between the two, if the corresponding transcendent term is found which names the unifying principle. The naming of this principle makes the two orders of associations more meaningful in their relationship to one another. As an illustration, Burke explains Jowett's difficulty with the Platonic dialogue *Phaedrus* as an inability to recognize this transcendent process.

> He has characterized the process of transcendence as it looks from without, rather than as it looks from within. For as seen from without, the change from one level of discourse to another would be a kind of jolt or inconsistency.... Yet as seen from within, this change of levels would be precisely what the dialogue was designed to trace....A Platonic dialogue is rather a process of transformation whereby the position at the end transcends the position at the start, so that the position at the start can eventually be seen in terms of the new motivation encountered en route. (*GM*, p. 422)

One outcome of a focus upon transcendence is to bring new insight to changes within a discursive text such as the *Phaedrus*. However, another result may be the ability to uncover the construction of identity, both materially and in language, since the several processes of association are so intimately tied to the production of the subject. Most of Burke's critical applications are dedicated to pursue both outcomes.

Applications of Association: Burke's Method

Two critical applications which illustrate Burke's use of the typology of association in identification particularly well are the aforementioned discussions of *Samson Agonistes* and the *Phaedrus*. While both applications use the terminology of identification, they avoid reducing the two texts to the same strategy; in other words, they accomplish what Lentricchia calls "recognizing the text as an 'event.'"[33] Further, these analyses succeed in deconstructing the authorial identity of the texts, without debilitating the power of either the subjects or the language.

Samson Agonistes features the character of a blind murderer-suicide, created by a blind poet. According to Burke, a mechanical association is established between Samson and Milton, because they incidentally share a common feature, blindness. However, the two men also have other, analogical, associations in common. Milton could associate himself with a motive for suicide because he identified with this Old Testament hero, even though the Christian religion forbids aggression against the self.

> Here, too, though still remotely, would be "literature for use": the poetic reenactment of Samson's role could give pretexts for admitting a motive which, if not so clothed or complicated, if confronted in its simplicity, would have been inadmissible. (*RM*, p. 5)

However, suicide is not the only motive exemplified in the poem. Aggression against oppressive enemies is just as powerful a motive. Burke argues that Milton associated the Philistines of the story with his own personal enemies, the British loyalists. Samson's conquering of the Philistines represents in language Milton's own aggression against the opposition party.

> In saying, with fervor, that a blind Biblical hero did conquer, the poet is "substantially" saying that he in his blindness will conquer. This is moralistic prophecy, and is thus also a kind of "literature for use." (*RM*, p. 5)

Christine Oravec

In effect, Milton has transferred the complex motivations he may have had in the "material" world to a set of motivations held by a character in a world of ideas.

To effect the transfer of motives from the substructural to the superstructural level, a transfer of motives occurs in language, between the two images of "suicide" and "murder." This transference of one term to the other describes the plot of the poem, while it reflects Milton's own subconscious motivations. The poem, then, can be read primarily as one author's successful sublimation into language of both historical and psychological determinants, and Burke does imply such a reading. The author's efforts at containing his purposes within the boundaries of a text, his project of self-construction, is thus undermined by the subconscious influences of "history and desire." But for Burke, such a diagnostic reading does not go far enough; it does not recognize the power of the text in constructing Milton's identity, and possibly that of his audience. As Burke says, the personality of the poet both determines and is determined by the quality and type of imagery she or he produces.

> The depicting of a thing's *end* may be a dramatic way of identifying its *essence*. . . . Then, in an aside, as an illustrative conceit, we proposed a project whereby personality types be defined in terms of the world's end, depending upon the type of such "eschatalogical" imagery with which a given person most readily identified himself. (*RM*, p. 17)

The poem *Samson Agonistes*, with its vision of a hero's end, strategizes the containment of, or transcends, Milton's most personal motivations, conscious and unconscious, determined and indeterminate. The text does reflect the unconscious and material determinations of its subject, but it also articulates, or "bodies forth," a strategy which encompasses its author's motivations. This is not to say that the poem escapes determination, exists, as it were, as a unique "subject." Rather, the poem, since it is subject to its author's own determinants, has the capacity to produce his identity in a way that transcends the explicit intentions of both the subject and the poem itself. The productive power of language must always be, in part, an unconscious power.

A similar process of association and transcendence occurs in Plato's *Phaedrus*. As mentioned above, Burke suggests that this work is an act of transcendence which critics like Jowett find hard to describe, "as it looks from without, rather than as it looks from within." In his analysis of the discourse "from within," Burke concentrates on the function of a particular image, "love," and its associations. From this he builds a critique of Socrates' personality and social context.

Burke discusses two metaphors or conceits that are repeated throughout the poem. As mentioned above in the discussion of "image," the first image, "feast of discourse," has mechanical associations of hunger, and analogical associations of "sociality" in the sharing of words and ideas. Similarly, the second image, "love," is introduced through a conceit, the first speech of the "nonlover." This conceit depends greatly upon the accidental associations of the concept "love," that is, physical passion. The nonlover is interested only in the material associations of the concept, not the ideological qualities. Burke writes,

> Lysias' speech on love, which is read with naive admiration by Phaedrus, is trivial. It is built around a conceit, the proposition that Lysias should gain his suit not because he is a lover but because he is a non-lover, and the non-lover will never cause the beloved the many disturbances that a lover would. (*GM*, p. 423)

Since the mechanical association of "feast" is hunger, and the mechanical association of "love" is passion, there is a common cluster of attitudes surrounding these two images, based on the material principle of "desire."

> Since love is similarly appetitive, we have a cluster of *food, love, hunger, enjoyment* experiences functioning at the roots of purpose. (*GM*, p. 424)

However, Burke suggests that if the critic completes the inquiry at the mechanical level, she or he does not understand the process of transcendence that transfers the general associations of "love" to the general associations of "feast of discourse." For not only does love occur at the physical level, but it is also expressed in "impassioned language," or rhetoric. Similarly, the feast of discourse is not a satiation of physical appetite but the receiving of "impassioned language." Through these analogizing associations, language is identified with love, and love with language, in the single transcendent term "rhetoric." The critic who works from "inside" the text sees this merging of love and discourse in one transcendent term, and the difference between the two concepts disappears.

The three speeches on love in the *Phaedrus* illustrate increasingly more analogical associations of the term "love." A fourth level of discourse illustrates how these same speeches function as examples of

Christine Oravec

impassioned discourse, or rhetoric. Burke characterizes the resulting transcendence of this fourth level as a discussion of rhetorical principles. The fifth level of transcendence in the text is a consideration of the virtues of the spoken word as the foundation of passionate discourse. The motivation of passion is transferred from love to the verbal persuasion of speechmaking; and the art of speechmaking is the "ideology" of the dialogue.

Finally, like *Samson Agonistes*, *Phaedrus* itself is a term of transcendence. As Milton as an authorial subject is constructed by the determining power of language, Plato is produced as an author through his traces in the Socratic dialectic. As Burke says,

> Socrates was thus accused of the "representative" transgression. And whatever may have been the realities of the case in the literal sense, the structure of the *Phaedrus* shows that he was a "corruptor of youth" in the transcendental sense. (*GM*, p. 426)

The power of the dialogue generates the power of Plato's own position. The dialogue, ostensibly stripped of material passion, contains an insidiously passionate motive, as Socrates' Athenian accusators undoubtedly sensed; in the guise of a lack of power, the language is determined to persuade the reader to a particular philosophical system. The *Phaedrus*, then, produces the very conditions of seductive discourse which gives effectiveness to Plato's philosophy and to his identity as "corruptor of youth."

By thus turning discourse on its head, Burke makes his two authorial subjects, Milton and Plato, products of their own productions. In the process, he deconstructs, through examination of the forces of historical determination and of language, the identity of the subjects. Milton, the pious Protestant, becomes the self-obsessed and passively murderous rebel, a figure not unlike his own Satan. Plato becomes the seductive and effective rhetor, of the kind which he himself castigates in the *Gorgias* and other dialogues. But by deriving the subject from its own language, Burke criticizes the received view of both Milton and Plato without reducing their positioning to random, arbitrary events in the subtext of history, or mere reflections of their material circumstances. The new characterizations are admittedly demythifying, yet open to the constructive power of the subjects and the language. Hence these identities are not opaque but determined by complex layers of forces, and mediated by the productive function of language.

Burke's notions of identity and association, while admittedly complex, have their shortcomings. Particularly in the later work, and in the early *Counter-Statement*, there is a tendency to focus upon the internal transformations of the text to the detriment of its material conditions. Further, as Lentricchia has noted, there is throughout Burke's writing a too-rapid escape into comic, transcendent, God-like perspectives, with the individualism and essentialism that implies. But the central Burke, the Burke of *Attitudes toward History, Permanence and Change, A Grammar of Motives,* and *A Rhetoric of Motives,* more likely takes the stance described by Lentricchia:

> Against our usual views of the interrelated conceptions of the autonomous subject, intention, and personal identity, Burke brings his central proposal of "action," not as the production of an "agent" who would be in turn conceived as the expressive origin and master of "action" but as a transpersonal, all-embracing process within which agents are already situated.[34]

If association implies a transcendence, it is a transcendence "of," and not exclusively "by," the individual subject.

Further, Burke's typology of association suggests some trenchant critiques of contemporary critical approaches. His mechanistic form of association recognizes yet criticizes the implications for the arbitrariness of language present in traditional structuralism, as well as the reductiveness of naive materialism. His analogic type of association acknowledges the productive power located in the individual subject, as does much rhetorical theory and criticism, while it proceeds to uncover the material and unconscious determinants of that power. In ideological association he would provide a location for a production/construction of the subject which transcends material processes, without idealizing either the subject or language itself. Finally, in his application of association he discovers ways to deflate, rather than debunk, the individual.

Burke's formulation answers some questions on the issue of identity while it obscures others; nevertheless, it appears that his concept is not as "serenely transparent to itself" as Jameson suggests. With regard to Marxist criticism of the rhetoric of class, Burke writes:

> We are not merely trying to strike a compromise between unreconcilable opponents, or treating the two positions as ideal opposites, with the truth somewhere in between. Rather, we are assigning a definite function to each of the positions—and we are saying that, insofar as each performs its function, they are no more at odds than the stomach and liver of a healthy organism. (*RM*, p. 137)

Christine Oravec

Burke knows the need for complexity in that relationship of historical determination, identity, and language for which so many contemporary theorists are striving. His conclusions are a model, if not of results, then of effort.

NOTES

1. The author wishes to thank David Williams, Susan Stewart, Richard Gregg, and Lloyd Bitzer for their help in developing this paper.
2. Kenneth Burke, *A Rhetoric of Motives* (1950; rpt. Berkeley: University of California Press, 1969), p. xiii.
3. Fredric R. Jameson, "The Symbolic Inference; or, Kenneth Burke and Ideological Analysis," *Critical Inquiry,* 4 (1978), 507–23; reprinted in Hayden White and Margaret Brose, eds., *Representing Kenneth Burke* (Baltimore: Johns Hopkins University Press, 1982), pp. 68–91, quotation on p. 86; "Critical Response II: Ideology and Symbolic Action," *Critical Inquiry,* 5 (1978), 417–22; and Frank Lentricchia, *Criticism and Social Change* (Chicago: University of Chicago Press, 1983). Citations in this text to the first Jameson article refer to the reprint in *Representing Kenneth Burke.*

In the follow-up exchange between Jameson and Burke printed in the Winter 1978 issue of *Critical Inquiry,* Jameson denies that his initial article was an "attack" against Burke, even less a "debate" or "dispute." Still, he differentiates his Marxist position from that of Burke by opposing "the alienated forces of human institutions" to Burke's " 'counter-finality' or human freedom" (p. 422). Thus, though he does not reopen the issue of identity, he distinguishes his position on the bases of the originating force of individual action versus the determination of external material and social factors. I choose to focus upon Jameson's initial argument because it is more thoroughly articulated.

Another statement in the same vein, that of Philip Wander in "The Ideological Turn in Modern Criticism," *Central States Speech Journal,* 34 (1983), 5–6, appears to confirm Jameson's position, but is primarily concerned with the compatible uses to which Burke was put by academic scholars of rhetoric. Wander's two major claims concerning Burke himself, that he "had, by the 1950's, begun to detach himself from radical politics to meditate on literary texts," and that during this later time " 'cultural texture' could mask if not entirely obscure political concerns in Burke's work," are not contested in this study. However, I agree with one of Wander's many respondents, namely Farrel Corcoran in "The Widening Gyre: Another Look at Ideology in Wander and His Critics," *Central States Speech Journal,* 35 (1984), 55–56, that neither "meditation on literary texts" nor absorption with "cultural texture" is necessarily incompatible with "political concerns," or even "radical politics," particularly when it comes to Burke's lifelong project.
4. Though Frank Lentricchia in *Criticism and Social Change* comes closest,

a comprehensive study of the relationship between Burke's key term, "identification," and his concept of "identity" has yet to be made, particularly in light of recent critical interest in issues of the "subject" (see n. 6). This paper does not attempt to provide such a comprehensive study. Rather, Burke's concepts of identity are read in and through various statements on identification published in *GM* and *RM*, with only some items taken from his earlier "Marxist" period. These selections, I believe, are the most relevant to Jameson's objections, being located in the "central" period of Burke's career with which Jameson appears to be concerned.

5. Jameson, "Symbolic Inference," p. 87; Lentricchia, *Criticism and Social Change*, p. 93.

6. One of the most complete discussions of contemporary ideas of the "subject" is Rosalind Coward and John Ellis, *Language and Materialism: Developments in Semiology and the Theory of the Subject* (London: Routledge and Kegan Paul, 1977), where they examine Barthes and Lacan. See also Michel Foucault, "What Is an Author?" in *Language, Counter-Memory, Practice* (Ithaca: Cornell University Press, 1977), pp. 113–38; and Gayatri Chakravorty Spivak, Translator's Preface, in Jacques Derrida, *Of Grammatology* (Baltimore: Johns Hopkins University Press, 1976), pp. xxiv–ix.

7. Jameson, "Symbolic Inferences," p. 88.

8. Lentricchia, *Criticism and Social Change*, p. 6.

9. Jameson, "Symbolic Inferences," p. 88.

10. The attribution of "complexity" to Burke's notion of identity occurs repeatedly throughout Lentricchia's study, particularly at those places where he is tracing the interface between Burke and contemporary critical theories. Thus, in noting the similarities of Burke's critique of capitalism to Gramsci's concept of hegemony, Lentricchia writes: "Alienation, Burke insists, is therefore a psycho-economic concept, synonymous with a need to reject reigning symbols of authority.... But... our identities are very nearly hopelessly complicated (beyond self-conscious control) by a hegemonic process that would enroll us in a range of corporate identities, some concentric, others in conflict. The result of such complicating and proliferating coordinations and corporations of identity is to clog and solidify identity to the point where change of the radical sort is almost unimaginable" (pp. 77–78). Burke himself uses the term in his consideration of Jameson's reading of "identification": "I have also indicated in what sense I would not call the 'centrality' of the 'self'...a mere 'optical illusion,' though I would grant that the individual, as a 'person,' dissolves into quite a complexity of *identifications* in the sociopolitical realm." "Critical Response I: Methodological Repression and/or Strategies of Containment," *Critical Inquiry*, 5 (1978), 413.

11. Frank Lentricchia, *After the New Criticism* (Chicago: University of Chicago Press, 1980), pp. 6–7.

12. Lentricchia, *Criticism and Social Change*, pp. 71–72.

13. Ibid., p. 143.

14. Ibid., pp. 159–60.

Christine Oravec

15. Marie Hochmuth Nichols cites Burke on the subject of dramatism in her book *Rhetoric and Criticism* (Baton Rouge: Louisiana State University Press, 1963), p. 89: "He remarks that the [dramatistic] approach, instead of being *epistemological* and thus centering upon perception, knowledge, learning, etc. shall be an *ontological* one, thus centering upon the *substantiality* of the act."

16. As indicated by Joseph Schwartz, "Kenneth Burke, Aristotle, and the Future of Rhetoric," in Douglas Ehninger, ed., *Contemporary Rhetoric: A Reader's Coursebook* (Glenview, Ill.: Scott, Foresman, 1972), pp. 254–55.

17. Kenneth Burke, *A Grammar of Motives* (1945: rpt. Berkeley: University of California Press, 1969), p. 424.

18. Lentricchia, *Criticism and Social Change*, pp. 148, 149.

19. I am indebted to David Williams for directing me to the *Biographia Literaria* and for his excellent suggestions on Burke's use of Coleridge.

20. S. T. Coleridge, *Biographia Literaria*, ed. J. Shawcross, Vol. 1 (London: Oxford University Press, 1954), p. 198.

21. Ibid., p. 202.

22. Coward and Ellis, *Language and Materialism*, p. 4.

23. Coleridge, *Biographia Literaria*, p. 202.

24. Lentricchia in *Criticism and Social Change* describes metaphor as the way in which "language asserts its collective, classless potentiality as it moves against a stubborn, constellated series of notions like origin, privacy, ownership, virtue, the bourgeois subject, the liberal individual—all of which undergird the cultural staying power of capitalism" (p. 147).

25. Coward and Ellis, *Language and Materialism*, p. 6.

26. *RM*, p. 130. In his response to Jameson, Burke reiterates his long-standing principle of the biological basis for individuation as a separate organism: "immediate sensations not...shared in their immediacy by other organisms." He goes on to argue: "Once the human organism has developed, by physiological mutations, the ability to impose a strong anthropomorphic imprint upon the nonhuman 'context of situation' in which humanity developed, the mere postulate that this aptitude for symbolic action is grounded in nonsymbolic (and by the same token nonhuman) nature does not imply that such a realm of symbolicity cannot be an originating force in its own right. Its 'ideas'...are not merely 'derived' from material conditions; they are positively 'creative' of material conditions." See "Methodological Repression," pp. 413, 414.

27. Kenneth Burke, *The Philosophy of Literary Form*, 3d ed. (1941; rpt. Berkeley: University of California Press, 1973), p. 311. A significant history and analysis of "Twelve Propositions" appears in Michael Feehan, "Kenneth Burke's Discovery of Dramatism," *Quarterly Journal of Speech*, 65 (1979), 405–11.

28. Lentricchia claims that Burke's use of the term "embodied by," as in a motivating principle "embodied by" groups of concerns, or thought being "embodied" in discourse, indicates a kind of Kantian idealism which views material existence as reflections of a higher ideal. However, I show later

how the term "embodies" connotes a reciprocal relationship between ideal and material when applied to the acting subject. See "Reading History with Kenneth Burke," In White and Brose, *Representing Kenneth Burke*, p. 132.

29. Lentricchia finds a similar ambiguity in the term "substance" as discussed in the *Grammar*. Most of Burke's key "action" words, such as "motivation," "strategy," "action/motion," etc., could be read as containing implications for activity or passivity by the agent. Perhaps this is why action terms are so central to Burke's dramatism. See *Criticism and Social Change*, pp. 73–75, and "Reading History with Kenneth Burke," pp. 138–40.

30. Coleridge, *Biographia Literaria*, pp. 183, 202.

31. Lentricchia, *Criticism and Social Change*, pp. 64–65.

32. Jameson, "Symbolic Inference," p. 86.

33. Lentricchia, *After the New Criticism*, p. 188.

34. Lentricchia, *Criticism and Social Change*, p. 137.

9 UNDER THE SIGN

OF (AN)NIHILATION

BURKE IN THE AGE OF

NUCLEAR DESTRUCTION AND

CRITICAL DECONSTRUCTION

DAVID CRATIS WILLIAMS

In a self-proclaimed "rhetorical defense of rhetoric," Kenneth Burke begins his essay "Semantic and Poetic Meaning" by considering the " 'dialectical process' whereby a difference becomes converted into an antithesis." "You have noted," he writes, "that when two opponents have been arguing, though the initial difference in their position may have been slight, they tend under the 'dialectical pressure' of their drama to become eventually at odds in everything." In this fashion, for example, we find "bourgeois" depicted as the "absolute antithesis" of "proletarian," or we see oppositions such as "poetry vs. science." The transformation of difference into opposition is occasioned by the dialectical structure of language itself, and as human agents identify with, or inhabit, those linguistic structures they engage each other dramatically as opponents. These polarizations not only may blind opponents to the dialectical processes at work in them, and dramatized by them, but also may cause critics, "accustomed to thinking by this pat schematization," to "become almost demoralized at the suggestion that there may be a 'margin of overlap' " between seeming antitheticals.[1]

The dialectical structure of language seems to encourage us to think in dialectical frames, in polarities and through oppositions, rather than to focus inward on the processes of dialectics itself. As such, it should come as no surprise that the lucubratious pundits of literary and social criticism, the "word people" of our era, have too frequently indulged themselves in the dramatic resources of dialectical opposition, in thinking by this pat schematization. While Burke has himself been the victim of such tendencies to convert difference into opposition,[2] the increasing interest in Continental rhetorical and literary theory, and particularly in the writings of Jacques Derrida, has created new oppositional theaters, inviting graphic depictions such as a recent *Washington Post* headline: "Humanities vs. The Deconstructionists," with the word "Deconstructionists" dripping down the page in the best tradition of horror movie titles.[3] Each critical camp has become an encampment, an enceinte, prompting a recent article in the *Chronicle of Higher Education* to describe the contemporary critical scene as a "battlefield."[4] Indeed, the Yale English department, noted for its own Americanized version of deconstruction, is often viewed as an Edenic garden-turned-jungle which now "shields a guerrilla camp from which armed nihilists have been launching raids on the academic countryside."[5]

The creation of well-demarcated camps within critical theory and practice illustrates the result of the dialectical pressures toward oppositional thought. The mosaic is one of battle lines, extreme fractures inviting conflict: "Humanities vs. Deconstruction," "Scientism vs. Dramatism," "Deconstruction vs. Dramatism." "How often," laments Wayne Booth, "have we heard gory talk about 'the battle of the new criticism,' about 'total war,' about 'firing broadsides' designed 'to blast the other side into oblivion,' about 'counterattacks,' 'missiles,' and 'barrages.' "[6]

Rather than accept such a landscape and prepare for a battle royal with the "opposition," perhaps critics should seek between encampments the "margins of overlap" which convert antithesis into difference. To reconstitute difference as something other than opposition is to confront headfirst the quandaries of dialectics itself and the processes of transformation which allow dialectics to function.

This essay will develop the argument that there are important "margins of overlap" between the perspectives of Kenneth Burke and those of Jacques Derrida, especially in their respective analyses of the antinomies of dialectics. The concept of "margin," prominent in the writings of both Burke and Derrida, suggests not a synonymizing but rather both a border of demarcation between "opposites" and a "molten" area of ambiguity wherein transformation occurs between polarities.[7] There is in a sense a double margin at work in this project: both Burke and Derrida, by concentrating on the dialectical process itself, are concerned with the functioning of marginality in dialectics, with how the "margin between" both constitutes difference and dissolves opposition; moreover, there is a margin between their respective perspectives on dialectics and margins which allows both for "intertextual" reverberation and enhancement and for recognition of nontranslatability, of the difference between the perspectives.[8]

Since both Burke and Derrida are concerned with the problematics of dialectics, perhaps the best way in which to seek the margins between their perspectives is through a dialectical analysis of dialectics. The most obvious polarity in any consideration of language and meaning is that between "pure determination," wherein the linguistic sign "contains" the fullest plenitude of its meaning, and "pure indeterminacy," wherein the sign communicates no meaning whatsoever; in this formulation, each pole is the end, the eschatology, of "opposing" interpretive moves, one embedded in authority and announcing truth and the other denying any copula and thus any embeddedness. Although, as will be shown later, there is a margin between these poles which problematizes their status as polarities, they function initially as coordinates by which to chart the general course in linguistic analysis taken by both Burke and Derrida.

In charting the perspectives of Burke and Derrida through this dialectical analysis of dialectics, the conceptual polarities of pure determination and pure indeterminacy will be treated as eschatological visions, as concrete "seeings" of the respective ends. The vision of the end, its unveiling, its apocalypse, is, in Derrida's terms, "a transcendental condition of all discourse," but for purposes of analysis, the apocalyptic genre proper is "an exemplary revelation of this transcendental structure." And the scrutiny of this vision, the deconstruction of its transcendentalism, is the apocalypse of the apocalypse.[9] Similarly, Burke sees in the eschatological a dramatic proclamation of a thing's "essence or nature," of its entelechial perfection or "finishedness."[10] In terms of analytic procedure, Burke formalizes his insights in the "representative anecdote," or that synecdoche which preserves both scope and reduction in its "representativeness," and which he describes as "so dramatistic a conception that we might call it the dramatic approach to dramatism" (GM, p.60). This essay will appropriate the procedure of the representative anecdote in developing its dialectic of dialectics.

There appear to be two varieties of representative anecdotes: the admonitory, which through its eschatological warnings provides clues to, and admonitions concerning, what is becoming or may become "substantial," and the constitutive, which "reveals indices to human-kind's ontological nature."[11] The anecdotes selected to "envision" the polar coordinates of this essay are both admonitory, warning of future conditions rather than substantially describing things as they are. The anecdotes selected for this study are "nuclear war," as the perfect form of, the eschatology of, the rigidification and determination of differ-ence as opposition and conflict, perfecting in degree only the form of the current logomachy in the "battleground" of criticism; and the "image of no image," the ultimate meaninglessness, the abyss or the void that we name nihilism. Since the ultimate nuclear conflagration would obliterate humanity, it would also literally obliterate: it would blot out all language, leaving only the haunting silence of death. Simi-larly, the meaninglessness of the abyss is also an obliteration: it erases the letter, the word, and leaves only the silence of solipsism. Silence, obliteration, the destruction of the sign and of meaning is thus "mar-ginal" to both pure determination and pure indeterminacy, and to that extent it problematizes the very dialectic which, through its con-ditioning of the border, of differentiation between, it helps to found.

The subsequent sections of this essay pursue the questions of mar-ginality raised above, in relation both to a "dialectic of dialectics" and, embedded in that, to a reading of Burke and Derrida. The first section discusses the relationship between determination, or the self-present realization of truth, and the motivational complex which culminates in perfect conflict, in the annihilation of nuclear war. The concerns therein are essentially epistemological in focus. The second section "undoes" the first: it pursues the logic of deconstructive and logologi-cal readings of what it is that is known, and in that focus its concerns are primarily methodological, emphasizing the process of knowing (and thus unknowing). In its depriveging of truth and knowledge, indeed of linguistic closure or self-assuredness of any kind, these methodologies may be read as "perfecting" indeterminacy and thus opening up not new vistas of meaning but rather the vista, the hori-zon, of nothingness itself. The final section will examine the *perspec-tives* of Derrida and Burke as they "see" the dialectic of dialectics, as they "locate" their own critical endeavors within (or without) that dia-lectic. While both perspectives problematize knowledge and truth, it will be argued that Burke's unique "inhabitation" of the dialectic of di-alectics, through the constitutive anecdote of "drama," enacts the "motto" of dramatism, "By and through language, beyond lan-guage,"[12] in its ontological proclamation that humans *are* "bodies that learn language."[13] While this statement certainly becomes "caught in

David Cratis Williams

its own traces," its explicit self-reflexivity, its self-definition, creates if not a self-identity, or ontological closure, at least perhaps an identity for, a dramatization of, self, privileged above and perhaps, if one accepts Burke's arguments, insulated from the metaphoricity of, and thus the deconstructions in, language.

I

Both Derrida and Burke work under the nuclear shadow in their elaborations of critical theory; that is, they view language in the context of, and as a potential motivation for, nuclear war. Each views language as a system "grounded in" duplicity and paradox in which either the "trace" of the "other" or the "principle of the negative" keeps meaning aswirl. Yet each also discerns a seductive side of language; each hears language's siren song of knowledge, in pursuit of which humans may lose consciousness of the sine qua non of language itself: its own dialectic, its own duplicity. As a result, we may pursue blindly that siren song of certitude, and in the process we risk crashing upon the rocks of overdetermination, confirming not our certitude but rather our own finitude. This section of the paper will chart first the perspective of Derrida and then that of Burke on language itself, on its fundamental duplicity, its siren song of certitude, and, ultimately, its potential to motivate humanity to annihilate itself and obliterate all meaning.

Derrida's critique of language may be seen to revolve around a consideration of the concept of difference and its involvement in the construction of meaning. From the Derridean perspective, language consists of an unstable, arbitrary structuring of difference between sounds, signs (signifiers/signifieds), and, ultimately, meanings. This difference necessarily invokes a sense of "otherness," in that *A* is different from *B* only when it is other than it. In this sense, "traces" of the other always weave playfully through the "meaning" of that which is under consideration, constituting that meaning but also disseminating the "presence" of that meaning through the myriad traces of alterity. For Derrida,

> The play of differences supposes, in effect, syntheses and referrals which forbid at any moment, or in any sense, that a simple element be *present* in and of itself, referring only to itself. Whether in the order of spoken or written discourse, no element can function as a sign without referring to another

element which itself is not simply present. This interweaving results in each "element"—phoneme or grapheme—being constituted on the basis of the trace within it of the other elements of the chain or system. This interweaving, this textile, is the *text* produced only in the transformation of another text. Nothing, neither among the elements nor within the system, is anywhere either simply present or absent. There are only, everywhere, differences and traces of traces.[14]

This linguistic play of traces is the precondition for meaning in that the shadow of the other provides a suggestion of demarcation, of difference. Yet because the traces recede infinitely through a maze of others, producing a dissemination of meaning, the boundaries of difference cannot be clearly marked: they are always overrun, and the differential margin is problematized. The element of the trace suggests the wavering possibility of such demarcation, but its fruition is deferred through the infinite regress of otherness. Recognition of the trace produces an awareness of the paradoxical structure of meaning itself: meaning is never present in and of itself, but rather it disseminates through its traces and traces of traces and, in that sense, is always absent. Derrida captures this sense of duplicity, this dialectical metaphoricity, in his own neologism/metaphor *différance.*

"*Différance,*" writes Derrida, "is the systematic play of differences, of the traces of differences, of the *spacing* by means of which elements are related to each other."[15] While the metaphor of *différance* appropriately enough defies precise definition, some efforts at description seem worthwhile. The French verb *différer* has two seemingly contrary meanings: "to differ," implying a nonidentity, and "to defer," suggesting a delaying but still within the "order of the *same.*" Derrida gives "the name *différance* to this *sameness* which is not *identical:* by the silent writing of its "a" it has the desired advantage of referring to differing, *both* as spacing/temporalizing and as the movement that structures every dissociation." Thus, *différance* is "the middle voice" which "precedes and sets up" structures of opposition, or dialectical pairs, such as activity/passivity, nature/culture, etc.: it refers to the "production of difference and the differences between differences, the *play (jeu)* of differences." The operation of *différance* "will therefore be seen wherever speech appeals to difference."[16] Indeed, the metaphor of *différance* itself enacts the duplicity which it accords to language in general. That is, just as *différance* functions in language to establish duplicity through its recognition of the trace, so too does the *a* in *différance* graphically keep the word unsettled, referring to neither difference nor deferral but simultaneously suggesting both. This duplicity of the trace, its invocation of alterity, is the very condition which permits meaning; as Derrida puts it, "without the trace retaining the other as other in the same, no difference would do its work and no meaning would appear." In this sense, *"The (pure) trace is différance."*[17]

The metaphor of *différance* also suggests the seductiveness of language, the siren call of certitude. While the *a* in *différance* keeps it graphically unsettled, or visually jarring, the *a* is silent; it has no voice. In spoken representation, then, there is no difference between difference and *différance*. This vocal "erasure" of the *a* allows inferences of difference *or* deferral; that is, the necessary graphic duplicity of *différance* may fade in speech before the illusion of dichotomy. In language such dichotomies, including "all the conceptual oppositions of metaphysics," amount to "a subordination of the movement of *différance* in favor of the presence of a value or a *meaning* supposedly antecedent to *différance*, more original than it, exceeding and governing it in the last analysis." It is this illusion of presence, this freezing of meaning outside of the play of the trace, which Derrida calls the "transcendental signified."[18] When a transcendental signified exceeds and governs *différance*, demarcations of difference become rigid, and the gesture toward deferral is forgotten. Difference has transformed into opposition, and opposition necessarily privileges one of the paired terms, necessarily institutes hierarchy. It becomes a matter of this instead of that; this rather than that. Opposition is therefore necessarily a "conflictual and subordinating structure."[19]

Structures of opposition rigidify when the duplicity of the trace, the play of signifiers, is effaced, when all that remains is the "pure" signified unencumbered by the processes of language which produced it. Values which exceed the linguistic processes that produced them become metaphysical; they step outside of language and seemingly exist independently of it, either ontologically, as conditions of being, or theologically, as conditions of meaning. As Ryan observes, "All of the conceptual oppositions of metaphysics...can be said to hang on the frame of the interiority/exteriority binary."[20] To be outside of language is to be in the realm of pure signification, of oracular knowledge received totally, in its fullest plenitude, from an unknown other. This illusion of pure signification is indeed the very "history of truth,"[21] and, as Truth, this illusion of the transcendental signified generates a sense of "absolute knowledge." Fortified with, and motivated by, transcendental knowledge, humanity may "run the risk, precisely because of that," of enacting the conflictual impulses contained within any ordained hierarchy, of speeding onward toward a nuclear end.[22]

Prompted by illusions of truth and knowledge, humanity may be willing to venture the risk of nuclear annihilation, for "those who contemplate such a catastrophe do so no doubt in the name of what is worth more in their eyes than life ('better dead then red')." But nuclear destruction would not only annihilate, it would also obliterate; it would erase all writing. It would be a "remainderless destruction," "without symbolicity."[23] Thus, the "name in the name of which war would take place would be the name of nothing, it would be pure name, the 'naked name.' " And that "would be the End and the Revelation of the name itself, the Apocalypse of the Name." As Derrida points out, "Apocalypse means Revelation, of Truth, Un-veiling." But nuclear war "in the name of..." reveals nothing. It does not unveil the sign of truth; rather, it obliterates all signs. Indeed, the illusion of truth, of "absolute knowledge," which follows from the effacement of the signifier may be the condition of obliteration. Or, as Derrida cryptically observes, reversing the standard chronology, "No truth, no apocalypse." But since the illusion of pure signification beckons from within language itself, humanity may not be able to resist the siren song of certitude. In this sense, the "worldwide organization of the human *socius* today hangs by the thread of nuclear rhetoric," and the prospect of nuclear destruction is therefore "*fabulously textual*, through and through."[24] We can either heed the moral, the admonition, implicit in the fable of obliteration or we can continue to run the risk of the silence of death.

The admonitory insistence of the nuclear anecdote also seems to emerge from Burke's analysis of the dialectical structure, the duplicity, of language and its encrustations of certitude, its entelechial drive toward perfection, toward "the end-of-the-line." Burke's perspective on language contains two distinct emphases, dramatism and logology. Why "*two* terms for *one* theory"? Burke maintains that " 'dramatism' and 'logology' are analogous respectively to the traditional distinction (in theology and metaphysics) between ontology and epistemology."[25] In my current consideration of aspects of language which generate the aura of truth, the focus is clearly more upon the logological than upon the dramatistic, although dramatism proper will emerge as a central focus of the third section of this essay. In charting the logological perspective, the duplicity of language is seen in its metaphorical and analogical structure, but, as was seen in the Derridean perspective, that duplicity tends to efface itself. In Burke's terms, language is "rotten with perfection," suggesting that each linguistic distinction contains a perfectionist impulse, an entelechial drive, which propels that distinction, that demarcation of difference, toward a pure state, toward a reification of its implications, toward an "end-of-the-line." And when the "ever-ready dialectical resource" in language converts "national 'differences' into national 'conflicts,' " the nuclear arsenal portends the "end-of-the-line" ("Linguistic Approach," p. 272).

There is a double sense of the term "logology": in one respect, "logology" is a "science of words," or a method of understanding how language works to create, or to problematize, "knowledge"; but in a second sense, logology "relates to the initial duplication that came into the world when we could go from *sensations* to *words* for sensations."[26] This second sense concerns the nature of words themselves, their duplicitous structure and their discriminating function. While the first sense is certainly concerned with knowledge, it is knowledge about the second sense, or knowledge about how words create illusions of knowledge. In the first sense, then, "logology" is concerned with the way in which we read words and understand language; it is methodological in its orientation. That sense of logology will be examined in the second section of this essay. Our concern here is with the second sense of logology, with the "*discriminations* that we make by language" and with how those discriminations "constitute our realm of *knowledge* ("Dramatism and Logology," p. 91).

While an ideal language might perhaps in theory be a duplication of external reality, Burke maintains that in fact language is but a selection, reflection, and deflection of that reality, and to that extent language is creative of that which we take as reality. The move from sensations to words for sensations does not merely duplicate the sensations; rather, it creates a whole new order of sensation, a whole new order of understanding and motivation. Burke writes, "the body receives, via the senses, reports of the surrounding world. When these sensations are backed by words, the range of interpretations is greatly increased." And in the increased range of interpretations arises a new order of motivation, one apart from, other than, the nonsymbolic realm of sensation and nature. Burke explains, when our primordial ancestors "added to their sensations *words* for sensations...they could duplicate the taste of an orange by *saying* 'the taste of an orange,' that's when STORY was born, since words *tell about* sensations. Whereas Nature can do no wrong (whatever it does is Nature) when STORY comes into the world there enters the realm of true, false, honest, mistaken, the downright lie, the imaginative, the visionary, the sublime, the ridiculous, the eschatological (as with Hell, Purgatory, Heaven, the Transmigration of Souls, Foretellings of an Inevitable wind-up in a classless society).... " This symbolic order of motivation *moralizes* nature, and it moralizes by creating a whole new range of interpretations which come to stand in the place of the sensations. In this sense, language is not a duplicature of sensation; rather, it stands in a duplicitous relationship with sensation, perfecting yet transforming the sensation. It is in this duplicitous relationship that logology is found: "Logology is rooted in the range and quantity of knowledge that we acquire when our bodies (physiological organisms in the realm of non-symbolic motion) come to profit by their peculiar aptitude for learning the arbitrary, conventional mediums of communication called 'natural' languages" ("Dramatism and Logology," pp. 89–92).

The duplicitous dimension of language may be seen more clearly in Burke's examination of the relationship between substance and definition, as that relationship is epitomized in the very definition of "substance." In "Antinomies of Definition," in *A Grammar of Motives*, Burke explores the pun, the deconstruction, in the term "substance," and through his reading of "substance" he illustrates the unresolvable paradox "underlying" language. After noting that "etymologically 'substance' is a scenic word," Burke observes, "Literally, a person's or a thing's sub-stance would be something that stands beneath or supports the person or thing." Thus, "To tell what a thing is, you place it in terms of something else. This idea of locating, or placing, is implicit in our very word for definition itself: to *define*, or *determine* a thing, is to mark its boundaries, hence to use terms that possess, implicitly at least, contextual reference. Here we take the pun seriously because we believe it to reveal an *inevitable* paradox of definition, an antinomy that must endow the concept of substance with unresolvable ambiguity" (*GM*, pp. 22–24). Such ambiguity facilitates linguistic transformations, for, as Burke notes in the introduction to *A Grammer of Motives*, "it is in the areas of ambiguity that transformations take place" (p. xiii). And, in turn, such transformations condition the very possibility of dialectic.

One of the more famous passages in that introduction develops further the issue of linguistic transformation and its embeddedness in the antinomies of definition:

> Distinctions, we might say, arise out of a great central
> moltenness, where all is merged. They have been thrown from
> a liquid center to the surface, where they have congealed. Let
> one of these crusted distinctions return to its source, and in this
> alchemic center it may be remade, again becoming molten
> liquid, and may enter into new combinations, whereat it may be
> again thrown forth as a new crust, a different distinction. So

> that A may become non-A. But not merely by a leap from one
> state to the other. Rather, we must take A back into the ground
> of its existence, that logical substance that is its causal ancestor,
> and on to a point where it is consubstantial with non-A; then
> we may return, this time emerging with non-A instead.

This cycling between moltenness, the alembic center where distinctions are merged, and encrusted differences captures the paradox of definition, the necessary duplicity in any demarcation of difference, and that duplicitousness is only heightened by the recognition that the "logical substance" underlying A and non-A must itself dissolve into the antinomies of its own constitution. Nonetheless, it is this dissolving substance, this molten, liquid ground, which founds the very possibility of dialectic: "From the central moltenness, where all the elements are fused into one togetherness, there are thrown forth, in separate crusts, such distinctions as those between freedom and necessity, activity and passivity, cooperation and competition, cause and effect, mechanism and teleology" (GM, p. xix). The central antinomy of definition, the pun lurking behind the concept of sub-stance itself, is the necessary invocation of an other in order to constitute a meaning. Thus, in the Burkean system, as well as in the Derridean one, meaning is disseminated: it retreats into the moltenness of the alembic center and reemerges as an other.

The duplicitous structure of language is further revealed in metaphor and analogy, which Burke sees as the creators of new distinctions and hence new meanings. New meanings are thus created from the context of the old; they are born from the old, but remain forever attached to, enveloped in, invaginated with the old, each feeding symbiotically from the other. They are grafted from, grafted with, and grafted onto old ones, replicating in this contextual, textual confusion the quintessential antinomy of definition. The process of interpreting, of gaining meaning from, metaphor is therefore the quintessential process of communication and meaning in general. Metaphor works through nonidentities grafted together to create a new "oneness," which is always already never a oneness. Each nonidentity "lends" itself to the oneness, but then, in reconstituting itself, it must "borrow" itself back, but with added value, new interest gained by its encounter in the "oneness." Interpretation of metaphor, the generation of meaning in metaphor, can occur without gross error "only if we know how to 'discount' a metaphorical term" ("Linguistic Approach," p. 298). Such discounting implies an awareness of the duplicity in language, a comfort with the inbred irony of language. Such discounting is, for Burke, explicable as "the principle of negativity":

The paradox of the negative, then, is simply this: Quite as the *word* "tree" is verbal and the *thing* tree is non-verbal, so all words for the non-verbal must by the very nature of the case, discuss the realm of the non-verbal in terms of *what it is not.* Hence, to use words properly, we must spontaneously have a feeling for the *principle of the negative.*[27]

This "principle of negativity" is that aspect of human language use which facilitates thought and linguistic interpretation. Burke writes, "Since language is extended by metaphor which gradually becomes the kind of dead metaphor we call abstraction, we must know the metaphor is *not* literal. Further, we cannot use language maturely until we are spontaneously at home in irony." To reach our linguistic maturity, to achieve our fullest development, to, like a mature wine, reach our desired condition, we must, it seems, be at home *in* irony, literally inhabit irony, dramatize irony; indeed, "dramatic irony carries such a principle of negativity to its most complicated perfection."[28] This inhabitation, this perfection of dramatic irony, especially as a critical or ontological posture, generates quandaries of its own, to which I will return in the conclusion of this essay. The pertinent question here, in pursuing epistemological interests, is: What happens when the metaphoricity of language, its duplicitousness, is *not* discounted?

As language becomes more abstract, as the pile of metaphors atop metaphors swells, the self-evidence of the nonliteralness of language fades, and the illusion of pure presence ascends. The encrusted differences are taken as realities rather than manifestations of the unreduceable paradox of definition itself. The symbol user may succumb to the symbol system, and the symbol-using animal becomes instead the symbol-used animal. Burke is fond of citing Coleridge in arguing that a "new distinction may become 'so naturalized and of such general currency that the language itself does as it were *think* for us.' "[29] Rather than our dramatically inhabiting language, living more or less *in* irony, language comes to live in us, to inhabit us, to consume us. Burke discusses it in terms of ideology:

> An "ideology" is like a god coming down to earth, where it will inhabit a place pervaded by its presence. An "ideology" is like a spirit taking up its abode in a body: it makes that body hop in certain ways; and that same body would have hopped around in different ways had a different ideology happened to inhabit it. (*LSA*, p. 6)

Language has taken over; language is no longer a tool of humanity, but rather, in a sense, humanity is a tool of language. Or in other

David Cratis Williams

Burkean terms, action has turned to nondramatic motion. (*LSA*, pp. 53–55).

Burke examines language's potential for inhabiting and dominating humanity in terms of the concept of "entelechy," or the inherent perfectionist pressure within the linguistic system. "Entelechy" means "the notion that each being aims at the perfection natural to its kind." As applied to language, entelechy suggests that each linguistic construct, each pile of metaphorical creations contains an internal and inherent perfectionist pressure: the figurative play created by metaphorical self-referencing begins to masquerade as truth, and such truth motivates its own enactment. Burke writes, "A given terminology contains various implications and there is a corresponding 'perfectionist' tendency for man to attempt carrying out those implications." Or, more strongly, "There is a kind of 'terministic compulsion' to carry out the implications of one's terminology" (*LSA*, p. 19). The image of the ideology-inhabited person dancing to the tune of his or her language is illustrative of such terministic compulsion: the necessity of "discounting" language has been forgotten, and the illusion of the ideological godhead has attained presence. Language has become theological, or demonic, and in its attainment of transcendent status it has taken humanity captive.

Entelechial perfection suggests that closure is a motivation for enactment. This perfectionist tendency of language is what transforms national difference into international conflict. Perhaps Burke's clearest statement of the nuclear dangers lurking in such perfectionist tendencies is in his ironic poem, "Old Nursery Jingle Brought Up to Date":

> If all the thermo-nuclear warheads
> Were one thermo-nuclear warhead,
> What a great thermo-nuclear warhead that
> would be.

> If all the intercontinental ballistic missiles
> Were one intercontinental ballistic missile,
> What a great intercontinental ballistic missile that
> would be.

> If all the military men
> Were one military man
> What a great military man he would be.

> If all the land-masses
> Were one land-mass
> What a great land-mass that would be.

And if the great military man
Took the great thermo-nuclear warhead
And put it into the great intercontinental ballistic
missile,
And dropped it on the great land-mass,

What great PROGRESS that would be.[30]

The entelechical impulse, in perfecting categories and in perfecting differences, may literally lead to "the end-of-the-line." The ironic twist at the end of the poem is exemplary of Burke's admonitory mode, for only in the ironic displacement by incongruity can the perfectionist pressure be released and the nuclear threat defused.

II

The prospect of annihilation, while perhaps The End for naive submission to the overdeterministic impulses in language, is the beginning point for a nuclear criticism, not a critique of war per se but rather a criticism of, an admonition concerning, linguistic determinacy itself. The critical assault on closure, on the illusions of presence, truth, and knowledge, embraces the openness of indeterminacy, and it suggests the emptiness of the nihilistic abyss. If, in the methodological perfection of indeterminacy itself, all meaning becomes problematic, becomes irretrievably mired in oxymoron and tropical doubleness, then silence also awaits in this direction as surely as it does in the "remainderless destruction" of nuclear holocaust. This section of the essay examines both Derrida's deconstructive critique of attitudes of certainty, of the illusion of absolute knowledge, and Burke's ironical, ultimately satiric critique of linguistic perfectionism. In this examination of "methodologies" of indeterminacy, I will focus on deconstructive and logological "strategies" for reversing hierarchical oppositions.[31]

Derrida argues that nuclear war "can only come about" if that war is waged in the name of something which is worth more than life. It is against dangerous certitude that Derrida launches his deconstructive critique of the transcendental center, or the nucleus. The irony, of course, is that the deconstructive program deprivileges the name, demystifies it; under deconstructive analysis, the name is shown to be already decentered, or denucleated. Such ultimate decentering occurs both in the nuclear war and in the thorough application of critical denucleation; in each anecdote, the name names nothing: it is silent.

This very dialectic illustrates the Derridean perspective. Pure determination and pure indeterminacy are paired in opposition, and Western metaphysics has privileged determination over, instead of, indeterminacy. Deconstruction works through the margins between these poles, in this instance the commonality of silence, of the end of the name. Through the genius of marginality, the hierarchy can and indeed must be reversed: overdeterminism is shown to be already decentered, denucleated in the very dehiscence of the name, in the apocalypse of the name. Indeterminacy, as the apocalypse of the apocalypse, as the unveiling of the unveiling, is already at work in determination. Indeterminacy thus, in a sense, governs determination, is privileged over it. Such a reversal, however, is only "an essential first step" in the deconstructive process, for to stop with the reversal is to "preserve hierarchized thinking." Rather, as is the case in all deconstruction, there must be a further deconstruction of the new hierarchy and a reinscription of the old, producing a never-resting oscillation between them.[32]

One major Derridean strategy for such denucleation is the recognition of the "supplement," especially as it functions, marginally, to erase but not destroy the borderlines. Although Derrida's use of the term "supplement" derives from his deconstruction of Rousseau's use of the term,[33] the idea of "supplementarity" remains an identifying strategy of deconstruction itself.[34] Like the term *differance*, "supplement" has a doubleness in its meaning: "it means both an addition and a substitute."[35] Or, the doubleness can be represented as suggesting that a supplement is something which both completes and makes an addition, thereby blurring all margins.[36] Derrida sees two functions in the supplement: first, it "adds itself" as a "plenitude enriching another plenitude" and thus achieves "the fullest measure of presence," and, second, it "adds only to replace. It intervenes or insinuates itself *in-the-place of*."[37] In a sense, the process of supplementarity is one through which the "perfection" of a category becomes its essence, its fullest measure of presence; yet, as in the Burkean frame, in the very attainment of that perfection it is transformed into something else, which now stands in place of the other. And much like the logological cycle, in which that which goes forth material returns spiritualized (perfected, graced, and therefore different), the process of supplementarity involves a continual perfection of and addition to itself; that is, the supplement creates a textile which endlessly weaves around itself and for that reason can never be closed. It always supplements itself.[38] For Derrida, then, the supplement can keep language unsettled; it can undo any movement toward overdeterministic closure. And by undoing movements toward determination, the supplement works in and through the margins to reverse hierarchically paired terms.[39]

For Burke, linguistic perfection, including the rigidification of differences into oppositions into conflicts, heightens the threat of nuclear destruction. Consequently, we should cultivate "a partially impious 'fear of symbol-using.' " Such a fear provides the admonition about the potential consequences of errant symbol use; methodologically, it attempts "to perfect techniques for doubting much that is now accepted as lying beyond the shadow of a doubt" ("Linguistic Approach," p. 272). From this perspective, Burke's entire project "is motivated by a 'humanitarian concern to see how far conflict (war) may be translated practically into linguistic struggle and how such verbal struggle may be made to eventuate in a common enactment short of physical combat' " ("Linguistic Approach," p. 268). The fundamental insight governing the doubting of what lies beyond a shadow of a doubt is the recognition of the paradox of substance as that paradox "plays out" in the metaphoricity, the duplicity of language. Guided by this recognition of the metaphorical, poetic nature of meaning, Burke formalizes his perspective methodologically in logology, which reaches its most forceful culmination in dramatic irony and satire.

The duplicitous structure of language, inaugurated by the negative and formalized in story, suggests that language is essentially metaphorical, or poetic, and as such language cannot be reduced to a "semantic ideal" in which each construct is self-identically fully and exclusively itself. In "Semantic and Poetic Meaning," Burke argues that " 'poetic' meanings" cannot "be disposed of on the true-or-false basis. Rather, they are related to one another like a set of concentric circles, of wider and wider scope. Those of wider diameter do not categorically eliminate those of narrower diameter. There is, rather, a progressive *encompassment*" (*PLF,* p. 144). This encompassment always completes and adds to that which it envelops; the poetic ideal of meaning transcends the "dialectical process" of opposition, and in doing so it suspends the either/or choice implicit in such opposition and supplants it with a both/and encompassment which, at a minimum, defers choice until such time as the transcendent merger fragments and the oppositional divisions reappear.[40] In this fashion, the perspective of meaning as "poetic" functions like Derrida's supplement; thus, as Atkins writes of Derrida, "instead of opposing 'A' to 'B,' as in logic, we see the work of supplementarity, by means of which 'B' is at once added to 'A' and substituted for it."[41] The metaphor of poetics, including drama, provides a critical frame through which to explore the metaphoricity of language itself, and it leads to a concentric "heaping up" of meaning in which each polar term is always already encompassed by its seeming opposite.[42]

The view of language as metaphorical, as essentially poetic, leads toward the development of a critical "methodology" designed to admonish us against naive language use, designed to reassert the duplicitousness of language and the need to "discount" its literality. Logology, in its methodological slant, names Burke's attempts to do precisely this. That is, methodologically, logology, as words about words, as a "science" of words, is designed to reveal the oppositions, the dialectics inaugurated by the negative: "logology's 'dramatistic' (or dialectical) view of language as symbolic action is in its very essence *realistic*—and such a view is necessarily dualistic, since man is the typically symbol-using animal, and the linguistic invention of the negative is enough in itself to build a dualism.[43]

Burke's most detailed development of logology as method, as a way of reading, comes in "On Words and The Word," in *The Rhetoric of Religion*. Here Burke posits six primary logological analogies, or six analogical categories of words about words, the ultimate or paradigm example of which is words about the Word.[44] The Word is the spiritual perfection of language; its motivation is not theological but rather entelechial. The Word is the end-of-the-line; it suggests a metaphysical move out of the realm of the linguistic and into a realm of spiritual absolutes. Logology, as Rueckert puts it, is "a methodology for the study of symbol systems which uses a kind of neutralized Christian theology as its paradigm."[45] Burke, the consummate wordman, phrases it thus: "When we are confronting so fundamental a problem of sociology, precisely then, in keeping with the methodology of logology the first principle of axiology advises us to look for some analogy of morphology in the realm of theology."[46] The analogy of theology, since it encompasses the hypostatizing move from words to The Word, is the analogy par excellence. The logological method, through both the doubleness of its analogic structure and its systematic invocation of the negative, highlights the self-referential and unstable structure of meaning: words may move to The Word, may become spiritualized, but they are always already materialized and thus must, at the same time, remain words. Logology builds in a discounting of language; in its analogy to the "pious 'fear of God,' " the logological "impious 'fear of symbol using' " reminds us that, whatever else they may strive to become, symbols always remain empirically symbols. In reminding us that words both are and are not The Word, logology forces us toward an ironic attitude, toward a methodological perspective designed to forever discount the literality, the semantic purity of language. As such, the insights of logology push us toward dramatic irony and, ultimately, satire.

Dramatic irony is that point in symbolic action where the direction of the action is suddenly undercut by the ironic generation of a counteraction that is other than, or that negates, the original direction; it is the "strategic reversal" when *A* is transformed into not-*A*: "We could lay it down that 'what goes forth as A returns as non-A.' This is the basic pattern that places the essence of drama and dialectic in the irony of the 'peripety,' the strategic moment of reversal" (*GM*, p. 113). The already cited "Old Nursery Jingle Brought Up to Date" illustrates such dramatic irony. Burke's focus on the peripatetic reversal, or the inevitable metaphoric doubleness of language even as it follows its entelechial impulses, produces a critical focus on dramatic irony. From an ironic perspective, the "perfection" of any given category, or word, invokes the negative of that category, creating the textual doubleness of the oxymoron. The critical resource of irony—that is, the critical location of ironic reversals already in the text—provides the critic with an admonitory tool, with an ability to turn the text against itself in order to demonstrate the adverse entelechial implications which may also be lurking in the text. The ironic mode is itself perfected in satire.

Satire seizes upon the entelechial principle and pursues it more rigorously than does the perfectionist impulse itself. Satire amplifies perfectionist tendencies, but it does so with a perverse twist. Burke suggests that the "major resource of satiric amplification is an *excess of consistency*. Taking conditions that are here already, the satirist perversely, twistedly, carries them 'to the end of the line' ." ("Why Satire," p. 318). In "Archetype and Entelechy," Burke urges the satirist to "set up a situation whereby his text can ironically advocate the very ills that are depressing us—nay more, he can 'perfect' his presentation by a fantastic rationale that calls for *still more* of the maladjustments now besetting us."[47] Through such a methodic perfecting of irony, satire provides a strong admonitory accent. Satire "can track down the entelechial principle. But it does so perversely, by tracking down possibilities or implications to the point where the result is a kind of Utopia-in-reverse" ("Why Satire," p. 315). Thus, in satire, hierarchies are violently and dramatically reversed through diligent pursuit of the necessarily ironic structure of the language itself. The satiric plucking of Hell out of the Utopia of Heaven in Burke's "Helhaven" essays exemplifies this procedure.[48]

The logological focus on linguistic form leads the critic toward a recognition of the textual evidence of ironic reversals, which in turn provide the openings for satire. Such reversals occur when the material is spiritualized, when the word turns toward The Word, when language becomes infused with the godhead of ideology; or, these transformations can themselves add to such completions, can destabilize the spiritual by revealing that it is always also material. In this manner, the logological perspective keeps meaning caught "in the turn" from words to The Word and thus keeps meaning indeterminate, in a "perpetual-motion" between words and The Word.[49] In this respect, Burke's critical orientation resembles the Derridean orientation: both deconstruction and logology impose rigorous methodological procedures on language, procedures designed to reverse the perfectionist movement toward hypostatization. In overturning such deterministic tendencies, however, both Burke and Derrida risk the "Utopia-in-reverse": the perfection of their very procedures to erode overdeterminism leads toward a "perfect" indeterminism, or the pure silence of the abyss.

III

If the specters of nuclear war and the denucleated image of no image constitute polar extremes between which a critical system must position itself, then any critical stance which is aware of the opposition is necessarily characterized by the tension of conflicting aversions: any move away from the specter of annihilation may be a move toward the ghostly embrace of nihilistic despair, and vice versa. While a Janus-like watchfulness of each extreme is desirable, such a pose is difficult for the mortal human subject. This section of the essay will examine how Derrida and Burke, in their respective articulations of a dialectic of dialectics which destabilizes the determination of opposition itself, attempt to position their critical systems in relation to the specter of nihilism implicit in any "methodology" of indeterminism.

In undertaking its deconstruction of "everything that ties the concept and norms of scientificity to ontotheology, logocentrism, phonologism,"[50] Derrida's program includes its own enactment: it cannot seek a privileged position outside the deconstructive movements of language. In his analysis of the metaphor in philosophy, for instance, Derrida argues that reflection upon the metaphor, or upon metaphoricity itself, leads not out of metaphor, not to a higher ground or a transcendental position, but rather into the endless regress of duplicity itself.[51] As Ryan puts it, any accounting for all metaphors, any "metametaphorics," is "impossible without recourse to yet one more metaphor." That is, "To account for the language of the account would require another account—and a potentially interminable repetition of the problem."⁵² Of course, this is precisely the functioning of the supplement, which "traverses its own field, endlessly displaces its closure, breaks its line, opens its circle, and no ontology will have been able to reduce it."⁵³ Deconstruction, then, is "a question or strategy because no transcendent truth outside the sphere of writing can theologically command the totality of this field." It becomes a "strategy without finality."⁵⁴ In this sense, "the enterprise of deconstruction always in a certain way falls prey to its own work."⁵⁵ Deconstruction literally consumes itself, preys off its own constitution. In its posture of preyer, however, deconstruction genuflects toward its own redemption, toward its own joyful affirmation.

Deconstruction problematizes the privileged concepts of our era; it demonstrates how these conceptions—Truth, Nature, etc.—always overrun their borders, how they always supplement themselves in the play of the linguistic trace. It takes concepts which have (seemingly) moved outside the problematics of language to a transcendental status above language and reimplicates them in the swirling antinomies of language. From the Derridean perspective, however, such a move does not abrogate meaning; rather, it focuses quite properly on the processes of meaning, on the process of *difference*. It keeps meaning inside itself, invaginated in the processes of its own production. In this posture, deconstruction can be seen as rigorously and methodically pursuing the conditions, the limits, of meaning itself. Conversely, the strategic decision to *not* deconstruct, to accept the plenitude and the priority of the privileged signifieds, *is* to abrogate the limits of meaning, for to accept "pure" signification detached from any process of its own production is to accept the radical, pure voice of the Other and its oracular decrees of Truth and Knowledge. Here there is no reasoning, no testing, no critical examination, for these are all processes embedded in the *production* of "truth." When truth arrives in ordained form freed from its own conditions, all limits are removed.

In its rejection of any hermeneutical bedrock, be it theological or ontological, which privileges itself outside of the play of signifiers, deconstruction plunges into not the abyss of nihilism, of silence, but rather into the oscillations of the processes of *difference*, the oscillation between difference and deferral, between reinscription and dissolution. In this sense, deconstruction urges an inhabitation of language, a living *in* irony. Such a posture may be joyful, deriving its joy not only from the "process of interpreting" but also from the liberating, freeing implications of deconstruction itself: "Without a final authority, determinate meaning is impossible; meaning is scattered, dispersed, disseminated. We are, it seems, thus *freed* by the endlessness of interpretation from *the dominion of* pre-existent meaning, authority, and a sense that reality is completed."[56] If deconstruction is freeing, however, it may be too freeing; in its dismantling of the transcendental authority of theology and ontology it has also dismantled any assurances we may have of who we are. If there is joy and freedom in deconstruction, it may be a joyfulness and a freedom in which few take solace, for the task of endless interpretation may be too onerous for a humanity long accustomed to the restful comforts of certitude.

Burke offers a somewhat similar vision of perpetual oscillation between words and The Word; neither the spiritual nor the material is privileged or definitive. In this sense, Burke's critical posture resembles that of Derrida, but Burke's system, encompassing both logology and dramatism, fights to avoid the progressive deconstruction ad infinitum which Derrida accepts with the understanding that there will always be a remainder, a trace, a living on. Burke grounds his perspective in what I call the "ontological loop" of dramatism; that is, dramatism, as Burke has decreed, is an ontological perspective: it tells us who we *are* in a substantial, constitutive sense. We *are* the symbol-using animal, suggesting that we inhabit, enact, dramatize the problematics of language, the duplicities of dialectic. The "loop" is the encompassing, self-authenticating structure of the definition. That is, whether we succumb to deterministic impulses, reify difference, and initiate war or whether we retreat into inhabitation of the ironic, enacting the paralysis of action characterized by Hamlet, we nonetheless affirm our very nature as symbol-using animals.

A return to the paradox of substance, by which all other certitudes may be seen to dissolve into their own traces, demonstrates Burke's privileging of his own ontology. In *A Grammar of Motives*, Burke selects "drama" as the representative anecdote of his undertaking because it "treats *language* and *thought* primarily as modes of action" (*GM*, p. xvi). The anecdote of "drama" is a constitutive one, telling us who we *are*; as such, it must prove substantial in itself. That encompassing substance, which transcends and *contains* the antinomies attendant to the pun in sub-stance, is "dialectical substance." " 'Dialectical substance,' Burke tells us, is "the over-all category of dramatism," and yet it is a category which exists only in its own absence, in its own non-presence: "Whereas there is an implicit irony in other notions of substance, with dialectical substance the irony is explicit. For it derives its character from the systematic contemplation of the antinomies attending upon the fact that we necessarily define a thing in terms of something else" (*GM*, p. 33). To possess dialectical substance is to be at home, literally, in irony: it is to *be* irony. Dialectical substance is the metametaphorics, the inhabitation of metaphor which, through its substantiality, through its being fully what it *is*—metaphor, dialectic, drama—is no longer metaphorical but *literal.*

In his 1968 article "Dramatism," Burke clarifies this ontological grounding of the human subject:

> In this sense man is defined literally as an animal characterized by his special aptitude for "symbolic action," which is itself a literal term. And from there on, drama is employed, not as a metaphor but as a fixed form that helps us discover what the implications of the terms "act" and "person" *really are.*[57]

Although such a grounding is explicitly *in* language, it suggests a movement *through* language to a position *on* language, and in that sense *beyond* language. Dramatism thus finds itself on empirically firm footing for the questioning *of* language, for the logological "methodology" of indeterminacy. The motto which Burke invokes for dramatism captures this: "By and through language, beyond language." The move beyond language, however, is an ontological move only, not an epistemological one. It privileges the human subject, not truth or knowledge.

One may question or deconstruct Burke's privileging of his unique onotological perspective; however, the tautological, self-referential structure of the anecdote of drama and its ontological implications suspends, but does not vanquish, the menace of ontodeconstruction, for even the observation, indeed the demonstration, that the linguistic structure of the anecdote unravels its own assertiveness, deconstructs its own story, can but be additional support for the claim that humans are the animals that use language (and indeed deconstructive prowess may be one of the most sophisticated forms of language use, perhaps suggesting that it is one of the more quintessentially human of human activities). From drama, the entire human problematic of language spins out and recoils; it is the ontological Word which moves by and through language to beyond language. It is a substantial anecdote, and it is resolutely affirmative of the human identity in the self-referential, self-identical, totalizing claim that we are the animal that uses language. In this context, Burke's claim that dramatism is not

David Cratis Williams

metaphorical but rather literal is perfectly explicable. Burke has privileged his self-reflexive ontological claim as beyond the subversion of language by virtue of being a subversion of that subversiveness, and he has carefully insulated his claim through the linguistic resources of tautology and self-referencing.

The "ontological loop" in dramatism affords it a ground on which to stand, but it is a ground of paradox, a molten and liquid ground wherein transformations are likely to occur. Questions of the marginal assert themselves; the movements of deconstruction are not thwarted. In a sense, Derrida's ontodeconstruction and Burke's ontological construction revolve around each other, arguing with each other in ways that at times, under the dialectical pressure of the conversation, seem to place them in opposition. But since each problematizes the rigidity of structures of opposition, the margin between— the margin of overlap—reasserts itself. In the end there is no end to the conversation: the revelation of the end, the apocalypse of the end, is to begin again, to engage in the endless process of interpretation, and to find what joy, what affirmation we may in it, for to cease the process of interpretation is to invite the Apocalypse without remainder, to enact the end that awaits at the end of the oppositional line.

The reconstitution of opposition as difference is, if there is legitimacy in the anecdote of nuclear war, an imperative at the societal level, for humanity can no longer afford the interpretive errors of hypostatization which heighten difference into conflict into war. The critical perspectives which pursue such a reconstitution, as exemplified by those of Burke and Derrida, appear in radical form as methodologies of indeterminacy which obliterate all meaning and all that is meaningful; such radicalization, such reduction of their perspectives, however, seems inappropriate given their respective efforts to "save" meaning, to keep meaning and our understanding of the possibilities for meaning situated within the processes of its own production. Tendencies of critics, conditioned by thinking in the "pat schematizations" of oppositional thought, to oppose, to attack, to declare logomachic war upon the questioners of dialectical opposition itself reflect in microcosm the tendencies which at a global level portend nuclear annihilation. This logomachy needs to be reconstituted as a dialogue, a conversation which is engaged in dialectically but which concerns the very processes of dialectic, one which seeks not the clarification and rigidification of difference but rather the murky margins between, those margins of overlap which inaugurate and which limit the very functioning of dialectic.

NOTES

1. Kenneth Burke, "Semantic and Poetic Meaning," *The Philosophy of Literary Form: Studies in Symbolic Action*, 3d ed. (Berkeley: University of California Press, 1973), pp. 138–39.

2. Burke has at various times been labeled "an irresponsible sophist," a communistic "apostle of linguistic skepticism," a "sceptic" whose "progress" is "headed toward total collapse," a "muddle-headed, undisciplined spinner of speculations," or even a "traitor" to classical Marxism. See Merle E. Brown, *Kenneth Burke*, Pamphlets on American Writers, no. 75 (Minneapolis: University of Minnesota Press, 1969), p. 5; Charles I. Glicksberg, "Kenneth Burke: The Critic's Choice," in William Rueckert, ed., *Critical Responses to Kenneth Burke* (Minneapolis: University of Minnesota Press, 1969), p. 75; Austin Warren, "The Skeptic's Progress," *American Review*, 6 (1935), 193–213, as cited in Brown, pp. 6–7; Robert Adams, "The Dance of Language," *TLS*, 8 July 1983, p. 715 (Adams does not represent this view as his own); and Ben Yagoda, "Kenneth Burke," *Horizon*, 23 (June 1980), 68. Burke recalls that Joe Freeman called him a traitor following Burke's address to the American Writers' Congress in 1935; for the text of Burke's address, see below.

3. James Lardner, "War of the Words," *Washington Post*, March 6, 1983, p. G1.

4. Ellen K. Coughlin, "Discontent with Deconstruction and Other Critical Conditions," *Chronicle of Higher Education*, 23 (1982), 27.

5. Reported in Colin Campbell, "The Tyranny of the Yale Critics," *New York Times Magazine*, February 9, 1986, p. 20.

6. Wayne Booth, *Critical Understanding* (Chicago: University of Chicago Press, 1979), p. 220. Booth is citing Serge Doubrovsky's discussion of the metaphor of "war" as it was used in the critical confrontation between "old criticism" and "new criticism" in France in the mid-1960s. See Doubrovsky, *The New Criticism in France*, trans. Derek Coltman (Chicago: University of Chicago Press, 1973), pp. 41–53. In many respects, Booth's appraisal of critical monisms "skewering" and "killing" each other prefigures much of my own discussion. Although Booth's concern remains more directly centered on squabbles within the discipline of literary criticism, he is aware that for Burke such literary conflicts may be but microcosms of the "kinds of conflict, symbolic and literal, that may destroy us" (p. 109). Viewed from this angle, Booth's search for a "pluralism of pluralisms" may seem to anticipate the current search for a "dialectic of dialectics." There may, however, be an important difference in emphasis. While Booth's pluralism works to supplant the either/or of monism with a both/and, the both/and of pluralism is a sequential one: first you inhabit one modality, then you inhabit a second, and each modality remains fundamentally irreducible in its own right. As Booth puts it, in what may be interpreted as a somewhat

David Cratis Williams

ironic "skewering" of deconstruction, "But there is a great difference between the exhausted swimmer who is convinced that the patternless waves he struggles through extend in all directions without limit, and the one who says to himself, 'There *are* islands. Swim a bit further, and you will certainly find another one, perhaps even more hospitable than the last one you rested on' " (p. 340). That is, the "world is built of many centers, irreducible to any one" (p. 348), and the pluralist migrates between them. The search for a dialectic of dialectics poses a slightly different question. Not "where are the islands, irreducible and distinct?" but rather "where are the margins which both problematize the distinction between islands and at the same time create the islands?"

7. See Jacques Derrida, "Living On," in Harold Bloom et. al, eds., *Deconstruction and Criticism*, trans. James Hulbert (New York: Continuum, 1979), pp. 75–176; also Michael Ryan, *Marxism and Deconstruction: A Critical Articulation* (Baltimore: Johns Hopkins University Press, 1982), esp. pp. 13–14. Burke discusses "margins of overlap" both in "Semantic and Poetic Meaning" and in *A Grammar of Motives* (New York: Prentice-Hall, 1945), esp. pp. xii–xvi.

8. While a comprehensive comparative study of Burke and Derrida has yet to be written, the name of each is increasingly invoked in relation to the other, sometimes sympathetically but, perhaps more often, antagonistically. For treatments which place Burke and Derrida in opposition to each other, see Denis Donoghue, *Ferocious Alphabets* (Boston: Little, Brown, 1981), esp. pp. 205–11, and James Arnt Aune, "Beyond Deconstruction: The Symbol and Social Reality," *Southern Speech Communication Journal*, 48 (1983), 255–68. For treatments which find more intertextual reverberations between the two, see Stephen Glynn, "Beyond the Symbol: Deconstructing Social Reality," *Southern Speech Communication Journal*, 51 (1986), 125–41, and Phillip Tompkins, "On Hegemony—'He Gave It No Name'—and Critical Structuralism in the Work of Kenneth Burke," *Quarterly Journal of Speech*, 71 (1985), 119–31. Frank Lentricchia's work also frequently draws parallels between Burke and deconstruction, although Lentricchia typically looks to Yale School deconstructionist Paul de Man rather than Derrida. See *Criticism and Social Change* (Chicago: University of Chicago Press, 1983) and "Reading History with Kenneth Burke," in Hayden White and Margaret Brose, eds., *Representing Kenneth Burke* (Baltimore: Johns Hopkins University Press, 1982), pp. 119–49.

9. Jacques Derrida, "Of an Apocalyptic Tone Recently Adopted in Philosophy," *Semeia*, 23 (1982), 87, 94.

10. Kenneth Burke, *A Rhetoric of Motives* (1950; Berkeley: University of California Press, 1969), pp. 13–16.

11. V. William Balthrop, "The Representative Anecdote as an Approach to Movement Study," unpublished paper, p. 11n.

12. Kenneth Burke, "Linguistic Approach to Problems of Education," in Nelson B. Henry, ed., *Modern Philosophies and Education*, 54th Yearbook of

the National Society for the Study of Education, pt. 1 (Chicago: University of Chicago Press, 1955), p. 263.

13. Kenneth Burke, *"Permanence and Change:* In Retrospective Prospect," *Permanence and Change,* 3d ed. (Berkeley: University of California Press, 1984), p. 138.

14. Jacques Derrida, *Positions,* trans. Alan Bass (Chicago: University of Chicago Press, 1981), p. 26. See Gayatri Chakravorty Spivak, Translator's Preface, in Jacques Derrida, *Of Grammatology* (Baltimore: Johns Hopkins University Press, 1976), p. xvii.

15. Derrida, *Positions,* p. 27.

16. Jacques Derrida, "Differance," *Speech and Phenomena,* trans. David B. Allison, Northwestern University Studies in Phenomenology and Existential Philosophy (Evanston: Northwestern University Press, 1973), pp. 129–30.

17. Derrida, *Grammatology,* p. 62.

18. Derrida, *Positions,* p. 29.

19. Ibid., p. 41.

20. Ryan, *Marxism and Deconstruction,* p. 13.

21. Derrida, *Grammatology,* p. 20.

22. Jacques Derrida, "No Apocalypse, Not Now (full speed ahead, seven missiles, seven missives)," *Diacritics,* 14, no. 2 (1984), 31.

23. Ibid., pp. 30–31. Burke offers a similar argument: "The ironic likelihood is that, if we fought another great war to 'save' capitalism, capitalism would be done for, regardless of who 'won' the war." See Burke, "Ideology and Myth," *Accent,* 7 (1947), 204.

24. Derrida, "No Apocalypse," pp. 23–31. See also Derrida, "Of an Apocalyptic Tone," esp. pp. 80–95.

25. Kenneth Burke, "Dramatism and Logology," *Communication Quarterly,* 33, no. 2 (1985), 89.

26. Burke, "Dramatism and Logology," p. 89. Emphasis in original. Burke cites the *Oxford English Dictionary* 1971 ed. as the source of the definition of *logology* as the "science of words."

27. Kenneth Burke, *The Rhetoric of Religion* (1961; Berkeley: University of California Press, 1970), p. 18.

28. Kenneth Burke, *Language as Symbolic Action* (Berkeley: University of California Press, 1966), p. 12.

29. Burke, "Afterword," p. 305; citing Coleridge, *Biographia Literaria,* chap. 4.

30. Kenneth Burke, *Collected Poems, 1915–1967* (Berkeley: University of California Press, 1968), p. 175.

31. The specific "strategies" explicated, while only parts of the respective critical wholes, are taken as "representative" of those wholes. For both Burke and Derrida, entry into their systems at virtually any point soon leads one through the whole system; or, to suggest it differently, the examination of any of their key terms tends to lead to an examination of all of

their strategic terms, since one usually implies another. Thus, while this treatment is admittedly partial, it is hoped that it adequately suggests the flavor of the respective systems.

32. G. Douglas Atkins, " 'Count It All Joy': The Affirmative Nature of Deconstruction," *University of Hartford Studies in Literature*, 15 (1984), 125–26.

33. Derrida, *Grammatology*, esp. pp. 141–64.

34. Christopher Norris, *Deconstruction: Theory and Practice* (New York: Methuen, 1982), pp. 32–33.

35. G. Douglas Atkins, *Reading Deconstruction, Deconstructive Reading* (Lexington: University of Kentucky Press, 1983), p. 22.

36. Jonathan Culler, *On Deconstruction* (Ithaca: Cornell University Press, 1982), p. 102.

37. Derrida, *Grammatology*, pp. 144–45.

38. Ibid., p. 150.

39. Vincent Leitch, *Deconstructive Criticism: An Advanced Introduction* (New York: Columbia University Press, 1983), pp. 170–71.

40. See *GM*, pp. 403–18. The dialectical resource in language which leads to oppositional thinking can be reversed by the same resource: "Or, dialectical resources being what they are, we can readily propose that any troublesome *either-or* be transformed into a *both-and*" ("Linguistic Approach," p. 293). Such encompassments, however, remain unstable and are subject, through dialectical pressure, to fragmentation. Burke says, "the crumbling of hierarchies is as true a fact as their formation" (*RM*, p. 141). Or, in a similar vein, identification always, ironically, implies division (see *RM*, p. 23).

41. Atkins, *Reading Deconstruction*, p. 22.

42. In "Metaphorical View of Hierarchy," Burke suggests that the hierarchical oppositions might profitably be metaphorically reversed; see *RM*, pp. 137–42. Such reversals can provide an insight by catachresis or incongruity in that they clearly violate "the 'proprieties' of the word in its previous linkages" (*PC*, p. 90). For a similar discussion in Derrida, see "White Mythology," *Margins of Philosophy*, trans. Alan Bass (Chicago: University of Chicago Press, 1982), pp. 207–71.

43. Kenneth Burke, "Theology and Logology," *Kenyon Review*, n.s., 1 (1979), 184.

44. The five analogies are: the "Matter-Spirit," the "Negative," the "Titular," the "Time-Eternity," the "Formal," the "Creativity," the "Courtship," and the "Reversible." In addition, "several others" lie "about the edges" of these (perhaps in the margins?). See *RR*, p. 38.

45. William Rueckert, *Kenneth Burke and the Drama of Human Relations*, 2d ed. (Berkeley: University of California Press, 1982), p. 264.

46. Kenneth Burke, "Why Satire, with a Plan for Writing One," *Michigan Quarterly Review*, 13 (1974), 323.

47. Kenneth Burke, *Dramatism and Development* (Worcester, Mass.: Clark University Press, 1972), p. 52.

48. See "Why Satire" and Kenneth Burke, "Towards Helhaven: Three Stages of a Vision," *Sewanee Review,* 79 (1971), 11–15.

49. Geoffrey Hartman, *Criticism in the Wilderness* (New Haven: Yale University Press, 1980), pp. 90–91.

50. Derrida, *Positions,* p. 35.

51. Derrida, "White Mythology," esp. pp. 261–71.

52. Ryan, *Marxism and Deconstruction,* p. 20.

53. Derrida, "White Mythology," p. 271.

54. Derrida, "Differance," p. 135.

55. Derrida, *Grammatology,* p. 24.

56. Atkins, " 'Count It All Joy,' " p. 123.

57. Kenneth Burke, "Dramatism," *International Encyclopedia of the Social Sciences,* ed. David L. Sills (New York: Macmillan, 1968), p. 448.

10 THE RHETORIC OF ALLEGORY

BURKE AND AUGUSTINE

DAVID DAMROSCH

I am tempted to begin by defining Burke's "logology" as follows: the essence of logology is the perception that anything that can be said about God can also be said about Kenneth Burke. Thus (to use the sort of negative definition which Burke describes as typical of speech about God), Burke's intellectual range is infinite, his energy is unbounded, and he is clearly immortal as well. Adapting a more positive definition, we can say that he is a one-man hermeneutic circle, whose center is nowhere and whose influence is everywhere.

This said, it remains true that "logology" has not found as wide acceptance as many of Burke's ideas, and *The Rhetoric of Religion: Studies in Logology*, in which this new field of inquiry is unveiled, has earned more respect than active use. It is a puzzling book. Why does Burke derive logology from, or against, Augustine's *Confessions?* What interest remains for us, once Burke has derived his theory, in retracing the ins and outs of his readings of Augustine and the opening chapters of Genesis? Is logology only another shape in which the Protean Burke cloaks theories already developed elsewhere, or does it have independent value for students of interpretation? I wish to argue that logology does cast significant light on "dramatism" and indeed on much critical practice, and that we have much to learn from watching Burke reading Augustine and the Bible.

In general terms, it appears that there is a natural affinity between dramatism and logology, between a dramatic reading of rhetoric and a theological reading. This affinity can also be observed in the other major dramatistic theoretician of interpretation, Hans-Georg Gadamer. In his *Truth and Method* Gadamer develops at length an analogy between the reading of a text and the playing of a game; in the course of his discussion, he plays heavily on the German *Spiel*, which means "play" in the two senses of "game" and "theater piece." At the same

224

time, Gadamer's language is heavily theological ("The poem...does not describe or signify an entity, but opens up to us a world of the divine and the human").[1] Working within the philosophical tradition that has its roots in the theologically based hermeneutics of Schleiermacher, Gadamer is concerned, like Burke, to allow for a range of meaning in texts, but at the same time to assert that some defined truth persists in the range of meaning—meaning, like the Trinity, is simultaneously multiple and uniform. Ultimately for Gadamer the secular concept of drama or play is grounded in the theological experience of ritual, in which the ancient, sacred text is brought alive in the present: "Hence contemporaneity is something that is found especially in the religious act, and in the sermon....Now I maintain that the same thing is basically true for the experience of art."[2]

Like Gadamer, Burke finds a natural grounding for his dramatism in religious experience: the view of reading a text as performance can be fruitfully assimilated to the religious view of God's language as performative. Where Gadamer focuses on theological language *in* performance (the rite, the sermon), Burke looks directly, in Augustine, at theological language *as* performance.

The dramatistic reading of theological language can thus be seen as a logical next step for Burke as he developed his ideas after *A Grammar of Motives* and *A Rhetoric of Motives*. What is surprising is his choice of Augustine as the basis of his study. If "what we say about *words*, in the empirical realm, will bear a notable likeness to what is said about *God*, in theology,"[3] then any theologian is a potential starting point. Yet among the many possible choices, Burke picked for his dramatistic reading one of the writers most hostile to drama in all of Western writing.

In the *Confessions*, Augustine's exposure to the theater coincides with his immersion in the "hissing cauldron of lust" of Carthage. No sooner has he plunged into the pleasures of immoral and illicit sexuality, muddying "the stream of friendship with the filth of lewdness," than he starts going to the theater:

> I was much attracted by the theater, because the plays reflected my own unhappy plight and were tinder to my fire. Why is it that men enjoy feeling sad at the sight of tragedy and suffering on the stage, although they would be most unhappy if they had to endure the same fate themselves? Yet they watch the plays because they hope to be made to feel sad, and the feeling of sorrow is what they enjoy. What miserable delirium this is![4]

David Damrosch

From this moral and intellectual debauchery it is but a step to outright heresy, and soon Augustine has fallen into the clutches of the Manichees, the great villains (apart from his own desires) of his youth. Thus theater forms the connecting link between Augustine's unrestrained sexual passions and his apostasy from the true faith, and the very feature of drama which Gadamer will consider central to his theory of reading, the fusion of horizons between reader and performance, is the worst thing of all for Augustine, a "miserable delirium." As the *Confessions* proceeds, theater is associated with a series of increasingly debased rituals: Manichaean services, public performances of rhetoric, and gladiator fights. Is this a work on which to base a dramatistic reading of theology?

As surprising as Burke's choice of the *Confessions* is, equally surprising is the fact that he simply passes in silence over Augustine's hostility to drama. In a hundred and thirty pages of close reading of "Verbal Action in St. Augustine's *Confessions*," he entirely sidesteps Augustine's diatribes against drama. Is Burke having a little joke at Augustine's expense? Why use Augustine at all?

One answer would be to see Burke's project as the deconstruction of Augustine. In this view, it would be precisely because Augustine is Burke's worst enemy that Burke is moved to treat him, to set himself the task of deriving his principles from the opposite camp. This is the position taken by John Freccero in his essay "Logology: Burke on St. Augustine." Freccero is brought to this view in considering Burke's general project of discussing theology as rhetoric:

> Burke's interest in theology is the reverse of the theologian's and is essentially deconstructive of the theological edifices of the past. It includes exposing the workings of the principle of perfection in those systems while acknowledging that none of us can escape it entirely, certainly not in expository prose.... The dismantling of Augustine's work is a prodigious task that Burke accomplishes with a thoroughness and a rapidity that sometimes leaves the reader behind.[5]

Having raised this issue, Freccero moves into a direct discussion of Augustine, arguing that many of Burke's ideas are presented more openly in Augustine than Burke would seem to allow. I don't believe, however, that Burke's project is really deconstructive at all; at the same time, there is much evidence that does suggest that Burke is turning Augustine on his head. Whatever Burke's purposes, many aspects of his argument indicate a systematic series of inversions of Augustine;

these inversions require some examination if we are to understand Burke's use of the *Confessions*.

Overall, Augustine presents his story as the account of his maturation from physical, intellectual, and spiritual infancy to adulthood in behavior and faith. Yet Burke's account of this process stresses the return of infancy in Augustine's "mature" faith. In the twelfth chapter of his analysis, Burke discusses Augustine's conversion in terms of "five 'instinctual responses' of infants; namely: crying, smiling, sucking, clinging, and following," and concludes:

> We are not suggesting that Augustine's ideas of rest (and silent words) in the afterlife are reducible simply to terms of an infant clinging to its mother. But we are saying: As regards the sheerly *verbal behavior* of his pages, the references to *clinging* indicate that such associations characterize one notable strand in the complex of meanings that "eternity" represents in his particular terminology. (*RR*, pp. 131, 133)

Further, in the process of developing his reading of Augustine's progressive-regressive development, Burke highlights Augustine's rhetorical strategies in ways that treat the *Confessions* as a very "pagan" literary work, in Augustine's terms. Repeatedly in the *Confessions* Augustine stresses the evil of pagan rhetoric, such as he himself taught before his conversion, in which beauty of style was ranked far above truth; gradually he learns that the stylistic simplicity of the Bible does not at all decrease its value, for content is what finally matters, not form. In Burke's reading of the *Confessions* and Genesis, by contrast, the formal relations of terms are more significant than their specific theological content; late in his study of Genesis, he is even willing to claim that the form alone matters: "though the believer studies [theology's] answers for their matter, logology loves them solely for their form" (p. 268).

As for Burke's reading of Augustine's formal structures, we may note that he discounts Augustine's open generic model, that of the psalm. In effect, Augustine casts his whole book as an extended psalmic prayer, as Freccero points out.[6] What Burke emphasizes, however, are implicit dramatic structures; Augustine's psalmic answer to the evils of dramatism is cast as a drama itself, and indeed as a five-act—pentadic—Shakespearean drama. Thus the conversion episode is presented, in the heading to Burke's ninth section, as "The Middle (Conversion, Turn, Peripety)," and Burke dramatistically sets the stage for us: "The year: A.D. 386. Augustine is thirty-two" (p. 101). Having

David Damrosch

opened in Aristotelian terms, Burke gives several analogies to the moment of decision of Augustine's conversion, all from Shakespeare. The choice is far from random, for, Burke tells us,

> we are interested here in . . . the kind of development that usually takes place in the third act of a five-act drama. Despite his great stress on the will, and despite his extraordinary energy in theological controversy, Augustine seems to have felt that, at the critical moment of his conversion, something was decided for him. Act III is the point at which some new quality of motivation enters. (P. 102)

It is noteworthy that Burke's three Shakespearean examples are further determined in selection: they come from *Macbeth, Othello,* and *Hamlet,* and Burke goes on to draw an extended analogy between the end of the *Confessions* and the last two acts of *Othello.* ("Othello's suspiciousness would correspond perversely to Augustine's state of conviction following his conversion. . . . Iago's fatal suggestions to Othello would correspond perversely to the role of Monica in leading towards his conversion," and so on [pp. 103–4].)

Why this evocation of Shakespeare's major tragedies? Certainly Burke's perverse sense of humor shows through in his development of analogies between Iago and Monica, Desdemona and Augustine's pagan mistress; at bottom, though, as always with Burke's humor, there is a serious critique at work. We see here the heart of his dramatistic revision of Augustine: within the professedly "comic" mode of Augustine's life story, with its movement from error and misery to truth and fulfillment, Burke sees a story of loss. Since his analysis is concerned with motivation, with acts of will, Augustine's happy surrender of his will to God takes on tragic overtones for Burke, who sees this consequence of the conversion: "however active one may be henceforth, the course is more like a rolling downhill than a straining uphill"—clearly a tragic movement.

In keeping with this new emphasis on the tragic loss inherent in conversion, whereas Augustine comes to see that evil is nothing in itself, merely the absence of good and not the pervasive substance described by the Manichees, Burke begins his book with a discussion of the importance of the negative as the ground of all meaning—an essentially Manichaean position. (See Burke's introductory chapter, "On Words and The Word.") It is no coincidence, indeed, that the Manichaean drama of Burke's book ends with a dramatic dialogue entitled "Prologue in Heaven"—a title taken from the opening scene of Goethe's *Faust.* The figure of Faust, and his very name, appear ultimately to derive from Faustus, the chief spokesman for the Manichees in the *Confessions* (book 5). If Augustine's search is ultimately for a theology of love which will transcend the sciences of knowledge and of the will expounded by Faustus, Burke reverses the process and identifies Augustine with Faust. It is, moreover, Goethe's Faust who enunciates the central tenet of modern dramatism, when he emends "In the beginning was the Word" to: "In the beginning was the Act."[7]

We may well conclude that, if the *Confessions* tells of a conversion experience, reading "Verbal Action in St. Augustine's *Confessions*" gives us more of an *in*version experience. However, as God constantly tells Satan in Burke's prologue/epilogue in heaven, "It's more complicated than that." As Freccero has shown, in reading theology logologically, "If we assume that we are second-guessing Augustine'...as Burke sometimes does, then we are likely to miss an essential point about the text.... Augustine himself provides us with a logological interpretation" of his central concerns.[8]

I would argue that Burke only rarely makes this mistake, which would be pervasive if his reading were genuinely deconstructive; rather, I would describe Burke's method not as deconstructive satire but as parody, a parody so thoroughgoing and sincere as to resemble a Renaissance *imitatio*. It is true that Burke is essentially indifferent to the truth claims of Augustine's theology, and even hostile to its consequences for human motivation, but he is altogether a disciple of Augustine's hermeneutics. Burke is, in fact, quite open about the parodic nature of "perverse" readings such as his equation of Augustine with Othello; as we will see, in his parodic reformulations of Augustine Burke sees himself as following in Augustine's own footsteps.

Before I discuss Burke's motivations for this imitation, something of the specific nature of his parodic method should be shown. The process is perhaps most clearly seen in the eighth section of Burke's essay "Adolescent Perversity," in which he discusses, brilliantly, Augustine's most famous sin, the stealing of pears from an orchard as an adolescent. The pears are worthless, the crime trivial; Augustine highlights the episode to show the senselessness of sin, and to discuss its various motivations (choosing, of course, an episode that resonates against the forbidden fruit in Eden). As Burke sums up the incident, "It was his foremost sin because it was, in substance, the complete perversion, or perfect parody, of his religious motives" (p. 94). Burke goes on to discuss Augustine's band of fellow pilferers as a parodic church community.

What is most notable for our purposes in this equation of perversity with parody is the fact that Burke here presents his own discussion as a parody as well, thus clearly linking his reading to Augustine's "perversity." The whole section is introduced as a parody of Aquinas: "VIII. Adolescent Perversity. On the Stealing of the Pears, as recounted in Augustine's *Confessions*, Book II. (Treated after the fashion of a *Quaestio* in the *Summa Theologica* of Thomas Aquinas)" (p. 93). The section proceeds in classic Aquinine fashion, with a question followed by three objections, followed by a counterstatement and replies to the three objections, one of them even quoting "The Philosopher," Aristotle.

The explicitness of this parody, in the very section discussing sin's perversity as parody, reminds us that Burke's entire *Rhetoric of Religion* is organized as a parody, or imitation, of the *Confessions*. Like Augustine, Burke moves from an autobiographical discussion to an analysis of the opening chapters of Genesis, and his essay on the *Confessions* begins with an "Outline of the Inquiry," a detailed summary of each section which imitates the summaries of the books of the *Confessions* at the beginning of Augustine's text.

The *Confessions* is an ideal choice for Burke precisely because of this movement from autobiography to textual interpretation, for Burke has always tended to intermingle these two genres. As Hayden White has noted, "There is something densely *autobiographical* in everything he has written, so that any effort to come to terms with his work requires that we come to terms with the man who made it."[9]

There is much in Burke's essay, in fact, that suggests that his analysis of Augustine's autobiography has directly autobiographical overtones for himself as well. To introduce this topic, I cannot do better than cite a letter Burke sent me—by return mail—in February 1984, after receiving a first draft of this paper. His letter is largely concerned to refute any imputation that he is a deconstructionist. In the course of developing this point, Burke mentions that he first read the *Confessions*, in Latin, when he himself was an adolescent and could identify directly with the author.[10]

Interestingly, after leaving the direct discussion of Augustine, Burke writes of the role of chance in his own life. His letter describes a scene which any reader of Augustine will find highly evocative:

> When writing my "anti-novel," *Towards a Better Life*, I needed to imagine, for my character who was falling apart, a stage of regression to adolescence. I was stumped. Then lo! from out my jumble of notes and papers, I chanced upon an adolescent story I had written of a guy falling apart. "Given" my ability to transform it for my later purposes, it was *exactly* what I needed.

Since, as I interpret the whole narrative, it is a kind of symbolic predestination, I do feel that "luck was with me" there in that enterprise. The whole ex*peee*rience with and of such doings makes me feel that. . . extra-/non-theological as my study of Augustine is, a "deconstruction" angle can't be quite the accurate way of getting at it. . . .

Indeed not—even in his late eighties Burke is casting a scene in his own life as a writer into a form that directly recalls the critical moment of Augustine's conversion when, paralyzed by his divided will, he hears a mysterious child's voice urging him to "Take it and read, take it and read" and goes and reads at random in Paul, applying the text to his own life. In a nice variation, the sacred text Burke hit on was not the Bible but one of his own adolescent writings.[11]

There is ample evidence within *The Rhetoric of Religion* itself for the autobiographical overlap between Burke and his subject. Frequently his characterizations of Augustine remind us of Burke himself, as when he speaks of Augustine's "extraordinary energy in. . .controversy," or tells us that "if Augustine's only choices were between chance and order, for all his emotional turbulence he was temperamentally bound to choose order" (pp. 102, 78). Most interesting is Burke's most extended sketch of Augustine's life before conversion:

> Looking over Augustine's long series of quests, questions, and "inquisitions," we see the self-portrait of an inquirer who, though he did not say so in so many words, had experimented tirelessly. Infant spontaneity; childish play; adolescent perversity; imaginative engrossment in the poetry of Rome and Greece; aesthetic liberalism; amours both rowdy and conscience-laden; metropolitan careerism as a rhetorician (a mixture of teaching and salesmanship); . . .skepticism or systematic doubt (in the style of the Academics); Stoicism. . . "colony-thinking". . .Manichaeanism; the Platonists; and even a touch of Aristotelianism. . . .
>
> All told. . .we have. . ."an ardent seeker after the good life" . . .and "a most acute scrutinizer of the most difficult questions. . . ." (Pp. 91–92)

Such autobiographical resonances would not in themselves, of course, be sufficient to keep Burke returning to Augustine. Equally important is the relation between Augustine's interpretive practices and Burke's own. Burke himself suggests as much, in the letter quoted above, in denying that he is out to undo Augustine:

David Damrosch

> Conceivably Augustine might conceive of me as his worst
> enemy. But although I never really *liked* the guy, I consider him
> an outstanding genius in the ways of verbalization.... I'm not
> trying to "deconstruct" anything. I'm trying to say what I think
> is going on, in my terms for saying what is going on. I wd.
> *parallel* it.

This activity of paralleling Augustine's discourse, which I have been describing as parodic or imitative, can also be described, as Burke does here, as a process of translation of Augustine into other terms. To speak in terms of Greek rhetoric, this is a process of *allegoria*, the description of one thing under the image of another. Here I believe we come to the heart of Burke's interest in Augustine, since it is Augustine who is a seminal theorist of allegorical interpretation. The last three books of the *Confessions* advance an allegorical interpretation of the first chapter of Genesis, in which the creation of the physical world is presented as an allegory for the spiritual development of the soul. Burke could, of course, find any number of allegorical expositions of Genesis in the church fathers; Augustine's is of particular interest to him for two reasons. First is the autobiographical setting of this discussion, through which the interpretation of Genesis becomes a universalized version of the personal evolution Augustine has just shown us; second, and equally important, is the fact that as he introduces his reading of Genesis, Augustine is inspired to his remarkable explorations of the nature of time and of memory (see books 10 and 11).

The conclusion Augustine is most concerned to demonstrate is that time has no objective existence: "time is merely an extension, though of what it is an extension I do not know. I begin to wonder whether it is an extension of the mind itself" (11. 26). "It is in my own mind, then, that I measure time. I must not allow my mind to insist that time is something objective" (11. 27). The importance of this conclusion for interpretation is that it provides a theoretical justification for typological allegorical readings. Events of the "Old" Testament can foreshadow those of the "New," since their temporal separation is merely illusory.

This perspective, modernistically adapted, becomes the basis of Burke's logology. As he expounds the opening chapters of Genesis his general concern is to undercut the narrative force of the story and show that the narrative development can best be read as an exfoliation of logical priorities rather than of temporal sequences. Thus,

> the purport of our entire essay is to the effect that "myth" is
> characteristically a terminology of quasi-narrative terms for the

expressing of relationships that are not intrinsically narrative, but "circular" or "tautological." (P. 258)

Logology, then, relies upon an essentially allegorical atemporality, and as Burke says, allegory "is a mode of thought to which logology is always, though somewhat coyly, prone" (p. 159).

Through logology, as through traditional allegory, figures and events in a narrative transcend any merely literal significance (the role assigned them within the temporal framework of their narrative), and are liberated for a more general, atemporal, symbolicity. The divine figure of Burke's closing "prologue," TL, describes the result as

a wholly ample dialectic, with each moment of a man's life being seen (or glimpsed) in terms of the entire conglomerate complexity.... Things thereby transcend their nature as sheer things. They are found to move men not just by what they are in their blunt physicality, but also by what they *stand for* in the farthest reaches of symbolicity. (P. 301)

So far, Burke is exposing the achronicity of any symbolic reading. But his own practice does not show only this general analogy to typological allegory; many of his symbolic interpretations are quite directly typological, and in these readings we see that "the farthest reaches of symbolicity" are, for Burke, highly Augustinian in kind. Thus, he is quite willing to follow Augustine and other church fathers in linking the serpent in Eden with Lucifer: "the search for a cause is the search for a scapegoat, as Adam blames Eve, Eve blames the serpent, the serpent could have blamed Lucifer, and Lucifer could have blamed the temptations implicit in the idea of Order..." (p. 191). Any modern biblical critic would take exception to the lofty disregard of history visible in this comment, as Lucifer, and indeed Satan, are nowhere to be found in Genesis; Lucifer and Satan are identified together only in much later texts, and only in Christian times was their presence read back into the Eden story.

Such direct evocations of Augustinian allegory are, however, only a stage en route to a somewhat wider allegorizing, for Burke does not limit himself to Augustine's traditional typology, whereby the Old Testament prefigures the New. The passage just quoted shows this stage in the serpent's blaming of Lucifer (an option opened up to the serpent in the era of Christian typology), but then goes on to say that Lucifer himself could have blamed a still more distant principle: "the temptations implicit in the idea of Order (the inchoate 'fall' that...is intrinsic to the 'creation of the non-absolute')" (pp. 191–92). Lucifier, then, has an option opened up for him in the nineteenth century,

David Damrosch

when Coleridge could read the Fall dialectically, as "the creation, as it were, of the non-absolute" (quoted on p. 174). Burke's ultimate typology does not show the Old Testament prefiguring the New, but instead shows the whole Bible prefiguring modern dialectical thought, specifically in the philosophy of history. From this perspective, in discussing the central Pentateuchal concept of the covenant, Burke does not need to spend any time discussing ancient Near Eastern concepts of covenant, but moves directly to Hobbes, in the very first lines of his section on Genesis:

> Hobbes's *Leviathan* well serves our purposes here. . . . it makes us acutely conscious of the Biblical stress upon *Covenants* as motives. And we want to so relate the ideas of Creation, Covenant and Fall that they can be seen to implicate one another inextricably. . . . (P. 174)

Burke presents this Hobbesian insight as though the centrality of covenants would not be obvious to every biblical scholar, and indeed to any careful reader of the Pentateuch. But Hobbes is not merely the starting place; when Burke needs a definition of covenants, he takes it from Hobbes, quoting him at length (pp. 197–99), not pausing to note that the Hobbesian idea of covenant as a mutual agreement among equals is radically different from the ancient Hebrew idea of covenant, *b'rith*, which is a treaty between a superior and his inferiors. This difference would be of major significance for a literalistic, historicist reading of the relations between God and man in Genesis; but such a reading is clearly not Burke's aim. Other and even more striking examples of Burke's typological readings could be given,[12] but enough has been said to make the pattern evident.

An understanding of Burke's allegories in *The Rhetoric of Religion* is valuable in two ways: as an aid to understanding Burke's methods in his other writing, and as suggesting certain patterns that are widespread in interpretive analysis generally, though rarely seen so openly.

Readers of Burke will need few hints as to the applicability of my theme to Burke's writings in general; I will content myself here with one particularly striking example, from *A Rhetoric of Motives*. A passage which has more than once been cited by hostile critics, as evidence for claims that Burke is an interpretive lunatic, is his reading of Keats's "Beauty is truth, truth beauty," a line which, Burke says, many readers have found displeasing:

> The resistance is probably due in large part to the fact that idea, rather than mythic image, becomes the final stage in the

unfoldment. And other kinds of analysis are needed, to make such an "ultimate" acceptable.

As regards Keats's line, we have an uneasy hunch that it contains an "enigmatic" meaning. And this meaning, if we are right, could best be got by "joycing," that is, by experimentally modifying both "beauty" and "truth" punwise until one found some tonal cognates that made sense, preferably obscene sense, insofar as the divine service to beauty may, with a poet who has profoundly transformed the Christian passion into the romantic passion, be held in an *ecclesia super cloacam*. A combination of pudency and prudence has long prevented us from disclosing how we would translate this Orphic utterance. (However, to give an illustration of the method, we would say that *one* of the meanings we quickly discern in "beauty" is "body," while "truth" could be joyced meaningfully by a metathesis of two letters and the substitution of a cognate for one of the consonantal sounds.)[13]

So body is turd, turd body; the enigma is solved. Here we have Burke at his wildest; yet it is just here that we also have Burke at his most traditional, if we are attuned to the right tradition, that of ancient allegorical interpretation of Scripture. Consider this parallel from one of the classical texts of rabbinical Midrash, *Sifre*, a sober commentary on the book of Numbers. In Numbers 12:1, Moses' wife, Zipporah, is described as a Cushite. The problem for the rabbis was that she had already been described, in Exodus 2, as a Midianite. What then could "Cushite" mean? Unwilling to admit even a minor inconsistency in the sacred text, the rabbis proposed the following solution: "Cushite" is not meant as a literal place name, but signifies that everyone who saw Zipporah praised her beauty.

This conclusion is demonstrated by the method Burke would later dub "joycing." From "Cushite" take the root *Cush*. Change the *sh* (a single letter in Hebrew) to an *s* (compare Burke's *th* to *d*) and metathesize the consonants (again compare Burke), arriving at *s-c*, the root of *sacah*, "to look out." The rabbis clinch this point by reminding us that Abraham's wife, Sarah, was admired by the Egyptians (Genesis 12:15, which uses the same verb); clearly "Cushite" means to suggest that Zipporah received a similar admiring attention.[14]

The parallel is striking because of the coincidence of the close similarity of the phonetic operations performed on "Cush" and "truth"; it is instructive if we consider the similarities in motivation for these operations. The rabbis have a dual motive, intellectual and moral: they wish to resolve an inconsistency in the text, and they wish to defend

David Damrosch

Zipporah against her attackers within the text itself. In Numbers 12:1, the passage in question, Moses is being criticized by his brother Aaron and his sister Miriam because he has married a foreign ("Cushite") wife—a serious issue, as so many Hebrew leaders are led astray by pagan wives. The rabbis, then, are showing that Moses is not in the wrong, that Zipporah really is not foreign after all. The issue had pressing political significance for the rabbis, writing during the period of Roman domination of Palestine, a period of particular danger for Jewish cultural identity.

It seems fair to say that in the usually quite sober and interpretively cautious *Sifre* this forced interpretation is inspired by an unusual pressure of concerns, simultaneously textual, moral, and political; we are reminded of Burke's multivalent interpretive interests. Furthermore, Burke, like the rabbis, is seeking to justify what he calls an "ultimate" meaning by grounding it in a hidden, "enigmatic" truth, with the ground of meaning here seen not as God but as the body, as mediated by the unconscious, whose processes are to be exposed through "joycing."

A few pages later in the *Rhetoric* Burke directly discusses the allegorical nature of his quest for meaning:

> The veil of Maya is woven of the strands of hierarchy—and the poet's topics glow through that mist. By "socioanagogic" interpretation we mean the search for such implicit identifications. . . . The new equivalent of "moral" or "tropological" criticism would probably be found in a concern with the poem as a ritual that does things for the writer and reader. . . . Any sense in which one order is interpreted as the sign of another would probably be the modern equivalent of the "allegorical." (Pp. 219–20)

Thus the *Rhetoric of Motives* in 1950 is already announcing the essence of Burke's project in *The Rhetoric of Religion*, and is asserting the commonality of allegory and general critical practice. By embracing the ahistoricity of Augustinian allegory Burke makes room for his many-sided, and always autobiographical, critical activity. The importance of his procedures for interpretation generally lies in his methodological openness and self-awareness, and in the thoroughness, one might say the perversity, with which he employs his methods. Burke's interpretations highlight concerns and techniques that are implicit in much critical activity, and can help us become better aware of the complexities inherent in our attempts to offer interpretive readings of texts, however literal a translation we attempt. Burke is willing to go farther out than most, but, as the parallels to the rabbis and Augustine show, he is never more central than when he appears most eccentric.

NOTES

1. Hans-Georg Gadamer, *Truth and Method* (New York: Seabury, 1975), pp. 427–28.
2. Ibid., p. 113.
3. Kenneth Burke, *The Rhetoric of Religion* (Berkeley: University of California Press, 1970), pp. 13–14.
4. Augustine, *Confessions*, trans. R. S. Pine-Coffin (New York: Penguin, 1961), 3.2.
5. John Freccero, "Logology: Burke on St. Augustine," in Hayden White and Margaret Brose, eds., *Representing Kenneth Burke* (Baltimore: Johns Hopkins University Press 1982), pp. 52–67, 52–53.
6. As Freccero says, "the psalms are explicitly mentioned at the beginning of the *Confessions* and serve as its models throughout" ("Logology," p. 63).
7. See *Faust*, pt. 1, lines 1178–1237. The Faustian/Manichaean reading of Augustine as Othello is rendered only more parodically perverse by Burke's downplaying of the associations made in the play between Iago and the Devil, in favor of the supposed parallel to Monica. When he does mention the Devil, Burke makes the strange claim that "despite the intensely devilish role of Iago, the play is not 'Manichaean'—for Iago is allowed by his creator to exist only because of his contribution to the 'good' of the play as a whole" (p. 105). By this reasoning, no Manichaean could ever have written a book that would illustrate Manichaeanism.
8. Freccero, "Logology," p. 58
9. Hayden White, Preface to *Representing Kenneth Burke*, pp. vii–viii.
10. Burke writes: "as an adolescent who loved Latin and, starting to branch out on my own, was 'naturally' attracted to a book with 'Confessions' as a title, I began reading him (with the added attraction of its being 'in the original,' while there were the sexual itches, too, for me to 'identify avec')." Note that this account parallels Augustine's description of being drawn to the theater as an adolescent "because the plays reflected my own unhappy plight and were tinder to my fire."
11. The autobiographical dimension of Burke's concerns is also evident in a later discussion of the *Confessions*, in the course of a review of B. F. Skinner's autobiography, *Self-Portrait of a Person*. Burke's extensive analysis, running to twenty long pages in the journal *Behaviorism* (Fall 1976), would merit an extended discussion in itself. For the moment, I will only note that Skinner, as well as Augustine, takes on Burkean overtones in the course of the review, as a youthful would-be novelist turned social analyst.

David Damrosch

12. My favorite example occurs on p. 213, when Burke interprets the Genesis account of the mist watering Eden as representing an infant's pre-linguistic attempts at communication; he supports this idea by references to mist in Flaubert and to the Rhine in Wagner's *Das Rheingold*.

13. Kenneth Burke, *A Rhetoric of Motives* (Berkeley: University of California Press, 1969), p. 204.

14. *Sifre zu Numeri*, trans. and ed. Karl Kuhn (Stuttgart, 1959).

11 REREADING KENNETH BURKE

DOCTRINE WITHOUT DOGMA,

ACTION WITH PASSION

WILLIAM H. RUECKERT

Epilogue as Prologue

Every career has its own logic and integrity. At one point—in the fifties and sixties—it seemed as if Burke's career was going to reach or achieve its culmination in the building of his dramatistic system. But, from a later vantage point in the late seventies and early eighties, it became clear that this was but a stage in, rather than the culmination of, his career. Criticism as a way of life, rather than system building, is what accounts for the logic and integrity of Burke's career. That was the discovery I made while conceiving and writing this paper. Its double purpose is to characterize the role of the critic, and to characterize more overtly the nature of Burke's enduring legacy to us. If I have used myself in this essay, it is not because I wanted to intrude myself upon the reader, but because I am one of Burke's primary legatees, and I have tried throughout to think of Burke in history—mine as well as his. A critic, as Burke well knows, is a historical counteragent, or a counteragent to history, taking what his own time provides him with and subjecting it to the scrutiny of the critical intelligence. A critic does not deny history but accedes to it by asserting through his actions as a critic the role of the critical intelligence in history. No critic can escape his own time, but he can, as Burke most clearly has done, transcend it, rising above it to provide us, his legatees, with a critical doctrine free of destructive dogma, and to show us, by the passion of his repeated critical actions, what it means to be a true critic.

"Legacy: anything received from or passed on by an ancestor, predecessor, or earlier era." Well, at least Burke is not yet an earlier era, so

William H. Rueckert

we can ignore that part of the definition. Ancestor and predecessor: Yes, by all means. What, exactly, has he left us, passed on to us? To be literal minded about it, he has left us his verbal symbolic acts, and they are what will survive and endure.

When I first began getting ready to do this essay, I subjected myself to a huge new infusion of Burke: I read as much of the new criticism as I could, I talked and corresponded with Burkeans, and reread many of the sacred texts. This huge new infusion caused a massive confusion in my head, and a condition which Burke has described as "counter-gridlock."[1] Gridlock is when, in monumental traffic jams, you can't go any way at all: counter-gridlock is when, confused out of your mind, you go every which way. Anxious for some way to end my counter-gridlock—because the more I read, the worse I got—I decided on refusion. If we joyce this term a bit, we get re*fuse*, re*fuse*, and refuse (as trash or garbage), a pun that should delight Burke. In order to bring about re*fusion*, you have to re*fuse* and try to get rid of the refuse. You have to say NO to some of those seductive YESES. So that is what I did. I refused exposition in any sustained form, since I think we are beyond that in our work on Burke and ready for synthesis, placement, application, and evaluation. I refused the powerful temptation to dissolve Burke in particular into an elaborate discussion of genius in general, especially American genius. I refused synecdoche, or the detailed treatment of Burke in terms of one representative text—which is his own favorite way of doing things; and I refused the exploitation of my knowledge of a Burke few others seem to know—the Burke of the unpublished "Symbolic." I decided instead that I would shoot the moon and attempt refusion. I would try to put Burke together for myself in a new way and then characterize his legacy to us by spinning out an essay strung on the titles of his major symbolic acts. What better way to break a counter-gridlock than to lock onto the relentless irreversible rectilinear forward movement of Burke's titles; what better way to arrive at the tautological cycle of terms implicit in the idea of Kenneth Burke.

Counteragent

For my purposes, Burke's first significant symbolic act is *Counter-Statement* (1931). I prefer to leave *The White Oxen* lowing contentedly in the fictional world Burke created for them. *Counter-Statement* is another matter. It identifies an essential ingredient of everything that Burke has done and said as a critic from the twenties to the present. From the very beginning, Burke conceived of the critic—not just the literary critic, but the critic at large—as a counteragent, and of his writings as counterstatements and counteractions. To be a counteragent is always to be in a dialectical relationship to one's culture. Twenty years after most people retire, Burke, tireless as ever, is still on the road as a counteragent, admonishing us, educating anyone who will listen. His ferocious energy has fueled him, and his driving, corrective ironic goal (to counter and correct what is wrong, mistaken, destructive) has motivated him throughout. This has been very clear from the thirties on, and is perfectly embodied in the title of his only novel, *Towards a Better Life.*

Realistic Idealist

The "towards" in this title is as essential as "a better life," for Burke has always moved, and tried to move others, toward some nondogmatic conception of a better life. Burke has spent a lifetime fighting the tyranny of dogma—as can be studied in his efforts to secularize God and turn him into a linguistic marvel. (I'm not being entirely facetious here: Burke, a great pluralist in his own way, has always wanted to have his divinities and secularize them too. An inveterate empiricist, he will die with his words on.)

But let's not lose track of the better life; let's not stray back toward counter-gridlock. Whatever *Towards a Better Life* (1932), is about (and Burke has said many times that of all his symbolic acts this one most perfectly names his number), it is quite clear that writing this novel enabled Burke, at a time of great personal difficulty and anguish, to move himself toward both the conception and the reality of a better life. If we must search for a motive as to why the critic, following out his own entelechy, keeps writing, I think we can find it here. If the critic is a counteragent working for the good of society—the noblest of all human motives, we are told—then he must work against the factional disputes that keep humans at war, with themselves and others, and thus prevent them from moving, progressing toward a better life. In some essential way, the work of Burke the critic—as was true of Burke the novelist, and will later be true of Burke the poet—is purgative-redemptive. Catharsis is absolutely essential to any understanding of Burke's legacy to us.

We may tend to discount Burke's many rhetorically elegant statements about the overall purpose of his work because we find them overly idealistic and perhaps a bit naive, but in doing this we forget that behind Burke the idealist is Burke the realist, and ever and always Burke the dualist. The motto for *A Grammar of Motives*—"Towards the Purification of War"—should be understood in the most literal way. Millions were killed while Burke was writing this book. Such a brute reality might make any thoughtful critic wonder about what his words should do.

Burke has never defined the better life, nor is he likely to. He has, however, often described the worser life and written about those ideas and forces that distract us from and, worse, corrupt our view of the better life. What is important is that we have some idea of the better life that does not contradict our nature as symbol-using animals, and keep striving to move toward it. Stasis is as antithetical to Burke as dogmatism; and process, that great Whitmanian and pragmatic good, is probably more important than any final truth. Almost every major Burkean proposition is a process/towards one. He has had a lifelong concern with moving on, with purification, with dialectic, with locating and taking on new antagonists. Even his latest definition of human beings as bodies that *learn* language is a process definition. We should remember that Burke ends his wonderful "Epilogue: Prologue in Heaven" with an unfinished word-in-process. And we should recall the many *towards* titles in Burke: *Towards a Better Life,* "Towards the Purification of War," *Attitudes toward History,* "Towards Looking Back," "Towards Helhaven." I cannot think of a single point in Burke's development where he is not moving on toward something new, some more perfect way of saying or doing it. If we have to identify the salient characteristics of his genius, this application of energy and creativity to a single sense of mission and purpose is certainly one of them.

Poetic Anatomist

Burke's turn toward social criticism (and far beyond that) occurred in the early thirties. It was a turn he never turned back from. Burke's next title is *Permanence and Change: An Anatomy of Purpose* (1935). There are probably more terms for this opposed pair than there are for any of the many other dualities we find in Burke. Just to list some of these oppositions would take one a long way toward understanding the always dualistic, always dialectical nature of Burke's thought.

Like many Americans, Burke is divided between a conservative body and a radical mind. There are some things which he does not want to change. Though Burke has been everywhere in his head and, of late, thanks to modern technology, practically everywhere in the United States, his "sickly selph" has spent most of its life in rural New Jersey. While he was conceiving and writing his most radical books, he lived in Andover without running water, flush toilet, or electricity, and modernized his house there only when necessity forced his hand. Burke is profoundly conservative in the way he thinks about our biological, technological, and ecological needs. His dazzling learning makes us forget his homely life-style and simple country ways. All of his thought is deeply grounded in nature and the body.[2]

But let us not forget the subtitle of this book: *An Anatomy of Purpose.* Having studied and diagnosed the sickly body of society, Burke is now going to do us a detailed anatomy of human purpose so that he can suggest a cure. Burke was never one to shy away from the big questions. In this subtitle we have the first of many similar kinds of tropes Burke is going to use to describe his own purpose. Other obvious ones are philosophy, calculus, grammar, and dramatism. These figures give us variations of the same drive in Burke and also reveal a rather interesting progression (from body to mind to mathematics to drama to language.)[3] Every major title from the *Grammar* on has language in it, and all bring language and human purpose together in some way. From the thirties on, Burke was to keep on trying to define, in the most Occamistic way possible, just exactly what human purpose is. Purpose is but another term for motives, and the whole enterprise begun in *Permanence and Change* was brought to a systematic completion in the *Motives* books.

Permanence and Change is a radical book devoted to intense social analysis and organized around the ways in which we inherit, establish, and create our individual and collective identities. It is most appropriately dedicated to Burke's parents. Burke said that he put the book together to keep himself from falling apart. He clearly also did this in *Towards a Better Life*, but there he seems much more personal because he is intent on killing off an old self and an old relationship in order that a new one may be born. In *Permanence and Change*, we have a conjunction of individual and social, critic and society: Burke acts out in symbolic form a permanent individual human motive or purpose—the need to define the individual self and to have a larger sense of social purpose—in the midst of chaotic historical change. The larger purpose is reflected in the diagnostic and corrective intent of the book, which goes far beyond whatever therapeutic function the book may have had for Burke. It is the critic's way of turning his personal problems into policy, and so partially transcending them.

Burke defined the major overriding purpose of all his subsequent work in this book. If Burke defined the literary critic and his function in *Counter-Statement*, he defines and enacts the function of the social critic in this book. The critic must study human beings first to discover what their permanent psychophysical needs are, then he must try to determine if these needs are being met in the kingdom of necessity— that is, society at the critic's own point in history. If the critic finds that these permanent human needs are not being met, then he must undertake corrective action, both for himself and for such others as he can reach by means of the printed word. It seems almost inevitable, after the fact, that Burke's next book would be about attitudes toward history, history being the kingdom of necessity.

Comic Historian

We are up to 1937 now. Europe is killing itself in Spain in a trial run for the great slaughter of World War II—an event which is to have a profound effect on Burke. America is still working its way out of the Great Depression. The Russian communists are purging themselves. The Nazis are gathering strength. Burke is forty years old. I am eleven years old. My father has recently been killed in a stupid car accident. I have entered history. Ten years later I will first encounter Burke in print. Burke will later become one of my spiritual fathers. Later still, I will name one of my sons after him. Burke is studying history and making it. He has begun an amazing period of productivity that will last thirty years, on through the publication of *Language as Symbolic Action* in 1966. He will write and publish millions of words during this period in a sustained action of the critical intelligence that is unmatched (and as yet poorly understood and appreciated) by any other critic writing in America during this time. I will study and write about Burke during this period. Our histories will converge. I will become one of his legatees. He will remake my mind. I will carry on his work in my own way.

Part of Burke's legacy to us is the comic/ironic attitude toward history as he first worked it out in this wonderfully playful and intellectually resilient book. Many have adopted this comic/ironic perspective as part of their own equipment for living. Burke's true genius is perhaps first evident in *Attitudes toward History*. One characteristic of that genius—perhaps a characteristic of every genius—is its essentializing, entelechial, to-the-end-of-the-line nature: ask the *essential* questions; construct a dictionary of *pivotal* terms; identify the most *fundamental* psychological responses; determine the *basic, brute* realities; offer a corrective, a way of diagnosing and coping with our problems; give us ways of developing our own attitudes toward history so that we may move, knowingly, toward a better life. Vitality, variety, energy, boundary breaking, and creativity—all essential characteristics of Burke's mind—everywhere abound in this most Emersonian book.[4] Though this book was clearly an action of the critical mind upon a historical scene, it seems as fresh and relevant today as ever because there has never been a time, nor is it likely there will ever be one, in which we do not need and cannot use the comic frame and comic correctives Burke provides us within this book.

Philosopher of Symbolic Action

Strictly speaking, Burke probably cannot be considered a systematic philosopher.[5] In general, philosophers have negative reactions to him because they find his logic suspect and his methods much too unorthodox. Their loss, I think, is our gain, and Burke's great originality of mind will probably win out in the end. If Burke is not a systematic philosopher, he is certainly very philosophically inclined, because he asks so many essential, fundamental questions, and clearly has one of the great questing, questioning minds of our time. Looking up at the high peaks, he has not been one to fall backward into a faint, nor has he ever hesitated to enter and explore any labyrinthian text that he came upon. He began asking hard questions about literary form in the twenties. He kept asking them long after *The Philosophy of Literary Form* (1941) was published. He did not really get answers that satisfied him until he wrote his "Symbolic of Motives" in the fifties. In a culture dominated and almost suffocated by trivia, and in a discipline (the study of literature) devoted to trivia in a kind of monumental way, Burke, true to his idiosyncratic and philosophical bent, went his own way and went after first principles. In developing his theory of symbolic action and the methodology to apply it, he bewildered and offended many of his fellow workers in this most conservative of professions.[6] In an age of science, he asserted that all poems are highly subjective and deeply personal and that this subjective content could be got at by objective methods. In an era of the well-wrought urn—of the poem as dead artifact—he asserted that poems are acts, the dancing of an attitude, and that, furthermore, poems are an essential part of our equipment for living. Here, as elsewhere, he

William H. Rueckert

continued his role as counteragent, reminding us that we should take literature at least as seriously as do those who write it.

Consider these titles: *The PHILOSOPHY of Literary form; ATTITUDES toward History; ANATOMY of Purpose*, and *A GRAMMAR of Motives*. Do we not have here the powerful, fearless Aristotelian drive of Burke's mind, the impossible desire of the Sage of Andover to do for his time what Aristotle did for his? One could say that Burke has spent a lifetime trying to formulate first principles and the first principle of first principles—a new definition of man that would replace the Aristotelian one.[7]

What of the subtitle *Studies in Symbolic Action?* Symbolic action is a concept Burke introduced into the language and thence into our heads and critical terminology. Burke has added many terms to our language and critical vocabulary, but symbolic action is among the most potent. Everything that he wrote could be considered, as I have been doing here, as *his* symbolic actions. Let's favor one of these two terms as the foremost among equals: let's favor and talk about action for a bit.

One of Burke's major contributions to the way in which we think about ourselves, the texts we have inherited, and the way we interact with the world into which we were born has been his insistence upon the fact that in speaking and writing, especially in writing, we are engaging in authentic, essential human actions, and that in the written word, especially, the action remains active and can be reenacted by the reader—or the actors and spectators, if it is a play. There is a symbolic transfer from the agent into the act so that the symbolic action contains in itself not just its linguistic ingredients but its human, personal ingredients. This most fundamental Burkean conception has had a profound effect upon the ways in which we approach speaking, writing, literature, language, and all verbal symbolic acts. Burke gave us a theory of the text long before the current obsession with this question began proliferating supposedly "new" theories of the text.[8]

Everything that Burke writes from this point on will be tied to his theories of language, symbolic action, and texts. By 1941, he has discovered his main subject, which is not literature, but language. Everything that he does from here on will be language-centered. Like every other genius I have ever studied, Burke eventually found and then concentrated on his own special field. Faulkner wrote novels; Stevens wrote poems; Burke, the critic, studied and wrote about language and man as a symbol-using animal.

Grammarian/Antinomist/Dialectician

This is Burke's big book—all 517 pages of it. It is so big that most of us do not even know or fully understand what is in it. The *Grammar* (1945) represents a quantum leap forward from the previous book where Burke tried to work out a philosophy of literary form. To go from literature to language is to go from the part to the whole, from one kind of human symbolic action and its motives, to human symbolic action in general with its enormous variety and complexity of motives. Any lingering confusions that Burke was merely a literary critic were removed by this monument to human energy, adventuresomeness, ingenuity, and intelligence. As our teenagers say, this book is awesome. It is a true critical cornucopia and represents Burke the critic at his very best as grammarian, working out the grammars of many different systems; as antinomist, attacking reductionism wherever he finds it in terminological networks; and as dialectician, lining up the terms, pounding the paradoxes, revealing the ambiguities lurking in the apparently simple explanations of human motives. We can say of this book what Burke said of Freud: reading it, or rereading it, is suggestive to the point of bewilderment.

This book, after all, is the home of dramatism as a concept and method, of the pentad and ratios, of the paradox of substance, the representative anecdote, the paradox of purity, antinomies of definition, the noble critical motive of *ad bellum purificandum*, the demonic trinity, the temporizing of essence, tropes as a mode of perception, the concepts of act and substance so essential to dramatism, ambiguity as a necessary part of the human condition, admonition as a critical function, language as the essential human trait, reductionism and oversimplification as curable, correctable habits of mind (language), neo-Stoicism and linguistic skepticism as critical ideals, the dazzling analysis of Keats's "Ode on a Grecian Urn,"—and more. No other book of Burke's tells us so much about language and, if we take the metaphor of his title seriously, so much about the relation between language, terminological networks, motives, actions, and nonverbal realities. And no other book of his gives us so many different ways to deal with language as an action, and texts as symbolic acts.

Burke says of this book and the dramatistic project in general that it should help "towards the purification of war" through "encouraging tolerance by speculation." The book is addressed, he says, "to a speculative portion of the mind," and the work it does helps us to "transcend" our problems by teaching us to "appreciate them," by teaching us something about "the ways in which we are victims of our own and one another's magic."[9] This should remind us that Burke is a critic, not a politician, and that knowledge, not action, is his business. We may well act differently after reading this book; we are certainly liable to think differently after taking it into our heads and making it part of our equipment for living as critics in our own right.

Passionate Persuader

A Rhetoric of Motives (1950) is Burke's second big book. It, too, has proved to be awesome, and almost seems more persuasive now in the time of terrorism and resurgent fanatical fundamentalism than when it was first published. If we ever had any doubts about the passionate ethical-social motives behind Burke's rhetoric—that is, his conception of the social function of the critic—we need only refresh our memories from this socially conscious book with its relentless emphasis upon the hierarchic, especially the social hierarchy, and upon the ways in which motives, especially destructive social motives, may be manipulated by means of rhetoric.

> Order, the Secret, and Kill. To study the nature of rhetoric, the relation between rhetoric and dialectic, and the application of both to human relations in general, is to circulate about these three motives. . . . Starting from any one of them, you find a vast network of dialectical possibilities in the offing, whereupon you may tend to see the whole of the dialectic itself in terms of the starting point, thereby being conservatively slavish to Order, morbidly fascinated by the Secret, militantly envenomed for the Kill. We must consider how the fullness of dialectic ("reality") is continually being concealed behind the mists of one or the other of these rhetorical overemphases. Here would be the outer reaches of a Rhetoric of Motives.[10]

Without worrying too much about the syntactically ambiguous title—an ambiguity that is uncharacteristic of Burke and persists into his next title, *A Symbolic of Motives*—let's explore what Burke is doing here, since he seldom does the same thing twice, or anything in exactly the same way in any two books. This methodological and conceptual originality and variety are an essential part of his legacy to us. His mind has pushed forward with great American restlessness from book to book, and every book has taken him, and us, into new territory. He has a great westering mind and has, like Whitman, always been in search of his own passage to India.[11]

It is 1950 and cold war time. The superpowers are squaring off. We have entered the nuclear age. It seems somehow appropriate that Burke would write a book about dialectic during the terrible years of World War II, committing it to the purification of war; and that he would write a book about persuasion during the rancorous years following the war, committing it to "tolerance and contemplation." Every book of Burke's is tied in some way to the events of his own time—a fact we often forget when considering his work. *The Rhetoric of Religion*, for example, is filled with topical allusions and comments which cast quite another light on the apparently rather remote essays in that book.

A Rhetoric of Motives (1950) is too well known for me to offer what could only be a quick, foolish summary. I want to use it to make three points about the way in which Burke works. The *Rhetoric* is probably our purest sustained example of the action of Burke's mind. It is his most coherent and tidy book, written almost entirely without footnotes and appendages. Very little of it was published separately ahead of the book and almost none of it, so far as I know, is occasional or "on request" work. The book seems to have been conceived and written all of a piece. It is arranged in Burke's characteristic triadic structure, as is *A Grammar of Motives*.[12] Burke likes to begin with concrete examples—usually texts—which allow him to introduce the key terms for a given book and illustrate them and their relationships at the same time. Here, in part 1, "The Range of Rhetoric," Burke begins with examples of identification (what goes with what, what equals what) and different kinds of persuasions that are affected by various kinds of identifications. Ranging is one of the most characteristic actions of Burke's mind and is always related to his concept of scope (thoroughness) and his belief that one must always have an adequate (rather than reductionist, oversimplified) range of terms as well as examples, a truly representative anecdote. This is Burke's "way into" the subject of the book. The middle part of this book—"Traditional Principles of Rhetoric"—is, as is part 2 of the *Grammar*, Burke's attempt to ground himself in history. At least, that is what it begins as. Having established his own terms and the relationship between them, as he does in the *Grammar* with the pentad and the ratios, he begins to look at other similar endeavors in relation to his own terms. Somewhere around the middle of the book—say in the "Act" section of the *Grammar*, and pretty much dead center here—Burke introduces the concepts which constitute the Burkean conceptual center of the book.

William H. Rueckert

Burke is not a historian of ideas but an originator of ideas. As Burke says near the end of part 2: "We do not pretend that our foregoing pages have been a comprehensive survey of works on rhetoric. We have attempted to consider only those writers who, by one device or the other, could be brought to "cooperate" in building this particular "philosophy of rhetoric," and whose presence might prevent it from becoming too "Idiosyncratic." " (*RM*, p. 169). By the end of part 2, this "philosophy of rhetoric" with its sociolinguistic and psychological co-ordinates is well laid out, and we have been made aware of the essential sociopolitical concerns of the book.

Part 3, "Order," is a detailed working out of Burke's concept of hierarchy, in a series of characteristically text-centered analyses. Hierarchy is one of the most important concepts in all of Burke: it is linguistic (positive, dialectical, and ultimate terms), sociopolitical (socioanagogic), and theological (rhetorical radiance of the divine). The importance of this concept to Burke's way of thinking about language and the drama of human relations cannot be overestimated. Within this hierarchic concept Burke works out most of his dramatistic moral-ethical concepts: guilt, mortification, hierarchic awe, hierarchic psychosis, catharsis, social courtship, and the like. This book about rhetoric turns out to be considerably more than just a study of the linguistic or literary or even the psychological devices used in various forms of persuasion. According to this book, our very existence is essentially rhetorical, a kind of continuous drama of identification, persuasion, and transformation. This idea, of course, is the basis of Burke's other great book on rhetoric, *The Rhetoric of Religion* (1961).

One point of this structural summary—which seems to me to be an essential point about almost all of Burke—is that he always gives you at least triple value for your reading: universal formulas and methods, such as the identification-persuasion one, which one can use to one's own ends; his own dramatistic theory, as we get it in parts 2 and 3, which you can accept or reject, as you choose; and, overall, the sustained action of his mind as it works its way into, over, and out of a subject.

All three of these have proven to be valuable legacies. There are probably more usable formulas in Burke than in any other modern critic. Many—such as the late Hugh Duncan—have found Burke's dramatistic theory a powerful and persuasive conceptual frame and have applied it at great length in their own disciplines; and many of us have found the text-centered ranging action of Burke's mind a useful antidote to the constraints of conventional logic and have adapted it to our own uses.

Symbolicist and His Sinbolix

"A Symbolic of Motives" is Burke's most enigmatic ti-
tle and nonbook. The title is enigmatic because, unlike all of Burke's
other titles, this one is not comprehensible apart from Burke's dramatistic system. Reading this title, no one could possibly know that it describes a book about poetics, the original title of which was, rather
more prosaically, "Poetics, Dramatistically Considered." The nonbook
is enigmatic because Burke apparently intends it to be his secret post-
humous legacy to us. He calls it his "Sinbolix" because he feels guilty
about having bolixed this nonbook for all these years.

All this aside, let's examine the title: "A Symbolic of Motives."
Grammar, Rhetoric, Symbolic: we all know what grammar and rhetoric are because they conform to their lexical definitions. However,
nothing but confusion can result from trying to apply a lexical meaning to symbolic as it is used here by Burke in this syntactically incor-
rect and confusing title. What, we ask ourselves, does Burke mean by
"symbolic" here, and why would you entitle your poetics "A Symbolic
of Motives"? Here is what Burke says about the "Symbolic" in *A Rhetoric of Motives:*

> The *Grammar* was at peace insofar as it contemplated the
> paradoxes common to all men, the universal resource of verbal
> placement. The *Symbolic* should be at peace, in that the
> individual substances, or entities, or constituted acts are there
> considered in their uniqueness, hence, outside the realm of
> conflict. For individual universes, as such, do not compete.
> Each merely *is*, being its own self-sufficient realm of discourse.
> And the *Symbolic* thus considers each thing as a set of
> interrelated terms all conspiring to round out their identity as
> participants in a common substance of meaning. An individual
> does in actuality compete with other individuals. But within the
> rules of the Symbolic, the individual is treated merely as a
> self-subsistent unit proclaiming its peculiar nature. It is "at
> peace" in that its terms *cooperate* in modifying one another. But
> insofar as the individual is involved in conflict with other
> individuals or groups, the study of this same individual would
> fall under the head of RHETORIC. (*RM*, pp. 22–23)

Burke has said that in going from dramatism to logology he went
from ontology to epistemology. Yes and no. The epistemological emphasis in the *Grammar* is very strong. But there is a lot of truth to what
he says, and one way to understand "A Symbolic of Motives" is to see

William H. Rueckert

it as the culmination of the ontological concerns of dramatism with its emphasis on substance and act. We should remember that as Burke was finishing the "Symbolic" he was beginning *The Rhetoric of Religion*—the first of his logological works. The "Symbolic" completes or perfects dramatism, taking it to the end of the line, working out its entelechy by treating literary *works* or forms—that is, whole literary works—as ontological paradigms, as perfections of being and language for their own sake. Using Burke's terms, we can speak of literary forms—that is, completed symbolic acts—as the perfection of the ontological motive intrinsic to language and symbolic acts. Just as pure persuasion is persuasion undertaken for its own sake, to persuade itself, as it were, so literary work would represent pure verbal being, or verbal being interested only in being itself. As Burke has argued most eloquently, poetry is the realm in which we can be most completely free.

Conceptually, the "Symbolic" is exceptionally interesting, not just because of what it says about poetics, the poetic motive, and specific texts, but because it completes the dramatistic system as Burke originally conceived it in the mid-forties. And, whether we like systems or not, dramatism, as we get it in the trilogy of *Motives* books, is certainly one of Burke's major legacies to us, and a monumental achievement in its own right.

Godsaken Logologer

It is 1961 and a new term enters our vocabularies just as dramatisms and the pentad did in 1945. That term is logology, and gives *The Rhetoric of Religion* its subtitle: *Studies in Logology*. This new term indicates that, as usual, Burke is moving on again, moving on down the open road, exhorting us as Whitman did in "Song of the Open Road" to join him, to travel with him, because traveling with him we will find what never tires. One could keep quoting from this wonderful poem, and much of it would be true of Burke. "Listen, I will be honest with you," Burke-Whitman says, "I do not offer the old smooth prizes, but the rough new prizes." Isn't Burke the critic like Whitman the poet, trying out the road ahead so that we may follow him? If Whitman is our great democratic poet, then Burke is surely one of our great democratic critics, in the American grain, right from the start, calling us to intellectual battle, telling us to join him, follow him in the search for knowledge, taking such risks as are necessary.[13]

Logology, where is logology going to take us? It initially took Burke through a series of analogical permutations on the relation of words to The Word, and, by that route, right on up to the top of his range of mountings; it took him deep into the verbal action of Saint Augustine's *Confessions*, and back to the narrative of the creation itself and to a long mediation on the tautological cycle of terms implicit in the idea of order; it took him on up to heaven and a dialogue with God himself; and later, it took him beyond heaven to Helhaven and counternature, to what may be the furthest reaches of where Burke's kind of knowledge can take us, to the very end of his line of thought. If theology takes us to God in his heaven, then logology, in its relentless examination of the ways of man, the symbol-using species, takes us to man in Helhaven, which is the ultimate ironic creation of the symbol-using genius of human beings. If there are profound similarities between Burke and Whitman, there are equally profound differences, as Burke pointed out in his Helhaven satire. At the end, Whitman the poet finds his passage to India, sailing forth on the winds of his own ecstatic rhetoric in search of the secrets of the cosmos. At the end, or, at least, near the end, Burke the logologist, following the epistemological logologic of his lifelong calling—he was sometimes a poet but always a critic—finds what? Not his passage to India certainly, and not the secrets of the cosmos: he finds the secret, ironic, and paradoxical human species knowledge he has always been after. Knowledge is Burke's religion, empirical/theoretical secular knowledge. Burke is one of our truly great rhetoricians of knowledge. In studying the rhetoric of religion, Burke demonstrates the rhetoric of logology for us. If dramatism comes to its culmination in the study of ontological paradigms, in the study of words persuading themselves to perfect themselves in autonomous symbolic forms, logology comes to its culmination in the study and contemplation of man's entelechy as a symbol-using animal, of man persuading himself to perfect himself in accordance with the entelechy of a symbol-using animal, of man persuading himself to perfect himself in accordance with the entelechy of his symbol-using genius. This takes us beyond poetry, beyond theology, beyond words, to technology. As you may remember, Burke's ironic motto for logology is that man's entelechy is technology.

Dramatism and logology do not contradict each other; rather they complement each other by showing us two of the main ways of humans, the symbol-using species. Are not poetry and technology two of the highest manifestations of our creative genius? What could be more closely connected than being and knowing.

William H. Rueckert

Omniverous Critic at Large

Burke brings twenty-five years of productivity and creative thinking to an end with the publication of his omnibus collection *Language and Symbolic Action: Essays on Life, Literature, and Method* (1966). This book should remind us of *The Philosophy of Literary Form*, not only because both are omnibus collections, or because the subtitle of one is generalized into the main title of the other, but because both show us Burke as the omniverous critic at large. The *Motives* books show us Burke the systematizer.[14] This book shows us again the first Burke we ever met in *Counter-Statement*; the Burke who worked and wrote for a variety of journals all through the twenties and thirties; the Burke who has written hundreds of reviews over the past fifty years; the Burke who took to the road in the late sixties and has stayed on the road ever since, lecturing, talking, reading, thinking on his feet—the critic at large in the most literal and Emersonian sense of this phrase, which is: the thinker let loose in our midst.

In some ways, this is the most representative of Burke's books, and the many readers who know him through it have here met the essential Burke. Headnotes precede the sections of the book, and many of the essays are followed by comments and/or addenda. Many of the essays and comments contain poems by Burke, which are also commented on. He includes and analyzes his own dreams in some of the essays. The comments elaborately cross-reference Burke's other works. There are, as usual, numerous footnotes. In sum, Burke follows his own advice by using all that there is to use; and he follows an old habit of his, which is to return after the fact to comment on his own work, trying to make sure he has got everything straight. Burke's mind is almost compulsively self-reflective. The epitome of this is his long Helhaven essay in which he writes a satire, examines his reasons for wanting to write one, and analyzes the satire as he is writing it.[15]

A lifelong tendency of Burke's mind has been to make repeated attempts to understand the same thing. In a way, we could say that Burke has been writing the same book over and over again since the mid-thirties, but the subject matter of this book is so vast that one can never finish it. Burke has kept at this task with remarkable determination, intelligence, ingenuity, and energy. His mind has seldom faltered: it wants to be understood; it wants to come to real knowledge; it wants to talk things out, to share knowledge, to set the record straight. Burke really believes that this is important, and by his actions he constantly renews our often-faltering belief in the power of mind, the powers of the critical word, the ability of the intellectual to affect the course of human events.

Nowhere, I think, is this clearer than in *Language as Symbolic Action* where Burke takes on so many different topics, covers such a wide variety of subject matter, comments on himself, corrects himself (and others), doubles back on himself, quotes his own poems, explores the most minute details of his seemingly trivial dreams, discusses his own insomnia and bladder functions, and in many other ways tries to bring mind and language to bear upon events in a series of "metholical meditations," and in this way counteract the high-speed, high-tech, fast-knowledge journalistic culture of his native land.

Logophilous at Play in the Field of Words

No major critical book by Burke has been published since 1966, but all of his earlier works have been republished by the University of California Press. Though he has written and published numerous essays and reviews during this period, there are only two new books: *Collected Poems* (1968) and *Dramatism and Development* (1972), which contains the two splendid lectures he gave at Clark University. *Collected Poems* brings together the poems Burke wrote between 1915 and 1954, which were originally published under the title *Book of Moments*, and dedicated to his sparring partners; and the many poems he wrote between 1955 and 1967, which are collected under the title *Introduction to What*. It is always tempting to quote at length from these poems because Burke not only is a pretty good poet but has a wonderful sense of the comic, ironic, absurd, and satiric. What I want to do here is pause long enough to acknowledge Burke's legacy to us as poet, letter writer, and performer—performer, because Burke does not just stand up and lecture, he enacts a discourse. Though it may not be immediately obvious, there are remarkable similarities between Burke the poet, the letter writer, and the performer. Since I have known Burke in all three of these roles, I'll draw upon my own experience here.

"Dear Billions," his letters to me begin. If he is at home in Andover, his letters will usually have something above the address, like "Back at Clutcher's Gulch, 154 Amity Road, And/Or 07821; or more simply, Groove 154." His letters are usually written in a combination of standard orthography and Burke orthography, which is a phonetic manipulation that allows him to exploit every pun he can think of as he writes. If he writes you when he's a bit tanked, or the mood is on him, the whole letter may be in Burkese. Here is a typical opening: "Dear Billions, by heck your new stuffo in your book anent my Sickly Selph, and your friendly exercising in the REPRESENTING volume do make look as though somethinks is going on. Thanks slavishly." The letters vary, of course, but always attentive to formal proprieties, Burke closes his letters as deliberately as he opens them. Here is one random example: "But I must hobble-cobble back to my last, while I last, Bestest to thee and thine, K.B." Sometimes Burke will end his letters rather more startlingly, as in this short one about some troubles he was having with U. Cal Press: "Love, love, love, love—*Killkillkillkill* Holla! K.B." If I were the only person Burke was writing letters like this to, that would be one thing; but I am one among a great many who have gotten the attention of this most generous great man. His letters are like a visit to Burke in the old days when you shared his outhouse, with its pyramidal dung heap, with him, helped him draw water from his wonderful dug well by the side of the house, sat in the kitchen while his wife fixed dinner, haggled with him in the deck chairs in the yard, or walked the country roads with him in the middle of the night, while he talked on and on. This is part of the legacy of the living man which many of us have been lucky enough to enjoy.

Burke the poet is the critic at play in the field of words. Of course, we also encounter this playful, ironic, pun-loving Burke elsewhere: in his early satiric piece "Waste: The Future of Prosperity"; with the intellectual playfulness of his perspectives by incongruity and of his presentation of Western history as a five-act drama; in the wittiness of "Anthony in Behalf of the Play"; in the marvelous "Epilogue: Prologue in Heaven" which brings *The Rhetoric of Religion* to closure; and in the more recent Helhaven satires. But it is in the poetry that we experience the perfection of these playful, ironic, comic, satiric motives in Burke. Let me quote a single representative poem, and then move on.

> A HUGE TRIBUTE
> He had mighty bulges
> This poet
> With vigor of movement
>
> His output was substantial
>
> When he swished
> By god he swished—
> And better keep your distance.
>
> Magnitude?
>
> Solemnity?
>
> Poise?

Calm self affirmation?
This one had them all—
And curvature.
I mean
He was a horse's ass.[16]

Burke is a logo-philos—a lover of words. He is also a great believer in logo-power. Words are for play and power, for knowledge and purification, for edification and delight, for mediation and meditation. Burke has used them to all of these ends—and more. If variety and thoroughness are marks of genius, then Burke is a genius in his relationship to words. Anyone who has experienced a Burke performance is well aware of this. In one of these performances we move from the written word to the spoken word; we experience the overwhelming presence of the man himself; we come face to face with Burke in behalf of himself, dramatism, and logology. It would certainly be a mistake to think that his legacy to us consisted entirely of ideas. Some of us hardly touch our times and do little more than ripple the water as it flows by. But Burke—to use a phrase from William Carlos Williams—has been a great toucher of others, as Whitman was, using both words and himself to promote tolerance and contemplation, laughter and irony, a comic perspective, the free play of the mind, self-awareness, language awareness, earth awareness, global awareness.

Beginning and End in One: The Now Forever New

The legacy that I have just been discussing is the legacy of the living man. Some of us are lucky because we have experienced, enjoyed, and learned from his living presence. But it is the written word that lives on, and carries the legacy into the future. And that is what I want to end with.

Burke's tentative title for a collection of the work he has done since 1966 is "On Human Nature, a Gathering, While Everything Flows." Readers with good memories will recognize part of this as a rejected title for *The Philosophy of Literary Form*. And readers with better memories will recall that this same phrase appears in a long complicated poem by Burke entitled "Introduction to What," in the following context:

William H. Rueckert

> It's a wrangle
> It's a tangle
> It's a Jingle-jungle
> JANGLE
> This world of Mr. Seat-Up and Miss Seat-Down
> And their Ultimate Interminglings
> While everything flows
> (panta rhei to you)

Let's break this title down into its three parts and take them up separately:

"On Human Nature"—this has been Burke's subject since the thirties. If he has seemed to concentrate exclusively on language, it is because language provides him with his access to the study of human nature. Let us remember, as we move toward closure, Burke's latest definition of human beings as bodies that learn language. You could spin a lot of books out of this dualistic definition that grounds language in the body and never allows us to talk for long about one apart from the other or the whole human being apart from nature. "On Human Nature" recalls all the parts of Burke's titles that stress permanence, his long search for essential knowledge, and all of the hundreds of terms and formulas in his work that do the same.

"A Gathering"—a perfect term for all that any critic can hope for, which is to make a gathering, perhaps a number of gatherings, from out of his "scatterhoods." Every book is a gathering of time-fixed verbal actions by the critic at a particular point in time. "A Gathering" is both verb and noun, action and substance, the now forever new, beginning and end in one.

"While Everything Flows—the brute reality, the kingdom of necessity, the history which Burke has always acknowledged even as he tried to make a gathering against it. Time, history, flows relentlessly from the past into the present and on into the future producing changes so massive, brought about by causes so complex and widespread, that no single individual has much real power against them. But still you make your gatherings while everything flows. Your gatherings are your books; they stand against time and the flow; they do not stop it. Nothing Burke says about technology is going to prevent technology from fulfilling its entelechy—or, more accurately, nothing is going to prevent human beings from following out their technological genius to the end of the line.

Should this kind of knowledge lead you to cynicism, despair, misanthropy, suicide—no, though all of these are temptations lurking around the edges of our knowledge. Burke could have quit years ago, and rested on his gatherings. But he didn't, he hasn't, he won't. He drives on, perhaps more slowly than before, and not just because work is therapeutic and provides one with a daily sense of the renewal of purpose. It is more complicated than that. He drives on because he can't relinquish his belief in the power of knowledge to do good in some way for someone; and he cannot (and many of the rest of us cannot) relinquish his fundamental, irony-tinged American idealism. Why? Because that is *his* entelechy.

Let him speak his own closure from his poem "Introduction to What": "Yours," he says

for the Light, the Doctrine, the Rebirth, the Promise, the Great Praiseworthy, the Over-Flowing through Sheer Abundance, The Beginning-and-End-in-One, the Unfolding, the Homecoming, the Perfect Turn from Estrangement, the Revelation, the Moment Within the Moment (drawn out forever), the Ultimate, the Crossing, the Looking Back Into the Future and Forward Into Pastness, the Single Irreplaceable Meeting (the one-time miraculous combination, the very best of good luck), the Dirt Made Pure, the Flash of Blinding Super-Night, the Succession Jammed Together, the Forum of Sheer Form:

The Welling-Forth of Absolute Springtime, the Flowering in Winter, the Motionless Revolving, The Doctrine Without Dogma. The Law Without Lawyers, the Word sans Syllables, the Grant Without Strings Attached....

The sunrise at sundown, the New Forever Now

(*CP*, p. 109)

NOTES

1. See *All Area*, No. 2 (Spring 1983), pp. 4–32. There is a long interview with Burke there, which includes many wonderful pictures of Burke, his family, and friends. The title of the interview is "Counter-Gridlock."
2. See "The Anaesthetic Revelation of Herone Liddell," *The Complete White Oxen: Collected Short Fiction of Kenneth Burke* (Berkeley: University of California Press, 1968), pp. 255–310. One section of this story is called "Haunted by Ecology." The story is about the mind-body, self-nature relationships so central to Burke's thought. See Burke's comments on this story

in *Attitudes toward History,* 3d ed. (Berkeley: University of California Press, 1984), pp. 391–93.

3. The progression is from anatomy (body) to attitude (mind) to philosophy (mind) to grammer (language) to drama (action) to rhetoric (language).

4. Emersonian because these are also characteristics of such Emerson essays as "Nature," "The American Scholar," "Circles," "Self Reliance," and "The Poet," and because Emerson also thought of himself as a counteragent.

5. To my knowledge, no philosopher has taken up Burke, and those who have bothered to review his books have not been sympathetic. See the essays by Max Black and Abraham Kaplan in William Rueckert, *Critical Responses to Kenneth Burke, 1924–1966* (Minneapolis: University of Minnesota Press, 1969). See also Christian Susini, "Turbulence," *Recherches anglaises et américaines* no. 12 (1979), pp. 109–25, for an excellent discussion of why Burke can be considered philosophic but not a philosopher.

6. I write as a member of this most conservative profession with many years of experience of trying to discuss Burke with my colleagues. Anyone who has doubts about my remark about trivialization in the profession should examine a program for the annual meeting of the Modern Language Association.

7. Burke's best-known definition is that man is the symbol-using animal. His most recent definition is that humans are bodies that learn language.

8. Burke began developing a systematic theory of the text as early as *A Philosophy of Literary Form* (1941) in the title essay and in "The Rhetoric of Hilter's Battle." He continued this work in *A Grammar of Motives* in his speculations on substance and constitutions. The famous essay on Keats's "Ode on a Grecian Urn" is clearly written from a carefully worked out theory of the text, as are the analyses of Ibsen plays. The most fully worked out examples of Burke's theory of the text are to be found in such essays as *"Othello:* An Essay to Illustrate a Method" and "Fact, Inference, and Proof in the Analysis of Symbolic Action"—both of which were written for inclusion in "A Symbolic of Motives." These essays are most readily available in *Perspectives by Incongruity* and *Terms for Order,* a double volume edited by Stanley Edgar Hyman, (Bloomington: Indiana University Press, 1964). Another excellent example is Burke's long analysis of Saint Augustine's *Confessions* in *The Rhetoric of Religion* (Boston: Beacon Press, 1961), pp. 43–171. All of the single-text analyses in *Language as Symbolic Action* are also excellent examples.

9. *Grammar of Motives* (New York: Prentice-Hall, 1945), p. 442.

10. *A Rhetoric of Motives* (New York: Prentice-Hall, 1950), p. 265.

11. The reference is to Walt Whitman's great poem "A Passage to India."

12. All of Burke's books from *Towards a Better Life* on are arranged in this three-part form in their original editions. Some, like *The Philosophy of Literary From* and a *Grammar of Motives,* have an appendix. *The Rhetoric of Religion* has an epilogue. Later editions of the books, especially *Permanence and Change* and *Attitudes toward History* have an afterword or an appendix or both. However, this three-part form is certainly Burke's recurrent and char-

acteristic way of arranging his books, whether they were written all of a piece, as *A Rhetoric of Motives* was, or assembled from pieces written separately, like *Language as Symbolic Action*. Perhaps Burke, always a great lover of symmetry, simply likes the beginning-middle-end arrangement. Few critics have ever tried to analyze the structure of any Burke book as a symbolic action, though this would clearly be a useful and probably revealing critical exercise.

13. *In the American Grain* (1925) is the title of William Carlos Williams' book about what it means to be an American writer. Williams—a longtime friend and neighbor of Burke's—wrote this book in an attempt to explain what it meant to define oneself as a writer in relation to native American traditions rather than, as T. S. Eliot did, in relation to European traditions. Emerson and Whitman made similar attempts in their own time, most notably in "Nature," "The American Scholar," the preface to the 1855 edition of *Leaves of Grass*, and "Democratic Vistas." One of the arguments of this essay is that Burke is directly in this American tradition. An elaboration of this argument would require a separate book. However, there are many useful and illuminating ways in which one can see Burke in relation to Emerson, Whitman, Henry Adams, and William Carlos Williams—to name a few of the Americans Burke has written about.

14. Malcolm Cowley (in 1950) was the first to recognize and write about the extent to which Burke was building a dramatistic system in his *Motives* books. Hugh Duncan is perhaps the best example of a disciple who subscribed to this system and tried—in a number of books—to apply it systematically in his own discipline, sociology. Others have tried to use Burke's dramatistic system with various degrees of thoroughness in different disciplines. However, the main response to Burke has tended to be piecemeal: people have taken from Burke what proved to be useful to them in their own disciplines and work. For an account of how Burke has been responded to and used by others through 1966 see my *Critical Response to Kenneth Burke, 1924–1966*. A bibliographic account of responses to Burke after 1966 can be found in this volume. Other accounts can be found in *Ranam*, no. 12 (1979); in *Representing Kenneth Burke* Hayden White and Margaret Brose, eds., (Baltimore: Johns Hopkins University Press, 1982); and in Frank Lentricchia, *Criticism and Social Change* (Chicago: University of Chicago Press, 1983).

15. Burke's Helhaven satire and his comments on it can be found in "Towards Helhaven: Three Stages of a Vision," *Sewanee Review*, 79 (1971), 11–25, and "Why Satire, with a Plan for Writing One," *Michigan Quarterly Review*, 13 (Winter 1974), 307–37. The third edition of *Attitudes toward History* is also a classic example of the self-reflexive Burke with many footnotes from the original edition and its "Afterward to Second Edition," "Appendix: The Seven Offices," and "Afterword: *Attitudes toward History*: In Retrospective Prospect."

16. Kenneth Burke, *Collected Poems, 1915–1967* (Berkeley: University of California Press, 1968), p. 225.

12 POEM

KENNETH BURKE

BEING BODIES THAT LEARN LANGUAGE
THEREBY BECOMING WORDLINGS
HUMANS ARE THE
SYMBOL-MAKING, SYMBOL-USING, SYMBOL-MISUSING ANIMAL
INVENTOR OF THE NEGATIVE
SEPARATED FROM OUR NATURAL CONDITION
BY INSTRUMENTS OF OUR OWN MAKING
GOADED BY THE SPIRIT OF HIERARCHY
ACQUIRING FOREKNOWLEDGE OF DEATH
AND ROTTEN WITH PERFECTION

FROM WITHIN OR
FROM OUT OF
THE VAST EXPANSES OF THE
INFINITE WORDLESS UNIVERSE
WE WORDY HUMAN BODIES HAVE CARVED
MANY OVERLAPPING UNIVERSES OF DISCOURSE
WHICH ADD UP TO A
PLURIVERSE OF DISCOURSES
LOCAL DIALECTS OF DIALECTIC

APPENDIX

BIBLIOGRAPHIES

CONTRIBUTORS

INDEXES

APPENDIX

Revolutionary Symbolism in America. Speech by Kenneth Burke to American Writers' Congress, April 26, 1935

When considering how people have coöperated, in either conservative or revolutionary movements of the past, we find that there is always some unifying principle about which their attachments as a group are polarized. I do not refer to such mere insignia as tricolor, hammer and sickle, swastika, crucifix, or totem pole—but to the subtle complex of emotions and attitudes for which such insignia are little more than the merest labels.

From a strictly materialistic point of view, such symbols are pure nonsense. Food, tools, shelter, productive technique—these things are the "realest" part of our vocabulary; they correspond to objects that can be seen and felt, and to operations that can be clearly and obviously performed. But the communal relationships by which a group is bound do not possess such primary reality. However vital they are in promoting historic processes, they are "myths," quite as the gods of Homer were myths. To search for them critically is to dissolve them, while a few rudimentary "realities" take their place. If you find a man attached to some cause, and keep pressing him with questions, he will not be able to point out the nature of his attachment in the way he might if you asked him to point to his house. Yet for all the illusive character of his attachment, we know that it may be a genuine social motive behind his actions.

"Myths" may be wrong, or they may be used to bad ends—but they cannot be dispensed with. In the last analysis, they are our basic psychological tools for working together. A hammer is a carpenter's tool; a wrench is a mechanic's tool; and a "myth" is the social tool for welding the sense of interrelationship by which the carpenter and the mechanic, though differently occupied, can work together for common social ends. In this sense a myth that works well is as real as food, tools, and shelter are. As compared with the reality of material objects, however, we might say that the myth deals with a *secondary* order of reality. Totem, race, godhead, nationality, class, lodge, guild—all such are the "myths" that have made various ranges and kinds of

Appendix

social coöperation possible. They are not "illusions," since they perform a very real and necessary social function in the organizing of the mind. But they may look illusory when they survive as fossils from the situations for which they were adapted into changed situations for which they are not adapted.

Lasswell holds that a revolutionary period is one in which the people drop their allegiance to one myth, or symbol, and shift to another in its place. However, when a symbol is in the process of losing its vitality as a device for polarizing social coöperation, there are apt to be many rival symbols competing to take its place. A symbol probably loses its vitality when the kinds of coöperation it promotes—and with which its destiny is united—have ceased to be serviceable. The symbol of bourgeois nationalism is in such a state of decay to-day, for instance—hence the attempt of Communists to put the symbol of class in its place. Similarly the Technocrats, attempting to profit by the prestige which the technological expert enjoys in the contemporary framework of values, would polarize allegiance around the symbol of the engineer. A project like the Douglas Social Credit plan, whatever its economic feasibility may or may not be, has no such symbol—hence, movements of this sort become objects of popular allegiance only when some distinct personality arises to champion them, and to polarize group allegiance about himself as an *individual*. In this category fall the procedures of men like Huey Long and Father Coughlin—and I need not examine, before a pro-Communist audience, the tendency of such individual polarizations to trick the allegiance of the people by deflecting their attention from the principal faults of their system. It is wholesome to give allegiance, even to a crook—but the mere fact that the tendency is wholesome is no guaranty that the people will not suffer for their wholesomeness.

The Communists generally focus their scheme of allegiance about the symbol of the worker, which they would put in the place of a misused nationalism as the polarizing device about which our present attempts at historic coöperation should cluster. Accordingly, my paper will discuss this symbol, and to what extent it fulfills the conditions of attachment. I should also emphasize the fact that I shall consider this matter *purely from the standpoint of propaganda*. It may be that the needs of the propagandist are not wholly identical with the needs of the organizer. Insofar as a writer really is a propagandist, not merely writing work that will be applauded by his allies, convincing the already convinced, but actually moving forward like a pioneer into outlying areas of the public and bringing them the first favorable impressions of his doctrine, the nature of his trade may give rise to special symbolic requirements. Accordingly, it is the *propaganda* aspect of the symbol that I shall center upon—considering the symbol particularly as a device for spreading the areas of allegiance.

In the first place, I assume that a symbol must embody an *ideal*. The symbol appeals to us as an incentive because it suggests traits which we should like to share. Yet there are few people who really want to work, let us say, as a human cog in an automobile factory, or as gatherers of vegetables on a big truck farm. Such rigorous ways of life enlist our *sympathies*, but not our *ambitions*. Our ideal is as far as possible to *eliminate* such kinds of work, or to reduce its strenuousness to a minimum. Some people, living overly sedentary lives, may like to read of harsh physical activity (as they once enjoyed Wild West fiction)—but Hollywood knows only too well that the people engaged in such kinds of effort are vitalized mainly by some vague hope that they may some day escape it. "Adult education" in capitalist America to-day is centered in the efforts of our economic mercenaries (our advertising men and sales organizations) to create a maximum desire for commodities consumed under expensive conditions—and Hollywood appeals to the worker mainly by picturing the qualities of life in which this commercially stimulated desire is gratified. The question arises: Is the symbol of the worker accurately attuned to us, as so conditioned by the reactionary forces in control of our main educational channels?

I tentatively suggest that it is not. By this I do not mean that a proletarian emphasis should be dropped from revolutionary books. The rigors of the worker must certainly continue to form a major part of revolutionary symbolism, if only for the reason that here the worst features of capitalist exploitation are concentrated. But the basic symbol, it seems to me, should be focused somewhat differently. Fortunately, I am not forced to advocate any great change—though I do think that the shift I propose, while minor in itself, leads in the end to quite different emphases in our modes of propaganda. The symbol I should plead for, as more basic, more of an ideal incentive, than that of the worker, is that of "the people." In suggesting that "the people," rather than "the worker," rate highest in our hierarchy of symbols, I suppose I am suggesting fundamentally that one cannot extend the doctrine of revolutionary thought among the lower middle class without using middle-class values—just as the Church invariably converted pagans by making the local deities into saints. I should also point out that we are very close to this symbol of "the people" in our term "the masses," which is embodied in the title of the leading radical magazine. But I think that the term "the people" is closer to our

folkways than is the corresponding term, "the masses," both in spontaneous popular usage and as stimulated by our political demagogues. I should add that, in an interview published recently in the
New York *World-Telegram,* Clarence Hathaway frequently used a com-
pound of the two in the form: "the masses of the people."

The symbol of "the people," as distinct from the proletarian symbol,
also has the tactical advantage of pointing more definitely in the direction of unity (which in itself is a sound psychological tendency, for all
that it is now misused by nationalists to mask the conditions of disunity). It contains the *ideal,* the ultimate *classless* feature which the revolution would bring about—and for this reason seems richer as a symbol
of allegiance. It can borrow the advantages of nationalistic condition-
ing, and at the same time be used to combat the forces that hide their
class prerogatives behind a communal ideology.

The acceptance of "the people" as the basic symbol also has the
great virtue that it makes for less likelihood of schematization on the
part of our writers. So far at least, the *proletarian* novel has been over-
simplified, leading to a negative symbol (that enlists our sympathies)
rather than to a positive symbol (that incorporates our ideals). The
symbol of "the people" should make for greater breadth in a writer's
allegiance. By informing his work mainly from the standpoint of this
positive symbol, he would come to see, I believe, that a poet does not
sufficiently glorify his political cause by pictures of suffering and re-
volt. Rather, a poet makes his soundest contribution in this wise: He
shows himself alive to all the aspects of contemporary effort and
thought (in contrast with a certain anti-intellectualist, semi-
obscurantist trend among some of the strictly *proletarian* school, who
tend to imply that there is some disgrace attached to things of the
mind). I can understand how such resistance arises, since the many
channels of thought are in control of reactionaries—but to turn against
thought for such a reason would be like advocating illiteracy because
people that read are exposed to the full force of our newspapers and
magazines. The complete propagandist, it seems to me, would take an
interest in as many imaginative, æsthetic, and speculative fields as he
can handle—and into this breadth of his concerns he would inter-
weave a general attitude of sympathy for the oppressed and antipathy
towards our oppressive institutions. In this way he would ally his attitudes with everything that is broadest and fullest in the world to-day.
And he would argue for his political sympathies, not literally and directly, but by the intellectual company he keeps.

Much explicit propaganda must be done, but that is mainly the
work of the pamphleteer and political organizer. In the purely imagi-

native field, the writer's best contribution to the revolutionary cause is *implicit*. If he shows a keen interest in every manifestation of our cultural development, and at the same time gives a clear indication as to where his sympathies lie, this seems to me the most effective long-pull contribution to propaganda he can make. For he thus indirectly links his cause with the kinds of intellectual and emotional engrossment that are generally admired. He speaks in behalf of his cause, not in the ways of a lawyer's brief, but by the sort of things he associates with it. In a rudimentary way, this is what our advertisers do when they recommend a particular brand of cigarette by picturing it as being smoked under desirable conditions; it is the way in which the best artists of the religious era recommended or glorified their Faith; and I imagine it would be the best way of proceeding to-day. Reduced to a precept, the formula would run: Let one encompass as many desirable features of our cultural heritage as possible—and let him make sure that his political alignment figures prominently among them.... And I am suggesting that an approach based upon the positive symbol of "the people," rather than upon the negative symbol of "the worker," makes more naturally for this kind of identification whereby one's political alignment is fused with broader cultural elements.

I might also note that the symbol of "the people" (which, I repeat, is already tacitly approved in the analogous term, "the masses") suggests a partial fallacy in too strict adherence to the doctrine of "antithetical moralities" ("proletarian" as antithetical to "bourgeois"). We convince a man by reason of the values which we and he hold *in common*. Propaganda (the extension of one's recruiting into ever widening areas) is possible only insofar as the propagandizer and the propagandized have *kindred* values, share the *same* base of reference. If you and I agree on a criterion of justice, I may turn you against a certain institution, such as capitalism, by showing that it makes for injustice. But no matter how well put together my arguments might be, they would be pointless in this case unless you were relatively in agreement with me as to the desirability of justice. Particularly as regards the specific problems of propaganda, the emphasis upon the *antithetical* tends to incapacitate a writer for his task as a *spreader* of doctrine by leading him too soon into antagonistic modes of thought and expression. It gives him too much authority to *condemn*—and however human this desire to grow wrathful may be, and however justified it is by the conditions all about us, the fact remains that his specific job as a propagandist requires him primarily to wheedle or cajole, to practice the arts of ingratiation. As a propagandizer, it is not his work to convince the convinced, but to plead with the unconvinced, which requires him to use *their* vocabulary, *their* values, *their* symbols, insofar as this is possible.

For we must remember that among the contradictions of capitalism we must also include the contradictions of anti-capitalist propaganda. Marxism is war to the ends of peace, heresy to the ends of unity, organization to the ends of freedom, glorification of toil to the ends of greater leisure, revolution in the interests of conservation, etc. Such a confusion cannot be settled once and for all. It is our particular "burden" at this particular stage of history. In the last analysis, art strains towards *universalization*. It tends to overleap imaginatively the class divisions of the moment and go after modes of thought that would apply to a society freed of class divisions. It seeks to consider the problems of *man*, not of *classes of men*. We are agreed that the current situation militates against this tendency, which is all the more reason for artists to enlist in the work of changing it. For a totally universalized art, if established in America to-day, would simply be the spiritual denial of an underlying economic disunity (the æsthetic of fascism). The strictly proletarian symbol has the useful advantage of emphasizing the temporary antagonism—but it has the disadvantage of not sufficiently embodying within its connotations the *ideal* incentive, the eventual state of unification that is expected to flow from it.

For this contradiction there is no wholly satisfactory solution. The closest to a satisfactory solution I can think of is simply to suggest that the imaginative artist show, in a general way, a wholesome alignment of attitudes, both political and nonpolitical. Some may and should deal specifically with strikes, lock-outs, unemployment, unsavory working conditions, organized resistance to the police, etc.—but an attempt to focus all their imaginative range within this orbit must produce an over-simplified and impoverished art, which would defeat its own purposes, failing even as propaganda, since it did not invigorate audiences by incorporating sufficient aspects of cultural glorification in its material.

I believe that the symbol of "the people" makes more naturally for such *propaganda by inclusion* than does the strictly proletarian symbol (which makes naturally for a *propaganda by exclusion*, a tendency to eliminate from one's work all that does not deal specifically with the realities of the workers' oppression—and which, by my thesis, cannot for this reason engage even the full allegiance of the workers themselves). And since the symbol of "the people" contains connotations both of oppression and of unity, it seems better than the exclusively proletarian one as a psychological bridge for linking the two conflicting aspects of a transitional, revolutionary era, which is Janus-faced, looking both forwards and back. I recognize that my suggestion bears the telltale stamp of my class, the petty bourgeoisie. And I should not dare to make it, except for a belief that it is vitally important to enlist the allegiance of this class. But I should point out, in closing, that there are really two features in my present paper, and although I think that they *tend* to be interconnected, they may not *necessarily* be. I make this point because I hope that, even if my hearers may resist my first suggestion (and I see many just grounds for their doing so), they may still accept the second. The first was that we take "the people" rather than "the worker" as our basic symbol of exhortation and allegiance. The second was that the imaginative writer seek to propagandize his cause by surrounding it with as full a cultural texture as he can manage, thus thinking of propaganda not as an over-simplified, literal, explicit writing of lawyer's briefs, but as a process of broadly and generally associating his political alignment with cultural awareness in the large. I consider the first suggestion important primarily because the restricted proletarian symbol *tends* to militate against the full use of propaganda by inclusion. But I should not like to make your acceptance of the second absolutely dependent upon your acceptance of the first. Some writers may be able to dissociate them, and to surround the strictly proletarian symbol with sufficient richness of cultural ideals to make it appealing even as a symbol of allegiance for people who do not think of themselves primarily within the proletarian framework. But I still insist that their function as propagandists will not be complete unless they do thus propagandize by inclusion, not confining themselves to a few schematic situations, but engaging the entire range of our interests, even such interests as we might have at a time of industry and peace.

Discussion of Burke's Speech at the Congress, April 27, 1935

The second session of the American Writers' Congress opened on the morning of April 27 in the auditorium of the New School for Social Research. The chairman was John Howard Lawson. He announced that because of the number of papers, and the need to devote most of the last session to the organization of the League of American Writers, discussion of the individual papers would have to be grouped at the end of each session instead of occurring at the end of each paper. In the main this worked out well—speakers did not duplicate each other. Before presenting the first speaker, who was Joseph Freeman, Mr. Lawson read aloud the names of those writers who had been suggested, by those who had worked for months to prepare for the Congress, as the actual presiding committee of the Congress. The nominees, all of whom were accepted by the delegates, were: Michael Blankfort, Harry Carlisle, Jack Conroy, Malcolm Cowley, Joseph Freeman, Michael Gold, Eugene Gordon, Henry Hart, Granville Hicks, Orrick Johns, John Howard Lawson, Meridel Le Sueur, Isidor Schneider, Edwin Seaver, Bernhard J. Stern and Alexander Trachtenberg. Paul Romaine was appointed recording secretary.

Two papers at the session provoked most of the discussion. These were Edwin Seaver's "The Proletarian Novel," and Kenneth Burke's "Revolutionary Symbolism in America."

Martin Russak dissented from Seaver's contention that the proletarian novel, by definition, could be one that treated any subject matter provided it did so from the standpoint and in the interest of the proletariat. "I think the proletarian novel has got to be," he said, "and is already becoming, a novel that deals with the working class. I don't think our novels should be concerned with the emotions and reactions and values of the upper or middle classes or the lumpen proletariat. I don't think the life experiences of hoboes and tramps, as depicted in some of our writing recently, is legitimate subject matter.

"I think that, if we completely understood the nature of class division, we would not say that all people are the same. In the working class we have a distinct kind of human being, a new type of human being, with an emotional life and psychology that is different, and distinct, and with which we should deal."

Michael Gold, in discussing Jack Conroy's paper, took issue with

Mr. Russak, but also warned against the danger of "our literary movement becoming a petty bourgeois movement." He said:

"I think some of the discussion this morning was interesting because it again contrasted two points of view which have been battling in our world of proletarian literature as long as I can remember.

"We know that our enemies have taken up the cry that proletarian literature is a literature of men with hairy chests, of slums and so forth, and that no bourgeois writer can approach these things. On the other hand, we have had all the proletarians insisting that the bourgeois writers and their themes have no place in the revolutionary movement. I think we got a little conception of that from Martin Russak. If anything has been cleared up in the last few years, it has been this point: that the revolution is a revolution led by the working class, and the lower middle classes are its allies. There is therefore room in the revolution for literature from all these groups. The viewpoint, as Edwin Seaver said, is what is important. The man with the revolutionary mind and approach can write a revolutionary book.

"So I think we must stand equally against the idea that proletarian literature has a place only for novels about the working class, the idea that was more or less implied this morning, as well as against the idea that novels about the workers are not important.

"Some one said that when we are dealing with a class myth we can juggle this class myth around. The very acceptance of this conception, put forth by the bourgeois critic I. A. Richards, that the working class myth is on a par with other myths, with fascist myths, is a surrender at a very vital point. We cannot accept any such classification, as many of the liberals do, that communism and fascism are equal schemes for solving the problems of society, for socializing society. We cannot accept the idea that the class struggle is a myth, or that the working class is a myth.

"I think the tone of many of our papers this morning showed that our literary movement is in danger of becoming a petty bourgeois movement. I think we must guard against that. It cannot become that. It must not become that. It is our main task to see that a strong working class is developed in the United States to lead the revolutionary vanguard. We may not lead it. So I think one of the basic tasks of every writer is to stimulate and encourage and help the growth of proletarian literature which is written by workers.

"I think all of us must learn to become teachers of the working class. We must assemble around ourselves a group of talented workers who wish to write, just as Gorky did it twenty-five years ago in Russia. We must realize that only this literature can answer these intellectual abstractions into which petty bourgeois people fall.

"A great body of proletarian literature will show the concrete facts. It will show our face. It will be the greatest argument we can present to those people who juggle with the theories of communism and fascism. We must build up a picture of what the working class in this country looks like. We must use this as a final and clinching argument—this picture of real life, of real working class struggle. We must use this as the final answer we can give to the intellectual abstractions of the bourgeoisie."

The discussion of Kenneth Burke's paper centered chiefly around the reasons for resisting his suggested substitution of the symbol "people" for "worker."

It began with Allen Porter's observations that one of the propaganda devices employed by the exploiting class during periods of struggle was making the demands of the workers appear as antipathetic to the "good of the *people*."

"Distinguishing between the workers and the people," he said, "is deliberately undertaken to confuse, as, for example, when Father Coughlin and General Johnson last summer attacked the general strike in San Francisco on the grounds that the workers were 'holding up the people.' By using the symbol 'all of the people' the inference was made that the common interest was opposed to the interests of the workers. The same symbol was used during the general strike of 1926 in Great Britain in precisely the same way. The *workers* were attacking the *people*. The attempt to substitute 'people' for 'worker' is very dangerous from our point of view. Historically, it has been the ruse of the exploiting class to confuse the issue. Moreover, the word 'people' is historically associated with demagoguery of the most vicious sort."

Friedrich Wolf supported this view, saying:

"A great danger reposes in this formulation of 'the people.' Hitler and Rosenberg used it. They said, let us not talk any more about the workers, let us talk about the people. In 1918 it was precisely this very same thing that the German reformist leaders utilized. Scheidemen and Ebert said we must have a policy that will cover the worker and the small merchant and the middle bourgeoisie. Hitlerism is a continuation of this policy. Hitler knew enough to use this ideological device as a supplement to his blackjacks and machine guns. Utilization of the myth of '*das Volk*,' the people, is an essential part of the reformist approach. In my own country it has directly resulted in the fascists taking power. The symbol 'worker' must be reserved to indicate the preponderant mass of the population—the actual workers and farmers. Substitution of the symbol 'people' confuses the interests of this fundamental and all-important class and renders a picture of society that is not merely un-Marxian but one which history has proven to be necessary for the continuation of the power of the exploiting class."

Joseph Freeman, in agreeing with the attacks upon Burke's suggestion, declared that it was necessary to show why the proletariat "is the sole revolutionary class." "If we consider the matter from the viewpoint of reality first and then from the literary viewpoint it is possible we may have no disagreement with Burke," he said and continued:

"The symbol of the *people* came with the bourgeois revolution. The bourgeoisie demanded the abolition of class privileges. Therefore it had the following of all the people. Then it turned out that the people were divided into classes. The word people then became a reactionary slogan—not because of any philosophy of myths, but because it concealed the reality, the actual living antagonism between the social classes. The type of myth represented by the word *people* can go so far that reality can be concealed even in the name of the proletarian revolution, even in the name of Lenin. Consider carefully the demagogy of the fascist government of Mexico. When I was in Mexico, I found state governors—one of whom became president of the republic—who used to hand out Lenin's portrait to peasant delegations. The official organ of the ruling reactionary party published special pro-Soviet supplements on November 7. It also published in full the call for our own Writers' Congress. So revolutionary are the Mexican workers and peasants, that nobody in Mexico can play politics without saying 'three cheers for the red flag' and 'three cheers for the *proletarian* revolution.' Even the Catholic church and its political exponents do this.

"If the *proletariat* can become a dangerous political myth in the hands of the reaction, how much more dangerous is the vague symbol of the *people*. We must not encourage such myths. We are not interested in the myth. We are interested in revealing the reality. We set up the 'symbol' of the worker because of the role which the worker plays in reality. When Hitler first came into power, most of the American bourgeois correspondents in Berlin were against him. Why were Burchell of the *Times* and the other American reporters so enthusiastic about Dimitroff and the other Communist workers on trial? Because the workers are in the most effective position to fight the reaction. Even the most proletarian of writers and intellectuals cannot call a general strike. They cannot switch off the electric lights, halt the street-cars, stop the factories, tie up the ships; they can't go out into the streets and take rifles and fight. We heard Friedrich Wolf tell us last night why the German writers and intellectuals came over to the working class. He told us how the poet Erich Muhsam died in a Nazi prison singing the *International*. Why this change? Under the bloody repression of fascism, the intellectuals recognized this tremendously significant fact, that the workers alone are socially, industrially, politically in a position to shut off industry under capitalism, to take it over under socialism. The intellectuals learned that the workers alone can give militant and effective leadership to the fight against reaction.

"This is due to the social position of the proletariat. That is why it is the only revolutionary class in modern society. If some of us call for the 'positive' symbol of the people to replace the 'negative' symbol of the worker, it is because we feel that the proletariat is a concept too narrow to include the intellectuals. But we do not need to be afraid. There is no real conflict involved here. We want to be included in the progressive class—and we are included. The proletariat alone can create a just society for the whole of the people. The proletarian is not merely some one who works. An English journalist told me the other day the Prince of Wales is getting a nervous breakdown. He works too hard. As a matter of fact, the Prince of Wales does work hard—and we know what he is working for. But this does not make him a proletarian. The proletarian is the man who has nothing to sell but his labor power. He not only works but depends upon his labor solely for his existence. That is why he is the most exploited and oppressed man in capitalist society; that is why he is the only one in a position to break with that society completely. The intellectual cannot lead the fight for the new world. He has his own vested interests in the old. He finds it hard to break with the old culture. He goes to school for sixteen years, takes his Ph.D., absorbs the old ideas, functions with them—and now he feels that the proletariat wants to expropriate him of the old culture. That is terrible. He feels that the term *people* will include not only him but his old ideas. But he need not fear. The proletariat takes over all that is best in the old culture.

"What must be kept in mind above all is the leading role which the worker plays in the transformation of society. The worker has nothing to lose but his chains. He alone is forced by his position to be revolutionary, and he alone can liberate the people. If we do not get lost in 'myths,' if we stick to the reality, it is only in the working class that the other exploited classes of society—including the intellectuals—can find leadership."

Kenneth Burke was then asked to reply to these criticisms and in the course of doing so, said:

"I was not disappointed in the response I expected when bringing up this subject. But I wish that some one had discussed the issue from my point of attack, the problem of propaganda. I think we are all agreed that we are trying to defend a position in favor of the workers, that we are trying to enlist in the cause of the workers. There is no issue about that. The important thing is: how to make ourselves effective in this particular social structure? I am trying to point out that there is a first stage where the writer's primary job is to disarm people. First you knock at the door—and not until later will you become wholly precise.

"As for my use of the word myth, I was speaking technically before a group of literary experts, hence I felt justified in using the word in a special sense. A poet's myths, I tried to make clear, are *real*, in the sense that they perform a necessary function. They so pattern the mind as to give it a grip upon reality. For the myth embodies a sense of relationships. But relationships cannot be pointed to, in the simple objective way in which you could point to a stone or a house. It is such a sense of *relationships* (I have sometimes called them 'secondary reality') that I had in mind when using the word myth.

"As for the charge that I made Communism appear like a religion: It may be a weakness on my part, but I have never taken this matter very seriously. As the Latin *religio* signifies a *binding together*, I take religion and Communism to be alike insofar as both are systems for binding people together—and the main difference at the present time resides for me in the fact that the Communistic vocabulary does the binding job much more accurately than the religious vocabulary. Let us compromise by saying that Communism is an ethic, a morality. But whenever you talk about an ethic, you must talk about much the same sort of things as you would if your were talking purely and simply about religion.

"As for the use of the term *people*: one speaker in rebutting me actually corroborated me when he said that Lenin used the term *people* up to 1917. I think that we are exactly in the same position as Russia prior to 1917.

"I probably should not have used the words *positive* and *negative* to distinguish the two types of symbol. I did not mean that there is anything negative about the worker symbol in itself, but only insofar as it *tends to* overly restrict a writer's range of interests and emphases. In practice it *tends to* focus a writer's attention upon traits that enlist our *sympathies*—whereas by a *positive* symbol I meant one that enlists not only our *sympathies* but also our *ambitions*.

"Some speakers have made the point that there is no contradiction between the *worker* and the *people*. I emphatically agree. But it was pointed out that in California the demagogues were able to give the appearance of a contradiction, to make it seem as though the workers were aligned against the people. And it is precisely the demagogic trick which the propagandist must combat. I think your symbolism has to be so molded that this apparent contradiction between workers and people cannot be set up. If you emphasize the worker symbol exclusively you give the reactionaries the best opportunity to make it seem that the *workers* and the *people* are opposed. But if you amalgamate the worker symbol with the people symbol, the very thing that was done in California cannot be done.

"I think that finishes up all the points that were made. The fundamental thing that I want to emphasize again is my belief that there is a different problem confronting the propagandist from that which confronts the organizer. The propagandist's main job is to disarm. In the course of disarming, he opens himself to certain dangers. He cannot draw a distinct line because if he did, he would not be able to advance into outlying areas. The organizer must cancel off these other dangers. After getting these people into your party, you can give them a more accurate sense of what you are aiming at. But in the first stage, the propagandist must use certain terms which have a certain ambiguity, and which for that very reason give him entrance into other areas."

Analysis of Burke's Speech by Frank Lentricchia

The excerpt that follows is from *Criticism and Social Change*, pp. 21–38, and is pretty close to the heart of the book. I did not write the book in order to answer Fredric Jameson's critique of Burke, but I suppose that's one way of reading what I've done. I'm saying that Burke is a powerful thinker on the left. To call an American intellectual with roots in Emerson and the pragmatist tradition a powerful thinker on the left is certainly a problem, maybe even a contradiction. I tried to come to terms with the issue in the book as a whole by arguing that though there's a lot of Marx in Burke, Burke is not a Marxist—like the most interesting thinkers in America, he's a liberal on the wild side who does not fear the regions of antinomianism. To call Burke a "Western Marxist," as I have, misleads and angers only the Marxophobics among us (their name is legion). It did not mislead Perry Anderson, whose magisterial *Considerations on Western Marxism* I was alluding to when I made the characterization. My point was that Burke had independently thought through many of the ideas of the Frankfurt School. I think my readers will understand me best if they keep firmly in mind two reviews of *Criticism and Social Change*: one, by a declared Marxist, who thinks the book a betrayal of the Marxist perspective he thought he discerned in *After the New Criticism*; another, by an American idolater of Jacques Derrida, who considers the book a manifesto (his word) for the academic Marxist.

I want to begin my pursuit of the issue of criticism as social force with a look at an event in the life of Kenneth Burke, the publication of which in his books and collections he has to this point deferred; an event which, according to his testimony, produced hallucinations of "excrement... dripping from my tongue," of his name being shouted as a "kind of charge" against him, a "dirty word"—"Burke!"[1] I am referring to a brief paper Burke delivered to the first American Writers' Congress, held at Madison Square Garden in late April of 1935, organized and attended by the most engaged literary figures in the United States, and featuring a number of distinguished European guest speakers. The purpose of this first congress was to extend the reach of the John Reed Clubs by providing the basis for a much broader organization of American writers. The capitalist system was crumbling rapidly—that seemed undeniable. If writers could effectively band together, then maybe they could accelerate what had to happen anyway—the destruction of capitalism and the creation of a workers' government. In his "Call for an American Writers' Congress" in the *New Masses* of January 22, 1935, Granville Hicks characterized the radical writer as one who did not "need to be convinced of the decay of capitalism, of the inevitability of revolution." Hicks's radical was a writer committed in every sense. Enter, into this scene of left-wing confidence, Kenneth Burke.

Burke remembers leaving the convention and overhearing one woman saying to another: "yet he looked so *honest.'*[2] He remembers Joseph Freeman, one of the moving forces of the congress, standing up and saying, "We have a traitor among us!"[3] There is no record of Freeman's remark in the edited transcript of the discussion that was appended to the published proceedings of the congress; a remark does survive linking Burke's thought to Hitler's. However hysterical and inaccurate, however fictive or real these statements—those in print, those in Burke's memory—these reactions to Burke form one of the incontrovertible signs of the social effect of his critical writing and a hint that when Burke speaks the issues of the text involve a great deal more than pleasure.

The discourse that produced these startling effects on the official left of the 1930s was cunningly entitled "Revolutionary Symbolism in America." In those years of Marxist history (Gramsci was Mussolini's dying prisoner in 1935), Burke's speech had the discomforting feel of ideological deviance. Revolutionary *symbolism*? That is to confuse mere superstructural effect with the directive forces at the base, the economic motor principle of revolution. In *America*? That is to put on the blinders of nationalism which will prevent us from seeing the real world historical dimension of revolution. Was Burke forgetting one of the key Hegelian points of Marx's theory of history: that the process moves inexorably from the local to the global? To stand with the intellectual left in the United States in the early 1930s was to stand in a place where Burke's kind of Marxism could be received only as heresy—as the very discourse of excrement.

Burke opens his essay by reminding his radical audience that principles of collectivity, whatever their genetic relation to a society's mode of production, do not themselves possess "primary reality" from a "strictly materialistic point of view" (see above, p. 267). In effect what he does in the essay as a whole is to rewrite and elaborate Marx's immensely suggestive first thesis on Feuerbach, which was itself a dialectical rewriting of materialism as it had been hitherto understood: the thing, reality, sensuousness, must not be conceived, Marx argued, as an object exterior (and opposed) to practice, to intellection, to sub-jectivity, but as *"sensuous human activity, practice,''* with "practice" now understood as an integrated and indivisible whole of physical, intel-lectual, and emotional coordinates.[4] Marx's first thesis on Feuerbach may stand as a proleptic warning to all economist and mechanistic re-ductions of historical materialism to the mere materialism that would be performed in his name. The central paralyzing conflict in the his-tory of Marxism may be located in its repetitious, even compulsive staging of that agon. With hindsight, we can see Burke's participation at the first American Writers' Congress in such an intellectual theater, with Burke enacting the father's role of historical materialist and his hostile respondents playing the parts of purists, sons anxious to purge all idealistic and therefore, of course, all fascist misappropriations of the master's word. By "strictly materialistic point of view" Burke re-fers not, I believe, to the doctrine of historical materialism but to the historically conventional materialism of determinist character that Marx regarded as less intelligent than all-out idealism.

Although I think Burke one of the really superior readers of Marx and would place him among the group Perry Anderson called the "Western Marxists" (Anderson himself did not), it is not my purpose to suggest that Burke, not his respondents, best understood Marx. That sort of reading of the American Writers' Congress would only re-peat and enforce another of the hopelessly infertile and claustropho-bic dialogues within Marxism: "What did Marx really say, and who among us is the most faithful to his sacred books?" It appears to me that Burke's trouble with thirties Marxists in the United States stems from his deviant understanding of Marx—and by "deviant" I mean that Burke was doing something like New Left analysis within the anti-intellectualist, Second International intellectual context of the old left. One of his most significant contributions to Marxist theory (be-yond his lonely American performance of "Western Marxism") is his pressing of the difficult, sliding notion of ideology, bequeathed to us by the *The German Ideology*, out of the areas of intellectual trickery and false consciousness and into the politically productive textual realms of practical consciousness—rhetoric, the literary, and the media of what he tellingly called "adult education in America." The political work of the hegemonic, as well as that of a would-be counter-hegemonic culture, Burke saw (as Marx did not) as most effectively carried through at the level of a culture's various verbal and nonverbal languages. In 1935 Burke was saying to America's radical left not only that a potentially revolutionary culture should keep in mind that revo-lution must be culturally as well as economically rooted, but, as well, and this was perhaps the most difficult of Burke's implications for his radical critics to swallow, that a revolutionary culture must situate itself firmly on the terrain of its capitalist antagonist, must not attempt a dramatic leap beyond capitalism in one explosive, rupturing moment of release, must work its way through capitalism's language of domination by working cunningly within it, using, appropriating, even speaking through its key mechanisms of repression. What Burke's proposal in 1935 to America's intellectual left amounts to is this: the substance, the very ontology of ideology—an issue that Marx and Engels engaged with little clarity, to put it charitably—in a broad but fundamental sense is revealed to us *textually* and therefore must be grasped (read) and attacked (reread, rewritten) in that dimension.

Burke concentrates therefore on the linguistic instruments which produce our sense of community, the "symbols" of "communal relationship by which a group is bound," the "myth" of the collective that is the "social tool for welding the sense of interrelationship." Collective coherence is no psychic reflex of the economy but the effect of an active, fusing work of cultural production that organizes social cooperation—it is a "tool" that "welds"—by disseminating those myths and symbols, stories and words, which constitute our sense of ourselves in America as part of a social whole presumably ministering justly and equitably to its cooperative, individual subjects (see above, p. 267). The primary lure of all myths of collectivity is that they ask people to yield to what Burke thinks a wholesome human tendency: the desire to give ourselves to something beyond our isolate individual existences. But, he quickly qualifies, and we can provide our own examples of the danger, "the mere fact that the tendency is wholesome is no guaranty that the people will not suffer for their wholesomeness" (see above, p. 268). As a radical American intellectual, with a keen awareness of the liberal American political discourse of justice, equality, and liberty, Burke says in so many words to the literary left gathered in convention that an alternative discourse of justice, a socialist discourse of equality and liberty, if it is successfully to supplant (uproot, plow under) the reigning hegemonic discourse of traditional America—if the socialist cause in America is to triumph, it will have to move inside and infiltrate the duplicitous but powerfully entrenched language of liberty to which we in the "land of the free" have already given allegiance. Burke's wager in 1935—and it is too soon to say that time has proved him wrong—was that the adhesive force of bourgeois nationalist symbols of allegiance was entering a state of decay, that other symbolic agencies were competing to take their place: that, indeed, this very situation of fluidity signified an unstable or revolutionary period in which people were in the process of shifting their allegiances from one myth to another. It was a situation of maximum opportunity for the literary intellectual: a struggle for cultural position was fully underway, and the literary intellectual, with his mastery of the tools of discourse, might have found himself in strategic leadership as a director of rhetorical war.

How then shall the writer speak? And to whom shall he direct his speaking? Those are the questions that preoccupy Burke as an intellectual; they are questions which, typically, he framed with his abiding concerns for history, rhetoric, power, tradition, and canon-formation. The "literary" for Burke is always embedded in those concerns. As a form of action in the world the literary is fully enmeshed in the social—it is not an imaginative space apart. This latter, however difficult a point to accept for those working from formalist traditions, should presumably have found a receptive audience at the first American Writers' Congress. Writing, not as haven for an isolated aesthetic pleasure, but as instrument for social change; the writer as "propagandist" (a word Burke understands in its full etymological history and which—unlike most professors of literature—he is not afraid to use or to apply to high-brow "literature") (see above, p. 268). What literary vulgarian, what socialist realist would not consent to those proposals? How could a convention of thirties radicals have received such a plea with hostility? Here is Burke's definition of the writer's task:

> Insofar as a writer really is a propagandist, not merely writing work that will be applauded by his allies, convincing the already convinced, but actually moving forward like a pioneer into outlying areas of the public and bringing them the first favorable impressions of his doctrine, the nature of his trade may give rise to special symbolic requirements. Accordingly, it is the *propaganda* aspect of the symbol that I shall center upon—considering the symbol particularly as a device for spreading the areas of allegiance. (See above, pp. 268-69)

Burke's challenge to the Marxist intellectual ("Insofar as a writer really is a propagandist") is to stop making things easy for himself by talking into the mirror of the committed and to enter into dialogue with the uncommitted, the skeptical, even the hostile. His implied, bruising point—it was not misunderstood in 1935—was that the proletarian novel was both a literary and a political indulgence: applauded by the already convinced, unread by the working class, quietly alienating to the unconvinced, the proletarian novel took no risk of real dialogue. As intellectuals, proletarian writers and other Marxists, insofar as they are going to have a chance of disseminating doctrine, will have to move inward into examination of the rhetorical grounds of the dissemination of faith and simultaneously outward into critical scrutiny of the rhetorical structure of the dominant hegemony that inhibits the creation of new allegiances.

We can understand the hostility of American literary radicals to Burke's speech if we contextualize their feelings within the dramatic opposition that literary Marxists and formalists historically have tended to enact: Burke was asking his radical auditors to resist thinking of social doctrine as separable from its medium of dissemination. He was telling them that right social action, for a literary intellectual, was preeminently a literary act, because it was grounded in, its effectivity proceeded from, the rhetorical textures, strategies, and structures of discourse. The left intellectual represented, say, by Edmund Wilson had trouble making an integral, internal connection between radical social vision and literary discourse. Cleanth Brooks, Wilson's thirties contrary, knew that and criticized Wilson on that score. But Brooks could never see anything specifically political, left or right, in his formalist conception of the literary. The distinction and—to the old left—the anomaly of Burke's mind was that it refused both sides of this controversy; Burke simply negated and at the same time preserved the Marxist/formalist controversy in a dialectical maneuver that insisted that the literary was always a form of social action, however rarely it might be recognized as such.

Burke moves from this general point about literary action to the central social commitment of Marxism, the working class itself. Taking a huge chance with this most sensitive of all Marxist sentiments, he asks the intellectual left to consider the worker at the symbolic—not the existential—level, as the embodiment of an ideal, and then to weigh the rhetorical value of that symbol in its American setting, and to measure the extent to which that symbol is persuasively forceful, whether it disseminates revolution or perhaps something else, perhaps reaction. In effect Burke asks Marxists—and the real value of his question is that it is not limited to that audience—whether or not it is their ambition to become workers: "There are few people who really want to work, let us say, as a human cog in an automobile factory, or as gatherers of vegetables on a big truck farm. Such rigorous ways of life enlist our _sympathies_, but not our _ambitions_. Our ideal is as far as possible to _eliminate_ such kinds of work, or to reduce its strenuousness to a minimum" (see above, p. 269). Burke's nice point needs a little filling out: you can't expect, he says, in effect, to his progressive friends, on the one hand, to keep painting these riveting portraits of workers under capitalism, of degradation and alienation—you can't expect people to accept these portraits as the truth, which is your rhetorical desire, after all, and then, on the other hand, at the same time, expect people to want to identify with workers, or become workers, or even enlist their energies of intellect and feeling on behalf of workers. Even though your intention may be otherwise, the fact is that your representations of workers are being received as representations of "the other." Such portraits, when they do enlist our sympathies, often, at the same time, in ways too subtle to trace, create an effect of repulsion—which is always, after all, the effect of "the other" when perceived from inside the self-rationalizing norm. You must therefore attend to the machinery of representation; you must as Marx would urge, rethink your representations of workers.[5] You must somehow bring them within, make sure that their fate and ours are bound up with each other. In cultural struggle, we try to seize the means of representation—rhetorical strategies and the media of their dissemination—and though this act is not equivalent to the seizing of the means of production, if we are successful the quixotic action generally involved in the latter will be unnecessary.

If Burke could have cited *The German Ideology* in 1935—possible, but not likely—and if in addition he had known Jacques Derrida's Nietzschean critique of representation—likely, but not possible—he would have quoted the following sentences which crystallize (besides a Marx-Derrida connection that would later come to light) the heart of Foucault's message. Burke might have said to his audience: consider, in what I am about to quote, the surprising meanings of the words *represent* and *representative, universal* and *rational*; notice how these words, so epistemologically safe in their traditional setting, so isolated from the world of struggle, in their rationalist purity, are here involved as ideological weapons in the work of historical process and class warfare.

> For each new class which puts itself in the place of one ruling before it, is compelled, merely in order to carry through its aim, to represent its interest as the common interest of all members of society, that is, expressed in ideal form: it has to give its ideas the form of universality, and represent them as the only rational, universally valid ones. The class making a revolution appears from the very start, if only because it is opposed to a *class*, not as a class but as the representative of the whole of society; it appears as the whole mass of society confronting the one ruling class.

Appendix

The embarrassing irony that Burke implicitly extracts from his analysis of the rhetorical effort of Marxism on behalf of the working class is that Marxist rhetoric emerges as reinforcement rather than as subversion of the hegemonic work of advanced capitalist society. "Some people," he says, and I take him—given his audience—to be referring to a certain type of left intellectual, "living overly sedentary lives, may like to read of harsh physical activity (as they once enjoyed Wild West fiction)—but Hollywood knows only too well that the people engaged in such kinds of effort are vitalized mainly by some vague hope that they may some day escape it" (see above, p. 269). Marxist rhetoric, in its effort to set in motion a counter-hegemony, must among other things project an image of a dehumanized and impoverished working class; the image is not rejected but welcomed by the intellectual forgers of the dominant hegemony who turn it against revolutionary intention. " 'Adult education' in capitalist America," Burke writes, "to-day is centered in the efforts of our economic mercenaries (our advertising men and sales organizations) to create a maximum desire for commodities consumed under expensive conditions—and Hollywood appeals to the worker mainly by picturing the qualities of life in which this commercially stimulated desire is gratified" (see above p. 269). The intention of what he calls adult education in America is to train or, in Foucault's sense, to *discipline* desire in the working class, to move it within a normalizing and self-perpetuating structure of desire promoted by an economic system that knows how to protect itself and, in this way, to move desire away from realizing one of its disruptive implications: the structural transformation of society and its socialist redefinition. Instead of foregrounding and pressing one of the potentially fatal internal contradictions of consumer capitalism, which would move it dialectically against itself (consumer capitalism must, through its manipulation of discourse and the image, "commercially stimulate" a desire for the good life whose social and economic historical ground cannot be capitalist society), Marxist rhetoric instead falls unwittingly into the hands of the artists and intellectuals of Madison Avenue and Hollywood and thereby helps to extend the historical life of consumer capitalism.

The "desire" that I refer to is not the ontological sort, the historically unlocated "lack" that Sartre defined in *Being and Nothingness:* it is, rather, that utopian yearning generated on the ground of capitalist economy itself, a yearning triggered by the message to the "*free*" laborer that, unlike his ancestor in the medieval system, *he* has unlimited social and economic fluidity—the message, to stay with my metaphor a moment longer, of "fluidity" itself. Especially in its democratic forms, capitalism creates radical desire as the possibility of unrestricted movement and personal fulfillment, socially and economically—a movement that was not permitted in the hardened hierarchy of the feudalist "structure." At the level of its own hegemonic metaphor, capitalism is no "structure." But since the capitalist system must resist the historical fulfillment of such desire—must resist socialism—if it is to preserve its inequitable (highly "structured") distribution of the fruits of labor, the system must find a way to appropriate the monster of utopian yearning for itself and thereby block the historical shift that Marx had predicted would follow upon its dialectically necessary deterioration.

Capitalism does find a way; it does block the teleology of history according to Marx. The first step was Frederick Taylor's, who disciplined workers' bodies for the ends of maximum productive efficiency; the second step was taken by consumer capitalism's poet-intellectuals who, in the media, discipline workers' desire through the creation and strategic deployment of the image—the media now understood not as a reflection of a preexistent economic base, and as therefore conspiratorially directed to promote acceptance of ruling class ideas, but as cultural mechanisms which produce the possibility of endless economic expansion by constituting, motivating, guiding, and "educating" desire. In its earlier stages, capitalism produces alienation; in its later, consumer, stage, it appropriates that alienation, turns its internal contradiction to advantage by projecting a perverse utopia of commodity-gratification that functions as the instrument for structuring desire as intention directed not toward the commodity per se but toward the capacity of the commodity to confer romance and wonder. Our novelists (Dreiser and Fitzgerald are among the most acute) have grasped the poetry of capitalist economics, but so have the creators of television commercials who portray drinking beer on a yacht not as what it is but as the fulfillment of desire—"going for the gusto." The perpetual production of the "new" commodity ensures, of course, that commodity-utopia will not be achieved, that desire is unappeasable, which is what consumer capitalism is all about: turning the potentially revolutionary force of desire produced on capitalist terrain toward the work of conserving and perpetuating consumer capitalism.

Consumer capitalism, therefore, direly needs the Marxist image of working class degradation, minus, of course, the Marxist analysis of the causes of that degradation; where Marxism says "exploitation," capitalism says a "condition" that its economic system will alleviate for those who work hard. If the motor principle of consumer capitalism is the production of both desire for the commodity and the illusion of potential gratification, a quality of happiness transcending commodities, though mediated by them, then proletarian fiction may unfortunately be one of the conditions of such production. The deep message of adult education in America is that the economic desire of workers can be requited only within a capitalist economy, undergirded and forever reinforced by its production of commodity-desire which, as Burke's reference to Hollywood's dream factory would suggest, well in advance of Guy Debord and Christopher Lasch, is synonymous with the production of the image. As critical theorist of social change, speaking to the intellectual vanguard of social change, Burke poses this question: "Is the symbol of the worker accurately attuned to us, as so conditioned by the reactionary forces in control of our main educational channels?" (see above, p. 269).

His response is no. But by answering in the negative Burke was not taking sides against Marx's historical wager on proletarian revolution; what he was denying, rather, was the rhetorico-symbolic value of the "worker," in discourses putatively aimed at changing minds for revolutionary ends, within an American social and political context in which class consciousness has been more or less successfully repressed. From the American point of view, the rhetorico-symbolic weight of the "worker" is burdened with an irrelevant historicity that is put into play every time the word is uttered, for it tends to carry with it an attendant rhetoric, decidedly foreign to our ways—*proletariat, bourgeoisie, ruling class:* the stuff of the European experience, but surely not of ours. Thus, along with the other disadvantages that Burke has noted, we have to add that all *talk* of a working *class* in America, or even just of *class,* and certainly of the complex awareness of hierarchical economic relations called class-*consciousness,* tends to sound forced, which is not to say that the experience of workers is a fantasy of Marxist intellectuals, or that the economic interests of a few do not require the exploitation of many. To say all of this against a Marxist rhetoric in the United States is not to speak against Marxism per se but only to acknowledge the awesomeness of the hegemonic discourse of our capitalist democracy. Lacking the bitter but useful historical consciousness of a precapitalist phase of American history, and saturated as we are by a mythology of equality ("one people," "indivisible," "with liberty and justice for all"), the symbol of the worker in America, with its Old World context of social hierarchy, not only does not embody our ideals (it cannot enlist our ambitions, as Burke put it), but, from a rhetorical point of view, when such a symbol is inserted into an American discourse on social change, it tends to have a fragmenting, not a unifying effect. The tragic effect of a traditional Marxist rhetoric in the American scene might be this: instead of extending (spreading, disseminating, propagating) a doctrine of revolutionary thought, a discourse weighted with symbols of proletarian life and exploitation might succeed only in isolating—I mean "quarantining"—workers' agony. Having thus inadvertently segregated workers from the social whole—irony of ironies for a totalizing philosophy—Marxist rhetoric then inadvertently plays into the purposes of the reactionary rhetoric poured out through our main educational channels where the worker is bombarded by images of the "good life," translated as maximum commodities consumed under expensive conditions. Maybe the bitterest of ironies to emerge from this conflict of rhetorics is not the quarantining effect of Marxist doctrine but the internal self-revulsion of workers as individuals and as members of an exploited group.

In suggesting that the American Marxist intellectual discard the symbol of the worker as rhetorical sine qua non of a vanguard movement, Burke by no means suggests that the real human costs extracted from workers be ignored or even down-played: "The rigors of the worker must certainly continue to form a major part of revolutionary symbolism, if only for the reason that here the worst features of capitalist exploitation are concentrated" (see above, p. 269). Burke is here urging that the rigors of the worker be inserted within a rhetorically more encompassing ("representative") symbol, so that the fate of the working class will be organically integrated with the fate of society as a whole: a vision of totality, undergirded by the working class, must be produced by a rhetoric of totality. The role of such rhetoric is not the persuasion of doubters that "there is" totality but the creation and insemination of a vision—we may say a heuristic fiction—whose promised child is consenting consciousness for radical social change. More specifically, what this counter-hegemonic effort entails is the choice of a central symbolism that would permit the vanguard intellectual to move with some hope for success into those very areas of society not disposed to think that the first order of American social business is structural change. Burke's suggestion, what created all the outrage and brought down on his head charges that he was a dupe of fascism who naively employed the rhetorical methods of Hitler, is that American Marxists choose in place of "the worker" the symbol of "the people" (see above, p. 269).

If it hopes to get its political work done in the United States, a Marxist rhetoric must take pains not to rupture itself from the historico-rhetorical mainstream of American social and political values. A truly ruptured rhetoric on behalf of the working class, standing in moral purity and isolation from the evils of all other political discourses, would not succeed in bringing the new society to birth ex nihilo but would only cut itself off from potentially sympathetic reception as it created not dialogue but narcissistic reflection. A radical rhetoric of revolution, instead of attempting to transcend the historical terrain of repression, should—I appeal to etymology here—work *at* the radical, within the history it would remake "at the root." The way out, if there is a way out, can only be the way through. Hence Burke's plea that "one cannot extend the doctrine of revolutionary thought among the lower middle class without using middle-class values—just as the Church invariably converted pagans by making the local deities into saints" (see above, p. 269). Burke's appeal to Marxists to immerse their rhetoric of revolution in the historical and cultural specificity of American folkways, to sink deeper into history, not to try to leap beyond it, though angrily rejected by his auditors at the American Writers' Congress, is primarily, I believe, a profound appeal to dialectics. Not dialectics as the theory of the gross institutional movement of social and economic history that Marx and Engels had outlined in *The German Ideology* but dialectics as a theory of the discursive movement of social and political history, dialectics as the theory of the emergent process of a liberating discourse—a dialectical rhetoric, not a simple negating language of rupture but a shrewd, self-conscious rhetoric that conserves as it negates. To a group presumably committed to the idea that revolution is made at the level of mind, and only executed, if at all, at the level of armed bodies, Burke is saying: get yourself a dialectical rhetoric and fashion it out of the stuff of the history and culture in which you find yourselves; in this way you will have the chance to be understood, clearly understood. That, to speak anachronistically, is the heart of Burke's Gramscian message—his appropriation of those decidedly non-teleological moments in the theory of history embedded in *The German Ideology.*

As dialectical rhetorician, the revolutionary writer must seize the historically persistent bourgeois rhetoric, somehow unmask its structure of oppression while preserving its emergent utopian intention. In America this means the appropriation, in the symbol of "the people," of a unifying direction, a latent ideal of society, "the ultimate *classless* feature which the revolution would bring about" (see above, p. 270). At the same moment, such appropriation must be a revelation of the frightening nationalistic and class prerogatives which hide their abusive force "behind a communal ideology." The ultimate point of such rhetoric is to create a new social center, aligned with the working class by its intellectuals—a critical mass galvanized into active "sympathy for the oppressed and antipathy towards our oppressive institutions" (see above, p. 270).

"The people" must be understood as an ideological element within an ideological system whose palpable, hegemonic form is linguistic. Burke is saying in effect that the discourse this element inhabits is not reducible to the interests of a specific class; nor, I would add, is it an epiphenomenon of the economic infrastructure of society. As an isolable element in the discourse, "the people," as a later critical theory would have it, is fundamentally "undecidable", at the same time, from the systemic or ideological point of view, any ideological element necessarily plays a functionally determinate role. Burke in his address was saying that the literary seizing of the time involved, among other things, taking advantage of such latent undecidability by first extracting "the people" from its bourgeois nationalist system and then placing it onto a very different ideological terrain, one that it was not accustomed to occupying, where it could do the sort of very decidable work that the orthodox left then thought unimaginable. The function of the critical literary intellectual, Burke is arguing, is to engage in ideological struggle at the discursive level; to absorb and then rearticulate "the people" with a new organic ideology, where it might serve a different collective will. The fluidity, or undecidability, of the symbol is not, therefore, the sign of its social and political elusiveness but the ground of its historicity and of its flexible but also specific political significance and force.

Enabling this dialectical or historical work of rhetoric (the work of "argument") is one of the traditional resources of the rhetorician: the tropes, now manipulated not for ornamental purposes but for the ends of social change. The tropes must carry the argument of Marxism, which cannot be made "literally and directly" but only by the "intellectual company" it keeps. Literally and directly, the deployment of the general Marxist argument in the United States is subject to the same limitations that enervated the proletarian symbol—it appears foreign, disruptive to our culture's "unity" and "stability," an intruder into the "organic" social body. The revolutionary argument must be made implicitly, must be made to emerge as a necessary expression of our historical drift as a nation. Burke is urging a distinction between the work of the intellectual in his pamphleteering role, or in his role as political organizer—such work, in other words, that is explicit in its commitments—and the work of the intellectual as "imaginative" writer whose political contribution must be implicit. This distinction entails an unspoken judgment: Burke is betting that the writer's implied political alignment will ultimately do more effective political work because its literary-rhetorical matrix will make the force of radical vision difficult to resist (see above, pp. 270–71).

I think Burke is anticipating his later work on the connection between political authority and the tropes, the matter of "representation" in both its political and aesthetic meanings. The political, he is saying in so many words, must be embedded as a kind of synecdoche—as part of a larger cultural whole from which it cannot be extricated without violating the character of the whole, without also carrying out all the desirable features of the whole associated with it by necessity. That is the textual magic of synecdoche, and that is what Burke is getting at when he says that one's political alignment must be "fused" with "broader" cultural elements. To "represent" the larger cultural whole as fused with a radical political alignment that functions as a synecdoche, a "representation" of the whole itself, is to naturalize the political, make it seem irresistible. This is the work of rhetoric, and rhetoric, like theory, as Burke knows, is not necessarily in the service of radical change.

Let me draw out the implication: the radical mind has no privileged mode of persuasion available to it; there is no morally pure, no epistemologically secure, no linguistically uncontaminated route to radical change. Thus Burke's chief example of implicit poetic strategy: "this is what our advertisers do when they recommend a particular brand of cigarette by picturing it as being smoked under desirable conditions; it is the way in which the best artists of the religious era recommended or glorified their faith; and I imagine it would be the best way of proceeding today" (see above, p. 271). To attempt to proceed in purity—to reject the rhetorical strategies of capitalism and Christianity, *as if such strategies were in themselves responsible for human oppression*—to proceed with the illusion of purity is to situate oneself on the margin of history, as the possessor of a unique truth disengaged from history's flow. It is to exclude oneself from having any chance of making a difference for better or for worse.

The traditional humanist response to all of this is not difficult to imagine: Isn't what you and Burke call Marxism at bottom, then, sheer and brutal Nietzschean will to power? Are you not saying that the end justifies the means? What, therefore, makes you think that your theory will not do to others what you say other theories have done? I used to think those questions powerfully sobering; I now think they are merely frightened, for they imply individually and collectively a desire for a transcendental guarantee that action in this world can proceed in innocence, with no harm done on any side—a

desire, in other words, to know in advance that what we do can produce only good. Of course those who pose such questions know
better—that is why they do nothing, and in such quietude assume
that they do no harm. The means of rhetoric, in fact, are neither good
nor bad: they simply are.

The intellectual who would be self-consciously socially effective can
but proceed, then, in the hegemonic mode, creating consensus. Consensus cannot be created by the purist stance of "antithetical morality," and that is what is at stake in Burke's suggestion that the symbol
of the worker be replaced by an encompassing symbolism whose rhetorical force will be located on the common ground, the kindred values it "finds," by sleight of hand, for writer and audience, for only
within such a rhetorical relation, so structured by commonality of
value and purpose, is the reception of radical values possible. Here is
Burke on the rhetorical conditions of propagation:

> Particularly as regards the specific problems of propaganda, the
> emphasis upon the *antithetical* tends to incapacitate a writer for
> his task as a *spreader* of doctrine by leading him too soon into
> antagonistic modes of thought and expression. It gives him too
> much authority to *condemn*—and however human this desire to
> grow wrathful may be, and however justified it is by the
> conditions all about us, the fact remains that his specific job as
> a propagandist requires him primarily to wheedle or cajole, to
> practice the arts of ingratiation. As a propagandizer, it is not his
> work to convince the convinced, but to plead with the
> unconvinced, which requires him to use *their* vocabulary, *their*
> values, *their* symbols, insofar as this is possible. (See above, pp.
> 271–72)

Dialectics as rhetoric, as art of ingratiation—as *"propaganda by inclusion"*: the creation, in a revolutionary era, when symbols of allegiance
are being exchanged, of a revolutionary symbolism (see above, p. 272).
"Revolutionary" means fundamentally for Burke "transitional"—the
state, both historically and psychologically, of being "between" and,
fiction of all radical fictions, the state of "tendency," of being "on the
way." It is not a question of whether there is a teleology in history—a
question for metaphysicians and some Marxists—but a question of
forging the rhetorical conditions for change, a question of forging (and
I'll insist on the Joycean resonance of that term) a teleological rhetoric,
of creating, through the mediations of such discourse, a collective will
for change, for moving history in the direction of our desire. We need
a rhetoric, Burke concludes, that creates a psychological bridge, a

Appendix

Janus-faced language; "looking both forwards and back" it establishes—forges—its historicity, its continuity as the inevitable, emergent language—fiction of tendency—and by so doing becomes as well the Janus-faced psychological bridge that carries "the people" smoothly, without break, from bourgeois democratic location to the state of socialism (see above, pp. 272–73). This political symbolism becomes effective when it is surrounded by the fullest of cultural textures—when one's political alignment is associated with "cultural awareness in the large" (see above, p. 273). At such a moment, the war for cultural position will have been won and the hegemony in place, replaced.

One of the chapters of a full-scale history of Marxist thought will have to be on Kenneth Burke who, among other things, was doing Gramsci's work before anyone but Gramsci (and his censors) could read what would be called the *Prison Notebooks*. The real force of Burke is not limited, however, to his historically independent Gramscian practice or to his American discovery of the popular front. The real force of his thinking is to lay bare, more candidly than any writer I know who works in theory, the socially and politically enmeshed character of the intellectual. To put it that way is to say that Burke more even than Gramsci carries through the project on intellectuals implied by parts of *The German Ideology*. And Burke did this not just occasionally but repeatedly over a career that has spanned more than sixty years.

NOTES

1. Quoted in Ben Yagoda, "Kenneth Burke," *Horizon*, 23 (June 1980), 68.
2. Ibid.
3. Ibid.
4. Karl Marx and Frederick Engels, *The German Ideology*, ed. with an introduction by C.J. Arthur (New York: International Publishers, 1970), p. 121.
5. For Marx and Engels on "representation," see *The German Ideology*, pp. 65–66.

THE WRITINGS OF

KENNETH BURKE, 1968–1986

RICHARD H. THAMES

The definitive Burke bibliography is that of Armin Paul Frank and Mechthild Frank published in *Critical Responses to Kenneth Burke, 1924–1966*, edited by William H. Rueckert. With the exception of books by Burke (all of which are listed for convenience in their latest editions), the intent of this bibliography is to correct and update the Franks'; it should be used, therefore, in conjunction with theirs. Their format is followed in such a way as to continue where they left off. Their description of the format follows.

"The checklist is divided into the following parts: (1) books, (2) [short] fiction, (3) poetry, (4) essays, (5) music criticism, (6) reviews, (7) commentary, discussions, and miscellaneous, (8) letters and replies, (9) translations, and (10) anthologies containing writings by Mr. Burke. The order within each section is chronological by the date of first appearance; the items in each section are consecutively numbered. Cross-references are two-way except in Part 1, where cross-referencing would frequently have amounted to providing complete tables of contents. Tables of contents are, however, given in the case of selective translations of books....Whenever an item was collected more than once, the references are in strict chronological order, cutting across the categories."

The knowledge of Robert Wess and Robert Garlitz proved invaluable. Unfortunately, no one rescued me with knowledge of the whereabouts of Burke's review of Barbusse's *Stalin* referred to by Sidney Hook in a 1937 *Partisan Review* piece (see *Critical Responses*, p. 93). Perhaps in a future update.

Part 1. Books

2. *Counter-Statement*. New York: Harcourt, Brace, 1931; 2d ed., Los Altos, Calif.: Hermes Publications, 1954; Phoenix paperback, Chicago:

298

University of Chicago Press, 1957; paperback, Berkeley: University of California Press, 1968.
3. *Towards a Better Life: Being a Series of Epistles, or Declamations.* New York: Harcourt, Brace, 1932; 2d ed., Berkeley: University of California Press, 1966.
4. *Permanence and Change: An Anatomy of Purpose.* New York: New Republic, 1935; 2d rev. ed., Los Altos, Calif.: Hermes Publications, 1954; paperback, Indianapolis: Bobbs-Merrill, 1965; 3d rev. ed., Berkeley: University of California Press, 1984. The 1954, 1965, and 1984 editions contain an appendix, "On Human Behavior, Considered 'Dramatistically' "; the 1965 and 1984 editions, an introduction by Hugh Dalziel Duncan; the 1984 edition, a new afterword, "*Permanence and Change:* In Retrospective Prospect."
5. *Attitudes toward History.* 2 vols. New York: New Republic, 1937; 2d rev. ed., Los Altos, Calif.: Hermes Publications, 1959; Beacon paperback, Boston: Beacon Press, 1961; 3d rev. ed., Berkeley: University of California Press, 1984. The 1984 edition contains a new afterword, "*Attitudes toward History:* In Retrospective Prospect."
6. *The Philosophy of Literary Form: Studies in Symbolic Action.* Baton Rouge: Louisiana State University Press, 1941; 2d ed., 1967; rev. abr. ed., Vintage paperback, New York: Vintage Books, 1957; 3d ed., Berkeley: University of California Press, 1973.
7. *A Grammar of Motives.* New York: Prentice-Hall, 1945; London: Dennis Dobson, 1947; 2d ed., New York: George Braziller, 1955; Meridian paperback, Cleveland and New York: World, 1962 (together with 1.8); Berkeley: University of California Press, 1969.
8. *A Rhetoric of Motives.* New York: Prentice-Hall, 1950; 2d ed., New York: George Braziller, 1955; Meridian paperback, Cleveland and New York: World, 1962 (together with 1.7); Berkeley: University of California Press, 1969.
8a. "Akastely c. regenyenek elemzese" (analysis of Kafka's *The Castle*), trans. Zsofia Dobras, *Helikon: Vilagirodalmi Figyelo,* 24 (1978), 326–32.
10. *The Rhetoric of Religion: Studies in Logology.* Boston: Beacon Press, 1961; Berkeley: University of California Press, 1970.
11. *Perspectives by Incongruity.* Ed. Stanley Edgar Hyman, with the assistance of Barbara Karmiller. Midland paperback, Bloomington: Indiana University Press, 1964; a combined clothbound edition of 1.11 and 1.12, Indiana University Press, 1964.
12. *Terms for Order.* Ed. Stanley Edgar Hyman, with the assistance of Barbara Karmiller. Midland paperback, Bloomington: Indiana University Press, 1964; a combined clothbound edition of 1.11 and 1.12, Indiana University Press, 1964.
13. *Language as Symbolic Action: Essays on Life, Literature, and Method.* Berkeley: University of California Press, 1966.
14. *Collected Poems, 1915–1967.* Berkeley: University of California Press, 1968. [Includes 1.9]
15. *The Complete White Oxen: Collected Short Fiction of Kenneth Burke.* Berkeley: University of California Press, 1968. [Includes 1.1]
16. *Dramatism and Development.* Heinz Werner Series, Vol. 6. Worcester, Mass.: Clark University Press, 1972.

Part 2. Short Fiction

No new publications. See the Franks' bibliography.

Part 3. Poetry

56. "A Count-in." *Poetry,* 113 (October 1968), 29–30.
57. "A Juxtaposition." *Poetry,* 113 (October 1968), 30.
58. "Eye-crossing, from Brooklyn to Manhattan." *Nation,* 208 (June 2, 1969), 700–704. [Included in 4.135]
59. "Her will." *New Republic,* 161 (July 5, 1969), 28.
60. "Modernism so far is but peanuts." *New Republic,* 161 (November 8, 1969), 30.
61. "Two Poems of Abandonment." *New Republic,* 162 (May 30, 1970), 27.
62. "But for these lucky accidents." *Communication,* 1 (1974), 196.
63. "A Critical Load, Beyond That Door; or, Before the Ultimate Confrontation; or, When Thinking of Deconstructionist Structuralists; or, A Hermeneutic Fantasy." *Critical Inquiry,* 5 (Fall 1978), 199–200.
64. "Belated Entrance." *Recherches anglaises et américaines,* 12 (1979), 9.
65. "Invocation for a Convocation." *Kenyon Review,* n.s., 1 (Winter 1979), 3–4.
66. "Out of Backwards Sidewise Towards Fromwards (An Attitudinizing Winter-Solstitially)." *Kenyon Review,* n.s., 2 (Summer 1980), 92–93.

Part 4. Essays

15. "Thomas Mann and André Gide." *Bookman,* 73 (June 1930), 257–264. [1.2; 10.11; 10.15; 10.52]
42. "The Rhetoric of Hitler's 'Battle.'" *Southern Review,* 5 (Summer 1939), 1–21. [10.7; 1.6; 1.12; 10.44; 10.55; 10.58; 10.60] Translation: "Die Rhetorik in Hitlers 'Mein Kampf,'" 1.6b, pp. 7–34.
44. "Surrealism." *New Directions in Prose and Poetry,* 5 (1940), 563–79; *Surrealism pro and con,* New York: Gotham Book Mart, 1973.
50. "Motives and Motifs in the Poetry of Marianne Moore." *Accent,* 2 (Spring 1942) 157–69. [1.7, Appendix C; 10.9; 10.51]
53. "The Problem of the Intrinsic." *Accent,* 3 (Winter 1942–43), 80–94. [1.7, Appendix B; 10.44a]
63a. "Kinds of Sensibility." In *Paul Rosenfeld: Voyager in the Arts,* ed. Jerome Meliquist and Lucie Wiese, pp. 100–105. New York: Creative Age Press, 1948.
101. "William Carlos Williams, 1883–1963." *New York Review of Books,* 1 (special issue of spring and summer books, 1963), 45–47; *Stand,* 6 (1964), 15–23. [1.13; 10.47a]
102. "The Thinking of the Body: Comments on the Imagery of Catharsis in Literature." *Psychoanalytic Review,* 50 (Fall 1963), 25–68. [1.13; excerpt in 10.53]
124. "Dramatism." In *Communication: Concepts and Perspectives,* ed. Lee Thayer, pp. 327–352. Washington, D.C.: Spartan Books, 1967. A shorter

Richard H. Thames

version appears in *International Encyclopedia of the Social Sciences*, 7. 445–52. New York: Macmillian and Free Press, 1968.

125. "Order, Action, and Victimage." In *The Concept of Order*, ed. Paul G. Kuntz, pp. 167–90. Seattle: Published for Grinnell College by the University of Washington Press, 1968.

126. "Words Anent Logology." In *Perspectives in Literary Symbolism*, ed. Joseph Strelka, pp. 72–83. University Park: Pennsylvania State University Press, 1968.

127. "King Lear: Its Forms and Psychosis." *Shenandoah*, 21 (Autumn 1968), 3–18.

128. "Thoughts on the Poet's Corner." In *Poetry Therapy: The Use of Poetry in the Treatment of Emotional Disorders*, ed. Jack J. Leedy, MD. Philadelphia: J. B. Lippincott, 1969.

129. "Kermode Revisited" (essay-review of Frank Kermode, *The Sense of an Ending: Studies in the Theory of Fiction*). *Novel: A Forum of Fiction*, 3 (Fall 1969), 77–82.

130. "Poetry and Communication." In *Contemporary Philosophical Thought*, Vol. 3: *Perspectives in Education, Religion, and the Arts*, ed. Howard Evans Kiefer and Milton Karl Munitz, pp. 401–18. Albany: State University of New York Press, 1970.

131. "Towards Helhaven: Three Stages of a Vision." *Sewanee Review*, 79 (Winter 1971), 11–25.

132. "On 'Creativity'—A Partial Retraction." In *Introspection: The Artist Looks at Himself*, ed. Donald E. Hayden, pp. 63–81. University of Tulsa Monography Series, no. 12 (1971).

133. "Doing and Saying: Thoughts on Myth, Cult, and Archetypes." *Salmagundi*, 7 (Winter 1971), 100–119.

134. "As I Was Saying." *Michigan Quarterly Review*, 11 (Winter 1972), 9–27.

135. "An Eye-Poem for the Ear (with Prose Introduction, Glosses, and After-Words)." In *Directions in Literary Criticism*, ed. Stanley Weintraub and Phillip Young, pp. 228–51. University Park: Pennsylvania State University Press, 1973. [Includes 3.58]

136. "The Rhetorical Situation." In *Communication Ethical and Moral Issues*, ed. Lee Thayer, pp. 263–75. New York: Gordon and Breach Science, 1973.

137. "Communication and the Human Condition." *Communication*, 1 (1974), 135–52.

138. "Why Satire, with a Plan for Writing One." *Michigan Quarterly Review*, 13 (Winter 1974), 307–37.

139. "In Response to Booth: Dancing with Tears in My Eyes." *Critical Inquiry*, 1 (Fall 1974), 23–31. Slightly different versions of this essay and the one by Booth which provoked it appear in *Critical Understanding: The Powers and Limits of Pluralism* by Wayne C. Booth. Chicago: University of Chicago Press, 1979.

140. "William Carlos Williams: A Critical Appreciation." In *William Carlos Williams*, ed. Charles Angoff, pp. 15–19. Rutherford, N.J.: Fairleigh Dickinson University Press, 1974.

141. "Words as Deeds." *Centrum*, 3 (Fall 1975), 147–68.

142. "The Party Line." *Quarterly Journal of Speech*, 62 (February 1976), 62–68.

143. "On Literary Form." In *The New Criticism and After* (John Crowe Ransom Memorial Lectures delivered at Kenyon College, April 3–5,

1975), ed. Thomas Daniel Young, pp. 80–90. Charlottesville: University Press of Virginia, 1976.

144. "Towards Looking Back." *Journal of General Education*, 28 (Fall 1976), 167–89.

145. "Self-Portrait of a Person" (essay-review of B. F. Skinner, *Particulars of My Life*). *Behaviorism*, 4 (Fall 1976), 257–71.

146. "Above the Over-Towering Babble" (essay-review of George Steiner, *After Babel: Aspects of Language and Translation*). *Michigan Quarterly Review*, 15 (Winter 1976), 88–102.

147. "Post Poesque Derivation of a Terministic Cluster." *Critical Inquiry*, 4 (Winter 1977), 215–20.

148. "Rhetoric, Poetics, and Philosophy." In *Rhetoric, Philosophy and Literature: An Exploration*, ed. Don M. Burks, pp. 15–33. West Lafayette: Purdue University Press, 1978.

149. "A (Psychological) Fable, with a (Logological) Moral." *American Imago*, 35 (1978), 203–7.

150. "Questions and Answers about the Pentad." *College Composition and Communication*, 29 (December 1978), 330–35.

151. "(Nonsymbolic) Motion/(Symbolic) Action." *Critical Inquiry*, 4 (Summer 1978), 809–38. [Included in 10.59 and 10.60]

152. "Methodological Repression and/or Strategies of Containment." *Critical Inquiry*, 5 (Winter 1978), 401–16.

153. "Theology and Logology." *Kenyon Review*, n.s., 1 (Winter 1979), 151–85.

154. "Theology and Logology." *Journal of the American Academy of Religion*, 97, Supplement (June 1979), 235–50. Not the same as 4.153. The essay appears in a "Supplement" rather than the June 1979 issue which contains only the abstract (p. 298); it must be ordered with the form provided in the regular issue.

155. "Symbolism as a Realistic Mode: 'De-Psychoanalyzing' Logologized." *Psychocultural Review*, 3 (Winter 1979), 25–37.

156. "As One Thing Leads to Another." *Recherches anglaises et américaines*, 12 (1979), 13–17.

157. "The Interactive Bond." In *Rigor and Imagination: Essays on the Legacy of Gregory Bateson*, ed. C. Wilder-Mott and John H. Weaklund, pp. 331–41. New York: Praeger, 1981.

158. "Addendum on Bateson." In *Rigor and Imagination: Essays on the Legacy of Gregory Bateson*, ed. C. Wilder-Mott and John H. Weaklund, pp. 341–46. New York: Praeger, 1981.

159. "Variations on 'Providence.' " *Notre Dame English Journal*, 13 (Summer 1981), 155–83.

160. "Realisms, Occidental Style." In *Asian and Western Writers in Dialogue: New Cultural Identities*, ed. Guy Amirthanagam, pp. 26–47. London: Macmillan, 1982.

161. "Towards a Transcendent Immanence" (essay-review of Justus George Lawler, *Celestial Pantomime: Poetic Structures of Transcendence*). *Cross Currents*, 32 (Fall 1982), 329–36.

162. "Letter from a Gentile." *Dialectical Anthropology*, 8 (October 1983), 161–71.

163. "Dramatism and Logology." *Communication Quarterly*, 33 (Spring 1985), 89–93.

164. "In Haste." *Pre/Text*, 6 (Fall/Winter 1985), 329–77.

Richard H. Thames

Part 5. Music Criticism

See the Franks' bibliography.

Part 6. Reviews

14. "Heaven's First Law" (William Carlos Williams, *Sour Grapes*). *Dial*, 72 (February 1922), 197–200. [Included in 10.47a]
35a. "But They Have Settled" (Van Wyck Brooks, Alfred Kreymborg, Lewis Mumford, and Paul Rosenfeld, eds., *The American Caravan: A Yearbook of American Literature*). *New York Herald Tribune Books*, 4 (September 18, 1927), 2.
35b. "Little Men" (Ferenc Molnaar, *The Paul Street Boys*). *New York Herald Tribune Books*, 4 (December 4, 1927), 4.
36a. "Witchcraft in Our Day" (Jacob Wassermann, *World's End*). *New York Herald Tribune Books*, 4 (January 15, 1928), 2.
36b. "Werthers with a Future" (Frank Thiess, *The Gateway to Life*). *New York Herald Tribune Books*, 4 (February 26, 1928), 7.
36c. "Love Among the Ruins" (René Schicke, *Maria Capponi*). *New York Herald Tribune Books*, 4 (March 4, 1928), 7.
96. "Thurber Perfects Mind Cure" (James Thurber, *Let Your Mind Alone!*). *New Republic*, 92 (September 1937), 220–21. [Included in 10.56]
142. "Cult of the Breakthrough" (Ralph J. Mills, Jr., ed., *Selected Letters of Theodore Roethke*). *New Republic*, 159 (September 21, 1968), 25–26.
143. "The Serious Business of Comedy" (Elder Olson, *The Theory of Comedy*). *New Republic*, 160 (March 15, 1969), 23–27.
144. "Toward the Perfectly Poisonous" (Richard Ellmann, ed., *The Artist as Critic: Critical Writings of Oscar Wilde*). *New Republic*, 160 (May 31, 1969), 28–30.
145. "The Christ-Dionysus Link" (John Unterecker, *Voyager: A Life of Hart Crane*). *New Republic*, 161 (August 16, 1969), 24–26.
146. "More Probes in the Same Spot" (Marshall McLuhan, *Counterblast*). *New Republic*, 162 (February 7, 1970), 30–35.
147. "Swift Now? Swift Then" (Denis Donoghue, *Jonathan Swift: A Critical Introduction*). *New Republic*, 162 (May 9, 1970), 25–26.
148. "Irony Sans Rust" (Wayne C. Booth, *A Rhetoric of Irony*). *New Republic*, 171 (July 6 and 13, 1974), 25–26.
149. "Father and Son" (Harold Bloom, *The Map of Misreading*). *New Republic*, 172 (April 12, 1975), 23–24.
150. Untitled review of Harold Bloom, *Wallace Stevens: Poems of Our Climate*. *New Republic*, 176 (June 11, 1977), 24–27.
151. Untitled review of Denis Donoghue, *The Sovereign Ghost: Studies in Imagination*. *New Republic*, 177 (September 10, 1977), 29–31.

Part 7. Commentary, Discussions, and Miscellaneous

21. "Comments [on the 'Uses of Speech Criticism' Symposium]. "*Western Speech*, 32 (Summer 1968), 176–83.
22. "An Interview with Kenneth Burke," by John Woodcock. *Sewanee Review*, 85 (Fall 1977), 704–18.

23. "In New Jersey, My Adopted, and I Hope Adoptive, State." *New Jersey Monthly,* November 1981, p. 67 ff.
24. "Counter-Gridlock: An Interview with Kenneth Burke." *All Area,* no. 2 (1983), 6–33.
25. "Dramatism as Ontology or Epistemology: A Symposium." *Communication Quarterly,* 33 (Winter 1985), 17–33.
26. "Postscript." In *Criticism and Social Change,* by Frank Lentricchia, pp. 165–66. Paperback, Chicago: University of Chicago Press, 1985.
27. "Kenneth Burke and Malcom Cowley: A Conversation." *Pre/Text,* 6 (Fall/Winter 1985), 181–200.

Part 8. Letters and Replies

12. "An Ecological Proposal." *New Republic,* 161 (December 13, 1969), 30–31.
13. "An Exchange on Machiavelli." *New York Review of Books,* 18 (April 6, 1972), 35–36. In reference to Isaiah Berlin's article "The Question of Machiavelli" in the November 4, 1971, issue, pp. 20–32. Berlin's response follows Burke's letter.
14. "Dramatism and Logology." *TLS,* August 12, 1983, p. 859. In reference to Robert M. Adams' review of the 2d rev. ed. of William H. Rueckert's *Kenneth Burke and the Drama of Human Relations.*
15. "A Plea to Join the Fray and Make It Worth Our While." *Kenneth Burke Society Newsletter,* 1 (October 1984), 1.
16. "A Letter from Andover." *Kenneth Burke Society Newsletter,* 2 (July 1986), 3–5.
17. "A Comment on 'It Takes Capital to Defeat Dracula.'" *College English,* 49 (February 1987) 221–22.

Part 9. Translations

15. Thomas Mann, *Death in Venice.* New York: A. A. Knopf, 1925; reissue 1965; reissue 1973 (all include "Tristan" and "Tonio Kröger"); rev. ed. with a critical essay by Erich Heller, New York: Modern Library, 1970; New York: Bantam Books, 1971; illustrated with wood engravings by Felix Hoffmann, Avon, Conn.: Heritage Club, 1972, and New York: Stinehour Press for the Limited Editions Club, 1972.

Part 10. Anthologies Containing Writings by Kenneth Burke

27. Morgan, Frederick, ed. *Hudson Review Anthology.* New York: Vintage Books, 1961. [Includes 6.131] Cross-reference corrected.
27a. Parsons, Talcott; Edward Shils; Kaspar D. Naegle; and Jesse R. Pitts, eds. *Theories of Society.* New York: Free Press of Glencoe, A Division of Crowell-Collier, 1961. [Includes "An Incongruous Assortment of Incongruities," 1.4]
44a. Olson, Elder, ed. *Aristotle's Poetics and English Literature.* Chicago: University of Chicago Press, 1965. [Includes 4.53]
47a. Miller, J. Hillis, ed. *William Carlos Williams: A Collection of Critical Essays.* Englewood Cliffs, N.J.: Prentice-Hall, 1966. [Includes 6.14 and 4.101]

Richard H. Thames

51. Hollander, J., ed. *Modern Poetry: Essays in Criticism*. London: Oxford University Press, 1968. [Includes 4.50]
52. Howe, Irving, ed. *The Idea of the Modern in Literature and the Arts*. New York: Horizon Press, 1968. [Includes 4.15]
53. Phillips, Robert S., ed. *Aspects of Alice: Lewis Carroll's Dreamchild as Seen through the Critics' Looking-glasses, 1865–1971*. New York: Vanguard, 1971. [Includes excerpt from 4.102]
54. Johannesen, Richard L., ed. *Contemporary Theories of Rhetoric: Selected Readings*. New York: Harper and Row, 1971. [Includes "Introduction," 1.7 and an excerpt from "The Range of Rhetoric," 1.8]
55. Scott, Robert L., and Bernard L. Brock, eds. *Methods of Rhetorical Criticism: A Twentieth-Century Perspective*. New York: Harper and Row, 1972. [Includes 4.42 and "Mind, Body and the Unconscious," 1.13]
56. Harrison, Gilbert A., ed. *The Critic as Artist: Essays on Books, 1920–1970*. New York: Liveright, 1972. [Includes 6.96]
57. Winterowd, W. Ross, ed. *Contemporary Rhetoric: A Conceptual Background with Readings*. New York: Harcourt, Brace, and Jovanovich, 1975. [Includes "Lexicon Rhetoricae," 1.2, and "Introduction," 1.7]
58. Golden, James L.; Goodwin F. Berquist; and William E. Coleman. *The Rhetoric of Western Thought*. 2d ed. Dubuque, Iowa: Kendall/Hunt, 1976. [Includes 4.42]
59. Roland, Alan, ed. *Psychoanalysis, Creativity, and Literature: A French-American Inquiry*. New York: Columbia University Press, 1978. [Includes 4.151]
60. Tanner, William E., and J. Dean Bishop. *Rhetoric and Change*. Mesquite, Tex.: Ide House, 1982; rev. ed., Arlington, Tex.: Liberal Arts, 1985. [Includes first part of 4.151 with minor revisions as "Motion, Action, and the Human Condition"]
61. Shapiro, Michael, ed. *Language and Politics*. New York: New York University Press, 1984. [Includes 4.42]

A SELECTED BIBLIOGRAPHY

OF CRITICAL RESPONSES TO

KENNETH BURKE, 1968–1986

RICHARD H. THAMES

Items included in this bibliography have been selected because they exhibit quality, address significant issues, create or resolve controversy, exemplify interdisciplinary influence, and reflect international recognition. Consistent with the character of this volume, most items represent *critical responses* to Burke rather than applications of his methodology. For a listing of the latter see Foss, Foss, and Trapp, *Contemporary Perspectives on Rhetoric*, pp. 291–304.

When I volunteered to compile this bibliography, I assumed I would owe the greatest debt of gratitude to the library's computer. I discovered quite soon just how ignorant it was. Richly deserved thanks go instead to the knowledgeable Roberts (Professors Wess and Garlitz again) and the ever sagacious Trevor Melia.

Abdulla, Adnan K. *Catharsis in Literature.* Bloomington: Indiana University Press, 1985.

Adams, Robert M. "The Dance of Language" (Review of William H. Rueckert, *Kenneth Burke and the Drama of Human Relations*, 2d ed.). *TLS,* July 8, 1983, pp. 715–16. *See* Burke's letter (8.14) in response.

Aune, James. "Burke's Late Blooming: Trope, Defense, and Rhetoric." *Quarterly Journal of Speech,* 69 (August 1983), 328–40.

Baer, Donald M. "A Comment on Skinner as Boy and on Burke as S—." *Behaviorism,* 4 (Fall 1976), 273–77.

Baker, Lewis. "Some Manuscript Collections Containing Kenneth Burke Materials." *Pre/Text,* 6 (Fall/Winter 1985), 307–11.

Barat, Jean-Claude. "Kenneth Burke et les 'New Critics.' " *Recherches anglaises et américaines,* no. 12 (1979), pp. 45–64.

Richard H. Thames

Bennett, W. Lance. "Political Scenarios and the Nature of Politics." *Philosophy and Rhetoric*, 8 (Winter 1983), 23–42.

Bessière, Jean. "Kenneth Burke face à quelques ecrivains européens (1921–1932)." *Revue de littérature comparée*, 54 (April–June 1980), 174–95.

Bloom, Harold. "A Tribute to Kenneth Burke." *Book World*, May 31, 1981, p. 4.

Bloom, Harold. *A Map of Misreading*. New York: Oxford University Press, 1975.

Bloom, Harold. *Agon: Towards A Theory of Revisionism*. New York: Oxford University Press, 1982.

Bloom, Harold. *The Breaking of the Vessels*. The Wellek Library Lectures at the University of California, Irvine. Ed. Frank Lentricchia. Chicago: University of Chicago Press, 1982.

Booth, Wayne C. "Kenneth Burke's Way of Knowing." *Critical Inquiry*, 1 (Fall 1974), 1–22. See Burke's response, 4.139.

Booth, Wayne C. *Critical Understanding: The Powers and Limits of Pluralism*. Chicago: University of Chicago Press, 1979.

Bostdorff, Denise M., and Phillip K. Tompkins. "Musical Form and Rhetorical Form: Kenneth Burke's *Dial* Reviews as Counterpart to *Counter-Statement.*" *Pre/Text*, 6 (Fall/Winter 1985), 235–52.

Brown, Merle E. *Kenneth Burke*. University of Minnesota pamphlets on American Writers, no. 75. Minneapolis: University of Minnesota Press, 1969.

Burks, Don M. "Dramatic Irony, Collaboration, and Kenneth Burke's Theory of Form." *Pre/Text*, 6 (Fall/Winter 1985), 255–73.

Cain, William E. "The Kenneth Burke Problem." *The Crisis in Criticism: Theory, Literature, and Reform in English Studies*, pp. 139–46. Baltimore: Johns Hopkins University Press, 1984. Originally published in *Review 3*, ed. James O. Hoge and James L. W. West III, pp. 63–73. Charlottesville: University of Virginia Press, 1981.

Carrier, James G. "Misrecognition and Knowledge." *Inquiry: An Interdisciplinary Journal of Philosophy and the Social Sciences*, 22 (Autumn 1979), 321–42.

Carrier, James G. "Knowledge, Meaning, and Social Inequality in Kenneth Burke." *American Journal of Sociology*, 88 (July 1982), 43–61.

Coe, Richard M. "It Takes Capital to Defeat Dracula: A New Rhetorical Essay." *College English*, 48 (March 1986), 231–42. See Burke's response (8.17).

Combs, James E. *Dimensions of Political Drama*. Santa Monica: Goodyear, 1980.

Combs, James G., and Michael W. Mansfield. *Drama in Life: The Uses of Communication in Society.* New York: Hastings, 1976.

Crable, Richard E., and John J. Makay. "Kenneth Burke's Concept of Motives in Rhetorical Theory." *Today's Speech,* 20 (Winter 1972), 11–18.

Crocker, J. Christopher. "The Social Function of Rhetorical Forms." In *The Social Use of Metaphor: Essays on the Anthropology of Rhetoric,* ed. J. David Sapir and J. Christopher Crocker, pp. 33–66. Philadelphia: University of Pennsylvania Press, 1977.

Crusius, Timothy W. "Kenneth Burke's Theory of Form in Rhetorical Interpretation." *Recherches anglaises et américaines,* no. 12 (1979), pp. 82–97.

Crusius, Timothy W. "Kenneth Burke on His 'Morbid Selph': The Collected Poems as Comedy." *CEA Critic,* 43 (May 1981), 18–32.

Crusius, Timothy W. "A Case for Kenneth Burke's Dialectic and Rhetoric." *Philosophy and Rhetoric,* 19 (Winter 1986), 23–37.

Davis, Walter A. *The Act of Interpretation: A Critique of Literary Reason.* Chicago: University of Chicago Press, 1978.

Dickey, James. "Kenneth Burke." *Babel to Byzantium: Poets and Poetry Now,* pp. 28–31. New York: Farrar, Straus, and Giroux, 1968.

Dinneen, F. P., S.J. Review of *The Rhetoric of Religion. General Linguistics,* 13 (1973), 176–95.

Donoghue, Denis. "Enigma Variations." *New York Review of Books,* 11 (July 11, 1968), 39–41.

Donoghue, Denis. "Reconsideration: TBL." *New Republic,* 173 (October 18, 1975), 29–31.

Donoghue, Denis. *Ferocious Alphabets.* New York: Columbia University Press, 1984.

Donoghue, Denis. "American Sage." *New York Review of Books,* September 26, 1985, pp. 39–42.

Duerden, Richard Y. "Kenneth Burke's Systemless System: Using Pepper to Pigeonhole an Elusive Thinker." *Journal of Mind and Behavior,* 3 (Autumn 1982), 323–36.

Duncan, Hugh Dalziel. *Communication and Social Order.* New York: Bedminster, 1962; paperback, New York: Oxford University Press, 1968; New Brunswick, N.J.: Transaction Books, 1985.

Duncan, Hugh Dalziel. *Symbols in Society.* New York: Oxford University Press, 1968.

Duncan, Hugh Dalziel. *Symbols and Social Theory.* New York: Oxford University Press, 1969.

Duncan, Hugh Dalziel. "Literature as Equipment for Action: Burke's

Dramatistic Conception." In *The Sociology of Art and Literature: A Reader*, ed. Milton C. Albecht, James H. Barnet, and Mason Griff, pp. 713–23. New York: Praeger, 1970.

Durham, Weldon. "Kenneth Burke's Concept of Substance." *Quarterly Journal of Speech*, 66 (December 1980), 351–64.

Edelman, Murray. *The Symbolic Uses of Politics*. Urbana: University of Illinois Press, 1964.

Feehan, Michael. "Oscillation as Assimilation: Burke's Latest Self-Revisions." *Pre/Text*, 6 (Fall/Winter 1985), 319–27.

Feehan, Michael. "The Role of 'Attitudes' in Dramatism." In *Visions of Rhetoric: History, Theory, and Criticism*, ed. Charles W. Kneupper. Arlington, Tex.: Rhetoric Society of America, 1987.

Fiordo, Richard. "Kenneth Burke's Semiotic." *Semiotica: Journal of the International Association for Semiotic Studies*, 23 (1978), 53–75.

Fletcher, Angus. "Volume and Body in Burke's Criticism, or Stalled in the Right Place." In *Representing Kenneth Burke*, ed. Hayden White and Margaret Brose, pp. 150–75. Baltimore: Johns Hopkins University Press, 1982.

Foss, Sonja K.; Karen A. Foss; and Robert Trapp. "Kenneth Burke." In *Contemporary Perspectives on Rhetoric*, pp. 153–88. Prospect Heights, Ill.: Waveland Press, 1985.

Foss, Sonja K.; Karen A. Foss; and Robert Trapp. "Bibliography: Kenneth Burke." In *Contemporary Perspectives on Rhetoric*, pp. 291–304. Prospect Heights, Ill.: Waveland Press, 1985.

Frank, Armin Paul. *Kenneth Burke*. New York: Twayne, 1969.

Frank, Armin Paul, and Mechthild Frank. "The Writings of Kenneth Burke: A Checklist." In *Critical Responses to Kenneth Burke, 1924–1966*, ed. William H. Rueckert, pp. 495–512. Minneapolis: University of Minnesota Press, 1969.

Freccero, John. "Logology: Burke on St. Augustine." In *Representing Kenneth Burke*, ed. Hayden White and Margaret Brose, pp. 52–67. Baltimore: Johns Hopkins University Press, 1982.

Gabin, Rosalind J. "Entitling Kenneth Burke." *Rhetoric Review*, 5 (January 1987), 196–210.

Gallo, Louis, "Kenneth Burke: The Word and the World." *North Dakota Quarterly*, 42 (1974), 33–45.

Garlitz, Robert. "The Sacrificial Word in Kenneth Burke's Logology." *Recherches anglaises et américaines*, no. 12 (1979), pp. 33–44.

Geertz, Clifford. "Blurred Genres: The Refiguration of Social Thought." *Local Knowledge: Further Essays in Interpretive Anthropology*, pp. 19–35. New York: Basic Books. Originally published in *American Scholar*, 49 (Spring 1980), 165–79.

Gregg, Richard B. "Kenneth Burke's Prolegomena to the Study of the Rhetoric of Form." *Communication Quarterly,* 26 (Fall 1978), 3–13.

Griffin, Leland M. "When Dreams Collide: Rhetorical Trajectories in the Assassination of President Kennedy." *Quarterly Journal of Speech,* 70 (May 1984), 111–31.

Gusfield, Joseph. "The Literary Rhetoric of Science: Comedy and Pathos in Drinking Driver Research." *American Sociological Review,* 4 (February 1976), 16–34.

Hartman, Geoffrey H. "The Wild Man of American Criticism." *Book Week,* July 2, 1967, p. 9.

Hartman, Geoffrey H. "The Sacred Jungle 3: Frye, Burke, and Some Conclusions." *Criticism in the Wilderness: The Study of Literature Today,* pp. 86–114. New Haven: Yale University Press, 1980.

Heath, Robert L. "Kenneth Burke's Break with Formalism." *Quarterly Journal of Speech,* 70 (May 1984), 132–43.

Heath, Robert L. "Kenneth Burke's Perspective on Perspective." *Pre/Text,* 6 (Fall/Winter 1985), 275–89.

Heath, Robert L. *Realism and Relativism: A Perspective on Kenneth Burke.* Macon, Ga.: Mercer University Press, 1986.

Howell, Wilbur Samuel. "Kenneth Burke's 'Lexicon Rhetoricae': A Critical Examination." *Poetics, Rhetoric, and Logic: Studies in the Basic Disciplines of Criticism.* Ithaca, N.Y.: Cornell University Press, 1975. Howell's criticism provoked a response from Burke (4.142).

Howell, Wilbur Samuel. "The Two Party Line: A Reply to Kenneth Burke." *Quarterly Journal of Speech,* 62 (February 1976), 69–77. Response to 4.142.

Howell, Wilbur Samuel. "Peter Ramus, Thomas Sheridan, and Kenneth Burke: Three Mavericks in the History of Rhetoric." In *Retrospectives and Perspectives: A Symposium on Rhetoric,* ed. Turner S. Kobler, William E. Tanner, and J. Dean Bishop, pp. 91–105. Denton: Texas Women's University Press, 1978. Also in *Rhetoric and Change,* ed. William E. Tanner and J. Dean Bishop, pp. 57–77. Mesquite, Tex.: Ide House, 1982.

Hughes, Daniel. Review of *Language as Symbolic Action. Criticism,* 10 (Summer 1968), 251–53.

Hyman, Stanley Edgar. "Kenneth Burke at Seventy." In *The Critic's Credentials,* ed. Phoebe Pettingell, pp. 69–73. New York: Atheneum Press, 1978.

Hymes, Dell. Review of *Language as Symbolic Action. Language,* 44 (September 1968), 664–69.

nscher, William F. "Kenneth Burke." In *Traditions of Inquiry*, ed. John Brereton, pp. 105–36. New York: Oxford University Press, 1985.

Jameson, Fredric R. "The Symbolic Inference; or, Kenneth Burke and Ideological Analysis." In *Representing Kenneth Burke*, ed. Hayden White and Margaret Brose, pp. 68–91. Baltimore: Johns Hopkins University Press, 1982. Originally published in *Critical Inquiry*, 4 (Spring 1978), 507–23. See Burke's response (4.152).

Jameson, Fredric R. "Critical Response: Ideology and Symbolic Action." *Critical Inquiry*, 5 (Spring 1978), 417–22. Response to 4.152.

Jameson, Fredric R. *The Political Unconscious: Narrative as a Socially Symbolic Act*. Ithaca: Cornell University Press, 1981.

Jay, Paul. "Kenneth Burke: A Man of Letters." *Pre/Text*, 6 (Fall/Winter 1985), 221–33.

Jennermann, Donald L. "Some Freudian Aspects of Burke's Aristotelean Poetics." *Recherches anglaises et américaines*, no. 12 (1979), pp. 65–81.

Jennermann, Donald L. "Kenneth Burke's Poetics of Catharsis." In *Representing Kenneth Burke*, ed. Hayden White and Margaret Brose, pp. 31–51. Baltimore: Johns Hopkins University Press, 1982.

Kostelanetz, Richard. "A Mind That Cannot Stop Exploding." *New York Times Book Review*, March 15, 1981, p. 11 ff.

Kreilkamp, Thomas. *The Corrosion of the Self: Society's Effects on People*. Irvington: New York University Press, 1976.

Le Brun, Phillip. Review of *Language as Symbolic Action*. *Review of English Studies*, 20 (May 1969), 243–46.

Leff, Michael C. "Redemptive Identification: Cicero's Catalinarian Orations." In *Explorations in Rhetorical Criticism*, ed. G. P. Mohrmann, Charles J. Stewart and Donovan J. Ochs, pp. 158–77. University Park: Pennsylvania State University Press, 1973.

Lemon, Lee T. "Incompatible Virtues" (Review of *Towards a Better Life*). *Prairie Schooner*, 51 (Fall 1967), 350–51.

Lentricchia, Frank. "Reading History with Kenneth Burke." In *Representing Kenneth Burke*, ed. Hayden White and Margaret Brose, pp. 119–49. Baltimore: Johns Hopkins University Press, 1982.

Lentricchia, Frank. *Criticism and Social Change*. Chicago: University of Chicago Press, 1983.

Macksoud, S. John. "Kenneth Burke on Perspective and Rhetoric." *Western Speech*, 33 (Summer 1969), 167–74.

Mann, Charles W. "The KB Collection: The Penn State Library." *Pre/Text*, 6 (Fall/Winter 1985), 313–15.

McCloskey, Donald N. "The Rhetoric of Economics." *Journal of Economic Literature*, 21 (June 1983), 97–119.

McCloskey, Donald N. *The Rhetoric of Economics*. Madison: University of Wisconsin Press, 1985.

Meisenhelder, Thomas. "Law as Symbolic Action: Kenneth Burke's Sociology of Law." *Symbolic Interaction*, 4 (Spring 1981), 43–57.

Melia, Trevor. Review of *A Rhetoric of Motives*. *Philosophy and Rhetoric*, 3 (Spring 1970), 124–27.

Mullican, James S. "Kenneth Burke's Comic Attitude: Corrective to Propaganda Analysis." *Continuing Education*, 4, no. 2 (1971), 89–92.

Mullican, James S. "A Burkean Approach to *Catch-22*." *College Literature*, 8 (Winter 1981), 42–52.

Murray, T. C. "Kenneth Burke's Logology: A Mock Logomachy." In *Glyph 2*, Johns Hopkins Textual Studies, ed. Samuel Weber and Henry Sussman, pp. 144–61. Baltimore: Johns Hopkins University Press, 1978.

Neild, Elizabeth. "Kenneth Burke and Roland Barthes: Literature, Language, and Society." *Recherches anglaises et américaines*, no. 12 (1979), pp. 98–108.

Nemerov, Howard. "Everything, Preferably All at Once: Coming to Terms with Kenneth Burke." *Sewanee Review*, 79 (Spring 1971), 189–201.

Nemerov, Howard. "Gnomic Variations for Kenneth Burke." *Kenyon Review*, n.s., 5 (Summer 1983), 23–25.

Nichols, Marie Hochmuth. "Burkeian Criticism." In *Essays on Rhetorical Criticism*, ed. Thomas R. Nilsen, pp. 75–85. New York: Random House, 1968.

Nichols, Marie Hochmuth. Review of *Dramatism and Development*. *Quarterly Journal of Speech*, 59 (April 1973), 227.

Nimmo, Dan D. *Popular Images of Politics: A Taxonomy*. Englewood Cliffs, N.J.: Prentice-Hall, 1974.

Nimmo, Dan D. *Political Communication and Public Opinion in America*. Santa Monica, Calif.: Goodyear, 1978.

Nimmo, Dan D. *Subliminal Politics: Myths and Mythmakers in America*. Englewood Cliffs, N.J.: Prentice-Hall, 1980.

Nimmo, Dan, and James E. Combs. *Mediated Political Realities*. New York: Longman, 1983.

Osborn, Neal J. "Kenneth Burke's Desdemona: A Courtship of Clio?" *Hudson Review*, 19 (Summer 1966), 267–75.

Osborn, Neal J. "Towards the Quintessential Burke" (Review of *Towards a Better Life* and *Language as Symbolic Action*). *Hudson Review*, 21 (Summer 1968), 308–21.

Overington, Michael A. "Kenneth Burke and the Method of Dramatism." *Theory and Society,* 4 (Spring 1977), 131-56.

Overington, Michael A. "Kenneth Burke as Social Theorist." *Sociological Inquiry,* 47, no. 2 (1977), 133-41.

Parsons, Talcott; Edward Shils; Kaspar D. Naegle; and Jesse R. Pitts, eds. *Theories of Society: Foundations of Modern Sociological Theory.* New York: Free Press of Glencoe, A Division of Crowell-Collier, 1961. Parsons' comments on Burke can be found on pp. 970-71, 987-88, and 1166-67.

Pattison, Sheron Dailey. "Rhetoric and Audience Effect: Kenneth Burke on Form and Identification." In *Studies in Interpretation,* vol. 2, ed. Ester M. Doyle and Virginia Hastings Floyd, pp. 183-98. Amsterdam: Rodopi, 1977.

Paul, Sherman. "A Letter on Olson and Burke." *All Area,* 2 (1983), 64-65.

Poirier, Richard. "Frost, Winnicott, Burke." *Raritan: A Quarterly Review,* 2 (Fall 1982), 114-27.

Rod, David K. "Kenneth Burke and Susanne K. Langer on Drama and Its Audiences." *Quarterly Journal of Speech,* 72 (August 1986), 306-17.

Roig, Charles. "Kenneth Burke et le langage des sciences sociales." *Recherches anglaises et américaines,* no. 12 (1979), pp. 18-32.

Roig, Charles. *Symboles et société: Une introduction à la politique des symboles d'après l'oeuvre de Kenneth Burke.* Bern: Peter Lang, 1977.

Romano, Carlin. "A Critic Who Has His Critics—Pro and Con." *Philadelphia Inquirer,* March 6, 1984, sec. D., p. 1 ff.

Rueckert, William H. "Kenneth Burke and Structuralism." *Shenandoah,* 21 (Autumn 1969), 19-28.

Rueckert, William H. "Some of the Many Kenneth Burkes." In *Representing Kenneth Burke,* ed. Hayden White and Margaret Brose, pp. 1-30. Baltimore: Johns Hopkins University Press, 1982.

Rueckert, William H. *Kenneth Burke and the Drama of Human Relations.* 2d rev. ed. Berkeley: University of California Press, 1982.

Rueckert, William H., ed. *Critical Responses to Kenneth Burke, 1924-1966.* Minneapolis: University of Minnesota Press, 1969.

Schmitz, P. F. "Kenneth Burke: No, Yes, Maybe." In *Reisgidsen Vol Belluno's En Blaauwbaarden: Opstellen over S. Vestdijk en anderen aangeboden aan Dr. H. A. Wage,* pp. 122-30. Leiden: Vakgroep Nederlandse Taal & Letterkunde, 1976. Written in Dutch.

Schwartz, Joseph. "Kenneth Burke, Aristotle, and the Future of Rhetoric." *College Composition and Communication,* 17 (December 1966), 210-16.

Shaw, Leroy Robert. *The Playwright and Historical Change: Dramatic Strategies in Brecht, Hauptmann, Kaiser, and Wedekind.* Madison: University of Wisconsin Press, 1970.

Sivaramkrishna, M. "Epiphany and History: The Dialectic of Transcendence and *A Passage to India.*" In *Approaches to E. M. Forster: A Centenary Volume,* ed. Vasant A. Shahane, pp. 148–61. New Delhi: Arnold-Heinemann, 1981.

States, Bert O. *Irony and Drama: A Poetics.* Ithaca: Cornell University Press, 1971.

Susini, Charles. "Turbulence." *Recherches anglaises et américaines,* no. 12 (1979), pp. 109–28. Susini's *thèse d'etat,* "L'oeuvre critique de Kenneth Burke: Langage et Logologie" (Paris, 1978), is cited as indispensable by Barat in *RANAM* no. 12.

Susini, Charles, ed. *Recherches anglaises et américaines (RANAM),* no. 12. Strasbourg: Association strasbourgeoise des périodiques de sciences humaines, 1979.

Tacciu, Elena. Review of *The Philosophy of Literary Form. Romania Literara,* 6 (September [?], 1973), 15.

Tompkins, Phillip K. "On Hegemony—'He Gave It No Name'—and Critical Structuralism in the Work of Kenneth Burke." *Quarterly Journal of Speech,* 71 (February 1985), 119–31.

Tompkins, Phillip K. *Communication as Action: An Introduction to Rhetoric and Communication.* Belmont, Calif.: Wadsworth, 1982.

Tompkins, Phillip K.; Jeanne Fisher; Dominic A. Infante; and Elaine L. Tompkins. "Kenneth Burke and the Inherent Characteristics of Formal Organizations: A Field Study." *Speech Monographs,* 42 (June 1975), 135–42.

Valesio, Paolo. "Fine della Decostruzione." *Alfabeta,* 77 (October 1985), 35.

Valesio, Paolo. *Novantiqua: Rhetorics as a Contemporary Theory.* Bloomington: Indiana University Press, 1980.

Vitanza, Victor J., ed. *Pre/Text: An Interdisciplinary Journal of Rhetoric,* 6 (Fall/Winter 1985).

Wadlington, Warwick. *The Confidence Game in American Literature.* Princeton, N.J.: Princeton University Press, 1975.

Warnock, Tilly. "Reading Kenneth Burke: Ways In, Ways Out, Ways Roundabout." *College English,* 48 (January 1986), 262–75.

Wasserstrom, William. "Kenneth Burke, 'Logology,' and the Tribal No." In *Representing Kenneth Burke,* ed. Hayden White and Margaret Brose, pp. 92–118. Baltimore: Johns Hopkins University Press, 1982.

Watson, Edward A. "Incongruity without Laughter: Kenneth Burke's

Theory of the Grotesque." *University of Windsor Review,* 4, no. 2 (1969), 28–36.

Watson, Karen Ann. "A Rhetorical and Sociolinguistic Model for the Analysis of Narrative." *American Anthropologist,* 75, no. 1 (1973), 243–64.

Webster, Grant. *The Republic of Letters: A History of Postwar Literary Opinion.* Baltimore: Johns Hopkins University Press, 1979.

Wellek, René. "The Main Trends of Twentieth-Century Criticism." *Yale Review,* 51 (Autumn 1961), 102–18. Burke responds in 4.115.

Wellek, René. "Kenneth Burke and Literary Criticism." *Sewanee Review,* 79 (Spring 1971), 171–88. Also in *A History of Modern Criticism, 1750–1950,* Vol. 6, *American Criticism, 1900–1950,* pp. 235–60 (New Haven: Yale University Press, 1986). Burke responds in 4.134.

Wells, Susan. "Richards, Burke, and the Relation between Rhetoric and Poetics." *Pre/Text,* 7 (Spring/Summer 1986), 59–75.

Wess, Robert. Review of Hayden White and Margaret Brose, eds., *Representing Kenneth Burke. Modern Language Notes,* 98 (December 1983), 1315–18.

Wess, Robert. "Frank Lentricchia's *Criticism and Social Change:* The Literary Intellectual as Pragmatic Humanist." *Minnesota Review,* n.s., 27 (Fall 1986), 123–31.

Wess, Robert. "Utopian Rhetoric in *The Man of Mode.'' The Eighteenth Century: Theory and Interpretation,* 27 (Spring 1986), 141–61.

White, Hayden V. *Metahistory: The Historical Imagination in Nineteenth-Century Europe.* Baltimore: Johns Hopkins University Press, 1973.

White, Hayden V. *Tropics of Discourse: Essays in Cultural Criticism.* Baltimore: Johns Hopkins University Press, 1978.

White, Hayden, and Margaret Brose, eds. *Representing Kenneth Burke.* Baltimore: Johns Hopkins University Press, 1982.

Winterowd, W. Ross. "Dramatism in Themes and Poems." *College Education,* 45 (October 1983), 581–88.

Winterowd, W. Ross. "Black Holes, Indeterminacy, and Paolo Freire." *Rhetoric Review,* 2 (September 1983), 28–35.

Wise, Gene. *American Historical Explanations.* 2d rev. ed. Minneapolis: University of Minnesota Press, 1980.

Yagoda, Ben. "Kenneth Burke: The Greatest Literary Critic Since Coleridge?" *Horizon,* 23 (June 1980), 66–69.

315

A Selected Bibliography of Critical Responses

Zollschan, George K., and Michael A. Overington. "Reasons for Conduct and the Conduct of Reason: The Eightfold Route to Motivational Ascription." In *Social Change: Explorations, Diagnoses, and Conjectures*, ed. Zollschan and Walter Hirsh, pp. 270–317. New York: John Wiley, 1976.

CONTRIBUTORS

JANE BLANKENSHIP is professor of communication studies, University of Massachusetts–Amherst. She has written and edited a number of books, book chapters, monographs, and articles in scholarly journals such as *Philosophy and Rhetoric, Communication Monographs,* and *Quarterly Journal of Speech,* and in magazines such as *The Futurist.* She has served as president of both the Eastern Communication and the Speech Communication Associations.

DAVID DAMROSCH is associate professor of English and comparative literature, Columbia University. He is the author of *The Narrative Covenant: Transformations of Genre in the Growth of Biblical Literature* (1987), and of articles on modern literature and literary theory. He is now at work on a book on ancient and modern hermeneutics.

JOSEPH R. GUSFIELD is professor of sociology at the University of California–San Diego. His influential work *The Culture of Public Problems: Drinking-Driving and the Symbolic Order* (1981) incorporates a Burkean perspective. Other notable publications are: *Community: A Critical Response* (1975) and *Symbolic Crusade: Status Politics and the American Temperance Movement* (1986).

MICHAEL LEFF is professor of communication arts at the University of Wisconsin–Madison. His published scholarship mainly deals with the history of rhetoric and the relationship between the classical tradition and contemporary issues in theory and criticism. He is the editor of *Rhetorica,* the journal of the International Society for the History of Rhetoric.

FRANK LENTRICCHIA is professor of English at Duke University. He is best known for *After the New Criticism* (1980) and *Criticism and Social Change* (1983). His most recent book, *Ariel and the Police* (1988), was published by the University of Wisconsin Press.

DONALD N. MC CLOSKEY is professor of history and of economics at the University of Iowa, specializing in English economic history. He has written and edited books on economic theory, medieval agriculture, nineteenth-century industry, and, most recently, *The Rhetoric of Economics* (University of Wisconsin Press, 1985), and is a past editor of the *Journal of Economic History.* With colleagues at Iowa he is founding "Poroi," a Project on the Rhetoric of Inquiry.

317

318

TREVOR MELIA is associate professor of rhetoric and communication at the University of Pittsburgh and has taught previously at Tufts University. His early education in science and a Ph.D. in rhetoric have combined to produce an abiding interest in the rhetoric of science. He has studied, lectured, and written about Burke's work for two decades, and, with Nova Ryder, has written a "Burkean novel," *Lucifer State.*

CARY NELSON is professor of English and criticism and interpretive theory at the University of Illinois. He is the author of *The Incarnate Word: Literature as Verbal Space* (1973) and *Our Last First Poets: Vision and History in Contemporary American Poetry* (1981), the editor of *Theory in the Classroom* (1986), and the co-editor of *Marxism and the Interpretation of Culture* 1988 and *W. S. Merwin: Essays on the Poetry,* (1987). He is presently completing *Reading Criticism: The Literary Status of Critical Discourse,* portions of which have been published in *Critical Inquiry, PMLA, MLN,* and in the collections *What Is Criticism?* and *Psychoanalysis and the Question of the Text.*

CHRISTINE ORAVEC is associate professor of communication at the University of Utah. She has written on the rhetoric of the conservation movement, the epideictic genre of discourse, and recent developments in rhetorical theory. She is currently researching the implicit rhetorical theory in the early-nineteenth-century criticism of American public address.

WILLIAM H. RUECKERT is professor of English at the State University of New York at Geneseo. He has previously taught at the University of Rochester, the University of Illinois, and Oberlin College. He is the author of *Kenneth Burke and the Drama of Human Relations* (1963, 1982), *Critical Responses to Kenneth Burke, 1924–1966,* (1969), *Glenway Wescott* (1965), and numerous articles on literary criticism and American literature. He has recently completed a book-length study of the novels of William Faulkner.

VITO SIGNORILE is associate professor in the Department of Sociology and Anthropology, University of Windsor. His writings on "Sociology in a New Key" reflect the influence of Susanne Langer. His larger projects dealing with the general theory of symbolic action invariably mobilize the theories of Kenneth Burke.

HERBERT W. SIMONS is professor of rhetoric and communication at Temple University where he teaches persuasion and related subjects. Founder of the Temple "Discourse Analysis" conference series, Simons is editor or co-editor of four conference-related volumes, including, most recently, *Rhetoric in the Human Sciences* (Sage, 1989), and *The Rhetorical Turn: Invention and Persuasion in the Conduct of Inquiry* (Chicago, forthcoming). Simons is also the author of *Persuasion: Understanding, Practice and Analysis* (Random House, 1986, 2e).

Contributors

RICHARD H. THAMES is associate professor of rhetoric at Duquesne University. As a graduate student, he attended a seminar on Kenneth Burke co-taught by Burke himself and Trevor Melia. He subsequently wrote his dissertation tracing the influence of Spinoza on Burke's ontology.

DAVID CRATIS WILLIAMS is an assistant professor of speech communication at Northeast Missouri State University. In addition to his work on Kenneth Burke and Jacques Derrida, he has presented papers and published essays exploring both a rhetorical theory of ideological argumentation and a rationale for the practice of "nuclear criticism."

AUTHOR INDEX

Adams, R., 12, 26n19, 219n2
Adler, J. M., and Adler, M. J., 91n4
Andreski, S., 60–61, 72n18
Anscombe, G. E. M., and von Wright,
  G. H., 93n21
Auden, W. H., 3
Aune, J. A., 220n8
Austin, J. L., 105

Balthrop, V. W., 220n11
Barnes, B., and Edge, D., 53n30
Barthes, R., 17, 171
Bates, E., 76, 91n4
Bauman, Z., 88, 97n70
Bazerman, C., 104, 114n16
Beck, Z., 93n17
Becker, G., 104
Becker, G., and Stigler, G., 113n14
Bell, D., 70, 73n37
Bergmann, G., 83, 91n1, 95n46
Bidney, D., 91n4
Bitzer, L., 17, 157, 172n5
Black, M., 260n5
Bloom, H., 3
Blumer, H., 91n8
Booth, W., 4, 6, 17, 43, 92n13, 98n80,
  102, 114n21, 157, 172n4, 197, 219n6
Brisset, D., and Edgley, C., 51n1
Brock, B., 17, 157, 172n4
Brown, H., 93nn21,22
Brown, M., 219n2
Brown, R., 43, 51n1, 53n31, 84,
  96nn49,59, 97n63, 98n80
Bunge, M., 91n10, 92n12
Burns, E., 51n1

Cain, W., 173n13
Callie, W. B., 25n11
Campbell, C., 219n5
Camprone, J., 157
Cassirer, E., 71n3
Chihara, C.S., 94n22

Collingwood, G., 90, 96n48
Collins, H., 106, 114n19
Combs, J., 36, 17n52
Combs, J., and Mansfield, M. 51n1
Cooley, T. F., and Leroy, S. F., 114n18
Corcoran, F., 192n3
Coughlin, E. K., 219n4
Coward, R., and Ellis, J., 181–82, 193n6,
  194nn22,25
Cowley, M., 12, 261n14
Crane, R., 92n13
Culler, J., 222n36

de Man, P., 220n8
Derrida, J., 171, 176, 200, 220n7, 9,
  221n14–19, 21–24, 221nn14–19, 21–24,
  222nn33, 37, 38, 223nn50, 51, 53–55
Donoghue, D., 3, 17, 157, 172n4, 220n8
Doubrovsky, S., 219n6
Douglas, J., 60, 72n15
Dreyfus, H., 97n59
Dummett, M., 77, 94nn22, 24
Duncan, H. D., 29, 32, 46, 51nn3, 9,
  53n38, 250
Durkheim, E., 40, 81, 85, 88, 95n41

Edelman, M., 13, 34, 52n11
Elster, J., 113n11
Engell, J., and Bate, W. J., 171n1

Fletcher, A., 149n40, 158, 172n7
Fogarty, D., 157, 172n5
Fogel, R., 114n16, 137, 149nn36–39
Foucault, M., 162
Francis, R., 78, 94n27
Frank, A. P., 22
Frank, M., 23–24, 45
Freccero, J., 21, 27n30, 226, 229,
  237nn5,6,8
Freidman, M., 113n13
Frye, N., 41, 52n26, 102, 158

321

SUBJECT INDEX

Achronicity, 233

Action as drama, 34, 208

Action theory of, 71n3; versus motion, 36

Actor as agent, 19; actor-subject relation questioned, 18

Admonitory anecdote, 200

Adult education, 269, 283, 288, 290

Agency, 86–87, 163

Agent, 23, 178

Alembic code, 206

Algebra, 66–68

Allegory, 22

Animality, 71n5

Analogues, 130; analogy of theology, 212

Annihilation and nihilism, 214

Antinomies, 43; of dialectics, 197

Antitheticals, 196

Aquinas, 82

Aristotle, 13–14, 58, 74–76, 82, 84–87, 115–16

Arnold, M., 39

Association, 179–89

Atomistic philosophy, 60

Attitude, 72n1, 73n36, 89

Augustine, 21–22, 225–30, 232

Austin, J. L., 105

Authorial agent, 69

Autobiographical concerns in Burke's analysis, 237n11

Axiology, 212

Barthes, R., 171

Burke, as object of analyses/critiques/readings, 11–14, 69–70, 165

Burke, characterized as: Austrian School economist, 101; change agent, 290; Ciceronian or Aristotelian, 125n2; critical pathfinder, 5, 11; demystifier, 9; eccentric, 11; economistic, 14, 100; grounded in history, 249; humorist, 288, ironist, 244, 256; Leftist, 19;

lumper rather than splitter, 43; not anti-science, 14; originator of ideas, 250; pioneer, 50; poststructuralist, 170–71; "Prince of Saying," 100; radical writer, 282; self-critical, 164; self-reliant Marxist, 176; social critic, 10; social scientist, 31; sociologist, 4; sophist, 219n2; structuralist, 4; symbolist, 15, 77; "un-disciplined," 11; Western Marxist, 283, wordman, 63. See also Burke, as object of analyses/critiques/readings; Burkean theory, philosophy

Burke, compared/contrasted with: Aristotle, 76–89; 115–16, 246; Barthes, 171; Cicero, 26n22, 116–21; Coleridge, 14, 128–51; Derrida, 11, 17, 20, 171, 197–218 (See also Deconstruction); Einstein, 63; Emerson, 176; Freud, 7, 175–76, 247; Gadamer, 22, 225; Goffman, 36–37; Lévi-Strauss, 46, 170; McKeon, 26n17; Marxist literary critics, 69; Nietzsche, 7; radical Marxists, 175; Swift, 18, 167; Vico, 7; Whitman, 252–53. See also Burke's analyses/critiques/readings

Burkean concepts and distinctions: action/motion, 14, 34; association, 190–92; desynonymizing, 134; double vision, 23; dramatic irony, 67; dramatism, 21, 36, 46, 118; entitlement, 116, 128; identification, 174–76; identity, 174–75, 177–78, 190–92; idiolects, 17; logological entelechy, 78; logology, 21; pentad, 76–89; pollution, 143; principle of negativity, 207, principle of perfection, 78; representative anecdotes, 198; semantic and poetic meaning, 33; strategies of containment, 177; tropes, 108–10. See also Burkean theory, philosophy

Burkean influences: on refiguration of

325

Subject Index

Subject Index

Literary analysis, 42, 50
Literary criticism, 104
Literature, 50, 58–59; and sociology, 29
Logological: analysis, 222n44; approach, 128; entelechy, 14, 78; principle of perfection, 132–33; terms used to analyze Genesis, 67
Logology, 66–70, 146n13, 162, 164, 211, 253; compared to narrative, 67–68; definition of, 204–5, 212, 224; reliance on allegory, 233; self-reflexive, 166

Machiavelli, N., 133
McKeon, R., 26n17
Magic, 16, 128. See also Language
Man, 162, 260
Margin (marginality) and dialectic, 197–98
Marx, K., and Aquinas, 47; and Derrida, 287; and Freud, 16, 128; and Mannheim, 41; Burke critiques, 36; Burke's interpretation of, 174–77, 283; contribution to rhetorical theory, 10; influence on Burke, 14, 16, 282; thesis on Feuerbach, 282
Marxist: critics, 69, 186; rhetoric in America, 289, 291, 293
Master tropes, 161
Material cause, 86–87
Mathematics, 64
Mead, G. H., 31
Mechanical associations, 181–82
Mechanistic sense of causation, 74–75
Metadiscourse, 118–19
Metalanguages, 166
Metametaphorics, 215
Metaphor: and analogy, 206–7; defined, 194n24; extends language, 207; metonymy, synecdoche, and irony, 160; of poetics, 211
Metaphoric doubleness of language, 213
Metaphysics, 179–80; and poetics, 116
Metonymy, 120
Middle class values, 269, 292
Milton, 20, 39, 69, 187–88, 190
Misidentification, 10
Money, 35
Morphogenesis, 88
Motion, 14, 138
Mystery, 138–41

Mystification, 186; and demystification, 143
Myth of the collective, 284

Naming, 57, 129–30, 134
Narrative, 67–68, 253
Negative, 40, 133, 143, 164
New left, 283
New physics and new rhetoric, 63
Nietzsche, F., 9, 14
Nihilism, 20, 199
Nonlinguistic region, 79–80
Nonsymbolic motion, 56
Nuclear war, 199; danger, 208–9

"Old Nursery Jingle Brought Up to Date," 208–9
"On Human Nature," 257–58
Ontodeconstruction, 21, 218
Ontological: concerns of dramatism, 251; loop, 21, 212
Ontology: and epistemology, 203; of ideology, 284
Oratorism, 118
Order, 40, 47, 67, 250
Othello, 260n8
Oxymoron, 28, 44, 55

Paradox: in Helhaven, 167–68; of substance, 211, 218
Parody, 229
A Passage to India, 141
Passionate discourse, 190
Pentad: analyzed, 172–73; centrality of, 37–38; compared to Aristotle's tetrad, 14; exploratory system, 164; Goffman's social frame, 81; hexad, 27n3, 61; terms, 162–64; terms as characters in a play, 119
Pentodes, 81–82
"People" as ideological symbol, 19, 269, 271, 291, 293; used by Hitler, 276
Perfectionist tendency, 208
Perfection principle, 78, 164
Peripatetic reversal, 213
Peripety, 119
Perspective, 120; by incongruity, 44
Perspectivism, 18
Persuasion, 106–8
Phaedrus, 20, 174, 186

Subject Index